From Savage to Negro

From Savage to Negro

Anthropology and the
Construction of Race, 1896–1954

Lee D. Baker

UNIVERSITY OF CALIFORNIA PRESS

Berkeley / Los Angeles / London

University of California Press
Berkeley and Los Angeles, California

University of California Press, Ltd.
London, England

© 1998 by
The Regents of the University of California

Library of Congress Cataloging-in-Publication Data

Baker, Lee D., 1966–
    From savage to Negro : anthropology and the construction of race,
1896–1954 / Lee D. Baker.
       p. cm.
    Includes bibliographical references and index.
    ISBN 0–520–21167–7 (cloth : alk. paper).—ISBN 0–520–21168–5
(pbk. : alk. paper)
      1. Racism in anthropology—United States—History. 2. Anthro-
pology—United States—History. 3. Racism in popular culture—
United States—History. 4. Afro-Americans—Public opinion. 5.
Public opinion—United States. 6. United States—Race relations.
    I. Title.
    GN17.3.U6B35 1998
    305.8—dc21   97–31602

Printed in the United States of America
9 8 7 6 5 4 3 2

The paper used in this publication meets the minimum requirements of
American National Standards for Information Sciences—Permanence of
Paper for Printed Library Materials, ANSI Z39.48-1984.

I dedicate this book to Thurgood Marshall, Ida B. Wells-Barnett, W. E. B. Du Bois, and the countless others who possessed the audacity to believe in democracy and the courage to fight for justice.

Contents

Illustrations

Acknowledgments

I received tremendous support for this project, both material and intellectual. I began my initial research for it as a fellow at the W. E. B. Du Bois Institute for Afro-American Research at Harvard University. I would like to acknowledge Randall K. Burkett, Karen C. C. Dalton, Henry Lewis Gates, Jr., Elizabeth Guzmán, Richard Powell, and Manisha Sinha, as well as all of my fellow fellows. Everyone gave me great support, direction, and ideas. The following year I received a fellowship to continue my research and writing at the National Museum of American History, Smithsonian Institution. I had the tremendous opportunity to engage many people who supported my efforts, including Mary Dyer, Carolyn Goldstein, Johnathan Holloway, Tera W. Hunter, Charles McGovern, Niani Kilkenny, Doug Rossinow, Fath Ruffins, Marvette Perez, Peggy Schaffer, and Stephanie Thomas. During the ensuing year I was fortunate enough to completely rework the manuscript as a Mellon Scholar at the Institute for Global Studies in Culture, Power, and History at the Johns Hopkins University. I would like to acknowledge the support of Herman Bennett, Shelly Eversley, Sidney Mintz, Jennifer L. Morgan, Odeana R. Neal, Robert F. Reid-Pharr, Michel-Rolph Trouillot, Dorothy Ross, and Brackette F. Williams. Additional financial support came from Temple University and the Duke University Arts and Sciences Council. Other people, including anonymous reviewers, Jenifer Alvey, Ananth Ayer, Janaki Bakhle, Michael Blakey, Karen Brodkin, Valerie Cassel, Nahum D. Chandler, Kenneth B. Clark, H. Alexis Economou, Thelma Foote, Christine Ward Gailey, Alan H.

Goodman, Richard Handler, Robin D. G. Kelley, Sylvia Lim, William Murphy, Sarah K. Myers, Jack Nelson, Don Nonini, Peter Rigby, Robert Rydell, Audrey Smedley, Arthur Spears, Terrance R. Taylor, Nancy H. Tolin, Mark V. Tushnet, Kathy Walker, and Howard Winant, helped me in both broad and specific ways. I also want to acknowledge those who have contributed to my early foundations in both African American Studies and Anthropology: William A. Little, Thomas Patterson, and the late Daniel Scheans. Finally, I owe a debt of gratitude to the patience and perseverance of both Layli D. Phillips and Faye V. Harrison, who demonstrated overwhelming support for me and this project. Finally, thanks to Tracy Hammond, Bayo Holsey, Martha S. Jones, John L. Jackson, Jr., Erica Turnipseed, and my lovely wife, Sabrina L. Thomas.

Introduction

Race in the United States is at once an utter illusion and
a material reality, a fiction and a "scientific" fact. It is a political wedge
and a unifying force. It is structured by legislation yet destabilized by
judicial fiat, shaped by public opinion but also configured by academic
consensus. Though historically contingent, it is constantly being transformed. The history and reality of race and racism in the United States
force individuals to negotiate daily between the ideological pillars of
democracy—justice, freedom, and equality—and stark racial inequality.
Whether one looks to Alexis de Tocqueville or Studs Terkel, this negotiation is recognized as a fundamental character of U.S. society—what
Terkel calls "the American obsession."

In the United States, people use "commonsense" racial categories
every day to identify strangers and social situations or to help form their
own identities. Racial categories are often seen as "natural" or as having
some inherent biological component. But some have understood for
decades that categories of race in the United States have little to do with
natural history and a great deal to do with social and political history.

Although they often seem immutable, racial categories are always in
flux; indeed, sometimes they change rapidly. Racial categories are produced and reproduced ideologically and culturally: they are constructed.
In turn, these categories structure the access of specific groups to opportunities and resources. Complex political, economic, and cultural
processes on a global scale produce various racial constructs that vary
during particular periods in history from solid and generally accepted to

tenuous and vigorously contested. The dynamics of this variation will become clearer as this narrative unfolds.

Since the founding of the Union, contests over what racial groups in the United States signify have been political enterprises. Though dating to the colonial period, the politics of race was woven into the Constitution and continues to dominate American culture and politics. As with most political endeavors in the United States, various individuals, groups, and coalitions simultaneously wield power, marshal authority, and sway public opinion. The construction of race is no different. No political party, interest group, or scientific organization has itself structured racial inequality. Although various interests worked in concert, the structuring of racial inequality was not orchestrated. Yet ideas about race are articulated in ways that reinforce legal, social, and economic relations among groups.

Historically, there has been a certain "resonance" between laws regarding race passed by Congress and upheld by the Supreme Court, ideas about race articulated in the mass media, and studies on race published by scientists. These institutions share specific notions about race that converge, are sometimes linked, and often influence one another. Researching, theorizing, and classifying racial groups has always been the province of anthropology.

In this book I explore the relationships and linkages between the shifting discourse on race within anthropology and the racial constructs undergoing transformation in the United States. One of my goals is to explore how anthropologists and the texts they produce contribute to the various dynamics involved in the formation of the racial category used for African Americans. I focus on the first half of the twentieth century because ideas about racial inferiority were supplanted by notions of racial equality in law, science, and public opinion; each arena played off and reinforced the other. Anthropology also matured as a discipline during these years and was affected by these changes, yet it helped to effect them. Simply put, I integrate the history of anthropology and the history of the African American experience, and by doing so I reveal intersections and linkages that have not been considered previously.

The first half of the twentieth century is bounded by two landmark U.S. Supreme Court decisions concerning the Fourteenth Amendment. Each codified a significant shift in U.S. race relations. In 1896 *Plessy v. Ferguson* upheld racial segregation and put forth the doctrine known as separate but equal, which allowed unequal segregated public facilities. In 1954 the *Brown v. Board of Education* decision essentially overturned the separate-but-equal doctrine, and the Supreme Court began to mandate racial desegregation. This shift in the legal significance of racial categories coincided with a striking shift in anthropology, which provided scientific validation for first one, and then the other, interpretation of the U.S. Constitution. In 1896 Social Darwinist thought informed anthropological writings on race and offered scientific validation to proponents of racial hierarchies. By 1954, however, cultural relativism informed the anthropological research on race and culture and provided scientific support for champions of racial equality.

The relationship between the anthropological discourse on race and the prevailing racial construct has been close and often reciprocal. The processes that construct race have also helped to shape the field of anthropology; anthropology, in turn, has helped to shape various racial constructs. The social context from which turn-of-the-century constructs of race emerged—industrialization, poll taxes, public lynchings, unsafe working conditions, and Jim Crow segregation—at the same time gave rise to a professional anthropology that espoused racial inferiority and, as a consequence, supported and validated the status quo. Three decades later, social and political movements like the Great Migration, the rise of the National Association for the Advancement of Colored People (NAACP), the Harlem Renaissance, the African American alliance with the Democratic Party, and the struggle for desegregation all contributed to the rise of a new paradigm in anthropology that espoused, and in turn quickened the struggle for, racial equality.

Between 1896 and 1954 anthropology played an integral role in helping to change the meaning and structure of race for African Americans. Although one can never adequately document all facets of how racial categories transform, one can identify how the justices on the Supreme Court incorporate changing scientific ideas about race in their various interpretations of the Fourteenth Amendment. The variance of the Supreme Court's interpretations of the equal-protection clause of the Fourteenth Amendment is perhaps the best barometer of race relations and the changing significance of race in the United States.[1]

Since its inception in the eighteenth century, American anthropology has been the science that takes the explanation of race and culture as its central charge. Anthropological explanations of race and culture have changed in step with larger social transformations. These explanations have not been left idle in an ivory tower but have become an active part of the social machinery that constructs racial categories, and that machinery has helped sustain the discipline of anthropology.

The anthropological discourse on race feeds into the larger discourses out of which it is itself constructed. For example, lawmakers have used anthropology to write legislation that shapes public policy, and journalists have used it to produce media that shape public opinion. The discipline of anthropology, in turn, is validated by this sort of appropriation.

Science and law continue to play a leading role in the formation of racial categories. Both fields are largely shaped by powerful elites yet checked or curtailed by public intellectuals.[2] Each contributes to the processes that form and reform the permanent, though flexible, social modality of race. Race contributes to the shape and tenor of political parties, federal and state agencies, labor and financial markets; it plays an undeniable role in what we sometimes sum up with the phrase "life chances." In turn, these inspire cultural strategies, political initiatives, or organizational efforts to contest or reproduce these projects.[3] Science and law not only inform but also transform the boundaries of opportunity for the empowerment of racial groups. Science and law change over time, and individuals working with and within the methodologies and institutions of these disciplines actually effect the changes. Civil rights activists have used these fields to change how racial meanings are attributed, how racial identities are assigned or embraced, and what the various categories of race mean—psychologically, symbolically, and structurally.

During the first part of the twentieth century, scholars and activists engaged in fighting racial inequality were attracted to science and jurisprudence because the paradigms and doctrines of each field could ostensibly be changed with new arguments and evidence. They believed they could gather evidence to change scientific arguments about racial inferiority and gather evidence to change constitutional arguments for racial segregation.

Entry into the fields of law and science before World War II was difficult and almost exclusively limited to male members of America's elite. Those who obtained degrees that gave them the authority to challenge the prevailing scientific and legal arguments on race were mostly African American and White (often Jewish) men; Native American, Japanese American, Latino, and Chinese American men, as well as all women, faced almost insurmountable barriers to these fields. While this study investigates the construction of racial categories, it focuses specifically on how certain Black men and White men fought together in an effort to obtain equality for African Americans by transforming science and the law, which in turn changed how race was signified culturally and structured socially for all racial groups in the United States. The first four chapters generally show how anthropology became a professional and scientific discipline in the United States, in part because early ethnologists provided scientific support for widely held ideas about the racial inferiority of people of color and about the superiority of White American citizens.

The first chapter begins with some historical background of the dynamics that led to the unique construction of race in the United States. It also outlines the development of anthropology before it was an academic discipline associated with museums and universities. I review the racialized politics between the North and the South to demonstrate that sociobiological conceptions of racial inferiority served as an ideological glue to reunite these regions by 1896, when William McKinley was elected president and the Court handed down *Plessy*. Chapter 2 looks at John Wesley Powell, Daniel G. Brinton, and Frederic Ward Putnam, the American ethnologists who were the most instrumental in establishing anthropology as a professional discipline. I document how these men established anthropology through the articulation of notions of racial inferiority and a unique form of Social Darwinism. Chapter 3 details the role anthropology played in popular culture. I explore the world's fairs of 1893 and 1904 and then look at how journalists, editors, and legislators marshaled anthropological findings to shape opinions about racial inferiority in the media. I suggest in chapter 4 that the progressive movement, spearheaded by Theodore Roosevelt, merely recycled older notions of Social Darwinism; and I explain that the eugenics movement of the 1920s and 1930s was merely the practical application of ideas of inferiority by the state.

The fifth chapter shows the transition from an understanding of race embedded in evolutionist notions to a view grounded in concepts of racial equality and cultural relativity. I take up here how Franz Boas was instrumental in reshaping anthropological thinking about race and culture. Scientists steeped in Social Darwinism viewed race and culture as one and the same, arguing that cultural traits were merely race traits and tendencies. Boas built a heavily documented refutation of these ideas, asserting that culture was separate from biology and not reducible to it. I also show that Boas and W. E. B. Du Bois developed similar concepts of race and culture concurrently by detailing the often overlooked relationship between these two scholars. The final chapters discuss how members of the New Negro Movement used Boasian ideas about culture to promote cultural achievement and how members of the NAACP Legal Defense and Education Fund (LDEF) used Boasian theories on race to underpin arguments for school desegregation that culminated with *Brown*. Chapters 6 and 7 explore the role of anthropology "behind the veil" or within the cultural transformations that occurred during the New Negro Movement of the 1920s. Many intellectuals of the New Negro Movement or the Harlem Renaissance were interested in documenting African cultural continuities within the New World. Concurrently, Boas and several of his students were producing studies on Negro folklore doing the same thing. The *Journal of American Folk-Lore* (JAFL), under the editorship of Boas or one of his associates, was the vehicle in which these two enterprises converged. During the 1920s more than a dozen "Negro numbers" were published. These were special issues devoted to Negro life and culture and included contributions from Blacks and Whites in and outside of anthropology.

Chapter 8 discusses how Howard University emerged as the center for the study of race relations during the 1930s. While Boas and his students developed a tightly knit discourse on racial equality and cultural relativity, the scholars centered at Howard University unraveled it by jettisoning the idea about cultural relativity and embracing the idea about racial equality. The Howard scholars did not want to celebrate the African retentions in Negro culture; they argued that Negroes should assimilate so-called American culture. This same approach was incorporated in Gunnar Myrdal's 1944 *An American Dilemma*. Myrdal's work was influential and came on the heels of the Jewish Holocaust. Together they helped change the way in which many Americans thought about government-sponsored racism.

Chapter 9 examines the specific role anthropology played in the desegregation movement. The principal attorneys in the LDEF were trained or taught at Howard University. The arguments they employed during the late 1940s and early 1950s to fight against segregated schools in the court system rested on the social science produced by their colleagues from Howard. When *An American Dilemma* became widely acclaimed, the LDEF presented the premise of Myrdal's study as Exhibit A to the Supreme Court in *Brown*. The Supreme Court, in turn, relied on this social science to justify its reinterpretation of the Fourteenth Amendment, which theoretically overturned *Plessy* with regard to public education. The role anthropology played in *Brown* is the role it played in *An American Dilemma*. It was the basis for asserting that the environment shaped cultural differences and that there was no proof of any racial inferiority. This Boasian theme is a pillar for both the Howard studies during the 1930s and Myrdal's volume.

Framing Contemporary Discussions

In the late 1990s the United States is experiencing another racial realignment, in which, literally, the terms and conditions of being a member of any racial group are transforming. While anthropologists, sociologists, and psychologists continue to embrace Boas's critique of racial categories, the critiques of race as a biological concept have led many to embrace a color-blind thesis that denies the existence of even socially constructed racial categories. This approach eschews the simple question: Why does *racism* continue to exist if there are no races in the natural world?[4] The denial of categories of race can support arguments for a so-called color-blind society that has been used to erode affirmative action programs and majority-minority voting districts. Faye V. Harrison has suggested that since the late 1980s and early 1990s anthropologists have been "overcoming denial" and contributing to an intensifying multidisciplinary discourse exploring complex dimensions of race, racism, and identities.[5]

As part of this movement anthropologists are rehistoricizing race and uncovering previously buried anthropological contributions by people of color. To appreciate the current revitalization of the anthropology of racial meanings, structures of inequality, and forms of resistance, the interpenetrating pasts of both race and anthropology must be rehistoricized.[6] What can we learn by rehistoricizing science and, more specifically, rehistoricizing how anthropology contributed to processes of racial formation? I hope that by better understanding how and why racial science was used in the past, we can better understand the force behind racial science and racial politics today.

In the following chapters I unwittingly address two specific threads in the contemporary discourse on race coming from two important institutions — the U.S. Supreme Court and the American Enterprise Institute (AEI). I actually offer a counternarrative to Supreme Court Justice Clarence Thomas and AEI Resident Scholar Dinesh D'Souza's use of the history of anthropology.

Exposing the Right's Wrong

U.S. Supreme Court Justice Thomas rewrote the role social science played in *Brown* in his concurring decision to *Missouri v. Jenkins* in June 1995. In so doing he bolstered conservative ideas about race and culture and formulated a powerful revision of the once-sacrosanct ideal of racial equality embedded in *Brown*.

Missouri v. Jenkins was one of three decisions delivered during the Supreme Court's 1994–1995 term that crippled federal legislation to equalize opportunity for people of color in public education, congressional elections, and federal affirmative action programs. While narrow majorities prevailed in each case (5–4), the decisions came on the heels of the Republican takeover of the House and the Senate, the House Republicans' "Contract with America," a national debate on the merits of affirmative action, and the meteoric sales of *The Bell Curve: Intelligence and Class Structure in American Life.*[7] In *Missouri v. Jenkins*, the Court ruled that a Missouri federal district court improperly ordered the state to pay for a program to desegregate Kansas City's public schools.

In his concurring decision, Associate Justice Thomas framed his seemingly persuasive opinion by stating: "It never ceases to amaze me that the courts are so willing to assume that anything that is predominantly black must be inferior. . . . The mere fact that a school is black does not mean that it is the product of a constitutional violation." Thomas supported halting the district court's desegregation plan because it cited *Brown* as its rationale. "In *Brown v. Board of Education*," Thomas argued, "the Court noted several psychological and sociological studies purporting to show that *de jure* segregation harmed black students by generating 'a feeling of inferiority' in them." He concluded that "this approach not only relies upon questionable social science research rather than constitutional principle, but it also rests on an assumption of black inferiority."[8] By using only the term *black*, Thomas skillfully blurred the line between race and culture. As well, he sidestepped explaining how the arguments in *Brown* were based on ideas of racial equality *and* ideas of cultural assimilation. Thomas simply collapsed the concepts of race and culture into an ostensibly commonsense idea about "black inferiority." Thomas's entire argument, however, falls apart when one puts it in historical context or simply asks: What do you mean by *black*? My research demonstrates that LDEF members clearly distinguished race from culture, and they did not employ ideas that African Americans were somehow inferior racially or biologically.

Clarence Thomas has not been alone in recent attempts to reinvent U.S. social science to bolster a conservative political agenda. Dinesh D'Souza, in *The End of Racism*,[9] attempted to argue that "multiculturalism is a political movement based on a denial of Western cultural superiority."[10] He did this, in part, by leveling an indictment on Franz Boas and his students for challenging notions of Social Darwinism and advancing ideas of cultural relativism.[11] D'Souza suggested that "the logic of cultural relativism leads directly to proportional representation, which is the underpinning of American civil rights law." He deplores the fact that "relativism generates an expectation of group equality."[12] Like Thomas, D'Souza rewrote the history of social science that underpinned *Brown*. D'Souza argued that "Thurgood Marshall spearheaded a direct attack on segregation, and chose to premise it on the findings of Boasian relativism."[13] This is where D'Souza is not accurate. My research demonstrates how D'Souza failed to comprehend that Thurgood Marshall only employed the Boasian notion of racial equality and not his ideas of cultural relativity in the arduous litigation leading to *Brown*. D'Souza's entire argument falls apart as well if one puts it in historic context or simply points out that the LDEF attorneys rejected Boas's ideas of cultural relativity but embraced his idea of racial equality. Although Thomas and D'Souza articulated similar ideas about a so-called color-blind society, they used different interpretations of the history of anthropology—and neither was accurate. Even though I do not explicitly engage these holes in both Thomas's and D'Souza's work, it is clear that the historiography of science and its role in racial formation remain salient today.

CHAPTER 1

History and Theory
of a Racialized Worldview

I begin my narrative proper with a discussion of turn-of-the-century anthropologists in the United States and how they contributed to the formation of racial categories. The history and politics of race, however, predate the formation of anthropology as an academic discipline. The first half of this chapter is intended to foreground the twentieth-century material with a brief history of the origins of race in the United States and review the contributions of the first "American school of anthropology" in the mid–nineteenth century. The second part of this chapter outlines the turbulent racial politics in which turn-of-the-century anthropologists found themselves embroiled.

A Brief History of the Formation of Race

The origins of contemporary racial categories lie in sixteenth-century England and emerge from the age of exploration, the rise of capitalism, and the rise of science.[1] From the sixteenth through the eighteenth centuries the term *race* consisted of folk classifications that were interchangeable with concepts like nation, type, variety, or stock. These folk ideas about cultural differences were viewed as natural or biological differences and merged with the Anglican and Puritan belief in the sacredness of property rights and the individual. These ideological ingredients were transferred to the New World. They helped to shape colonial identities, the form of slavery, and the relationships between colonists and indigenous peoples.[2]

In the seventeenth century the English elite first imposed the idea of a less-than-human "savage" on the "wild" Irish, who were viewed as wicked, barbarous, and uncivil. Borrowed from the Spanish view of indigenous people in the New World, they reconfigured it in terms of their own ethnocentricity to label their subjected Gaelic neighbors. For example, members of the English gentry generally viewed the Irish as lazy, filthy, superstitious, and given to stealing, amorality, and crime. These traits constituted the antithesis of "civilized man" bound by laws. Imposing such traits dehumanized the Irish and allowed the English to forgo any ethical or moral considerations in their discrimination. According to Audrey Smedly, the same traits used to depict the Irish as savage in the seventeenth century were used to classify African Americans and Native Americans as savages during the following three centuries.[3] The critical difference between the seventeenth-century English ideas of savagery and the early-twentieth-century ideas in the United States was the authority: the former was religious; the latter, scientific.

The antecedents of contemporary notions of race are found not in the science of race but in the theology of heathenism, the saved, and the damned. Although many attempts were made by early North American colonialists to "save" the souls of indigenous people, the ensuing conflicts quickly changed the image of Native Americans from noble to ignoble savages. Religious doctrines inspired both colonization and malicious destruction of indigenous peoples' lives, land, and culture. It was God's will! John Winthrop, who established the Massachusetts Bay Company in 1630, claimed that the smallpox epidemic of 1617 was God's way of "thinning out" the Indians "to make room for the Puritans."[4]

The first Africans to reach the New World accompanied Columbus on his initial foray to the Americas. Africans also accompanied conquistadores, pirates, and immigrants venturing to the so-called New World. The first Africans to join a North American English colony were sold as "cargo" from a Dutch ship to colonists at Jamestown in 1619. By 1633 New England colonists also held Africans in servitude. In all areas in North America the numbers of Africans were relatively small, and their status as free, enslaved, or indentured was ambiguous. The numbers of Africans in the Americas increased when sugar plantations were established in the Caribbean after 1500 in the Spanish colonies and after 1640 in the French, Dutch, and English colonies. The successful plantations grew dependent on the labor of enslaved Africans. In North America there was a steady stream of enslaved African labor as the tobacco industry took hold. Beginning with the Virginia Assembly in 1661, the ambiguous status of Africans in North American colonies was quickly defined. Smedly and others argue that by the 1690s Africans were reduced to chattel slavery as a result of numerous laws, customs, and labor needs. The institution of slavery was swiftly codified into the legal framework of colonial society and became integral to its economy. Slavery also evolved as a social institution. English colonists developed a unique ideology about human differences as institutional and behavioral aspects of slavery solidified. These changes continued into the early eighteenth century. Slavery developed throughout the Americas as a system of bondage that was unique in human history. Its primary distinctiveness rested on the fact that this form of slavery was reserved exclusively for Black people and their children. The institutionalization of slavery and scientific ideas of racial inferiority were critical steps in the evolution of the formation of a racialized worldview.[5]

By the end of the eighteenth century a whole new body of intellectual endeavors termed "science" had begun to emerge as a distinct domain of Western culture that challenged theology and moral philosophy. Enlightenment writers saw science emanating from the "rational mind of man" unfettered by emotion or superstition, and by the middle of the eighteenth century science was becoming a dominant discourse on both sides of the Atlantic. Between the middle of the eighteenth century and the dawn of the twentieth century, science played an important role in establishing the "fact" that savages were racially inferior to members of civilized society. During the second half of the eighteenth century continental scholars such as Louis LeClerc, Comte de Buffon, and Johann Blumenbach fused their aesthetic judgments and ethnocentrism to form an elaborate system to classify the races into a rigid, hierarchical scheme. In North America this scientific system, coupled with colonists' popular thinking about racial hierarchies, buoyed existing power relationships, political goals, and economic interests, which in turn institutionalized racial inferiority and socially structured the categories in new and enduring ways.[6]

European scientists' ideas about racial inferiority became more influential in North America as revolutionary fervor began to sweep the colonies. As English and colonial relations became more antagonistic, revolutionary philosophies about citizens' rights, freedom, and liberty rose to a crescendo. The duplicitous contradiction of fighting the tyranny of England while denying freedom to enslaved Africans fueled antislavery attempts to challenge the institution of slavery. The morality claim presented by Abolitionists was eviscerated by using scientific studies about racial inferiority to explain that Negroes and Indians were savages not worthy of citizenship or freedom.[7] The Abolition movement was not easily curbed. At the dawn of the Civil War, Abolitionists insisted on juxtaposing the institution of slavery with the ideology of democracy, but this only motivated proslavery forces to construct an even more elaborate edifice of race ideology.[8]

The "American School" of Anthropology

The so-called American school of anthropology was developed in the midst of the political, financial, and ideological unrest that led to the Civil War. Until the mid–nineteenth century most scientists explained racial inferiority in terms of the "savages' " fall from grace or of their position in the "Great Chain of Being." The idea of monogenesis — that Negroes were fully human — was integral to both paradigms. U.S. scientists, however, revived earlier ideas of polygenesis — multiple origins of the human species — in the wake of the growing antislavery forces and slave revolts. The proponents of these arguments eclipsed the single-origin thesis prior to and following the Civil War, even after Charles Darwin's *On the Origin of Species by Means of Natural Selection* (1859) should have abated them.[9] The first American anthropologists advanced the polygenesis thesis within the highly politicized antebellum period, and these efforts were aimed at setting Negroes apart from Whites and defining the Negro's place in nature. The most influential scholars of this school were Samuel Morton, Josiah Nott, and Louis Agassiz.

Samuel Morton was a Philadelphia physician who also taught anatomy to medical students. He curated, for his private use, one of the world's foremost collections of human skulls. He used his collection as a database to write two major publications, *Crania Americana; or, a Comparative View of the Skulls of Various Aboriginal Nations of North and South America* (1839) and *Crania Ægyptiaca; or, Observations on Egyptian Ethnography, Derived from Anatomy, History and the Monuments* (1844). Morton linked cranial capacity with moral and intellectual endowments and assembled a cultural ranking scheme that placed the large-brained Caucasoid at the pinnacle. The impact of his research is reflected in a memoir published in the *Charleston Medical Journal* after his death in 1851: "We can only say that we of the South should consider him [Morton] as our benefactor, for aiding most materially in giving to the negro his true position as an inferior race."[10]

Josiah Nott was trained by Morton and was another physician who contributed to the original American school of anthropology. Nott hailed from Alabama and desperately believed that Negroes and Whites were separate species. In numerous publications and lectures during the 1840s, Nott discussed the natural inferiority of the Negro in an explicit effort to help proslavery forces fend off the Abolitionist movement. Nott advanced theories that were used widely to continue the enslavement of African Americans. One of the most pervasive was the idea that Negroes were like children who needed direction, discipline, and the parentlike care of a master. Negroes, he argued, were better off enslaved because this imposed at least a modicum of civilized culture. This very theme was recycled time and time again over the next eighty years by various public intellectuals and politicians during and after Reconstruction.

In 1854 Congress repealed the Missouri Compromise, enabling the new territorial governments of Kansas and Nebraska to decide the slavery question under the theory of popular sovereignty. A mini–civil war erupted instead of elections; known as Bleeding Kansas, it was a prelude to the Civil War. Also in 1854, Nott and George Gliddon compiled the available anthropological data on species variations for *Types of Mankind*, a celebrated book with ten editions by the end of the century. *Types of Mankind* was perhaps the most important book on race during the contentious antebellum period. Its "quantitative" data were used to strengthen proslavery arguments by scholars and laypeople alike.[11]

On the heels of Nott and Gliddon's first edition, and in the middle of the escalating tensions between the North and the South, the U.S. Supreme Court decided *Dred Scott v. Sandford* (1857). Chief Justice Roger B. Taney authored the majority opinion, which was supposed to be only about the right of a manumitted slave to sue across state lines in federal court. By broadening the scope of the case Taney decreed that all African Americans (enslaved or free) had no rights as citizens under the U.S. Constitution. Taney framed his argument by detailing how "far below" Negroes were from Whites "in the scale of created beings," in effect constitutionalizing the racial ideology articulated by the scientific discourse and the opinion of proslavery interests.[12]

The third and most prominent contributor to this American school of anthropology was the Harvard naturalist Louis Agassiz. Agassiz hailed from Switzerland and was an expert in paleontological ichthyology. In 1846 he was invited to join the faculty of Harvard University, where he developed an interest in the origins of the human species. Initially he advanced the single-origin or monogenesis approach. After four years in the racially charged antebellum climate, however, he underwent a conversion that led him to believe Negroes were a separate species altogether. Two important events led to this conversion. The first was meeting Samuel Morton and viewing his collection of skulls in Philadelphia. The second event also occurred in Philadelphia. Apparently, Agassiz had his first encounter with African Americans in a hotel in Philadelphia, and he was disturbed by their features. When a Black waiter approached his table, he wanted to flee. "What unhappiness for the white race," he exclaimed, "to have tied their existence so closely with that of Negroes. . . . [T]his [is a] degraded and degenerate race."[13]

Agassiz's legacy is not only the statues, schools, streets, and museums in Cambridge emblazoned with his name but also the bevy of students who were under his tutelage at Harvard University. He trained virtually all of the prominent U.S. professors of natural history during the second half of the nineteenth century. Nathaniel Southgate Shaler and Joseph Le Conte were two of his students who became influential in the political debates concerning racial inferiority.

As my research will demonstrate, Shaler was a prolific writer for the mass media, influenced many Harvard undergraduates (including Theodore Roosevelt), and had an important impact on the fledgling academic discipline of anthropology. Another student of Agassiz was Frederic Ward Putnam. At Harvard, Putnam established both the Department of Anthropology and the Peabody Museum of American Archaeology and Ethnology. Thus, the original American school of anthropology not only helped to shape the first generation of academic anthropologists but also gave scientific authority to proslavery forces.

Science successfully eclipsed religious and folk beliefs about racial inferiority once the physicians and naturalists established the so-called scientific fact of Negro inferiority. From the mid–nineteenth century on, science provided the bases for the ideological elements of a comprehensive worldview summed up in the term *race*. Audrey Smedley contends that the cultural construction of race only reached "full development in the latter half of the nineteenth century," when "the legal apparatus of the United States and various state governments conspired with science to legitimize this structural inequality by sanctioning it in law."[14]

My research begins at precisely this historic juncture. I do not suggest a conspiracy, but I do demonstrate that members of Congress used early anthropological studies to justify legislation that structured racial inequality. I begin with this particular convergence of politics and science in the 1890s because this period was quite literally a defining moment in the history of both racial formation and university-based anthropology in the United States.[15]

Smedley rightly argues that during the 1890s the racial worldview was solid and comprehensive. Not until the second half of the nineteenth century did a "fully developed" construct of race emerge, and between the two World Wars efforts to "dismantle" the cultural construct of race were effective. Although my view of the processes of racial construction is congruent with Smedley's, I suggest that there has always been a social construct of race in the United States, at the least since the Constitution was ratified. For Smedley's "not fully developed" I substitute the idea of "fractured." The ways in which we conceptualize race differ only slightly, however.

I suggest that a social construct of race can exist without having, as Smedley suggests, a comprehensive worldview in which the ideological ingredients form a shared cosmological ordering system. By proposing that at every moment in the racial formation process there is a construct of race, I mean that people experience every day the ways in which categories of race are signified and reified socially, structurally, and culturally (symbolically), in terms that range from the intrapersonal to the supranational. The way people are forced to negotiate racial categories, and the terms by which racial categories form, however, change over time. Given the dialogical nature of racial formation, I recognize that using the noun *construct* presents a logical problem because various groups, individual people, or institutions have always engaged in challenging or protecting the meaning of racial categories, thereby helping *to construct* the meaning of racial categories. I use the term both ways. Although I argue that early ethnologists helped to solidify the construct of race during the 1890s, I also argue that the appropriation of the Boasian discourse on race by the NAACP during the litigation that culminated in *Brown* helped to construct a different meaning for racial categories.

Constructing Race for the Twentieth Century

The more recent origins of the racial category used to categorize African Americans arise after the Civil War, during the Reconstruction era and the ensuing backlash in the 1890s. The academic discipline of anthropology also developed during this time, in some respects because it was the science that helped explain the "race problem," which the nation was figuring out.

Shortly after the Civil War, Congress passed the Reconstruction Act of 1867. This act ushered in the beginning of political empowerment for African Americans—Radical Reconstruction. The act divided all Confederate states, except Tennessee, into five military districts. It also required each new state government to follow certain procedures to be recognized by Congress. These involved rewriting state constitutions to include Negro suffrage and the ratification of the Fourteenth Amendment. During Radical Reconstruction, African Americans began to mobilize in political and labor organizations. On the labor front, workers from a variety of occupations organized and held strikes in cities throughout the South; on the political front, community leaders mobilized members of Black churches, clubs, societies, and leagues to form the Black arm of the Republican Party. By the end of 1867 it seemed that every Black voter in the South had joined the powerful, clandestine political organization called the Union League. For a short time, African Americans were becoming politically and economically empowered. With the help of paternalistic northern Republicans, African Americans in the South began to contest how southern Bourbons and the former planter class imposed racial inequality.[16]

Initially, African Americans voted straight Republican, never splitting a ticket. The fruits born from their party loyalty were African American delegations in each of the southern state's legislatures, congressional representation in Washington, and sundry political appointments. Although politically empowered, the Freedman's Bank debacle (when many lost their life's savings), the collapse of southern agriculture, and the lack of well-paying or union jobs left many African Americans economically desperate.[17] Notwithstanding, many White Republicans believed that *just* enfranchising African Americans would solve the so-called Negro problem. Senator Richard Yates even exclaimed that "The Ballot, will finish the negro question; it will settle everything connected

with this question. . . . We need no vast expenditures, we need no stand-
ing army. . . . Sir, the ballot is the freedman's Moses."[18]

During Radical Reconstruction, southern Democrats and ex-Con-
federates were politically impotent at the federal level. At the state level,
however, they obstructed the political empowerment of African Americans by any and all means. Although violence and terror were not new
to the South, numerous White supremacist organizations began to
flourish after the Reconstruction Act. To further White supremacy,
these organizations employed intimidation and bribery at the polls, ar-
son, and murder. Lynching became the tool of choice to keep African
Americans out of the polls and off the streets.[19] Congress passed three
bills designed to enforce the Fifteenth Amendment and stem the rising
tide of lynchings. These bills (collectively referred to as the force bills)
made it a federal crime to obstruct the election process. Additionally,
they placed the election apparatus within the jurisdiction of U.S. Attorneys. U.S. Attorneys began to prosecute election administrators who
allegedly disqualified voters based on race or "previous condition of
servitude" in the federal courts. Other bills passed by Congress included the Ku Klux Klan Act of 1871, which made the violation of citizens' rights a high crime, and the Civil Rights Act of 1875, which prohibited racial discrimination in inns, public conveyances, and places of
public amusement. Although Republicans at the federal level tried to
deploy U.S. Attorneys, federal marshals, the U.S. Army, and election
commissioners to enforce these acts, they did not squelch attempts by
the states and secret organizations to abridge African American suffrage.[20]

The main reason why the Republicans defended Negro suffrage with
federal force was to ensure the Black vote. Whereas the Supreme Court
challenged the role of the federal government in state and local elections
in *United States v. Reese* (1876) and *United States v. Cruikshank* (1876),
Congress tried to strengthen it. The tug-of-war over Negro suffrage
between state and federal government or Democrat and Republican
power continued.

Although Republicans relinquished federal control of southern states
in 1877, they lost partisan control of Congress in 1890.[21] Republicans
lost control of both houses in the Fifty-second Congress, in part because
the Populists launched an aggressive campaign in the South that split
the Republican vote. In the House alone, members of the GOP dropped
from 173 to 88, while Democrats surged from 156 to 231.[22] This dramatic
loss for the Republican Party and subsequently for African Americans

signaled the imminent Democratic backlash, but the backlash had begun even earlier.

The states began to rewrite their constitutions in an effort to explicitly limit the African American franchise, and the Supreme Court held many provisions of the Civil Rights Act unconstitutional because Congress attempted to create an impermissible municipal code which regulated the private conduct of individuals.[23] But as the Democrats swept into Congress, wave after wave of violence, policies, and legislation forced the disfranchisement of African Americans. In 1892 lynchings and terrorist attacks reached an all-time high, and the second Cleveland administration was elected on a platform that explicitly attacked the Federal Elections Bill. In 1892 the Democratic Party gained control of the House of Representatives, the Senate, and the White House. With the aid of a sympathetic Supreme Court they began to dismantle, section by section, the Federal Elections Bill. Between 1893 and 1894 Democrats in Congress repealed nearly all bills that federally protected the franchise of Negro men.[24]

Conservative Democrats, now in power at the state and federal levels, moved quickly to disfranchise the Negro completely. Their schemes, policies, and state constitutional amendments found ways to disfranchise African Americans while providing poor, illiterate, and landless Whites with the ability to vote. The overtures to politically empower poor Whites, coupled with zealous White supremacist demagoguery and propaganda, began to reunite poor and rich Whites in the South.[25]

The second Cleveland administration was in a quagmire of conflicts. Domestic issues — such as Free Silver, the rise of the Populist Party, and a severe depression in 1893 — and international issues — such as defining the United States' role abroad in places like Hawaii, Venezuela, Cuba, and the Philippines — all diverted federal attention from the Negro problem in the South. The southern states, which had implemented moderately restrictive election reforms prior to the surge of Democratic power, rendered the Fifteenth Amendment virtually void by various schemes and measures after the Republicans became embroiled in international issues.[26]

The structuring of African American inequality during the 1890s converged with the structuring of the working class. Between 1880 and 1900 there were close to 25,000 strikes involving more than 6 million workers. Several riotous strikes took place in the North during the same years in which riots at the polls took place in the South.[27] For example, in 1892 the Homestead and Carnegie Steel Company strikes both ended in fatalities. In the following year came a depression. The Pullman Palace Car Company, near Chicago, wanted to protect its shareholders, so it reduced workers' wages without reducing the cost of housing and services in the company town. The union went on strike, but the management had the staunch support of the Cleveland administration. On Independence Day 1894, Cleveland sent in federal troops, who used lethal force to crush the strike. Many union members were injured, and several died in the four-day confrontation.[28]

The locations where Cleveland chose to deploy federal troops were emblematic of the Democrats' agenda to disfranchise African Americans in the South and destroy organized labor in the North: the president began to pull federal troops out of the South, where they had been deployed to enforce Negro suffrage during elections; and in the same year he routinely deployed federal troops in the North to subvert union strikes and escort strikebreakers through picket lines.

The overwhelming victory of William McKinley and the Republican Party in 1896, without securing one electoral vote from the South, made it painfully evident that the party neither needed nor could secure the southern Black vote. With the backing of powerful capitalists, the Republican Party gained important support from the West, industrialists, and voters interested in procuring foreign markets. The Republican platform included planks that gainsaid lynchings and disfranchisement, but it did not use any language to enforce those planks.[29]

President McKinley immediately began to reconcile northern and southern animosities. In his inaugural address he stated:

The recent election not only most fortunately demonstrated the obliteration of sectional or geographical lines, but to some extent also the prejudices which for years have distracted our councils and marred our true greatness as a nation. . . . It will be my constant aim to do nothing, and permit nothing to be done, that will arrest or disturb this growing sentiment of unity and cooperation, this revival of esteem and affiliation which now animates so many thousands in both the old antagonistic sections, but I shall cheerfully do everything possible to promote and increase it.[30]

McKinley's inaugural address set the tenor for his administration's hands-off policies and attitudes toward race relations and his hands-on policies and attitudes toward international relations. Whereas Cleveland had only reluctantly taken the helm of the United States as a world power, McKinley gallantly seized it and subsequently assumed the role of admiral. The Spanish-American War, the occupation of Puerto Rico,

Cuba, Samoa, and the Philippines, all in 1898, plus the annexation of Hawaii in 1900, were hallmarks of McKinley jingoism.

Northern and southern animosity began to subside during McKinley's administration. One of the key components of this sectional unity was the acquiescence of northern Republicans to southern Democrats' strategies of disfranchisement, segregation, and ideas of racial inferiority. These were implicitly if not explicitly exchanged for Democrats' support in international matters. Senator Benjamin Tillman of South Carolina perhaps best summarized the North's accommodation of the South's ideas of racial inferiority in a diatribe on the Senate floor against northern Republicans during the Fifty-sixth Congress.

The brotherhood of man exists no longer because you shoot negroes in Illinois, when they come in competition with your labor, as we shoot them in South Carolina when they come in competition with us in the matter of elections. You do not love them any better than we do. You used to pretend that you did, but you no longer pretend it, except to get their votes. . . . You deal with the Filipinos just as we deal with the negroes, only you treat them a heap worse. You deal with the Puerto Ricans, or you propose to deal with the Puerto Ricans, just as we deal with the negroes, only you treat them a heap worse. . . . I will tell you that this is the difference: We of the South have never made any pretense of considering the negroes our equals or as being fit for suffrage. . . . You have changed; we have not.[31]

The acquiescence of northern Republicans to segregation and disfranchisement was reconciliatory and helped unify the country. A variety of interest groups integrated anthropology into their attempts to garner public support for foreign and domestic policies along these political lines. In addition, the anthropological discourse on race was (literally, in some cases) brought to life in magazines, museum exhibits, and world's fairs. These media were riddled with the writings of anthropologists, journalists, and so-called experts who appropriated early anthropological notions of race to buttress their propaganda. The American public voraciously consumed anthropology as popular culture. Similarly, world's fairs, magazines, and museum exhibits validated anthropology as a professional discipline in the academy because it provided a scientific justification for Jim Crow segregation and imperial domination.[32]

In 1912 John Daniels sagaciously identified the role of early ethnologists in the process of Southern redemption in his sociological study of Black Bostonians. He noted:

Whatever expectation had formerly been entertained that the Negro, endowed with equal rights, would forthwith rise automatically to the level of the other elements of the community and be received by them into full association, was now replaced by the conviction that the Negro was from these other elements and of a lower gradation. This change of view was in fact an approximation to the attitude held by the South. It was far more, however, than mere reconciliatory truckling to sectional opinion or prejudice. It amounted to an acceptance, in certain measure, of the South's anthropological theory with respect to the Negro,—the substance of which [assumed] . . . that he belonged to a "dissimilar" race, "unequal in intelligence and responsibility," [and] thus constituted a problem without precedent or parallel.[33]

A Constitutional Endorsement

One must first turn to the U.S. Supreme Court in the 1890s to fully understand how constitutional law structured and dictated the terms of racial categories through World War II. A series of Supreme Court cases actually codified the North's acceptance of the South's racial ideology into the law of the land.[34] Jim Crow statutes differed from the centuries-old de facto segregation and the Black Codes enacted after the Civil War because the U.S. Supreme Court endorsed these state laws and grafted the scientific understanding of racial inferiority onto the U.S. Constitution. The Supreme Court constitutionalized segregation by basing much of its rationale on popular conceptions of Social Darwinism, even though justices in the minority often dissented.[35]

During the 1896 session seven of the justices were liberal Republicans when appointed, and of the two Democrats, only one was from the South. Ostensibly, this would be a liberal court that would interpret the Constitution to uphold Negro rights and seek retribution from the South. The justices' liberal outlook regarding race seemingly waned in step with their legislative counterparts' because the Court consistently upheld southern segregation statutes.[36] One of these landmark cases was *Plessy v. Ferguson* (1896). This decision established the constitutionality of statutory segregation and helped to establish a climate for an onslaught of Jim Crow legislation and disfranchisement. It defied considerable precedent and created the disingenuous doctrine of separate but equal, which persisted for fifty-eight years.[37]

Associate Justice Henry B. Brown wrote the majority opinion for the Court; the object of the Fourteenth Amendment, he found, was to enforce equality between the two races before the law. "But in the nature of things" the amendment could not have intended to "abolish distinctions based upon color, or to enforce social, as distinguished from political equality."[38] The Court affirmed a Louisiana statute stating that conductors "shall have power and are hereby required to assign each passenger to the coach or compartment used for the race to which such passenger belongs."[39] Furthermore, any passenger insisting on going into "a coach or compartment to which by race he does not belong, shall be liable to a fine of twenty-five dollars, or in lieu thereof to imprisonment for a period of not more than twenty days in the parish prison."[40] If the conductor even failed to assign the passenger to the correct car, the conductor "shall be liable to a fine of twenty-five dollars, or in lieu thereof to imprisonment for a period of not more than twenty days in the parish prison."[41] In this sense, both Blacks and Whites were responsible for assigning and signifying social categories based on some scientific criteria that actually varied from state to state. Justice Brown failed to address the inherent ambiguities in the way he viewed race. The *color* of the plaintiff, Homer Adolph Plessy, was White or "in the proportion of seven eighths Caucasian and one eighth African blood" and "the mixture of colored blood was not discernible in him."[42]

The Court's opinion was validated by the growing commitment of White politicians and capitalists to the idea that the colored race was biologically inferior, which in turn helped to ensure their own political and economic power. The result became a construct of race imbued with notions of inferiority that promoted the repression of African Americans socially and structurally.

Associate Justice Henry Billings Brown decreed that "a statute which implies merely a legal distinction between the white and colored races — a distinction which is founded in the color of the two races, and which must always exist so long as white men are distinguished from the other race by color — has no tendency to destroy the legal equality of the two races."[43] The Court made a distinction between being equal and being equal before the law, and this distinction formed the basis of the so-called separate-but-equal doctrine. Brown asserted: "If one race be inferior to the other socially, the Constitution of the United States cannot put them upon the same plane."[44]

The state of Louisiana, with the affirmation of the U.S. Supreme Court, sanctioned the use of force to compel submission to those mechanisms that signified racial inferiority. The judicial branch of the federal government actually forced people — White and Black — to comply with the repression of African Americans in the social and cultural aspects of daily life, which helped to ensure African American repression in the political and economic aspects of daily life. Disfranchisement became the vehicle of oppression in state society, and racial segregation became the vehicle of oppression in civil society or the social and cultural sphere of daily life.[45] The idea of racial inferiority helped to define the terms, meaning, and significance for Negroes' racial construct, but statutory laws, pubic policy, and violence imposed those terms. Ethnologists in the United States at the turn of the century played an exceedingly important, albeit small, role in these complex processes because the self-styled discipline of American anthropology emerged as an authoritative source for expertise on natural laws and the scientific explanation of racial inferiority. In turn, anthropologists contributed to the solidification of the particularly oppressive construct of race that emerged in the late 1890s.

At the turn of the century a variety of ideas regarding racial inferiority served as a unifying ideology to guide the expansion of foreign markets and monopolies, the exploration and exploitation of natural resources, the imposition of American civilization on islands of "savages," and the promotion of disfranchisement and segregation for Negroes. Ideas of White supremacy, evolution, and racial inferiority routinized the notion that there was a natural and inevitable evolution of nations, races, and technology, from rude savagery into proficient civilization. This teleology was both encoded in discursive ideas of Social Darwinism and enacted in laws that structured race relations.

Southern interests marshaled the anthropological discourse on racial inferiority for propaganda and Jim Crow legislation, while Republican interests used the anthropological discourse on race to demonstrate that the inferior races of the Pacific and the Caribbean needed uplifting and civilizing.[46]

CHAPTER 2

The Ascension
of Anthropology as
Social Darwinism

The rise of academic anthropology in the United States occurred in the late 1880s and was concurrent with the rise of American imperialism and the institutionalization of racial segregation and disfranchisement. And like the anthropology that bolstered proslavery forces during the antebellum period, professional anthropology bolstered Jim Crow and imperial conquests during the 1890s. Before the 1880s the study of anthropology—or ethnology, as it was also called—tended to be an ancillary interest of naturalists and a romantic pastime for physicians interested in the so-called races of mankind. As discussed in the previous chapter, Samuel Morton, Josiah Nott, and Louis Agassiz contributed to the first school of American anthropology during the mid–nineteenth century, but these so-called men of science were not professional anthropologists employed by museums or departments of anthropology.[1] Anthropology moved from the margins of natural history into the center of the academy when other areas of natural history emerged as specific disciplines.

Following the Civil War, universities and government agencies quickly established departments of geography, physics, and geology when the proliferation of industries like railroads, steel, and mining demanded new technology.[2] Capitalists began to extol the virtues of science because it was the backbone for the development of technology, so important to the material ends of industrial development.

Industrializing America also needed to explain the calamities created by unbridled westward, overseas, and industrial expansion. Although expansion created wealth and prosperity for some, it contributed to conditions that fostered rampant child labor, infectious disease, and desperate poverty. As well, this period saw a sharp increase in lynchings and the decimation of Native American lives and land.[3] The daily experience of squalid conditions and sheer terror made many Americans realize the contradictions between industrial capitalism and the democratic ideals of equality, freedom, and justice for all. Legislators, university boards, and magazine moguls found it useful to explain this ideological crisis in terms of a *natural* hierarchy of class and race caused by a struggle for existence wherein the fittest individuals or races advanced while the inferior became eclipsed.

Professional anthropology emerged in the midst of this crisis, and the people who used anthropology to justify racism, in turn, provided the institutional foundations for the field. By the last decade of the nineteenth century, college departments, professional organizations, and specialized journals were established for anthropology.[4] The study of "primitive races of mankind" became comparable to geology and physics.[5] These institutional apparatuses, along with powerful representatives in the American Association for the Advancement of Science (AAAS), prestigious universities, and the Smithsonian Institution, gave anthropology its academic credentials as a discipline in the United States. The budding discipline gained power and prestige because ethnologists articulated theory and research that resonated with the dominant discourse on race.

The Laws of Science
and the Law of the Land

In January 1896 Daniel G. Brinton, the president of the AAAS and the first professor of anthropology in the United States, wrote in *Popular Science Monthly* that "the black, the brown and the red races differ anatomically so much from the white . . . that even with equal cerebral capacity they never could rival its results by equal efforts."[6] In April of the same year John Wesley Powell, the first director of the Bureau of American Ethnology (BAE) at the Smithsonian Institution, concurred with Brinton when he lectured at the U.S. National Museum

(USNM). Powell explained that "the laws of evolution do not produce kinds of men but grades of men; and human evolution is intellectual, not physical. . . . All men have pleasures, some more, some less; all men have welfare, some more, some less; all men have justice, some more, some less."[7]

Three weeks later, at the opposite end of the National Mall, Melville Fuller, the chancellor of the Smithsonian Institution and the chief justice of the U.S. Supreme Court, joined the Court's majority opinion in *Plessy v. Ferguson,* which stated that "if one race be inferior to the other socially, the Constitution of the United States cannot put them upon the same plane."[8] The Supreme Court constitutionalized segregation by grounding its rationale on notions of racial inferiority informed by Social Darwinism.[9]

Tenets of Social Darwinism emerged as important themes for the legal, scientific, and business communities—serving to glue one to the other.[10] Although ideas of racial inferiority and social evolution were not new to the United States, Social Darwinist ideas became increasingly dominant because they were viewed as scientific in an era when science reigned supreme. Early advocates of Social Darwinist (or, technically more accurate, Spencerist) thought retooled certain ideas of the Enlightenment for an industrializing society. Herbert Spencer, one of its chief proponents, grafted Thomas Hobbes's notion that the state of nature was a state of war—each individual taking what it could—onto Adam Smith's system of perfect liberty, later known as laissez-faire economics.[11] After Darwin's *Origin of Species* appeared, Social Darwinists blurred the idea of *natural* selection to scrutinize society and culture.[12]

Proponents of Social Darwinism believed that it was morally wrong for the government and charity organizations to provide public education, public health, or a minimum wage because these efforts only contributed to the artificial preservation of the weak.[13] A cross section of people, from politicians to world's fair organizers, White preachers to Black leaders, were influenced by this unique combination of social theory, and each used variations to explain inequalities in terms of the natural order of society. John D. Rockefeller even explained to a Sunday school class: "The American beauty rose can be produced . . . only by sacrificing early buds which grow around it."[14]

Two trajectories or planks emerged within Social Darwinian rhetoric in the United States. One emphasized the personal or individual struggle for existence; the other, racial and cultural evolution. The racial plank demarcated a hierarchy of races beginning with the inferior savage and culminating with the civilized citizen. The class plank presumed that the poor were biologically unfit to struggle for existence. Turn-of-the-century ethnologists took on the racial plank as their particular charge and played an important role in extending it.[15] And it was the racial plank that emerged as a means of reconciling animosity between the North and the South.

During the 1890s, ideas of Social Darwinism and racial inferiority were explicitly incorporated into political efforts to reunify the nation.[16] By 1896 the old ideas about Manifest Destiny, industrial progress, and racial inferiority (enlivened by Social Darwinism) served as an ideological cement that was able to form capitalist development, imperialism, scientific progress, racism, and the law into a rock-solid edifice within U.S. society. Social Darwinian ideas helped explain inequality in America, but Herbert Spencer's voluminous writings gave it scientific authority.

Herbert Spencer, America's Social Darwinist (1820–1903)

Herbert Spencer hailed from England, where Henry Ward Beecher adeptly wrote to him, observing that "the peculiar condition of American society has made your writings far more fruitful and quickening here than in Europe."[17] Spencer sold more than 300,000 copies of his books in the United States alone—a number unprecedented for nonfiction literature.[18]

The principal tenet of Spencer's synthetic philosophy was the organic analogy, an analogy drawn between biological organisms and society. The principles of biology, he argued, could be applied to society. Even before Darwin's *Origin of Species,* Spencer had worked out the basic elements for evolution. It was Spencer, not Darwin, who furnished the two famous phrases that became associated with the notion of evolution: "survival of the fittest" and "the struggle for existence." Spencer not only applied a biological analogy to society but also incorporated laws of astronomy, physics, geology, and psychology into a comprehensive scheme governed by something he called "the persistence of force."

The universe, as Spencer envisioned it, evolved from a state of homogeneity to one of heterogeneity. He argued that different scientific fields only explored certain facets of the evolutionary process. For example, astronomy and geology are distinct sciences, "but Geology is nothing more than a chapter continuing in detail one part of a history that was once wholly astronomic."[19] Likewise, sociology and psychology are extensions of biology, which are extensions of geology, astronomy, and physics.

Spencer devoted much of his attention to the evolution of human faculties, linking and ranking intellectual, social, and biological attributes. Minds, bodies, and social institutions (such as families and governments) thus fit neatly into an evolutionary framework. As he suggested, "Intellectual evolution, as it goes on in the human race [goes] along with social evolution, of which it is at once a cause and a consequence."[20] Within this evolutionary hierarchy, the most inferior were the savages; the next up the ladder were the semi-civilized, and finally we reached the civilized men.

Spencer applied this line of thought in "The Comparative Psychology of Man" (1876), presented to the London Anthropological Institute and circulated in the United States by *Popular Science Monthly*. In it, Spencer confidently ranked and ordered racial-cultural groups while detailing his familiar argument about the natural progress of societies. The labels he assigned to different people were concoctions of religions, continents, races, or languages, and he argued that anthropologists should thus prove whether his hierarchy was consistently maintained throughout all orders of races, from the lowest to the highest, "whether, say, the Australian differs in this respect from the Hindoo, as much as the Hindoo does from the European."[21]

This address revealed three particularly racist themes that were reproduced and canonized within U.S. anthropology. First, Spencer identified the "orders of races" by language, religion, or continent. This is important because race, language, culture, nationality, ethnicity, and so forth were all viewed as one and the same in Spencer's racial and cultural scheme. Second, Spencer asserted, with the conviction of a scientific law, that racial-cultural inferiority and superiority exist. For example, he advised the London Anthropological Institute to prove just how much inferiority there was based on his evolutionary assumptions.[22]

Finally, Spencer took his place in the long line of philosophers and scholars to scientifically affirm the association of *black* with evil, savagery,

and brutishness, thus recapitulating the widely held idea that the lighter races are superior to the darker ones. These themes were subsequently reproduced in the mass media as science, integrated into domestic and foreign policy, and appropriated by White supremacist demagogues. They were not successfully challenged until the United States entered World War II.

Anthropological Social Darwinists

As anthropology emerged in the United States as a discipline in the late nineteenth century, only a handful of ethnologists were influential in shaping it. The most influential were John Wesley Powell the research leader, Frederic Ward Putnam the museum builder, and Daniel G. Brinton the academician.[23] Between 1889 and 1898 each held the presidency of the AAAS, then the most powerful scientific organization in the United States. Although none of these ethnologists was a strict Social Darwinist in the Spencerian tradition, each was an evolutionist advancing ideas of the superiority and inferiority of particular races when Social Darwinism was a dominant ideology in the United States.[24]

The discipline of anthropology in 1896 was being carved out of various sciences and studies. The scope of the new discipline varied. Powell envisioned it as encompassing just about everything including somatology, esthetology, sociology, philology, and sophiology. The most significant scholars in the development of the field called themselves ethnologists, but for some time no real consensus existed as to what constituted ethnology. Brinton perhaps best captured the aim of the new science. Ethnology was to "compare dispassionately all the acts and arts of man, his philosophies and religions, his social schemes and personal plans, weighing and analyzing them, separating the local and temporal in them from the permanent and general, explaining the former by the conditions of time and place and the latter to the category of qualities which make up the oneness of humanity."[25]

Figure 1. Daniel Garrison Brinton. (Courtesy of the American Philosophical Society)

Daniel G. Brinton, Academician (1837–1899)

DANIEL G. BRINTON, A.M., M.D.,
PROFESSOR OF ETHNOLOGY AT THE ACADEMY OF NATURAL
SCIENCES, PHILADELPHIA, AND OF AMERICAN ARCHAEOLOGY AND
LINGUISTICS IN THE UNIVERSITY OF PENNSYLVANIA;
PRESIDENT OF THE AMERICAN FOLK-LORE SOCIETY
AND OF THE NUMISMATIC AND
ANTIQUARIAN SOCIETY OF PHILADELPHIA; MEMBER OF THE
ANTHROPOLOGICAL SOCIETIES OF BERLIN AND VIENNA AND THE
ETHNOGRAPHICAL SOCIETIES OF PARIS AND FLORENCE, OF THE ROYAL
SOCIETY OF ANTIQUARIES, COPENHAGEN, THE ROYAL ACADEMY OF
HISTORY OF MADRID, THE AMERICAN PHILOSOPHICAL SOCIETY,
THE AMERICAN ANTIQUARIAN SOCIETY, ETC., ETC.

This pillar of titles consumes the title page of Brinton's *Races and Peoples: Lectures on the Science of Ethnography* (1890) (Figure 1). The litany of titles framed the authority from which Brinton pioneered the discipline. The "etc." included being president of the AAAS and twice vice president and once president of the International Congress of Americanists.[26] Brinton only assumed these more powerful positions after the publication of *Races and Peoples.*

Brinton was largely responsible for changing anthropology from a romantic pastime to an academic discipline. He had an undaunted commitment to developing ethnology into a full-fledged scientific discipline, and he wielded his academic prowess, credentials, and reputation to develop and legitimate the field. Brinton had a penchant for source citation, demanded rigor, and maintained that ethnological research must adhere to standards of academic excellence. He also saw the need for a national organization of professionals with a publishing arm that explored all the fields of anthropology. Brinton developed the field, however, by advancing claims of the racial superiority of Whites and the racial inferiority of people of color. He anchored anthropology to an evolutionary paradigm, and he, perhaps more than any other early ethnologist, assimilated the current sociopolitical ideas about race and gender and restated them as science.

Like most ethnologists in the United States, Brinton was initially interested in Native American languages, customs, and prehistory and had only ancillary interest in evolutionary theory and racial classification. Although he first became interested in Native Americans when he discovered Delaware artifacts while wandering near his home in Thornbury, Pennsylvania, his first professional interest was medicine.[27] He graduated from Yale University in 1858 and pursued medicine at Jefferson Medical College in Philadelphia and postdoctoral research in Paris and Heidelberg. In 1862 he entered the Union Army and was soon commissioned as surgeon-in-chief of the Second Division, Eleventh Corps, of the Army of the Potomac.[28]

Even before the war Brinton was interested in Native American society and language. Although he never engaged in ethnographic fieldwork, he meticulously analyzed the mounds of the Mississippi Valley. He was one of the first scholars to ridicule the notion that previous races built the mounds, arguing that Native Americans from the Mississippi Valley engineered and built the structures.[29] Brinton became an expert on Native American linguistics and grammar, and his reputation, especially in Philadelphia, grew. He was elected to the American Philosophical Society in 1869, became professor of ethnology at the Academy of Natural Sciences of Philadelphia in 1884, and was named professor of American archaeology and linguistics at the University of Pennsylvania in 1886 (where he also sat on the board of what is now the University of Pennsylvania Museum of Archaeology and Anthropology). He was then elected president of the International Congress of Anthropology in 1893 and president of the AAAS in 1894. He published frequently in various journals and had a regular column in *Science* entitled "Current Notes on Anthropology."

The organs of the American Philosophical Society, the AAAS, and the Academy of Natural Sciences became regular outlets for Brinton's scholarship on racial inferiority, ethnology, and the grammar of Native Americans.[30] Regna Darnell, Brinton's biographer, explains that during the 1890s his career blossomed and he rose to power in the scientific community, which helped to validate and establish the scientific authority of ethnology.[31] During this period he shifted from Indian linguistics and grammar to evolutionary theory and ethnology. His writings on ethnology, published primarily in the 1880s and 1890s, explicitly articulated ideas of evolution by espousing racial inferiority. They were concurrent with, and congruent to, Social Darwinism, White supremacist demagoguery, increased lynchings, disfranchisement, and Jim Crow segregation. His shift from Indian linguistics to evolutionary theory correlated with his acquisition of unprecedented power for an ethnologist.[32]

By employing Darnell's distribution analysis of Brinton's publications, one can view the relationship between Brinton's rise to power and his scientific validation of racial inferiority. The total distribution of Brinton's ethnological writings included 13 articles in the 1860s, 10 in the 1870s, 78 in the 1880s, and 108 in the 1890s.[33]

The pivotal publication that solidified Brinton's national reputation seems to have been *Races and Peoples*. The book was a series of lectures on ethnography that consolidated the "latest and most accurate researches."[34] The first chapter, "Lectures on Ethnography," begins with a survey of craniology detailing a range of features used to classify and rank races. These characteristics included: cranial capacity, color, muscular structure, vital powers, and sexual preference. He summarized these under the subheading "Physical Criteria of Racial Superiority" and concluded: "We are accustomed familiarly to speak of 'higher' and 'lower' races, and we are justified in this even from merely physical considerations. These indeed bear intimate relations to mental capacity. . . . Measured by these criteria, the European or white race stands at the head of the list, the African or negro at its foot."[35]

In the next chapter, Brinton linked "physical elements of ethnography" to so-called social and psychological elements of ethnography. He proposed that the only way to accurately order and classify the races was to consider both mental and physical characteristics, explaining: "The mental differences of races and nations are real and profound. Some of them are just as valuable for ethnic classification as any of the physical elements I referred to in the last lecture, although purely physical anthropologists are loath to admit this."[36]

The entire first section of the book amounted to a periodic table of the "elements of ethnography," with instructions for ranking, ordering, and classifying races—literally a how-to guide. In chapter 3, "The Beginnings and Subdivisions of Races," he launched into a discussion of evolution, and he tended to favor the Lamarckian view that acquired characteristics were transmitted from parent to offspring.[37] He provided a detailed description of each race, beginning with the White or "the leading race in all history." For the various stocks and groups of Black people he merely restated rancorous racial stereotypes as science.

The tradition of racist imagery in the United States is long, of course, and he wove together science and imagery found in widely circulated magazines, minstrel shows, and the Uncle Tom's Cabin shows that were crisscrossing the country. Old stereotypes became scientific fact. Some were blatant: Brinton suggested that "The true negroes are passionately fond of music, singing and dancing."[38] Other statements were subtle but caustic. Brinton reproduced the stock stereotypes the entertainment and advertising industries had found profitable, including the idea that African Americans resembled apes. Brinton reiterated this image in his scheme for measuring cranial capacities and facial angles by placing the "African negro midway between the Orang-utang and the European white."[39] In another text he unabashedly stated that "the African black . . . presents many peculiarities which are termed 'pithecoid' or ape-like."[40]

The familiar ideas that Brinton recast as science were routinized in American popular culture by the myriad degrading images of African Americans used for everything from selling toothpaste to entertaining children.[41] These stereotypes drove industries like minstrel shows, trading cards, and sheet music of "coon songs."

Serious political ramifications followed when scientists like Brinton legitimated popular images within authoritative texts. Because Negroes were placed on the bottom rung of an immutable ladder to civilization, they were absolved of the responsibilities (voting) and denied the privileges (social equality) of civilization. This notion of a virtually permanent inferiority resonated with the logic of the Supreme Court's *Plessy* decision.

The parallels are striking. Brinton stated that the "Hottentot is rather a hopeless case for civilization efforts. He hates profoundly work, either physical or mental, and is passionately fond of rum and tobacco"; social equality among the races is not possible because of the *natural* inequality between the races.[42] Such was the line of thought articulated by the Supreme Court when it interpreted the Fourteenth Amendment in *Plessy*. The Court decided that the amendment was intended to enforce equality between the two races before the law. The amendment was not intended to impose an unnatural or impossible social equality. Just as Brinton elicited the notion of evolutionary rungs, Justice Brown used the term *plane* to evoke a similar symbol of racial inequality.[43]

Brinton did not stop at perpetuating racist stereotypes to buttress the logic for racial segregation. He provided the "scientific" justification for the "lynch law." The number of lynchings was steadily increasing in 1890, when *Races and Peoples* was published.[44] The Republicans had just lost control of Congress, cotton prices were plummeting, and the acts to secure African American suffrage were on the chopping block. Terrorists of the Democratic Party effectively used the lynch law to ensure home-rule and White supremacy (Figure 2). In both popular and scientific literature African American men, in particular, were depicted as savages who harbored a bestial lust for White women. These depravities, many believed, could be curbed only by sadistic tortures and lynchings.[45] The routine violence perpetrated by lynch mobs was always portrayed as justice served in the name of chivalry and the "protection" of White southern women.[46] Brinton goaded White supremacists with one more justification:

It cannot be too often repeated, too emphatically urged, that it is to the women alone of the highest race that we must look to preserve the purity of the type, and with it the claims of the race to be the highest. They have no holier duty, no more sacred mission, than that of transmitting in its integrity the heritage of ethnic endowment gained by the race throughout thousands of generations of struggle. . . . That philanthropy is false, that religion is rotten, which would sanction a white woman enduring the embrace of a colored man.[47]

Brinton's call to preserve White womanhood must be viewed as White supremacist demagoguery knighted by scientific authority. Ethnology

Figure 2. Justice? A lynch mob preparing to burn a man alive in Paris, Texas, ca. 1890. (Courtesy of the Library of Congress)

as a science gave to rich and poor southern Whites symbols of pure nationality while it helped to reinforce the cult of White womanhood.[48] Brinton's cloaked assertion that women need men and are inferior to men exemplifies Sandra Harding's assertion that science helps to interlock gender, race, and class hierarchies.[49]

After *Races and Peoples* was published, Brinton articulated these ideas from positions of national leadership. In his 1895 presidential address to the AAAS he espoused the same rhetoric that he had detailed in his 1890 book. However, this address had a much wider audience than the book because it was published by *Popular Science Monthly* (1896). Brinton employed the same evolutionary construct based on racial inferiority and insisted that anthropology "offers a positive basis for legislation, politics, and education as applied to a given ethnic group."[50]

The president of the AAAS issued a call for laws and educational reform which applied the scientific fact that Negroes were inferior. That same year the highest court in the land seemingly answered the call and ruled on *Plessy,* thereby codifying into constitutional law the idea of racial inferiority that forced African Americans into inferior schools, bathrooms, and the train cars of Jim Crow.

John Wesley Powell,
Research Leader (1834–1902)

In the late nineteenth century the BAE and the Anthropological Society of Washington mobilized more men, women, and resources to pursue ethnology than did any other organization in the nation.[51] John Wesley Powell was the person directly responsible for generating interest, dollars for research, and the growing body of research (Figure 3). In 1888 he was elected president of the AAAS. Although Native American ethnology was his sideline interest, he leveraged prestige, political savvy, and healthy budgets to establish the new field.

Powell was a powerful man in the elite circles of Washington, establishing almost single-handedly both the U.S. Geological Survey (USGS) and the BAE. The power he wielded in the House Appropriation Committee, the AAAS, the Smithsonian Institution, and the National Academy of Sciences was contingent on maintaining a strong alliance of support within these organizations. His base was made up of a coterie of Washington insiders, Harvard naturalists, government bureaucrats, BAE ethnologists, and members of Washington scientific societies. He had to continually shore up these alliances with favors, contracts, publications, and grants.[52]

Although Powell used ideas of evolution and racial hierarchies to produce his own theory and research, he did not espouse the rhetoric that was characteristic of Brinton and other scientists. Powell explicitly distanced himself from scientific racism. The distance was chimerical, because the people who supported him simply did not share his benign outlook toward people of color. In fact, Powell embraced some of the most ardent champions of racial inferiority to ensure his power and develop the research needed to legitimate the new field.

The Bureau's (Theoretical) Foundation

John Wesley Powell was born in 1834 and grew up in the Midwest. As a youth he wanted to make a career out of natural history, and in 1858 he went to Oberlin College to launch it. Oberlin had a long tradition of racial and gender integration, and it was a bastion of radical

Figure 3. John Wesley Powell at his desk at the Bureau of American Ethnology. (Courtesy of the National Anthropological Archives, Smithsonian Institution)

abolitionist thought and action when Powell attended. Although sympathetic to the radical students of Oberlin, Powell devoted himself full-time to natural history.[53]

When the Civil War broke out, Powell was forced to decide between his commitment to natural history and his commitment to the Union. He decided to answer Abraham Lincoln's call for volunteers and joined the Twentieth Regiment of Illinois Volunteers. He was quickly promoted and served courageously, even after he lost his right arm in combat. He was also one of the few officers who trained and outfitted an African American regiment for the Union Army.[54]

After the war Powell continued to pursue his chosen field. He envisioned a museum of natural history for the state of Illinois and successfully lobbied the Illinois legislature for an appropriation. Powell wanted his museum to be the "best in the West," so he immediately orchestrated a specimen-collecting expedition to the Rocky Mountains. He understood that a scientific expedition on the scale he envisioned needed unprecedented financial support. He was able to parlay his access to President Ulysses S. Grant (which he gained from the war) into the underwriting of his expedition by the public and private sectors.[55] Before he unpacked from his first expedition, he undertook the preparations for his second one, a geological and ethnological survey of the Grand Canyon. Between 1867 and 1877 Powell made more than thirty federally funded expeditions, and he emerged as the expert on the geological and ethnological classification of the Rocky Mountains and the Great Basin.[56]

Powell began as a dispassionate scientist, but he developed into a crusader to save public land and Native American societies. In the late 1870s he began to lobby the scientific community and Congress to reform land-acquisition legislation. He worked to convince the National Academy of Sciences to draft legislation to reform the way the federal government disposed of land and to consolidate the various federal surveying agencies.[57]

Although the National Academy of Sciences sponsored the bill, the land-reform legislation was not passed because it was hotly contested by railroad and development interests.[58] When the bill was in committee, Powell submitted his *Report on the Methods of Surveying the Public Domain* (1878) to the Department of the Interior, and it was reviewed during the congressional hearings for the bill. In the report he justified establishing the USGS and the BAE. Although the land-reform bill died, his report formed the basis from which both the USGS and the BAE were established under the Sundry Civil Appropriation Bill of March 3, 1879.[59]

In the report, Powell made seemingly contradictory statements for the justification of the BAE. Above all, he looked to science to remedy the Indian problem.[60] The theoretical position he took fits squarely within an anthropological strand of Social Darwinism, even though it challenged some of the assumptions Brinton and Spencer put forth regarding people of color. Powell opposed the idea that members of Indian societies were inferior to members of civilized societies and explained that "Savagery is not inchoate civilization; it is a distinct status of society with its own institutions, customs, philosophy, and religion" (Figure 4). He immediately, however, anchored the crux of the BAE

Figure 4. John Wesley Powell inquiring about water in the Southwest.
(Courtesy of the National Anthropological Archives, Smithsonian Institution)

justification to notions of evolution. Federal agents, he explained, must study indigenous customs because they "must necessarily be overthrown before new institutions, customs, philosophy, and religion can be introduced."[61]

Although Powell may have been benevolent toward Native Americans, there was no doubt about what race he viewed as superior. In an 1888 article for the first issue of the *American Anthropologist,* entitled "From Barbarism to Civilization," he explained that "in setting forth the evolution of barbarism to civilization, it becomes necessary to confine the exposition . . . to one great stock of people—the Aryan race."[62]

As director of the BAE Powell contracted and hired an array of scientists to conduct research on Native Americans under the rubric of what he called "anthropologic knowledge." The projects and studies sponsored by the BAE were compiled into large annual reports and distributed liberally throughout academic institutions around the world. Under Powell's direction the BAE published nineteen annual reports full of multicolored lithographs and scientific papers, forming the first comprehensive corpus of research for ethnology.

Ethnological research, under Powell, became field research and departed from Brinton's ethnography, which sought only to classify the races. Brinton could not compete with the sheer magnitude of research generated by the BAE and its collaborative approach. Actually, he did not attempt to compete with the bureau because he was philosophically opposed to the utilitarian approach of government science.[63]

Although Brinton was ostensibly not competing, he wrote the definitive text on Native American grammar. This effort culminated in *The American Race: A Linguistic Classification and Ethnographic Description of the Native Tribes of North and South America* (1891). While conducting research for the book, Brinton met resistance from the BAE and was denied access to unpublished manuscripts in its collections. Brinton exposed the rift between the two emerging axes of anthropology when he indicted Powell in his introduction. He lamented the fact that "access to this [material at the BAE] was denied me except under the condition that I should not use in any published work the information thus obtained, a proviso scarcely so liberal as had expected."[64]

Powell did not share Brinton's approach to ethnography, his disdain for applied research, or his view of people of color as perpetually inferior. The only thing Brinton and Powell shared were results presented at scientific meetings and in published papers. Powell believed that the federal government ought to shoulder the moral responsibility to uplift Native Americans to a status approaching civilized society. Unlike Brinton, Powell's later work did not attribute the state of savagery to racial inferiority.[65] For example, in "Sociology, or the Science of Institutions,"[66] he explicitly confronted the way savagery was viewed in the popular culture:

To the ethnologist a savage is a forest dweller. In common conception the savage is a brutal person whose chief delight is in taking scalps. Sometimes the sylvan man is cruel, — but even civilized men are sometimes cruel. Savagery is a status of culture to the ethnologist, who recognizes four such states, of which savagery is the lowest. Some of the Amerindian tribes belong to this lowest stage; while others belong to a higher stage which is called barbarism. . . . [C]onsider the savage not as a man of cruelty, but as a man who takes part in a regularly organized government, with laws, that are obeyed and enforced.[67]

However paternal, this passage represents a departure from his views in 1888 and from Brinton's notion that culture and race were one and the same. It also was consistent with the views of Lewis Henry Morgan.

Powell was largely self-taught in natural history and held no advanced degrees. Though not his formal teacher, Morgan influenced many of Powell's views, and most of the research at the BAE was shaped by Morgan's ideas about race and culture.[68]

Lewis Henry Morgan, Powell's Ally (1818–1881)

Lewis Henry Morgan also made a tremendous contribution to the foundation of U.S. ethnology, and in 1879 he was the first in a line of ethnologists to use the presidency of the AAAS as a bully pulpit to validate and legitimate ethnology in the United States (Figure 5). A longtime resident of upstate New York, he was trained in law, served in the state assembly and senate, and invested in railroads serving the Great Lakes region.

Morgan's contributions to ethnology were made somewhat earlier than were those of Brinton, Powell, and Putnam. And although he had an important theoretical impact, he did not play a major hands-on role in establishing the institutional foundations of the field. His accolades came late in his life. *Ancient Society, or Researches in the Lines of Human Progress from Savagery through Barbarism to Civilization,* his magnum opus, was published in 1877; he was elected to the presidency of the AAAS in 1879 but died a year after his term ended. He was interested in ideas of progress as well as Native American social organization and turned to ethnology to unite them.

He published widely on Native American kinship systems, but his most influential work was *Ancient Society,* in which he developed an elaborate evolutionary scheme to portray the development of human society. He argued that the road to civilization passed through a series of stages, each with its own distinctive culture and mode of subsistence. Morgan also seemingly observed that "with the production of inventions and discoveries, and with the growth of institutions, the human mind necessarily grew and expanded; and we are led to recognize a gradual enlargement of the brain itself."[69] He thus argued that there was a correlation between "cranial capacity" and social as well as technological development, asserting the belief that contemporary races were arranged hierarchically and reflected different stages in the evolution to civilization. Though similar to Spencer's ideas of the racial-cultural

Figure 5. Lewis Henry Morgan, ca. 1877. (Courtesy of the National Anthropological Archives, Smithsonian Institution)

evolution, Morgan differed because he linked cultural evolution to materialist development. He claimed that the development of technology and modes of production led to civilization, which suggested that races of people were not necessarily shackled to a permanent status of inferiority.

Powell worked closely with Morgan, and he supplied Morgan with ethnographic information about the kinship organization of the Hopi and other Great Basin groups for *Ancient Society*.[70] Morgan, like Powell, was influential in government circles. Prior to the Civil War—before Powell and Brinton were national figures—Morgan was regarded as *the* authority on Native American affairs.[71] It appears that Morgan was looked to as an expert on African American affairs as well. When the Compromise of 1850 was being made in Congress, Morgan advised William Seward—an old friend and U.S. senator from New York—that

it is time to fix some limits to the reproduction of this black race among us. It is limited in the north by the traits of the whites. The black population has no independent vitality among us. In the south, while the blacks are property, there can be no assignable limit to their reproduction. It is too thin a race intellectually to be fit to propagate and I am perfectly satisfied from reflection that the feeling toward this race is one of hostility in the north. We have no respect for them whatever.[72]

Although Morgan has been championed for his "materialist conception of history," this letter reveals the White supremacist perspective embedded in *Ancient Society* that later emerged as the theoretical underpinning of the BAE.[73] Powell distributed copies of the book to the members of his staff, who used it as an ethnographic handbook in the field and a guide for organizing museum exhibits.[74]

Morgan was not the only colleague in Powell's alliance who advanced the notion of racial inferiority: others had an even more devastating impact. One of the most outspoken scientists in the late nineteenth century on the inferiority of African Americans was Nathaniel Southgate Shaler.

Nathaniel Southgate Shaler, Powell's Ally (1841–1906)

Nathaniel Southgate Shaler was initially trained by Louis Agassiz and became a geographer, geologist, and dean of the Lawrence

Scientific School at Harvard University. By the turn of the century he was one of the most respected scholars in the country.[75] Powell, who was always looking, found powerful support in Shaler. Powell secured Shaler's support by granting him research funding and an appointment as director of the Atlantic Coast Division of the USGS.[76] The funding and appointment paid off.

In 1884 both the BAE and the USGS were in jeopardy because Congress was investigating the necessity of all scientific agencies. Powell's integrity, the bureau, and the survey were each scrutinized. The joint commission, chaired by Senator William B. Allison, investigated Powell's appointments and his fiscal responsibility. Simultaneously, the Treasury Department scrutinized every ledger under Powell's authority. The investigations lasted for a year, and Powell emerged victorious with the staunch support of Shaler.

From the beginning of the investigation Powell took the offensive by showcasing a myriad of statistics about aridity and settlement patterns and confirming them with an array of topographic maps. He challenged the commission on one point after another.[77] During the whole scandal Shaler aligned himself with Powell.[78] On Powell's behalf, Shaler admonished his Harvard colleague, Alexander Agassiz, who testified against Powell.[79] Their performance in the Allison Commission investigation propelled both of them into the national spotlight, and together they were regarded as national leaders in the applied sciences.[80] Although Shaler's reputation was fashioned in the academic community as an applied scientist, around the country middle-class Americans knew him as the Harvard professor who made science accessible to the general public. Shaler was recognized as the "purveyor of science to the nation" because of his widely circulated scientific exposés in magazines like the *Atlantic Monthly, Popular Science Monthly,* and the *North American Review.*[81] He did not limit his exposés to geology: he wrote widely on social issues and provided a scientific analysis of the so-called Negro problem for the American public.

For the 1890 volume of the *Atlantic Monthly,* Shaler wrote "Science and the African Problem." It appeared just months before the elections for the Fifty-second Congress (which repealed many of the federal election bills). It illustrates how popular versions of anthropology buoyed racist political projects. Shaler the geologist turned into Shaler the anthropologist to advocate "the study of the negroes by the methods of modern anthropology."[82] Like Brinton, Shaler entwined stereotypes with anthropology, but he did so in the mass media:

But it is not only as an experiment in practical anthropology that this trans-plantation of the negro in America will interest our successors. . . . We can see how English, Irish, French, Germans, and Italians may, after time of trouble, mingle their blood and their motives in a common race, which may be as strong, or even stronger, for the blending to these diversities. We cannot hope for such a result with the negro, for an overwhelming body of experience shows that the third something which comes from the union of the European with the African is not as good material as either of the orig-inal stocks; that it has not the vital energy and the character required for the uses of the state. The African and European races must remain distinct in blood.[83]

Shaler also reproduced the image that the affairs of "darkies" inevitably degenerate into chaos:[84]

But experience shows us that if we could insulate a single county in the South, and give it over to negroes alone, we should in a few decades find that his European clothing, woven by generations of education, had fallen away, and the race gone down to a much lower state of being than that it now occupies. In other words, the negro is not as yet intellectually so far up in the scale of development as he appears to be; in him the great virtues of the superior race, though implanted, have not yet taken firm root, and are in need of constant tillage, lest the old savage weeds overcome the tender shoots of the new and unnatural culture.[85]

Moreover, Shaler presented the stereotype of Negroes' mythic sense of rhythm as science:

There are reasons for believing that the negroes can readily be cultivated in certain departments of thought in which the emotions lend aid to labor; as, for instance, in music. There is hardly any doubt that they have a keener sense of rhythm than whites of the same intellectual grade,—perhaps than any grade whatever. . . . [T]hese considerations lead me to think that music may be one of the lines on which careful inquiry may develop great possi-bilities for the race.[86]

In "The Negro Problem" (1884), also published in the *Atlantic Monthly,* Shaler offered a scientific rationale to support disfranchise-ment and segregation. He based the article on a common premise that African Americans were inherently incapable of shouldering the re-sponsibility of citizenship.[87] The dean of the Lawrence Scientific School reported to the American public that African Americans were "a folk, bred first in a savagery that had never been broken by the least effort towards a higher state, and then in a slavery that tended almost as little to fit them for a place in the structure of a self-controlling society. Surely, the effort to blend these two people by a proclamation and a constitutional amendment will sound strangely in the time to come. . . . [R]esolutions cannot help this rooted nature of man."[88] Based on this framework, Shaler justified the many statutes declaring Negroes "unfit" to vote, sit on juries, and testify against White persons in a court of law, explaining, "I hold it to be clear that the inherited qualities of the negroes to a great degree unfit them to carry the burden of our own civilization."[89]

Shaler was the decipherer of science for the nation and the instructor of more than 7,000 Harvard graduates; he dispensed racial stereotypes in the classroom as science and saturated the most popular monthly publications with the same.[90] More than Brinton, Powell, and Putnam, it was Shaler who marshaled anthropological ideas to sway public opinion against Negro suffrage. Shaler was a self-proclaimed "practical anthropologist." By articulating the racial plank of Social Darwinism he helped foster the acquiescence of the North to southern ideas of racial inferiority and provided the scientific stamp of approval for McKinley's overtures to White supremacy, the Republican Party's abandonment of African American interests, widespread disfranchisement, and Jim Crow segregation.[91]

Powell's public association, support, and appreciation of Shaler must be scrutinized. Powell implicitly supported Shaler's agenda and did not explicitly reject Shaler's "practical anthropology." The ethnologist on whom Shaler relied for credibility was Powell, not Frederic Ward Putnam, who was also at Harvard as the curator of the Peabody Museum of American Archaeology and Ethnology. Similarly, Powell's connection with Harvard's powerful lobby in Washington was Shaler, not Putnam. Indicative of these relationships, Shaler was the Harvard faculty member who hosted Powell when he accepted an honorary degree at the university's 250th anniversary in November 1886.[92]

Powell's greatest contribution to the discipline of anthropology was a successful negotiation of Washington's political and bureaucratic terrain, which allowed him to lay an institutional and financial foundation to sustain the discipline. Although Powell challenged particular notions of racial inferiority, he never attacked the members of his elite circles who embraced Social Darwinian ideas of racial inferiority. Powell accommodated White supremacist ideology as he carried out the BAE's congressional mandate to study Native American institutions so they could be overthrown and replaced.

Frederic Ward Putnam, Museum Builder (1839–1915)

Frederic Ward Putnam anchored the New England axis of the institutional and curricular development of anthropology at the Peabody Museum of American Archaeology and Ethnology. He was also instrumental in the development of three later institutional foci for the discipline. These included the Department of Anthropology at the American Museum of Natural History (AMNH) in New York City, the Department of Anthropology at the Field Museum of Natural History in Chicago, and the Phoebe Apperson Hearst Museum of Anthropology at the University of California, Berkeley. Putnam's academic focus was American archaeology, which differed from Powell and Brinton's focus on ethnology and linguistics. Putnam forged Native American archaeology, linguistics, and ethnology together, insisting on the term *anthropology* to encompass all three.[93]

Like Brinton, Putnam "had to wrench the study of 'early man and his work' out of the hands of the amateur and of the dilettante and place scientific foundations under a structure which, at first, had only very vague outlines."[94] Following Morgan, Powell, and Brinton, Putnam also became the president of the AAAS in 1898.

Putnam was born in Salem, Massachusetts, in 1839. Both of his parents were descendants of the early New England elites. In his obituary the *Harvard Graduate's Magazine* boasted that "the father, grandfather, and great grandfather of Professor Putnam were all graduates of Harvard College, and the associations of his mother's family had been close with the institution from its beginning."[95]

Putnam entered Harvard College in 1856 but never formally matriculated into a degree program. The following year he became an assistant to Louis Agassiz at the Museum of Comparative Zoology, where he founded the journal *American Naturalist* in 1867. Although he established the Salem Press to publish that journal, the press also started publishing the *Proceedings of the American Association for the Advancement of Science*.[96] Putnam was the permanent general secretary of the AAAS for twenty-five consecutive years beginning in 1875, and his editorial leadership—which came with owning the press—helped define the direction of science during the final quarter of the nineteenth century.[97]

Anchoring the New England Axis

Three distinct institutional axes formed as the discipline matured: Powell anchored government anthropology in Washington at the BAE; Brinton anchored linguistic and evolutionary anthropology in Philadelphia at the University of Pennsylvania; and Putnam anchored archaeological anthropology in New England at Harvard University. As we will see, a power struggle over the direction of anthropology developed when Franz Boas dropped an anchor for cultural anthropology in New York City at Columbia University.

George Foster Peabody, an American-born London financier, provided the impetus for the New England axis. He endowed three Peabody Museums, one at Harvard University, another at Yale University, and the third in Salem, Massachusetts. Putnam was the first director of the Peabody Museum in Salem and later became the director of the one at Harvard.[98] In 1866 Peabody endowed Harvard University for a museum and professorship of American archaeology and ethnology. Putnam became curator of the Peabody Museum in 1875 and was appointed professor in 1885.[99]

Once in a position of leadership, Putnam orchestrated massive expeditions all over the Western Hemisphere to collect artifacts and conduct research for the Peabody Museum. He organized archaeological research in Central America, Ohio, New Jersey, and the Plains States. To publish the findings, he established the *Papers of the Peabody Museum of American Archaeology* in 1876 and a series of *Memoirs* in 1896. Like Powell's annual reports for the BAE, Putnam's *Papers of the Peabody* formed the corpus of research from which Native American archaeology advanced.

Another significant contribution Putnam made was to expose the public to anthropology through museums and world's fair exhibits; this was also his most significant contribution to the social construction of race. The organizers of the 1893 World's Columbian Exposition selected Putnam as the chief of Department M (anthropology). He began in earnest to fashion an ethnographical exhibition of the past and present peoples so that each stage of evolution could be observed.[100] He successfully lobbied top administrators for an anthropological building dedicated to the three-field approach to the discipline. The structure was simply called the Anthropological Building, and it was the first time the term *anthropology* was introduced widely to the American public.[101]

Under the rubric of anthropology and under the roof of the Anthro-pological Building, the images of racial inferiority imposed on the "lesser races" were brought to life for millions of Americans by "living ethno-logical exhibits." Putnam hired agents to collect indigenous people from all over the world and then instructed the "native representatives" where to set up their "habitations." He deliberately positioned their encamp-ments along the Midway Plaisance to reflect his idea of an evolutionary hierarchy. As Harlan I. Smith, one of Putnam's assistants, stated, "From first to last, the exhibits of this department will be arranged and grouped to teach a lesson; to show the advancement of evolution of man."[102] The images Putnam produced for popular consumption helped solidify the notion of racial and cultural inferiority imposed on African Ameri-cans, Native Americans, and other "savages" the world over.

Although the *Papers of the Peabody* and the world's fair were impor-tant, it was Putnam's organizational skills and institution building that created his important legacy, which includes initiating new regional cen-ters of anthropology, in Chicago, New York, and Berkeley. He was important in Chicago because he helped to curate the first collections of the Department of Anthropology at the Field Museum of Natural History. The Field Museum's first acquisitions were the collections dis-played at the 1893 Chicago world's fair. As chief of Department M, he was responsible for curating the fair's anthropological collections as well as overseeing the museum's adoption of them.

Putnam also helped institutionalize anthropology in New York City. In April 1894, immediately after the fair, the AMNH appointed him curator of the Department of Anthropology, where he served until 1903. He assembled a staff who developed a series of explorations and pub-lications for the museum. One of the most influential staff members was Franz Boas, Putnam's assistant at the world's fair in Chicago. Under the joint leadership of Putnam and Boas, the Department of Anthropology conducted the Jesup North Pacific Expedition and the Hyde Expedi-tions to the Southwest, up to that point the most far-reaching anthro-pological investigations ever conducted.[103]

Putnam also helped institutionalize anthropology in California. In 1903 Phoebe Hearst endowed the University of California, Berkeley, to establish an anthropological museum and a chair of anthropology. Hearst invited Putnam to assemble the museum and assume the chair. From 1903 to 1909 he was professor of anthropology and director of the Phoebe Apperson Hearst Museum of Anthropology.[104]

Although Putnam extended his talent, skill, and commitment around the country, the Department of Anthropology and the Peabody Museum of American Archaeology and Ethnology at Harvard remained under his fastidious tutelage. Charles Peabody summarized Putnam's commitment to forging the foundations of anthropology: "He started movements, societies, methods, plans, — anything to help anthropology, anything to help our knowledge of man and his works."[105] Similarly, Franz Boas wrote that Putnam "took up anthropological studies with that enthusiastic worship of material data as the indispensable basis for inductive studies that has dominated his life and that, together with his skill as an organizer, have made him the most potent factor in the development of anthropological institutions all over the country."[106]

The Prevailing Construct of Race and Anthropology

No one can deny the formidable contributions Brinton, Powell, and Putnam made to developing anthropology from a romantic pastime into an academic discipline: they established anthropology in the United States. However, one cannot divorce the institutionalization of American anthropology from its historical context. Anthropology was legitimated as a rigorous and practical science in prestigious universities and national museums—the very loci where intellectuals produce and promote ideological hegemony. An examination of how Putnam, Powell, and Brinton established the academic foundations for U.S. anthropology in a way that resonated with prevailing views about race will help us better understand how anthropologists of the next generation used those same institutions to challenge those views.

The historical specifics of the three "founding fathers" of American anthropology make it clear that there was not an orchestrated effort to develop a unified approach to the study of race. Yet the texts, images, and exhibits produced by Brinton, Powell, and Putnam clearly worked in concert. The anthropology they produced complemented and reinforced other projects by intellectuals, artists, and journalists that contributed to a larger discourse on race which converged to bolster the late-nineteenth-century views held by a large swath of Americans about civilization, people of color, the Fourteenth and Fifteenth amendments, and Jim Crow statutes.

Each of these men articulated an evolutionary paradigm imbued with ideas of progress and racial inferiority. In turn, politicians and others within specific institutions used these or similar ideas to justify the oppression of people of color. During this process each of these early anthropologists was awarded the presidency of the AAAS, endowed chairs, directorships, and funds to conduct more research along these very lines. Each of them took advantage of their powerful positions, appointments, and networks to establish the institutional and theoretical foundations for the discipline — anthropology.

CHAPTER 3

Anthropology in American Popular Culture

Here physical type, heredity, blood, culture, nation, personality, intelligence, and achievement are all stirred together to make the omelet which is the popular conception of "race."
M. F. Ashley Montagu, 1962

Chapter 2 has demonstrated how the anthropology produced by the first ethnologists reproduced ideas of race and culture consistent with Social Darwinism, racial segregation, and global expansion. I want to emphasize that I am focusing on the intersections between the formation of anthropology and processes of racial formation by exploring how the "fathers of anthropology" established the discipline in part by reproducing and reinforcing popular ideas about racial inferiority. In return, ethnologists received both tacit and direct institutional support. For example, the way Brinton shifted his research focus from linguistics to the evolution of the races, the way Powell supported explicitly racist scholars, and the way Putnam popularized anthropology each, in a sense, "paid off" and contributed to the institutional foundations of the field.

Turn-of-the-century anthropological science not only responded to but also intensified the signification of U.S. racial categories.[1] In this chapter, I attempt to identify the historically specific roles anthropology played in the complex social processes that foster racial inequality by demonstrating how politicians, world's fair organizers, and media magnates inserted the ethnological sciences into legislation, popular culture, and foreign and domestic policies.

When anthropology became an academic discipline, there were two areas of popular culture in which its scientific authority became particularly important: world's fairs and widely circulated magazines. Both were suffused with images and narratives that affirmed ideas about the racial inferiority of people of color.

The World's Columbian Exposition, Chicago — 1893

The 1893 World's Columbian Exposition was framed by prosperity for the rich and violence against the poor. During that year New England alone produced more manufactured goods per capita than any other country in the world. The United States had surpassed every country in steel manufacturing, oil refinement, meatpacking, and the extraction of gold, silver, coal, and iron. The country led the world in the number of telephones and incandescent lights, as well as in miles of telegraph wire. There was not, however, peace and prosperity for all. In May 1893 the National Cordage Company failed, and the ensuing financial panic created thousands of business insolvencies, hundreds of bank closures, scores of railroad bankruptcies, and record high unemployment with record low reserves of gold in the national treasury. The year also brought a realignment of political power. With Grover Cleveland winning the bid for the presidency, Democrats seized control of the executive and legislative branches of the government for the first time since before the Civil War. The November elections that ushered the Democrats to Washington was a miscarriage of a participatory democracy because the measures for enforcing the Fifteenth Amendment had been repealed. African Americans in the South witnessed wholesale disfranchisement accompanied by routine lynchings. During the year proceeding the fair, 1892, fifteen election-related murders took place during state elections in Georgia, and riots erupted at polls in Virginia and North Carolina. In the North, conflicts between striking union members and Pinkerton sheriffs resulted in deaths at Homestead and Pittsburgh, Pennsylvania.

In a brilliant and pointed analysis, Robert Rydell has documented how U.S. world's fairs trumpeted the ideals of political and financial leaders between the end of Reconstruction and the United States' entry into World War I. Large corporations, as well as state, federal, and foreign governments, underwrote the many commissions and delegations that promoted and organized the events. Fair organizers presented to more than a million visitors an optimistic view of the world in the wake of financial depressions and outbursts of class and race warfare.[2]

The 1893 fair depicted the ascendancy of the United States among the world powers and the self-confidence and optimism of the country, which its White citizens believed to be the most advanced in history.[3] Ideas of racial and cultural superiority and inferiority were reified by the architecture and physical layout of the expansive exposition. The exteriors of the large beaux-arts edifices were painted ivory. The White City, as the fair was designated, was the crowning achievement of this civilization. The latest in architectural styles and military hardware was exhibited, along with the newest mining and agricultural technologies, to demonstrate American cultural and industrial progress. The emphasis on hard science, high art, and exacting technology evidenced the material progress of American civilization and the progress of the civilized mind.

Across the river from the White City and segregated from the practical exhibits were the entertainments along the Midway Plaisance, where visitors could experience the thrills and chills of the Ferris wheel, the hootchy-kootchy, Dr. Welch's tangy grape juice, and the villages of the savage. Under the direction of Frederic W. Putnam, the Midway was a lattice of exotic, erotic, and wondrous excitement. Putnam sanctioned a blend of familiar forms of entertainment with ethnology in an attempt to popularize anthropology. The end result was a mile-long midway that fused the honky-tonk bar with the freak, minstrel, and Wild West show to form a "practical study of ethnography." Segregating the living ethnological exhibits into a dark ghetto away from the White City was symbolically important. The accomplishments of the civilized mind—art, architecture, and technology—were counterposed to ignorance, dirt, smells, and brown bodies. As Rydell points out, the White City and the Midway were not antithetical constructs. The depiction of the non-White world as savage and the White world as civilized were "two sides of the same coin—a coin minted in the tradition of American racism, in which the forbidden desires of whites were projected onto dark-skinned peoples, who consequently had to be degraded so white purity could be maintained."[4]

The 1893 exposition is generally recognized for its contributions to urban planning and innovative technology. But equally important, the fair introduced the American public to a new anthropology and its old evolutionary ideas about race. The popularity of the Midway transformed the ethnological exhibits along its course—and in the Anthro-pological Building—into vehicles of popular culture that shaped con-cepts of racial inferiority by framing them in an evolutionary hierarchy. The Smithsonian's William H. Dall reported to *The Nation* that the Midway constituted an "anthropological collection hitherto unequaled and hereafter not likely to be surpassed."[5] Curators displayed skulls and measurements of all races in the laboratory housed in the Anthropolog-ical Building. But visitors who questioned what constituted the epitome of the civilized race were directed to "the well-known statues of the Harvard boy and [Radcliffe] girl." As Dall explained, "these [statues] attract a constant stream of visitors, and are generally acknowledged to form one of the most instructive exhibits in the [Anthropological] build-ing."[6]

The living ethnological exhibits were arranged in an obvious evolu-tionary hierarchy that resonated with many White Americans' seemingly intuitive understanding of racial inferiority. The darker races were at the bottom of the midway and the lighter races at the top—closer to the White City. As Otis T. Mason reported to the Smithsonian Institution, "from the rude human habitations about the Anthropological Building to the results of co-operative architectural dreams which constituted the White City, was a long way on the road of evolution."[7]

Julian Hawthorne, writing for a special Columbian Exposition edi-tion of *Cosmopolitan,* detailed how the Department of Ethnology de-humanized people of color by providing him a conveyance to frolic up and down the evolutionary ladder while "playing" with "the elements" from which the civilized races developed: "The catalogue calls [it] 'Department M.—Ethnology. Isolated Exhibits—Midway Plaisance. Group 176,' this I say, I call the 'World as Plaything.' Here are the elements out of which the human part of the planet has been developed; it is all within the compass of a day's stroll; . . . Roughly speaking, you have before you the civilized, the half-civilized and the savage worlds to choose from—or rather, to take one after the other."[8] Hawthorne glee-fully guided *Cosmopolitan* readers through a wild trek down the evolu-tionary ladder, quipping, "[L]et us have done with Europe and try a cycle of Cathay. Beyond the great wheel, as to spatial distance, and who can tell how many thousands years away from us to appearance, modes of life and traditions, is the [African] Dahomey village."[9]

Fair organizers presented the racial plank of Social Darwinism in an entertaining and simple framework. The ethnological exhibits provided easy answers for many Americans who were groping for ways to explain the violent chaos that erupted at the massacre at Wounded Knee in 1890, race and labor riots in 1892, terrorizing lynch mobs, and reports that African Americans composed the most criminal element in society.

There was "no doubt that the Dahomans [were] more closely allied with the cruel and superstitious practices of savagery than any other country represented in [the] Midway."[10] John Eastman issued a stern warning to all visitors that these Africans were dangerous. He forewarned them that "the women are as fierce if not fiercer than the men and all of them have to be watched day and night for fear they may use their spears for other purposes than a barbaric embellishment of their dances."[11] The stern warning reinforced many Americans' fears that African Americans could not be trusted and were naturally predisposed to immoral and criminal behavior and thus kept away from White people through segregation. Edward B. McDowell, writing for *Frank Leslie's Popular Monthly,* made the connection explicit:

Sixty-nine of them are here in all their barbaric ugliness, blacker than buried midnight and as degraded as the animals which prowl the jungles of their dark land. It is impossible to conceive of a notch lower in the human scale than the Amazon, or female Dahomey warrior, represents. . . . Dancing around a pole on which is perched a human skull, or images of reptiles, lizards and other crawling things, their incantations make the night hideous. . . . In these wild people we can easily detect many characteristics of the American negro.[12]

While the evolutionary scheme of the Midway supported the belief that physical and moral characteristics were one and the same, it also reinforced the belief that slavery created a thin veneer of civilized characteristics for American Negroes. Lurking behind the veneer was the savage from Africa, incapable of morality and civilized behavior and predisposed to crime. The Italian criminologist Cesare Lombroso explained this as "the greatest obstacle to the negro's progress": "For notwithstanding that garb and the habits of the white man may have given him a veneer of modern civilization, he is still to often indifferent to and careless of the lives of others; and he betrays that lack of the sentiment of pity, commonly observed among savage races, which causes them to regard homicide as a mere incident, and as glorious in case it is the outcome of revenge."[13]

Frederick Starr, a new assistant professor of anthropology at the University of Chicago, echoed Lombroso by linking criminal behavior and morality to the evolution of the savage mind.[14] In Starr's view, Negroes were only half a step ahead of their savage brethren, and because American Negroes possessed the same morals as their savage brethren, they were naturally predisposed to criminal activity. Starr was adamant that "Race characteristics are physical, mental, [and] moral."[15] As a University of Chicago professor, Starr patiently explained to the readers of *Dial* magazine the "facts" of African American criminality. "Study of criminality in the two races gives astonishing results. Of the total prisoners in the United States in 1890, nearly 30 per cent were colored; the negro, however forms but 11 per cent of the population. . . . Conditions of life and bad social opportunities cannot be urged in excuse. In Chicago the conditions of life for Italians, Poles, and Russians are fully as bad as for the blacks, but their criminality is much less. The difference is *racial*."[16]

Although anthropology gave scientific justification for old ideas of racial inferiority, it was a new science for many visitors to the fair. The term *anthropology* was in many respects first introduced to the American public during this exposition.[17] Fair organizers drew on the growing authority and prestige of anthropological theories about natural and social progress to make ideas of America's progress more persuasive.[18] The budding discipline of anthropology also drew on the popular exposure and prestige associated with the fair. According to Dall, because of "the active exploration instituted by the Directors of the Exposition into matters connected with American anthropology, it is probable that this department of science will permanently profit by the anniversary thus celebrated to a greater extent than any other line of research."[19]

While anthropology bathed in the public prestige at the fair, Putnam attracted controversy and adversaries. Several Native American associations took issue with his vision. In the early planning stages of the exposition an amiable agreement had been struck between the U.S. Department of the Interior and Department M of exposition. It was agreed that Department M would erect "strictly scientific" representations of the primitive conditions of indigenous life. The Indian Bureau of the Department of the Interior would display the education and citizenship of modern Indians. However, Emma Sickles, chair of the Indian Committee of the Universal Peace Union, protested against the ethnological displays and tried to derail Putnam's efforts.

Sickles played a key role in passing a federal appropriations bill for the fair; in return, she was given a political appointment in Department M, over objections levied by Putnam. She attempted to persuade the staff of Department M that it should represent the process of civilization among Native Americans. As a result, Putnam fired her for insubordination. She immediately sent officials at the fair a resolution drafted by the Indian Committee of the Universal Peace Union which stated: "In the interests of the preservation of the peace and the progress of civilization I do hereby protest against the presentation of low and degrading phases of Indian Life."[20] She would not quit and relentlessly attacked Putnam and the fair in the press. For example, on October 8, 1893, the *New York Times* published one of her scathing editorials:

[E]very effort has been put forth to make the Indian exhibit mislead the American people. It has been used to work up sentiment against the Indian by showing that he is either savage or can be educated only by government agencies. This would strengthen the power of everything that has been "working" against the Indians for years. Every means was used to keep the self-civilized Indians out of the Fair. The Indian agents and their backers knew well that if the civilized Indians got a representation in the Fair the public would wake up to the capabilities of the Indians for self-government and realize that all they needed was to be left alone.

Native Americans were not the only Americans who were denied access to demonstrating their "progress." African American leaders demanded fair and equitable representation, but they too were rebuffed.

No Progress—No Negroes

Although the fair was dubbed the White City, the African American press dubbed it "the great American white elephant," or "the white American's World's Fair."[21] To ensure equitable representation of Negroes' "progress," Black leaders repeatedly asked for administrative appointments. To stem their pressure, fair organizers appointed a number of token African American commissioners with no real power.

Frederick Douglass, the dean of African American affairs, and Ida B. Wells-Barnett, the prolific antilynching crusader, were compelled to explain to international visitors why African Americans were "studiously kept out of representation in any official capacity and [only] given menial places." They envisioned printing a pamphlet written in German, Spanish, and French to explain their position. They secured enough funds to publish *The Reason Why the Colored American Is Not in the World's Columbian Exposition* in English, but they did not have enough money to print the foreign-language editions. They did, however, manage to print the introduction to the pamphlet in several different lan-guages.[22] The lack of African American representation and the degrading image of Africans left Frederick Douglass to conclude that exposition managers evidently wanted the Negro American to be represented only by the "barbaric rites" of Africans "brought there to act the monkey."[23]

As a concession for jettisoning plans for Negro exhibits, the fair or-ganizers suggested that one day in August be set aside as Colored Jubilee Day. Many African Americans were already infuriated by the discrimi-nation, and the idea of a "Nigger day" was not tolerable. Douglass seized the opportunity at the Jubilee Day to deliver a major address to vindicate the progress made by African Americans despite injustice, violence, and persecution. He also lambasted fair organizers who fostered the belief "that our small participation in the World's Columbian Exposition is due either to our ignorance or to our want of public spirit." "Why in Heaven's name," he appealed, do you "crush down the race that grasped the saber and helped make the nation one and the exposition possible?"[24]

Fair organizers drew a particular social blueprint for the throngs of visitors. This blueprint becomes unmistakable if one juxtaposes Fred-erick Douglass and Emma Sickle's appeals for the recognition of prog-ress among people of color with the Department of Anthropology's evolutionary scheme. The fair organizers eclipsed the progress of Afri-can Americans and Native Americans while Frederick Ward Putnam attempted to reveal how thin the veneer of progress actually was by showcasing the Negroes' savage brethren in a exotic, immoral, and ghet-toized Midway Plaisance.

Two years later, the representation of African Americans in Atlanta at the 1895 Cotton States and International Exposition gave rise to a new form of African American leadership. At the Atlanta exposition Booker T. Washington gave a speech that initiated his meteoric rise to power. As with Putnam and anthropology, Washington used the Cotton States Exposition as a platform to popularize his agenda—industrial education and accommodating White supremacy as a means to "uplift" the race. Washington framed his agenda for African Americans with concepts of cultural and racial progress that were also consistent with ideas of Social Darwinism.[25] As a result, he won the praise of both Democrat and Republican interests and helped articulate these notions across racial lines.

Booker T. Washington and the Cotton States and International Exposition—1895

In 1881 Washington founded and built Tuskegee Institute, a training school for African Americans that emphasized the virtues of hard work, thrift, and industry (Figure 6). In 1895 he was asked to deliver the opening address at the Cotton States Exposition. The address catapulted him to international prominence, and for the next twenty years, until his death in 1915, no other African American commanded comparable power and influence.[26]

The largely White exposition audience was concerned with finding sources of inexpensive labor and new markets for industrial and agricultural products; Washington, however, was concerned with finding more philanthropic support for Tuskegee Institute.[27] In his speech he suggested that Negroes could help the United States progress if they "learned to dignify and glorify common labor and put brains and skill into the common occupations of life."[28] He also warned Negroes not to migrate North because in the South "the Negro is given a man's chance in the commercial world."[29] Members of the White race could help U.S. progress, Washington surmised, if they utilized Negro labor instead of immigrant workers "of foreign birth and strange tongue and habits . . . [because the Negro, after all, has] without strikes and labor wars, tilled your fields, cleared your forests, builded your railroads and cities, and brought forth treasures from the bowels of the earth."[30] Washington did not challenge segregation statutes and disfranchisement, and he even suggested "in all things that are purely social we can be as separate as the fingers, yet one as the hand in all things essential to mutual progress."[31]

Washington's so-called Atlanta compromise provided important African American support for racial segregation and disfranchisement.[32] Without compunction, he couched his arguments in ways consistent with Social Darwinist ideas. Typical of Washington's many public statements was his allegation that "a race, like an individual, must pay for everything it gets—the price of beginning at the bottom of the social scale and gradually working up by natural processes to the highest civilization."[33] He continued for years along these same rhetorical lines, knowing that it was an effective way to gain support for his vision of Negro uplift.

Figure 6. Booker T. Washington at the Tuskegee Institute, ca. 1897. (Courtesy of the Library of Congress)

A number of ethnological and anthropological exhibits were displayed at the Atlanta Cotton States and International Exposition (1895), the Tennessee Centennial Exposition in Nashville (1897), the Trans-Mississippi and International Exposition in Omaha (1898), and the Pan-American Exposition in Buffalo (1901), but none matched the Midway of Chicago. Not until a decade after the Columbian Exposition was the scale and centrality of living ethnological exhibits surpassed.

The Louisiana Purchase Exposition, St. Louis — 1904

The St. Louis fair was pitched as the largest the world had ever seen — nearly double that of Chicago. After a decade of constricting monopolies, the Spanish-American War, and periodic depressions, the overarching theme the fair organizers promoted was still unbridled

American progress—but not for the Negro. African Americans were systematically erased from the representation of American industrial and cultural progress. Every effort to represent African American achievements at the fair was thwarted, save for one or two exhibits by Black colleges. Emmett J. Scott noted this in the *Voice of the Negro,* "as at Chicago where the African Dahomey Village, with its exquisite inhabitants, was the sole representation of the Negro people, so at St. Louis, . . . 'A Southern Plantation,' showing Negro life before the War of the Rebellion, is all there is to let the world know we are in existence."[34]

St. Louis, Missouri, was the Jim Crow South. The cosmopolitan tenor of the fair did nothing to stem the provincial customs and laws of segregation. Negroes were constantly "being turned away by concessionaires, sometimes courteously, sometimes with the brutal statement, 'we do not serve "niggers" here.' "[35]

W. S. Scarborough noted that Jim Crow statutes at the St. Louis fair applied only to African Americans: "There will be Indians, Chinese, Japanese, Mexicans, Hindoos, Italians, Cubans, Hawaiians, Filipinos, even down to the Negritos of the islands in the Pacific, in whom some wiseacres have thought to have discovered the missing link—all these will be received officially and entertained as others, no notice being taken of their presence in cars, on grounds, in cafes—in fact, anywhere, unless suspicion arises in the mind of some that they belong to the wonderfully mixed race that we call the American Negro."[36] Scarborough sardonically concluded, "Such is the irony of the American situation."[37]

Like the Chicago exposition, the St. Louis fair used anthropology to depict the inferiority of people of color and demonstrate American ascendancy. Explicitly, the directors wanted to develop "a comprehensive anthropological exhibition" to depict "the barbarous and semi-barbarous peoples of the world, as nearly as possible in their ordinary and native environments." These were to contrast the Departments of Education, Art, Liberal Arts, and Applied Sciences. The juxtaposition was planned not only to exhibit how far Americans had progressed in industry and culture but also, and more important, to demonstrate the need to rescue America's newly acquired vassals from the vestiges of savagery.[38] As a result, the Department of Anthropology emerged as a keystone in the most grandiose world's fair to date.

Defining Nationalism, Defending Imperialism

By 1904 Brinton and Powell had died and Putnam was spending his final years between Berkeley and Cambridge. There were four prominent ethnologists who had experience as world's fair organizers and could have assumed the job of organizing the Anthropology Department in St. Louis: Otis T. Mason and WJ McGee (Figure 7) at the BAE, Frederick Starr at the University of Chicago, and Franz Boas at Columbia University. Each of these leading ethnologists gained experience and most of their national notoriety by working as exhibit organizers at the expositions. The fair directors selected McGee. Not surprisingly, his elaborate vision of human progress was consistent with the organizers' optimism of a new century and view that foreign intervention would help to advance the "lesser races." While Americans witnessed the devastation, poverty, and unrest brought on by the so-called civilized races, McGee proposed that Americans were now at the cusp of the final culture grade: Enlightenment. This was the precise message the fair directors wanted to deliver.

McGee was not an anthropologist but a self-taught glacial geologist at the USGS. In less than a decade he emerged as an influential professional in anthropology. His entrée into anthropology came in 1893, when Powell resigned from the USGS under congressional pressure initiated by mining and timber lobbyists. McGee was Powell's protégé at the survey and resigned too. Powell did not, however, resign from his directorship at the BAE, and he hired McGee as his heir apparent.[39] As BAE ethnologist-in-charge, McGee rose to power within Washington's scientific societies during the following decade, but his fiscal mismanagement and opportunistic style led to his downfall at the Smithsonian. In 1903 he was forced out of government science because of public controversy and an indictment leveled by a Smithsonian investigation. When the fair organizers gave McGee the nod, he welcomed the opportunity to maintain his stature in the field and, perhaps more important, the opportunity to fashion a national identity out of his idea of racial progress.

McGee's ideas regarding progress were detailed in two 1899 addresses. The first, "National Growth and National Character," was delivered to the National Geographic Society; the other, "The Trend of Human Progress," was delivered to the Washington Academy of

Figure 7. WJ McGee conducting fieldwork among the Seri in Sonora, Mexico, for the Bureau of American Ethnology, ca. 1890. (Courtesy of the National Anthropological Archives, Smithsonian Institution)

Sciences. The latter was selected for publication in the inaugural volume of the new series of the *American Anthropologist,* the journal "representative of the science of Anthropology, and especially of Anthropology in America."[40] Quite explicitly, McGee's theory of racial progress advanced in "The Trend of Human Progress" represented the anthropological discourse on race. Five years later this discourse was literally brought to life for millions of people at the 1904 St. Louis world's fair by exhibiting people as if they were in a zoo.

In "The Trend of Human Progress," McGee tried to develop the argument that

there has been somatic development from race to race, from antiquity to modernity, and from generation to generation. . . . [T]he skull has risen from the simian type, the skeleton has become more upright and better adjusted to brain-led activities, the muscles have gained and are still gaining in efficiency if not in absolute strength, the faculty for work (or for normal exercise of function) is multiplied, the constitution is improved in vigor, life has grown longer and easier, and perfected man is overspreading the world.[41]

McGee asserted that the entire human race was progressing to the "culture grade" of "enlightenment," which he conveniently tacked onto the familiar savage-barbarian-civilized evolutionary scheme. Whites in the United States, he mused, had only achieved enlightenment "during recent decades," whereas Whites in Britain were beginning to experience "budded enlightenment." White Americans were on the "high road to human progress" and were the only ones to experience "full-blown enlightenment." Unfortunately, he remitted, the darker races were much farther behind and on a much slower trek.

McGee hung his argument regarding the converging evolution of all races on an analogy of tributaries that flow into one great stream. He argued that "if the racial lines towards progress were projected futureward, they [would] converge in consanguineal union transcending tribal and racist distinctions; projected backward, they divaricate to a indefinite number of confluent currents coming up from proto-human sources to successively merge in the great stream of living humanity."[42] He was quick to note that

interracial union is often apparently injurious, generally of doubtful effect, only rarely of unquestionable benefit . . . [although the] mixture of white and black has produced a Frederick Douglass, a Booker T. Washington, a Blanche K. Bruce, a Paul Lawrence Dunbar, and other makers of progress in the most progressive nation. By far the greater part of the interracial matings have been illicit, and between the lower specimens of one or both lines of blood, so that the evil of miscegenation may well have been intensified.[43]

The system of racial classification that McGee proposed was confusing. To begin with, he did not clearly state whether he attempted to assign culture grades to races, tribes, or nations. Nor was it clear whether individuals, regardless of race, could advance to a higher culture grade. He was clear that "human activities form the best basis for the classification of human kind."[44] He believed that the more complex the technology, the higher the culture grade. Racial classification, he insisted, was indexed by what he termed "activital products," or technological innovations, and these "products" were predetermined by innate and/ or acquired coordination. The evidence McGee chose to support this argument included his observation that

the yellow or red or black artisan draws his cutting tool toward his body, the white artisan pushes knife and saw and plane outward; . . . the less cultured scribe writes from the right, the more cultured toward the right; the plodding coolie plants his feet in the line of his path, the high-bred mandarin turns his toes outward at right angles to his front; the clumsy cook wipes the dish toward her and often drops the crockery, the deft dishwasher wipes outward and can be trusted with costly china.[45]

McGee explained that two different evolutionary processes determined one's coordination: cephalization and cheirization. He believed that cephalization was quite obvious and drew his evidence for it from the way in which the "human cranium has increased in capacity and changed in form from that of *Pithecanthropus erectus* to that of enlightened man; that arms and hands have shortened and acquired greatly increased amplitude of movement; that the jaws have condensed from prognathic type to the human form; [and] that the pelvis and leg bones have become better adapted to the erect attitude."[46] From this process of cephalization he concluded that cranial capacity has increased among all peoples and nations and decreased among none. But, he quickly retorted, "the records show that cranial capacity is correlated with culture-grade so closely that the relative status of the peoples and nations of the earth may be stated as justly in terms of brain-size as in any another way."[47]

The amount of coordination was not contingent solely on cranial capacity. In McGee's view it was correlated with and augmented by cheirization, which McGee explained in one rather lengthy sentence:

It is the process involved in manual training, both subconscious and pur-
posive; its mechanism appears in the wide range of action in the human
hand as compared with the paw of the animal, and no less strikingly in the
increasing range in manual capacity found in ascending the scale of human
development from savagery to enlightenment; its effects are displayed in the
better development of the forearm among white men than among yellow
or black men; and its prevalence is shown in the hundred manifestations of
manual dexterity among cultivated men to each half-dozen found among
primitive men.[48]

Although the logic and examples that McGee used to make his arguments were somewhat confusing, he came dangerously close to posing ideas that could have challenged the racial plank of Social Darwinism. For instance, he delinked race from culture, or he classified people
"in terms of what they *do* rather than by what they merely *are*."[49] By the
nature of his argument, he also implicitly supported certain interracial
unions. The way he circumvented these apparent contradictions enabled
anthropology to champion American imperialism in the Pacific and defend Jim Crow in the South. McGee fashioned an anthropological version of the White man's burden.

The logical extension of McGee's idea of convergent human progress
was racial equality; however, he mollified any question, even of its potential. He assured the readers of the *American Anthropologist* that "the
progenitors of the white man must have been well past the critical point
before the progenitors of the red and the black arose from the plane of
bestiality to that of humanity."[50] The White man, he argued, had a special responsibility to these lesser races of the world because they were
the only people to experience "full-blown enlightenment." White Americans had to shoulder the White man's burden and therefore were ob-
ligated to uplift the lesser races in the Pacific.

Considered as races, the peoples are evidently approaching community,
partly through blending of blood, partly through the more rapid extinction
of the lower races who lack the strong constitution (developed through
generations of exercise) enjoyed by the higher races; so that the races of the
continents are gradually uniting in lighter blend, and the burden of humanity is already in large measure the white man's burden—for, viewing the
human world as it is, white and strong are synonymous terms.[51]

The themes of the White man's burden, America's leadership into the
new culture grade, and evolution as a product of technological advancement were consistent with the sense of nationalism and defense of im-

perialism that the organizers of the 1904 Louisiana Purchase Exposition wanted to help foster.

McGee turned his theory into practice at the fair when he began to deploy various agents to bring savages and barbarians to St. Louis. He secured pygmies from Zaire, Patagonian giants from Argentina, primitive Ainu from Japan, and an assortment of Indians. These ethnological specimens complemented the U.S. government exhibit with more than 1,200 Filipinos. To carefully measure the ethnological specimens, McGee fashioned psychometric and anthropometric laboratories to calibrate the racial inferiority of people of color in terms of strength, endurance, sensitivity to temperature, touch, taste, and vision.[52] Franz Boas and Clark Wissler from Columbia University, Aleš Hrdlička, the newly appointed director of physical anthropology at the USNM, and Frederick Starr from the University of Chicago all gave their approval and advice to the laboratories and exhibits.

Starr actually arranged for students to receive course credit at the University of Chicago for attending the fair. His class, appropriately titled "The Louisiana Purchase Exposition Class in Ethnology," was composed of talks, lectures and "direct work with material, living and not."[53] During the decade between the Chicago fair and the St. Louis fair, the focus of the discipline moved from museum collections to university instruction.[54] Not only did anthropology have scientific merit, it also had value as education.[55]

Party politics quickly engulfed the didactic value of the discipline. Both expansionist Republicans and protectionist Democrats used anthropological research to bolster their agendas.[56] Their respective agendas were framed by a simple question: Does the Constitution follow the flag? Or, are the rights of people in U.S. territories protected under the Constitution? The protectionist Democrats argued that the Constitution must follow the flag. They looked at the nearly 1,200 Filipinos on the forty-seven-acre reservation on the fairgrounds as proof that they were naturally unfit to shoulder the responsibilities of citizenship and that, therefore, the United States should have protective tariffs and no interest in overseas expansion. Senator G. G. Vest summed up this popular position: "The idea of conferring American citizenship upon the half-civilized, piratical, muck-running inhabitants of two thousand islands, seven thousand miles distant, in another hemisphere . . . is so absurd and indefensible that the expansionists are driven to the necessity of advocating the colonial system of Europe."[57] Even though the Supreme Court ruled in some fourteen cases called the Insular Cases (1901–

1904) that the Constitution does not follow the flag, the American people had to judge for themselves. President Theodore Roosevelt stepped in to help.[58]

In 1904 Roosevelt, who had assumed office after McKinley was assassinated, was waging his first presidential campaign. He had to convince the electorate that the United States should stay in the Philippines to help civilize the islands. His Democrat opponent was Alton B. Parker, a conservative federal judge from New York. The protectionist Democrats were about to insert a plank into the party's platform suggesting that Filipinos were "inherently unfit to be members of the American body politic," and the 1,200 Filipinos wearing native loincloths reinforced this plank.[59]

Roosevelt became embroiled in a controversy between anthropologists and the fair organizers that was extensively covered by the press. The president demanded that short trunks replace the native loincloths worn by the Igorots and the Negritos. The anthropologists protested the president's attempt at "over night civilization." Starr warned that forcing the savages to don western attire would compromise the scientific authenticity of the exhibit and might kill the natives. By forcing the Filipinos to wear traditional garb, the visitors would have perceived these savages as unable to progress toward civilization, which buttressed the Democrats' opposition to the occupation of the islands.

Rydell has suggested that the Philippine Exposition Board evaded party politics by driving an ethnological wedge between the Igorots and the Negritos. The board arbitrarily placed the lighter-skinned Igorots on a rung above the dark-skinned Negritos. According to various official descriptions, the Negritos were "extremely low in intellect" and were on the way to extinction. To reinforce this notion, one of the Negritos was named "Missing Link." The Igorots were depicted as capable of attaining a state of civilized culture. Scientists, according to an official souvenir guide, "have declared that with the proper training they are susceptible of high stage of development, and, unlike the American Indian, will accept rather than defy the advancement of American Civilization."[60]

This ethnological wedge was not new. For a 1898 cover story, the *Scientific American* included a front-page montage of Filipinos in various states of civilization. Subtitles on the pictures ranged from "Savages of North Luzon, with Their Arms" to "Civilized Indians Pounding and Cleaning Rice, Luzon."[61]

Although the Negritos were remanded to a lower stage, the Pygmies from Zaire were relegated to the lowest form of savagery. One of McGee's special agents was the missionary and explorer S. P. Verner. McGee charged Verner with collecting and returning an ethnological exhibit of Pygmies from Zaire. He executed this order and brought several Mbuti to the fair. The Pygmy exhibit was one of the most popular in the ethnological menagerie. After the fair, Verner befriended one of his wards, Ota Benga, on the journey back to Zaire. Benga, who had lost his family to ivory pillagers, convinced Verner not to leave him in Africa but to bring him back to the United States. Verner agreed, but he was in financial ruin and could not support Benga. When the two returned to the United States with no means, Verner decided to sell his "African collectibles—artifacts, beetles, monkeys, and implicitly his pygmy to the American Museum of Natural History in New York."62 Ota Benga actually lived in the museum as more or less a visitor. He roamed freely and unobtrusively throughout the museum but was eventually transported to the Bronx Zoological Gardens after a series of mishaps. Initially he was just a live-in domestic worker at the zoo. Then, in a scheme to increase revenue, the director of the zoo displayed the thirty-seven-year-old Ota Benga in a cage with an orangutan. The sign above the cage read:

> THE AFRICAN PYGMY, "OTA BENGA." AGE, 23 YEARS
> HEIGHT, 4 FEET 11 INCHES. WEIGHT, 103 POUNDS.
> BROUGHT FROM THE KASAI RIVER,
> CONGO FREE STATE, SOUTH CENTRAL AFRICA
> BY DR. SAMUEL P. VERNER.
> EXHIBITED EACH AFTERNOON DURING SEPTEMBER.

Thousands of people saw Ota Benga in the Bronx Zoo in September 1905. The *New York Times* ran articles posing questions like "Is it a man or monkey?"63 New York City's African American community vehemently protested and eventually ensured Ota Benga's release.

In 1905 a fine line was drawn between the zoological construction of animal and the ethnological construction of other. The line was thin because of the immense popularity and entertainment value of the ethnological exhibits at consecutive world's fairs. It was stretched even thinner by the authoritative anthropologists who consistently depicted a close affinity between African savages and their "primate brethren." The administrators at the Bronx Zoo crossed the line with impunity and without reservation.

The ethnological exhibits at the world's fairs of 1893 and 1904 provided "living proof" of racial inferiority by explicitly exhibiting a Social

Darwinian evolutionary ladder for literally millions of fairgoers. The public's adoration of anthropology was due in part to the way its scientific authority resonated, converged, and reproduced popular ideas about race.

Images and Experts
in the Illustrated Monthlies

Ideas of racial inferiority sustained saliency within the proliferating mass media. During the mid-to-late 1890s, there was an explosion of printed material of all kinds. It was driven by new technology, increased literacy, concern with market share, and the efficacy of advertising. Americans consumed muckraking and sensationalism along with social commentary and international affairs by buying record numbers of newspapers and new low-priced books. Of the vehicles of popular information, none experienced a more spectacular increase in sales and circulation than magazines.[64] Prior to the 1890s, most magazines were literary, and all were marketed to affluent and well-educated audiences. The price of thirty-five cents assured that even middle-class Americans would not be privy to the cultured insights and literary digests of the moneyed elite. These magazines maintained a certain aloofness, unlike newspapers, which fostered a sense of urgency.

The entire genre changed during the 1890s. The price of the most popular magazines dropped to fifteen or even ten cents a copy, and circulations soared. Coverage of current events and social issues increased as the circulation grew. The *North American Review, Century Magazine,* and *Forum* were so-called high-brow magazines that had always addressed current events. The new middle-class readership demanded more timely topics from *Harper's,* the *Atlantic Monthly,* and *Dial,* which continued its focus on literature but increased its coverage of current events. During the 1890s, *Popular Science Monthly*'s editors even included articles on current events—tackling social problems with science. Fifteen-cent monthlies, like the world's fairs, emerged as fin-de-siècle vehicles of popular culture that cemented the ideas and values of the nation's political, financial, and intellectual elite to the middle and working classes.

The inexpensive and newsworthy illustrated monthlies came into direct competition with newspapers. The low newsstand price and even lower mail-order price (made more attractive by the special premium offers that accompanied subscriptions) forced newspapers to retaliate. They did so by publishing Sunday literary supplements or Sunday magazines, which were included in most metropolitan newspapers by 1894.[65] The magazines were able to carve out a niche in the popular-information market because they offered detailed lithographs and erudite and expert authors, and they managed to keep the prestige associated with the medium.

African Americans were routinely portrayed in these magazines by such epithets as *nigger, darky, coon, pickaninny, mammy, buck,* and *yaller hussy.* African Americans were also made out to be buffoons and conferred preposterous titles such as Apollo Belvedere, Abraham Lincum, and Prince Orang Outan, let alone Henri Ritter Demi Ritter Emmi Ritter Sweet-potato Cream Tarter Caroline Bostwick.[66] Derisive literature, images, and folklore have all had a long history in the United States, but consistent and pervasive stereotypes were contingent on mass media. The degree to which the format can replicate and duplicate ideas, sounds, and images created a shared experience and produced widespread stereotypes. The circulation, authority, and prestige of the magazines lent themselves to the appearance of truth. The better the copy, the greater the sense of truth and the more convincing the stereotype.[67]

The sense of truth was not based solely on the copy quality. The fifteen-cent illustrated monthly relied on expert and authoritative sources, as opposed to a journalist's rendition, to analyze current issues. The degrading cartoons, contemptuous literature, and racial epithets were complemented by experts who discussed such issues as Negro suffrage, education, and criminality, as well as the new South and imperialism.[68] The experts often recast the stereotypes that were being perpetuated within the literary genres and grounded them in science or expertise.

Anthropology, at the turn of the century, was not distributed to the American public in magazines by anthropologists. It was appropriated and then rearticulated by policy pundits and legislators. Senators and House representatives were perhaps the most powerful people to use ideas generated by anthropologists in these magazines. They used ethnology to sway public opinion in the North and fuel race antipathy in the South. In this respect, legislators contributed to the anthropological discourse on race while making it even more valid.

Senator John T. Morgan from Alabama warned the audience of *Arena* "that there is extreme danger, under existing conditions, in confiding to negro voters the representation of white families in the ballot box."[69] He wanted to make it clear that the tactics of disfranchisement were not born of southern prejudice but were implemented because "the inferiority of the negro race, as compared with the White race, is so essentially true, and so obvious, that, . . . [it] cannot be justly attributed to prejudice."[70] Morgan illustrated how obvious this inferiority was by using rhetoric similar to that of Brinton and McGee:

The mental differences and differing traits, including the faculty of governing, forecast, enterprise, and the wide field of achievement in the arts and sciences, are accurately measured by the contrast of the civilization of the United States, with the barbarism of Central Africa. . . . The negro race, in their native land, have never made a voluntary and concerted effort to rise above the plain of slavery; they have not contributed a thought, or a labor, except by compulsion, to the progress of civilization. Nothing has emanated from the negroes of Africa, in art, science, or enterprise that has been of the least service to mankind. Their own history, at home, demonstrates their inferiority when compared with that of other peoples. . . . Their social development has never risen so high as to repress human sacrifices and cannibalism; while their religion is a witchcraft that is attended with every brutal crime.[71]

John Sharp Williams, the freshman senator from Mississippi and former Speaker of the House, used anthropological ideas of race in an article entitled "The Negro and the South," published in the 1907 volume of the *Metropolitan Magazine*. Williams wanted "to endorse the repeal of the fifteenth amendment" and was clear that anthropology offered a simple rationale: "The reason seems plain to me. No race ever succeeded in reaching civilization by the superposition of the civilization of another race unless that superposition were by force. Then only a veneering of the civilization is put on, and it comes off when the veneered race is left to itself."[72]

Although Williams understood the need for Negro labor in the South, he favored sending "the negro somewhere where he could develop undisturbed along his own racial lines of evolution."[73] Williams's good friend from the state of South Carolina, Senator Benjamin Tillman, echoed the same thoughts in the 1907 volume of *Van Norden's Magazine*. In his article entitled "The Race Question" Tillman suggested that "The negroes were changed from barbarians to a degree of civilization under the coercive power of slavery."[74] He even suggested that "Those who have read Booker Washington's book, 'Climbing up from Slavery' [*sic*] ought to consider the title of a book which has not yet been written, 'Climbing up from Barbarism through Slavery.' "[75] He concluded his discussion of the race question with the statement that "Negroes are great imitators and many of the mixed blood have shown great aptitude and capacity."[76] He quickly jettisoned any idea of race mixing because "Ethnologists warn us against the degeneracy, physical and mental, which comes from the mixture of different races."[77] This line of thought was echoed by another notable author, Marion L. Dawson,[78] the former judge-advocate-general of Virginia, who wrote "The South and the Negro" for the *North American Review*.

For the readers of *Arena,* Congressman William C. P. Breckinridge of Kentucky attempted to explain the reason why northerners were less likely to harbor "race prejudice" than were southerners. Breckinridge believed that it was not a question of prejudice, but that the North had different Negroes. Based on the tenets of neo-Lamarckism, he explained that Negroes in the North acquired better race traits and tendencies than did Negroes in the South because of their contact with Whites. Breckinridge suggested that "where the negro was less numerous he was a much better man."[79] The better race traits of northern slaves, he speculated, were acquired by more contact with Whites, because slavery in the border slave states consisted "almost entirely of domestic slavery; that is, the slaves were comparatively few, and lived in the family and in daily association with the family of their owners. . . . And the daily contact with the white families to whom they belonged was an education. In the planting States there were domestic slaves; but there were also very large numbers of plantation slaves who lived at 'quarters,' isolated from the whites and the influence of daily contact with them." [80] He even assessed that "ethnologically it is perhaps true that there were differences between the early importations which settled in Virginia, and from which largely came the negroes of the border slave states, and the late importations from which the majority of the 'plantation' slaves in the cotton and sugar growing states came."[81]

Educational reform was another issue that received a considerable amount of press. Booker T. Washington's plan for Negro uplift through industrial education was scattered throughout popular magazines.[82] The central question posed was: Could Negroes uplift themselves or progress by education? During the Democrat backlash of the 1890s, Negro education received little money or public support. Although Negro education in the South was contingent on northern philanthropy, southerners still controlled how the money was allocated.

Jabez L. M. Curry was the general agent for both the Peabody Education Fund and the John F. Slater Education Fund.[83] In 1899 he also had the distinction of being one of the two surviving organizers of the Confederate government.[84] Curry was an influential leader in the South and an expert on Negro education, and he shaped the philanthropic policies for Negro education.[85] In 1899 he shared his expertise on the Negro with the audience of *Popular Science Monthly* by writing a timely article on "The Negro Question." The article was intended to explain the differences between "the Caucasian and the negro" in an effort to marshal evidence to support African American disfranchisement. The differences, Curry explained, were born of "irreconcilable racial characteristics and diverse historical antecedents."[86] Curry introduced the article with a short historical description of what he called the Negro menace from colonial times through Reconstruction. He asserted that Negroes were racially inferior and did not possess the moral and intellectual fortitude to participate in the political process. To support this assertion, he turned to anthropological notions of race:

Ethnologically they are nearly polar opposites. With the Caucasian progress has been upward. Whatever is great in art, invention, literature, science, civilization, religion, has characterized him. In his native land the negro has made little or no advancement for nearly four hundred years. Surrounded by and in contact with a higher civilization, he has not invented a machine, nor painted a picture, nor written a book, nor organized a stable government, nor constructed a code of laws. . . . For thousands of years there lies behind the race one dreary, unrelieved, monotonous chapter of ignorance, nakedness, superstition, savagery. All efforts to reclaim, civilize, Christianize, have been disastrous failures.[87]

The policy experts and legislators who wrote for the illustrated magazines also used anthropology to defend Native American policies. For example, Henry L. Dawes, author of the 1887 Dawes Severalty Act, wrote "Have We Failed the Indians?" for the *North American Review*,[88] in which he defended the preceding twenty-five years of Native American policies set forth by the federal government. He then outlined the rationale for the current administration's Native American policies:

It was plain that if he were left alone he must of necessity become a tramp and beggar with all the evil passions of a savage, a homeless and lawless poacher upon civilization, and a terror to the peaceful citizen. . . . Inasmuch as the Indian refused to fade out, but multiplied under the sheltering care of reservation life . . . there was but one alternative: either he must be endured as a lawless savage, a constant menace to civilized life, or he must be fitted to become a part of that life and be absorbed into it. To permit him to be a roving savage was unendurable, and therefore the task of fitting him for civilized life was undertaken.

This is the present Indian policy of the nation,—to fit the Indian for civilization and absorb him into it.[89]

Theodore Roosevelt also chimed in with a review of Benjamin Kidd's *Social Evolution* (1894) for the 1895 volume of the *North American Review*, which revealed his theoretical views on progress and evolution. His main criticism of Kidd's argument was the way he connected the struggle for existence with racial progress. Roosevelt explained that the "great prizes are battled for among the men who wage no war whatever for mere subsistence, while the fight for mere subsistence is keenest among precisely the classes which contribute very little indeed to the progress of the race."[90] Roosevelt was consistent with Brinton, Powell, Starr, Putnam, and McGee, because he was optimistic about the progress for most races but saw no hope for African Americans. He believed that "a perfectly stupid race can never rise to a very high plain; the negro, for instance has been kept down as much by lack of intellectual development as by anything else."[91]

The racial discourse articulated in the fifteen-cent illustrated monthlies was not limited to politicians, public-policy moguls, and budding presidents. It was also forcefully levied by scientists–cum–popular theorists who were generally outside the general purview of anthropological fields. The role of Nathaniel Southgate Shaler has already been addressed, but other scientists took to the monthlies and used their own renditions of theories on race to transform the popular medium into a bully pulpit to champion American progress and racial inferiority.[92]

To assert that early anthropology dominated racist science and theory in the popular arena would be misleading. Early anthropology should be viewed as an integral and significant participant in the veritable cottage industry of racist theory and science at the turn of the century. The anthropological discourse on race is distinguished from other leading Social Darwinist texts because ethnologists linked anthropometric measurements and cranial capacities to language, social institutions, kinship, morality, and technology and then positioned people into grades of race and culture. Ethnologists attempted to distinguish racial variations, say, between Great Basin "root diggers" and the Mississippi "mound builders" and then place them accordingly into an evolutionary hierarchy. This differed from other scientists who did not consider so-called activital activities and kinship systems. Notwithstanding this slight distinction, anthropology was influenced by, consistent with, and contributed to the larger public discourse on race.

In *Race Traits and Tendencies of the American Negro* (1896), Frederick L. Hoffman presented a scientific view of racial inferiority that did not draw directly from anthropological ideas.[93] Hoffman was a statistician for the Prudential Life Insurance Company and was convinced that the seemingly high incidence of tuberculosis, syphilis, gonorrhea, illegitimacy, and criminal activity among inner-city Negro populations was caused by abject morality, which, he asserted, was a heritable race trait. The statistics Hoffman used led him to conclude that "the colored race is shown to be on the downward grade."[94] The American Economic Association published his work in three consecutive issues of its journal, giving Hoffman a badge of authority. Hoffman proposed that no public expenditures be allocated for better access to medicine, fair housing, or education because they would only provide a temporary stay for the imminent extinction of the Negro race. Although Du Bois pointed out that Hoffman's conclusions were "of doubtful value" because of "the unscientific use of the statistical method," writers for the monthlies routinely cited Hoffman's call to abandon the "modern attempt of superior races to lift inferior races to their own elevated position."[95]

Like Hoffman's *Race Traits and Tendencies,* influential Social Darwinian books on race were cited, abridged, and serialized in the popular monthlies. Such books included Charles W. Carroll's *"The Negro a Beast"; or, "In the Image of God"* (1900), William Patrick Calhoun's *The Caucasian and the Negro in the United States* (1902), William Benjamin Smith's *The Color Line: A Brief in Behalf of the Unborn* (1905), and Robert Wilson Shufeldt's *The Negro: A Menace to American Civilization* (1907).

The fifteen-cent illustrated monthlies were sent to millions of middle-class American homes, and they were one of the first vehicles of popular culture to create a shared experience—each and every month. These magazines became useful outlets for politicians, scientists, satirists, muckrakers, and, through letters to the editors, everyday folk, to provide insight, shape opinions, and garner support for various agendas. The editors and publishers were always conscious of their bottom line and their advertisers. The content was largely confined to perpetuating the values of the nation's political, financial, and corporate interests. Sometimes, however, the editors included opposing views on the race question. Although editors consistently ran articles supporting ideas of racial inferiority, they occasionally ran articles supporting notions of racial equality.[96]

The specific lines of thought generated within the discipline by a relatively small and innocuous group of ethnologists had an important impact on the social construction of race. Politicians, fair directors, and magazine editors effectively appropriated and reproduced anthropological ideas for public consumption. Thus they used anthropology to promote and reify the ideas of racial inferiority that were so integral to the construction of race at the turn of the twentieth century.

CHAPTER 4

Progressive-Era Reform

Holding on to Hierarchy

WJ McGee and fair organizers held onto notions of Social Darwinian evolution while fantasizing about reaching "enlightenment" to create a sense of nationalism and reflect the ascendancy of the United States for millions of visitors to the 1904 St. Louis Exposition. Perhaps working-class fairgoers believed that their station in life was the highest in the world once they contrasted themselves to the Pygmies and Negritos, but the euphoric sense of superiority soon dissipated.

In the years before the fair and in the wake of debilitating depressions that concentrated finance and industry, many Americans began to challenge laissez-faire economic policies and the callous deference given to the "survival of the fittest."

Although it is impossible to identify a single or concerted progressive movement, the concerns of agrarian populists, labor activists, and settlement-house organizers in the 1890s gained momentum and galvanized nationwide initiatives to repudiate laissez-faire economic policies, support poor people, and develop regulations for industry and finance.

A new generation of economists and sociologists played an important role in shaping government regulatory reform. Obviously, economics was used to help regulate industry and finance, and sociology was used to help urban planning and relief agencies, but what was anthropology used for in the Progressive Era? Once government regulation of industry and finance became politically popular, it did not stop. State and federal governments began to regulate peoples' bodies and reproductive organs. Crime, immoral behavior, alcoholism, and so-called feeblemindedness were all viewed as social problems with a genetic source. These problems, regulators thought, could be curbed by government controls on "better breeding." During the Progressive Era anthropology and eugenics were used to help develop immigration restrictions and sterilization laws.

Change on the Horizon?

The perils born from unscrupulous and unregulated capitalism were thrown into vivid relief by sensationalist authors and journalists who demanded reform and ushered in the Progressive Era during the first decade of the twentieth century. These authors were collectively known as "the muckrakers." Frank Norris exposed corruption and attacked the Chicago Grain Market in *The Pit: A Story of Chicago* (1903) and maligned the Southern Pacific Railroad in *The Octopus: A Story of California* (1901). Ida B. Wells-Barnett detailed the horrors of lynching in *A Red Record: Tabulated Statistics and Alleged Causes of Lynchings in the United States, 1892–1893–1894* (1895) and *Mob Rule in New Orleans* (1900). Lincoln Steffens exposed graft in various municipal governments in *The Shame of the Cities* (1904), and Upton Sinclair condemned the reprehensible conditions of the Chicago meatpacking plants in *The Jungle* (1906). Ray Stannard Baker's *Following the Color Line: An Account of Negro Citizenship in the American Democracy* (1908) was also representative of this genre, but his book did not have the same impact as the others. Unlike the other muckrakers, Baker did not advocate legislative reform. He merely suggested that education, tolerance, patience, and following "the golden rule" would resolve the deplorable conditions he exposed. In addition to these novels, the same magazines that provided a forum for proponents of racial inferiority also served as a forum for the muckrakers' call for reform.

The public sentiment aroused by the muckrakers was complemented by Theodore Roosevelt's ability to arouse Americans to an awareness of their civic duties. The president fused the need for reform and regulation with appeals for social justice to form a doctrine called the "Square Deal." The deal called for government intervention to ensure equitable relations among four competing interests or sides of a square: farmers, business, labor, and the consumer. Roosevelt's Square Deal emerged as the backbone of his domestic agenda. Racial minorities and women were kept out of the deal and, to a large extent, the purview of the muckrakers' public scorn.

The plight of African Americans during the first decade of the twentieth century was not much better than in the previous decade. Although many Africans Americans in the South were struggling in business, most were relegated to eking out an existence in the lose-lose cycle of sharecropping. Lynchings were slowly decreasing, but attacks on entire communities were on the rise, and these attacks wreaked havoc and terrorized entire Black communities in the South and the North. Labeled as race riots, these pogroms were virtually condoned by public officials as a way to keep Blacks subordinated.

The small town of Statesboro, Georgia, was rocked in August 1904 by an angry mob when two African Americans were accused of the brutal murder of a White farmer's wife and children. The two accused men were sent to Savannah for two weeks of safekeeping in an effort to keep a lynch mob from executing justice with a rope and fagot. When the men returned to Statesboro for trial, they were convicted and sentenced to be hanged. Outside the courtroom the White citizens had worked themselves into a frenzy of race hatred that heightened to a feverish pitch amid aimless chatter about insolent Niggers. When the sentence was delivered, the angry mob surged upstairs, forced itself into the courtroom, overpowered the militia, dragged the two convicted men out to the street, and burned them alive. A wild rampage ensued: innocent bystanders were flogged, a woman with a three-day-old infant was kicked as her husband was killed, homes were destroyed, stores were wrecked, and people and property were set on fire.[1]

Atlanta's most infamous race riot was in September of 1906. During this melee, rural and urban elements of the White community joined together to besiege Black community leaders, destroy property, and wreak havoc. In the following days the riot spilled into the Black section of Atlanta known as Brownsville. Several African Americans in Brownsville attempted to protect themselves and fired rifles at the attackers, killing one police officer and wounding another. The mob threw aside any discretion they had left and set out to level the section. Many people were injured and four were slain in the carnage that rocked Brownsville.[2]

The South was not the only location where riotous carnage took place. Pogrom attacks on African American communities occurred in Philadelphia, Pennsylvania; Syracuse, New York; Springfield, Ohio;

Greensburg and Indianapolis, Indiana; and Decatur, Illinois.[3] Although reform was on the horizon for unscrupulous labor practices, corrupt politicians, and unsanitary food production, heinous crimes committed against African Americans went unabated. The Progressive Era—a watershed in U.S. history—proved to be a nasty backwash for Negroes.

The Racialized Worldview of Theodore Roosevelt

African Americans were cautiously optimistic when Roosevelt assumed the Oval Office after an assassin's bullet took President McKinley's life in 1901. The urgency with which Roosevelt sought to address the Negro question was clear in a letter when he wrote to Booker T. Washington on the day he was sworn into office. "I must see you as soon as possible," Roosevelt insisted. "I want to talk over the question of possible future appointments in the South."[4] This letter set the tenor for the Roosevelt administration's race-relation policies. As Roosevelt stated: "the salvation of the Negro lay in the development of the Booker Washington theory—that is, in fitting him to do ever better industrial work."[5]

Roosevelt did not confront race relations head-on, and the bulk of his efforts were meted out through political appointments that were always made under the advisement of Booker T. Washington.[6] Washington emerged as Roosevelt's advisor on all matters concerning the Negro.[7] After a month in office, Roosevelt invited Washington for dinner at the White House. Although African Americans applauded the gesture, the reaction from the southern press was deafening.[8]

Before his dinner with Washington the southern press gave Roosevelt good marks. Newspapers touted Roosevelt's southern background and military exploits and bragged how he crossed the party line to appoint a Democrat, Thomas Jones of Alabama, to the federal bench. The positive comments came to an abrupt halt when the news broke that Roosevelt had invited Washington to dinner. Benjamin Tillman, senator from South Carolina, suggested that the dinner would "necessitate our killing a thousand niggers" to put them back in their place.[9] Roosevelt's calculated response to the affair was denoted in a letter he wrote to Albion W. Tourgée: "I have consulted so much with him [Washington] it seemed to me natural to ask him to a dinner to talk over this work.

. . . I did not think of its bearing one way or another, either my own future or on anything else. As things turned out, I am very glad that I asked him, for the clamor aroused by the act makes me feel the act was necessary."[10] Washington's plan for the slow process of Negro uplift through thrift and industry was congruent with Roosevelt's ideas of rugged individualism and the natural inferiority of the Negro race. The president believed that the right to vote should only be bestowed on individual men of the race who worked hard to obtain the vestiges of civilization.[11]

Roosevelt's views and policies concerning African Americans, Native Americans, and the darker races within the protectorates never escaped the vise of turn-of-the-century racialist thought.[12] He framed his notions of race early in life, but they were honed by Spencerian-inspired scientists during the mid–nineteenth century. As a Harvard student, Roosevelt was instructed by Nathaniel Southgate Shaler, who cloaked White supremacy in rhetoric with science.[13] Roosevelt later acknowledged that Shaler strongly influenced his views of race.[14] He tempered Shaler's rhetoric in public, but in private correspondence he did not hold back. In 1899, for instance, he publicly reproduced common stereotypes in a *Scribner's Magazine* serial he wrote about his Rough Riders' charge of Cuba's San Juan Hill during the Spanish-American War:[15]

[U]nder the strain the colored infantrymen (who had none of their officers) began to get a little uneasy and to drift to the rear. . . . This I could not allow, as it was depleting my line, so I jumped up, and walking a few yards to the rear, drew my revolver, halted the retreating soldiers, and called out to them that I appreciated the gallantry with which they had fought and would be sorry to hurt them, but that I should shoot the first man who, on any pretense whatever, went to the rear. . . .

This was the end of the trouble, for the "smoked Yankees" . . . flashed their white teeth at one another as they broke into broad grins, and I had no more trouble with them.[16]

Roosevelt erroneously concluded that the action taken by the Negro soldiers (the result of jumbled orders) was a display of their innate fear. Although he did not explicitly employ Shaler's views of Negro inferiority in this context, he recounted them practically verbatim when describing the same situation privately: "I attributed the trouble to the superstition and fear of the darky, natural in those but one generation removed from slavery and but a few generations removed from the wildest savagery."[17]

In a 1905 address to the Republican Club of New York, Roosevelt demonstrated that his notion of "separate but equal" was similar to Daniel G. Brinton's ideas in *Races and Peoples* (1890), Booker T. Washington's at the Cotton States Exposition (1895), and Justice Brown's in *Plessy* (1896). He cautioned that Republicans had to "keep in mind the fact that there must be no confusing of civil privileges with social intercourse. . . . Full recognition of the fundamental fact that all men should stand on an equal footing, as regards [*sic*] civil privileges, in no way interferes with recognition of the further fact that all reflecting men of both races are united in feeling that race purity must be maintained."[18]

Although Roosevelt's racial ideology was influenced by Shaler, it was also aligned with more tolerant speculations of the day.[19] He adhered to the same neo-Lamarckian view as did Brinton, McGee, Powell, and Putnam—a view espousing racial inferiority but not dismissing the equipotentiality of different races.[20] For example, Roosevelt believed that it was necessary to "give fair play to those [African Americans] who individually rise above the general level,"[21] but "as a race and in the mass they are altogether inferior to the whites."[22] He rejected the vulgar struggle for existence and degenerative theories proposed by scholars like Kidd and Hoffman. Roosevelt's ideas on race *can* be distinguished from the hucksters of White supremacist demagoguery like Madison Grant, Charles Carroll, and William Calhoun, and their legislative cronies, such as Benjamin Tillman, John Sharp Williams, and John T. Morgan.

In 1904 Roosevelt accepted the Republican Party's nomination to head up the ticket. In his acceptance speech he stated that "this government is based on the fundamental idea that each man, no matter what his occupation, his race, or his religious belief, is entitled to be treated on his worth as a man, and neither favored nor discriminated against because of any accident in his position."[23] We can see here a mix of neo-Lamarckian equipotentiality, rugged individualism, and the belief that individuals could pull themselves up by their bootstraps.

Roosevelt's rhetoric about the potential of equality did nothing to erode the construction of race solidified during the 1890s; rather, this construction was strengthened during his administration. Roosevelt's policies were not antiracist. His big-stick diplomacy, assimilationist policies for Native Americans, and overtures to Jim Crow were ways in which people of color were repressed during his tenure. He implemented policies and steered legislation born of the scientific and public discourses of racial inferiority. In turn, he helped create racial inequalities in the United States but explained them as products of nature.[24] The same administration that sought to reform so many other social ills did virtually nothing to reform racism.

The virtual hegemony of Roosevelt's ideas on race was reflected by the fact that many African Americans appropriated the idioms of rugged individualism, self-help, and Social Darwinism. Many African Americans believed that to uplift the race they had to engender racial solidarity. The idea of racial solidarity, during this historic juncture, amounted to focusing on self-help while deferring to ideas of Social Darwinism and consenting to racial segregation and disfranchisement. Struggling entrepreneurs, recipients of political patronage, and the coterie of Washington's Tuskegee Machine found the philosophy of both Washington and Roosevelt congenial to their experiences and their pecuniary interests. The loudest proponents of this view were mostly self-made entrepreneurs whose economic vitality depended on segregation.[25]

Critical to an understanding of the processes of racial construction during this period is acknowledging how pervasive and virtually uncontested the idea of a naturalized racial hierarchy was throughout U.S. society. This ideology pervaded social and educational institutions (both Black and White), popular culture, legislation, literature, and the thought and actions of the president of the United States. Anthropologists were articulating a truly ubiquitous notion of racial inferiority as science, reinforcing it.

Eugenics: Social Darwinism in the Age of Reform?

One of the most popular preachers during the 1880s, Henry Ward Beecher, thought that the cultural and religious differences of immigrants were inconsequential to their enrichment of American blood.[26] Herbert Spencer even provided a direct confirmation of this in an 1882 interview, when he derived from "biological truths" that European immigration to the United States would produce the finest and most adaptable man in the world.[27]

During the Gilded Age hardly any Social Darwinist directly challenged this attitude. The combination of Anglo-Saxonism and U.S. nationalism merged in an optimistic belief that the Anglo-Saxon had a remarkable capacity for assimilating similar races and absorbing their most valuable qualities. Also, European race traits and tendencies seemed too closely connected with the great Gothic family to inspire alarm.[28] Notions about the possibility of assimilating European immigrant populations and the consequent downplaying of differences within and among European nations were necessary components in an effort to contrast, delineate, and categorize the so-called savagery and technological retardation of the lesser races. Racial categories were demarcated by the color line, and it was not until the subjugation of people of color was complete and clearly institutionalized that Eastern European immigrants were fashioned into distinct racial hierarchies. Not until color was, literally, ratified as a badge of inferiority were racial categories constructed for people not considered colored. For example, federal lawmakers denied equality and freedom to people of color by enforcing acts and decisions like the Chinese Exclusionary Act (1882), *Plessy v. Ferguson* (1896), the Dawes Servility Act (1887), and the Insular Cases (1901–1904). After these acts and constitutional interpretations had time to make people of color separate and unequal by vanquishing their claim to civil rights, fair housing, participatory democracy, and equal opportunity, then and only then did notions of racial inferiority become associated, for a generation, with European immigrants. Science was then used to construct buffer races or intraracial categories of inferiority that were imposed on Italians, Sicilians, Slavs, Hungarians, and Russian Jews during the first two decades of the twentieth century — the height of Eastern European immigration to the United States.[29] However, processes of racial construction stopped short of long-term and widespread institutionalized Eastern European racial categories.[30]

The formation of racial categories along the color line during the 1880s and 1890s was facilitated by the fact that roughly 80 percent of the immigrants who came to the United States between the 1860s and 1900 were from northern and western Europe. But as the century came to a close the number of eastern and southern European emigrants grew two hundredfold, increasing from 2 percent to 70 percent of all arriving immigrants.

By the mid 1890s people began to fear the "vast hordes of ignorant and brutalized peasantry thronging to our shores."[31] Francis Walker, writing for the *Atlantic Monthly,* urged readers to convince the president and Congress to protect "the American rate of wages, the American standard of living, and the quality of American citizenship . . . [from] the peasantry from the countries of eastern and southern Europe."[32] Typical of nativist rhetoric, Walker fueled the fear of immigrants by suggesting that the "millions of Hungarians, Bohemians, Poles, south Italians, and Russian Jews" would destroy the Nordic purity of the American stock because they were all "beaten men from beaten races; representing the worst failures in the struggle for existence."[33]

The arriving immigrants did present a political and financial threat to more established Americans because they increased the incidence of diseases in impoverished and crowded inner cities, worked for nonunion wages, and filled the voter rolls, becoming cogs in Democrat political machines. However, powerful nativists couched these threats in terms of the immigrants' contribution to so-called blood chaos in the American stock. Immigrants' party affiliations were even coded with blurred markers of racial and class distinction. For example, one pundit mused:

> The real distinction between the two parties lies in, or perhaps we should say, rather, springs from, the elements of which they are composed. The average or typical Democrat is a very different kind of man from the average or typical Republican. . . . Thus, if a person at all familiar with American politics were walking down Broadway, in the city of New York, he would certainly assume that the laborer digging up the street with a pickaxe was a Democrat; and so of the policeman at the crossing, of the fireman rushing past on his engine, of the bus driver. . . . When he reached the lower part of Broadway, where lawyers and bankers abound . . . the greater number of lawyers and bankers would be Republicans. . . . It is a frequent saying among Republicans that the great body of uneducated voters are found in the ranks of their opponents; the Democrats, they declare, represent the ignorance of the country. . . . The Republican has more money, and he occupies a position which is thought to be higher in the social scale.[34]

As urban areas became overcrowded and filled with non-English-speaking, cheap laboring, and culturally distinct people, pre–Civil War nativism was rekindled and fueled anxieties regarding the future of the so-called American stock.[35] Many native-born Americans feared that the "old stock American" would be forever compromised by these lowly peasants. These new immigrants did not completely change identities but preferred to identify themselves by language, food, customs, and neighborhood, which aided new concepts of race that began to take shape in the minds of uneasy nativists. But only the broadest outlines were clear; the pernicious details about immigrant character remained blurred and obscure, the gaps being filled by rumor and stereotypes.[36]

With perfect timing, a new scientific field emerged to fill in the gaps that rumor and stereotypes could not: eugenics, the science of the improvement of the human race by better breeding. The eugenics movement was conceived by scientists in an age of reform to manage a vast array of social problems. Eugenics was employed to stay so-called genetic pathologies, including alcoholism, feeblemindedness, manic depression, rebelliousness, prostitution, nomadism, criminality, and immorality. During the Progressive Era eugenics emerged as a major breakthrough in the application of scientific methods to solve social problems, justify immigration restrictions, and support sterilization laws in more than thirty states. Eugenicists shared with progressives the notion that society could no longer afford to be governed by laissez-faire principles, that it had to be planned and managed according to modern principles of anthropology, sociology, and biology. Eugenicists also shared the rationale that planning and tough-minded legislation would produce an improved society.[37] In this respect, Sir Francis Galton was to Herbert Spencer what John Maynard Keynes was to Adam Smith, both suggesting that the government should manage "natural" competitive processes.

During the first decade and a half of the twentieth century there was movement toward federal regulation. Eugenicists envisioned a way to regulate and manage the racial composition of the United States through better breeding. The shifts from laissez-faire to managed capitalism and from Social Darwinism to eugenics were not merely a matter of chance. The shifts in social and economic paradigms were parallel, each reinforcing the other.[38]

Coming to America:
Eugenics and the New Immigrants

Like Social Darwinism, the eugenics movement originated in England and became popular in the United States only when it was used as a scientific buttress for legislation and policies born of racist and nativist sentiments. Francis Galton (1822–1911) initiated the modern eugenics movement late in his life. Galton was born in 1822 and devoted the first half of his career to an array of scientific pursuits: statistics, meteorology, geography, and the study of fingerprints. After reading his cousin Charles Darwin's work *On the Origin of Species* (1859), he committed the balance of his life to raising "the present miserably low standard of the human race" by regulating the evolutionary process.[39] Galton first used the term *eugenics* in 1883 and insisted that each individual receives at birth a "definite endowment" of certain qualities like "character, disposition, energy, intellect or physical power." It is these, he argued, "that go towards the making of civic worth."[40] When Galton first developed eugenics he did not attract much attention on either side of the Atlantic. In 1901, however, he won critical acclaim for delivering "The Possible Improvement of the Human Breed under the Existing Conditions of Law and Sentiment," as the Huxley Lecture at the British Anthropological Institute, which was subsequently printed in both *Nature* and *Popular Science Monthly*.[41] In it he explained how "the possibility of improving the race of a nation depends on the power of increasing the productivity of the best stock," a goal "far more important than that of repressing the productivity of the worst." Galton wanted "to improve the race . . . by granting diplomas to a select class of young men and women."[42] He went on in great detail about how to award these special "diplomas" to individual men and women entrusted with advancing the race. The criteria, he suggested, "would take into consideration all favorable points in the family histories of the candidates, giving appropriate hereditary weight to each."[43] For Galton and other eugenicists, women were reduced to objects that only contributed germ plasm to men. Although Galton suggested giving young women special diplomas too, he warned:

The opportunities for selecting women in this way are unfortunately fewer, owing to the smaller number of female students between whom comparisons might be made on equal terms. In the selection of women, when nothing is known of their athletic proficiency, it would be especially necessary to pass a high and careful medical examination; and as their personal qualities do not usually admit of being tested so thoroughly as those of men, it would be necessary to lay all the more stress on hereditary family qualities including those of fertility and prepotency.[44]

Galton concluded by urging people to use science to develop programs for the "improvement of the race," no matter how morally suspect: "We are justified in following every path in a resolute and hopeful spirit that seems to lead toward that end."[45]

The address generated a flurry of public interest in eugenics throughout the United States, at the precise moment many Americans feared the "new" immigration as record numbers of Eastern Europeans were being processed on Ellis Island.[46] Galton's ideas resonated so strongly with the fears of nativist Americans that during the next few years journals were developed, fellowships were endowed, organizations and societies were created, and laboratories were established with the explicit goal of advancing eugenics.

Many of these new institutions honored Galton's contribution to the field by naming their organizations after him.[47] Enthusiasts who took up eugenics came from an array of professional backgrounds, including animal breeding, psychology, anthropology, and economics, and included professionals in social and criminal administration as well as activists for overtly racist and nativist organizations. Although the movement could never claim broad-based popular support, leaders of race-betterment societies shaped important social and immigration policies for the first thirty-five years of the twentieth century by using science, deploying powerful lobbies to Washington, and procuring strong financial support.[48]

Was the eugenics movement another strand of Social Darwinian thought? Eugenics delineated essentially the same racial categories with new jargon. With the misuse of Mendelian genetics, eugenicists attempted to rank-order races and racial characteristics to explain racial inferiority.[49] Similarly, eugenics linked social and cultural characteristics to "prove" that different races were positioned in a natural hierarchy, and they revived the long-standing class bias of science by linking poverty to genetic inheritance.[50] Eugenics research was also popularized in the mass media, which in turn helped to spur legislation that institutionalized the repression of people in poverty and of color. What most distinguished practitioners of eugenics from Social Darwinism was the use of Mendelian inheritance, the use of racial categories for Eastern Europeans, and the use of state regulations to "manage" evolutionary processes.[51]

Eugenics researchers also produced results that were identical to those of earlier Social Darwinism when African Americans fell under their probing gaze. In 1918 Paul Popenoe and Roswell Hill Johnson (students of America's most ardent spokesperson for eugenic research, Charles B. Davenport) wrote a definitive work entitled *Applied Genetics,* which soon became the most popular eugenics textbook in the United States. The authors included a chapter on "The Color Line," in which they proposed that Negroes were inferior to Whites because they had made no contributions to civilization. Moreover, they argued that African Americans' resistance to disease and capacity for intellectual achievement were inferior to those of Whites. Their evidence was gleaned from health statistics gathered in poverty-stricken urban ghettos and scores generated from the new IQ test.[52] Popenoe and Johnson stated that "we feel justified in concluding that the Negro race differs greatly from the White race, mentally as well as physically, and that in many respects it may be said to be inferior, when tested by the requirements of modern civilization and progress."[53]

Theodore Roosevelt was critical of some aspects of eugenics but chimed in to win support for his views on race suicide.[54] In a letter written to Charles B. Davenport on January 3, 1913, he stated that

any group of farmers who permitted their best stock not to breed, and let all the increase come from the worst stock, would be treated as fit inmates for an asylum. Yet we fail to understand that such conduct is rational compared to the conduct of a nation which permits unlimited breeding from the worst stocks, physically and morally. . . . Someday we will realize that the prime duty of the good citizen of the right type is to leave his or her blood behind him in the world, and that we have no business permitting the perpetuation of citizens of the wrong type.[55]

The eugenics movement also intersected with anthropology. Specifically, it merged with new ideas developing within physical anthropology, spearheaded by Aleš Hrdlička at the USNM. In 1903 Hrdlička (1869–1943) became the first curator of physical anthropology at the USNM, and in 1918 he founded the *American Journal of Physical Anthropology*. He was largely responsible for making physical anthropology a well-defined field within the discipline and in 1929 established the American Association of Physical Anthropologists.

Hrdlička's early work on evolution blended ideas from Lamarck and Darwin. He proposed that the environment "excited germ plasm," which in turn produced certain traits that offspring could then inherit. When Hrdlička's results were inconsistent with his predictions, he changed his methods or omitted certain assumptions.[56] He eventually allied himself with influential eugenicists in an effort to bolster his institutional power and strengthen his financial support. Although he has been considered "America's most distinguished physical anthropologist," he was compelled to ask the notorious racists Madison Grant and Charles B. Davenport to serve on the Anthropology Committee for the newly formed National Research Council (NRC).[57] He also permitted John H. Kellogg, industrialist and founder of the Race Betterment Foundation, to buy his way onto the editorial board of the *American Journal of Physical Anthropology*. Hrdlička only began to oppose Davenport and company when they began to compete with him for professional power and influence.[58] The intersection between physical anthropology and the eugenics movement was expressed by Hrdlička in a speech he delivered at American University in May 1921:

From now on evolution will no longer be left entirely to nature, but will be assisted . . . and even regulated by man himself. This is into what we are coming, and I think it will be one of the greatest manifestations of human-ity—the fact of assisting intelligently in its own evolution along the right lines, and thereby doing away with the immense waste which would oth-erwise happen. . . . This particular line of activity is known to-day under the name Eugenics . . . [which] is merely applied anthropological and medical science—applied for the benefit of mankind.[59]

The nativist-racist thrust in both science and politics steamrolled through World War I and the Roaring Twenties. The propaganda-style scholarship of Henry Cabot Lodge, Nathaniel Southgate Shaler, Mad-ison Grant, Henry Fairfield Osborn, Charles Davenport, Lothrop Stod-dard, and so forth, together with sundry eugenic and racial-betterment societies, fostered beliefs in papal conspiracies, communist threats, and international Jewish financial plots. In addition, they composed a pow-erful lobby on Capitol Hill and in state legislatures. Eugenicists helped to write sterilization laws and anti-immigrant legislation, including the sweeping immigrant-quota scheme embodied in the Immigration Re-striction Act of 1924.[60]

Freedom and Liberty, Reform and Racism

The unique separation of powers in the United States fos-ters clashes between state and federal governments, as well as among branches within the federal government. Many of these conflicts arose during the Progressive Era, particularly between states' police powers (the ability to maintain laws to ensure health, welfare, and morals) and the Supreme Court's interpretation of section 1 of the Fourteenth Amendment.[61]

During the first decades of the twentieth century state governments, the president, and Congress responded to the country's tumultuous changes, but the majority on the Supreme Court did not. The Court held onto ideals and doctrines established during Reconstruction. Lais-sez-faire constitutionalism was an ideological view that dominated the Court from 1873 to 1908 and remained influential until the New Deal.

It was a perspective that integrated several overlapping precepts united by a belief in an ordered society governed by natural laws.

This view had many sources, and some justices reflected it more than others. Its chief component was classical liberal economics, with its commitment to market control of the economy, entrepreneurial liberty, and hostility to government regulation. Social Darwinism was an overlapping element, with its commitment to a natural hierarchy of races and justifications for economic disparity. Laissez-faire constitutionalism also reflected so-called traditional American values like individualism, federalism, and untrammeled competition. Finally, proponents feared social unrest, especially if immigration, labor strikes, and race mixing were not severely curbed.[62] Although these views challenged Roosevelt's Square Deal and state laws mandating reform, they did not challenge the president's approach to race relations or state laws mandating Jim Crow segregation. Whereas the Supreme Court routinely held state laws regulating industries unconstitutional under the Fourteenth Amendment, it upheld state laws mandating racial segregation using the same amendment.

Relying on different themes of Social Darwinism, the Court used similar doctrines to interpret the Fourteenth Amendment cases concerning state laws to regulate businesses and state laws to segregate Negroes. As discussed earlier, the Court found state laws mandating segregation constitutional using the doctrine of separate but equal. Simultaneously, it routinely found state laws mandating business regulations unconstitutional using the doctrine of substantive due process or liberty of contract. Under this doctrine the Court devised a test for the due process clause that evaluated the substantive effect of regulating wages, hours, product quality, and prices.[63] The test used a "reasonableness standard" that weighed states' police power against the common or natural law of an individual's liberty to contract his or her labor. The test tended to privilege the individual but benefit business.

The controversial *Lochner v. New York* (1905) case exemplifies how the doctrine of substantive due process was applied. In this case, the Court invalidated a New York law limiting the hours bakers could work to ten per day or sixty per week. In 1895 the state of New York passed this legislation after journalist Edward Marshall detailed the squalid conditions of New York City's bakeries in the *New York Press*. As with other muckrakers, Marshall received support for his crusade. The New York state legislature responded by enacting the Bakeshop Act, which ensured that the health of the workers and the quality of products were not compromised in the tuberculosis-ridden bakeries of tenement-house cellars. Many master bakers, including Joseph Lochner, were affected by this legislation because they ran small bakeshops by working journeymen bakers up to one hundred hours a week. Lochner claimed that the act violated the Fourteenth Amendment by depriving him of life, liberty, and property without due process of law. Opponents of the Bakeshop Act (and other government regulation) based their arguments on laissez-faire economics reinforced by Social Darwinism. Proponents of the regulation based their arguments on the public's right to health and safety.[64]

Justice Peckham, who wrote for the bare majority, recognized that "the employee may desire to earn the extra money which would arise from his working more than the prescribed time, but this statute forbids the employer from permitting the employee to earn it."[65] Like other substantive due process cases, the Court had to decide "which of two powers or rights shall prevail, — the power of the state to legislate or the right of the individual to liberty of person and freedom of contract."[66] The Court found the Bakeshop Act "an illegal interference with the rights of individuals, both employers and employees, to make contracts regarding labor upon such terms as they may think best."[67] In a famous dissent, Oliver Wendell Holmes, Jr. challenged the majority's narrow construction of police powers and its effort to expand the liberty of contract. He recognized that these doctrines reflected the ideas of both Social Darwinism and laissez-faire economics and explained that the Constitution "is not intended to embody a particular economic theory." He attacked what he called the majority's major premise and implored: "The Fourteenth Amendment does not enact Mr. Herbert Spencer's Social Statics."[68]

Under the doctrine of substantive due processes, legislation that regulated child labor, dangerous conditions, endless hours, and abysmally low wages was found unconstitutional because one's liberty was denied. One's liberty was not denied, however, by legislation that segregated Negroes, forcing them to sit in Jim Crow cars, use "colored-only" bathrooms, and attend inferior schools because that legislation was found constitutional under the doctrine of separate but equal.

The way in which members of the Supreme Court used laissez-faire constitutionalism was hostile to the health and safety of working men but policed women's right to "liberty of contract" because they were viewed as inferior to men. Only three years after Lochner, the Court in Muller v. Oregon (1908) upheld an Oregon statute limiting the maximum number of hours that a woman could work. Louis D. Brandeis, a tenacious reform lawyer, argued the case. It was similar in many respects to *Lochner* but involved women in factories and laundries. Brandeis submitted an unusual brief including three pages of legal argument, more than one hundred pages of sociological data, and anecdotal evidence "proving" that women were inferior to men physically and morally. Using his unique brief (a style soon to be known as a Brandeis brief), he convinced the Supreme Court to uphold Oregon's regulatory legislation, forgoing their sacrosanct belief in the liberty of contract.[69] This was a tremendous victory for the National Consumer League and women's rights more generally, but it was not a victory won in the name of equality.

In the Court's unanimous opinion (which, of course, included Holmes's), Justice David J. Brewer explained: "[T]hat woman's physical structure and the performance of maternal functions place her at a disadvantage in the struggle for subsistence is obvious." The state's police powers could therefore abridge women's liberty of contract because "healthy mothers are essential to vigorous offspring, [and thus] the physical well-being of women becomes an object of public interest and care in order to preserve the strength and vigor of the race."[70] Social science was used explicitly by the Court for the first time in *Muller* to help police a woman's right to work by confirming what many then believed about women's inequality. The Court did not stop at upholding the control of the maximum hours women could work but affirmed the control of particular women's reproductive rights through sterilization. Eugenics was soon accepted by the Court as a justification to uphold sterilization laws imposed on women by state legislators.

Although Holmes vociferously challenged the majority's Spencerian views used to decide *Lochner,* he was quite sympathetic to notions of evolution and Social Darwinism. He actually believed that the law was both an instrument and a result of natural selection.[71] But he also believed that states should have full sweep of their police powers. Both of these views were made painfully evident when Holmes delivered the majority opinion in *Buck v. Bell* (1927), affirming a Virginia sterilization statute.

This case concerned Carrie Buck, who gave birth to a child after being raped. Both she and her mother were confined to Virginia's State Colony for Epileptics and Feeble-Minded in Lynchburg because they had scored poorly on the revised Simon-Binet IQ test. The superintendent, Albert Priddy, was ensconced in the eugenics movement and thus believed that Carrie Buck inherited her poor morals and low IQ from her mother and subsequently passed them on to her illegitimate daughter. As a result, he recommended Carrie Buck as a candidate for the eugenical sterilization program at the colony. Buck protested: this program was to mutilate her body and reproductive rights to "prevent those who are manifestly unfit from continuing their kind."[72] The Supreme Court heard the case in 1925. The attorney for Buck argued that new classes or even races may be brought within the scope of the statute, which would make for more "forms of tyranny . . . inaugurated in the name of science."[73] Holmes rejected the arguments to prevent Buck's sterilization, and the state cut her fallopian tubes without consent. Holmes explained: "She is the daughter of a feeble minded mother in the same institution, and the mother of an illegitimate feeble minded child." Accepting eugenic research, he suggested that "experience has shown that heredity plays an important part in the transmission of insanity, imbecility, etc."[74] Holmes thus provided his rationale for constitutionalizing the application of eugenic research: "We have seen more than once that the public welfare may call upon the best citizens for their lives. It would be strange if it could not call upon those who already sap the strength of the state . . . in order to prevent our being swamped with incompetence. It is better for all the world. . . . Three generations of imbeciles are enough."[75]

During this period of rapid transformations the Court played an active role in structuring race, class, and gender in different but interconnected ways. Although never a consistent majority, the Court's imposition of laissez-faire constitutionalism amounted to literally picking and choosing arguments and doctrines to impose its view of an ordered society governed by natural laws. Sometimes they relied on a formalism—using logic and precedent—to defend corporations, but at other times they used social science to justify the inferiority of women. Members of the Court rejected social science, public opinion, and state laws to decide against regulating labor conditions and product quality but deferred to social science, politics, public opinion, and state laws to affirm segregation and sterilization. Whereas the Court used ideas integrated into laissez-faire constitutionalism to defend liberty and freedom during this period, these same ideas were elements of a comprehensive racial worldview that blinded the Court's majority to its abrogation of these same pillars of democracy, thus structuring inequality as the law of the land.

CHAPTER 5

Rethinking Race at the Turn of the Century

W. E. B. Du Bois and Franz Boas

Eugenics was one particular project during the reform movement; other projects intersected and clashed with applied tooth-and-claw evolutionism. Intellectuals of all stripes were contesting nineteenth-century paradigms during the decades that straddled the dawn of the twentieth century. In education, John Dewey synthesized American pragmatism with stimulus-response theory to pioneer functional psychology, which helped to formulate new teaching methods and school curriculums.[1] In economics, Thorstein B. Veblen wrote *The Theory of the Leisure Class: An Economic Study of Institutions* (1899), in which he introduced the notion of conspicuous consumption, insisted that economics be studied in terms of cultural institutions, and critiqued the incompatibility between the modern industrial process and the irrational ways of business and finance. Also in economics, John R. Commons challenged previous ideas about the relationship of labor to economic institutions.[2] In history, Charles A. Beard challenged the democratic ideals of the constitution in *An Economic Interpretation of the Constitution of the United States* (1913), and Louis Brandeis challenged conventional ideas of jurisprudence when he fought tenaciously against giant corporations by defending a minimum wage and labor unions. To a large extent these scholars were muckrakers in an ivory tower. They were liberal reformers crusading against the untrammeled captains of industry, bolstered by ideological themes of Social Darwinism. In anthropology, the leading spokesperson against Social Darwinism and for liberal reform was Franz Boas; in sociology, W. E. B. Du Bois.

During the first decade of the twentieth century Boas began to take over and centralize the leadership of his field. He effectively directed the anthropology of race away from theories of evolution and guided it to a consensus that African Americans, Native Americans, and other people of color were not racially inferior and possessed unique and historically specific cultures. These cultures, he argued, were particular to geographic areas, local histories, and traditions. Furthermore, one could not project a value of higher or lower on these cultures—cultures were relative.

Franz Boas began to drive a wedge into the solid construct of race when he courageously challenged the ascendancy of ideas of racial inferiority within the academy. His wedge did not fracture it: only after the studies pioneered by Boas and Du Bois were appropriated by African American intellectuals engaged in the processes of razing America's racial edifice did anthropology turn the corner and begin to be used in the struggle against racial inequality.

Although anthropology continued to merge with nativism and reinforce racism well into the 1920s, much of its racial discourse had been redirected by 1910. Boas orchestrated this shift in racial theory within anthropology by distinguishing race from culture and language and by proving that racial hierarchies were scientifically untenable. With the help of his students he effectively orchestrated a paradigmatic shift in the discipline and subsequently in the social sciences, and the Supreme Court eventually embraced the "new" scientific claims about racial equality, ending Jim Crow segregation in public schools in 1954.

Boas's contributions were singularly significant, but he did not work alone. Without the wider social and political efforts of Du Bois, the NAACP, and scholars at Howard University, Boas's contributions to the changing signification of race would have been limited to the academy. The only way to fully understand the important role social science played in *Brown* is to examine the early relationship between anthropology and the NAACP, and the only way to do that is to explore the unique relationship between Du Bois and Boas in the first decade of the twentieth century. The efforts of Boas and Du Bois to change how scientists and the public understood race and culture were not simply efforts to shift a paradigm, they were struggles to secure the principles of democracy.

Boas's Early Attack

Franz Boas was born in Minden, Germany, on July 9, 1858 (Figure 8), the same year as Émile Durkheim and Georg Simmel; Booker T. Washington and Sigmund Freud were two years older than he, and John Dewey was a year his junior. Boas grew up in financially secure, socially and intellectually rich surroundings; however, he faced prejudice, anti-Semitism, and political persecution as a young Jew in Bismarck Germany, which was one of the factors that motivated him to migrate to the United States.[3]

From his teens on, Boas was interested in geography, the natural sciences, and cultural history, and he acquired exceptional skills in math and statistics. He pursued his education at the universities of Heidelberg, Bonn, and Kiel and was influenced by neo-Kantian philosophers as well as scholars who were committed to empiricism and positivism. He completed a doctorate in physics with a minor in geography at the age of twenty-three.[4]

In 1883 he joined a geographic expedition to the Cumberland Sound in Baffinland, Greenland, where a community of Eskimos transformed his life and shaped the balance of his career:

After a long and intimate intercourse with the Eskimo, it was with feelings of sorrow and regret that I parted from my Arctic friends. I had seen that they enjoyed life, and a hard life, as we do; that nature is also beautiful to them; that feelings of friendship also root in the Eskimo heart; that, although the character of their life is so rude as compared to civilized life, the Eskimo is a man as we are; that his feelings, his virtues and his shortcomings are based in human nature, like ours.[5]

This simple and seemingly axiomatic statement stood in stark contrast to Powell's and Brinton's contemporaneous musings about similar peoples. It also framed the philosophical positions and theoretical questions from which Boas would transform anthropology. How does the environment affect the institutions, beliefs, rituals, and social rules of a society? How can people with different physical types and widely different forms of existence and beliefs be so similar in many ways? How can physical and mental endowments—so-called racial differences—determine behavior when the environment seems so determinate? In many respects Boas committed the balance of his life to providing answers to

Figure 8. Official World's Columbian Exposition portrait of Franz Boas, 1893. (Courtesy of the American Philosophical Society)

these questions. He insisted that, to answer them, anthropologists should conduct painstaking, inductive ethnographic, anthropometric, and linguistic research so that one could cull generalizations from the universe of data. His Baffinland experience not only helped to frame his scientific questions, it also crystallized his political commitment to equal rights, which drove much of his scientific investigations. Writing to his future wife during his Baffinland fieldwork, he professed: "What I want to live and die for, is equal rights for all, equal possibilities to learn and work for poor and rich alike! Don't you believe that to have done even the smallest bit for this, is more than all science taken together?"[6]

In 1886 Boas embarked on his second field trip. This time he went to the Pacific Northwest and studied members of the Bella Coola. Instead of returning to Germany, he went on to New York and joined the editorial staff of *Science*. During this period he conducted more research in the Pacific Northwest. In 1888, and now married, he met G. Stanley Hall on a train to a professional meeting in Cleveland. Hall was presiding over assembling the faculty for the new Clark University in Worcester, Massachusetts, and invited Boas to join the inaugural faculty. Boas taught at Clark between 1889 and 1892 and launched a series of investigations comparing the growth patterns of U.S. immigrants and their children. In 1892 he resigned from Clark to join Putnam as assistant chief at the World Columbian Exposition. After the fair Boas suffered setbacks trying to secure steady employment. Anti-Semitism pervaded the nation, and German Jews witnessed declining status and narrowing opportunities, which perhaps explains why he was denied a position at the newly formed University of Chicago.[7]

In 1896 Boas followed Putnam to the AMNH, where he served as assistant curator; in 1901 he was promoted to curator. In 1896 he also joined the faculty of Columbia University as a lecturer in physical anthropology, and by 1899 he was a member of the full-time faculty. At the AMNH he undertook major research expeditions, including the Jesup North Pacific Expedition.

The Jesup expedition made scientific breakthroughs that included establishing the links between indigenous people of North America and Arctic Siberia.[8] The investigation was wide-ranging; as Melville Herskovits recounted, it was "designed to throw light on some of the basic theoretical and methodological problems of anthropology—the relation between race, language, and culture, the mode of diffusion of custom, and the ways in which historical relations between nonhistoric peoples, without written records, can be established."[9] In a significant but tangential way, the expedition influenced how race was constructed. Boas curated and exhibited the material gathered at the AMNH in a way that challenged ideas of racial inferiority.

As early as 1887 Boas began to combat scientific racism by challenging museum organizers' representations of other cultures. He argued that arranging artifacts into categories depicting degrees of savagery, barbarism, or civilization employed a fraudulent logic "not founded on the phenomenon, but in the mind of the student."[10] The debates were conducted through letters to the editor of *Science,* involving Otis T. Mason, president of the Anthropological Society of Washington, and John Wesley Powell, director of the BAE.[11] Boas argued that an "ethnological phenomenon is not expressed by its appearance, by the state in which it *is,* but by its whole history[;] . . . therefore arguments from analogies of the outward appearance, such as shown in Professor Mason's collections, are deceptive."[12] Boas's logic, which was not completely clear, became a cornerstone for the inductive ethnographic studies that he and his students pursued:

> The outward appearance of two phenomena may be identical, yet their immanent qualities may be altogether different; . . . these remarks show how the same phenomena may originate from unlike causes, and that my opinion does not at all strive against the axiom, "Like effects spring from like causes," which belongs to that class of axioms which cannot be converted. Though like causes have like effects, like effects have not like causes. . . .
>
> It is my opinion that the main object of ethnological collections should be the dissemination of the fact that civilization is not something absolute, but that it is relative, and that our ideas and conceptions are true only so far as our civilization goes. I believe that this object can be accomplished only by the tribal arrangement of collections.[13]

These thoughts were important precursors for much of his work after 1887. One of the grandest examples of these AMNH installations was the Northwest Coast Hall, in which, by bringing together collections of artifacts of specific linguistic groups, he demonstrated both their similarity and their complex diversity.

In 1894 Boas delivered his first public address in which he outlined the racism of the dominant anthropological discourse. "Human Faculty as Determined by Race," delivered to Section H of the AAAS, raised this question: Does race limit the ability to achieve civilization? Boas warned, cautiously, that the problem with simple evolutionary theories was the liability "to interpret as racial character what is only an effect of social surroundings."[14]

He detailed how various civilizations arose either independently or through cultural diffusion and emphasized that civilizations arose in various parts of the world regardless of racial disposition. Although deferring to findings of physical anthropologists about racial inferiority, Boas demonstrated there was considerable overlap of "so called" racial characteristics, imploring that no fact "has been found yet which would prove beyond a doubt that it will be impossible for certain races to attain a higher civilization."[15] He also explained that the primary reason for African American inequality was racism, suggesting "that the old race-feeling of the inferiority of the colored race is as potent as ever and is a formidable obstacle to its advance and progress." He advised scientists to focus on how much Negroes have "accomplished in a short period against heavy odds" because "it is hardly possible to say what would become of the negro if he were able to live with the whites on absolutely equal terms."[16] Boas concluded that "historical events appear to have been much more potent in leading races to civilization than their faculty, and it follows that achievements of races do not warrant us to assume that one race is more highly gifted than the other."[17]

Boas's approach was a direct challenge to most anthropologists during that period. Brinton essentially accepted this challenge: the following year he delivered "The Aims of Anthropology" as the presidential address to the AAAS, which seems to be a rebuttal to Boas's 1894 address to Section H. Boas pulled together his growing concerns about the discipline of anthropology to respond to Brinton the following year, 1896, when he issued a detailed critique entitled "The Limitations of the Comparative Method of Anthropology." He was concerned about the lack of methodological rigor in ethnology and believed that the comparative method only attempted to link disparate traits and failed to study cultures holistically. He concluded that the object of study should not be individual traits or customs but "a detailed study of customs in their relation to the total culture."[18] The best way to conduct this kind of investigation, Boas asserted, was the "new historical method," which "affords us almost always a means of determining with considerable accuracy the historical causes that led to the formation of the customs in question."[19]

Boas's arguments at this point did not have a significant impact on the scientific community and did not circulate in the more popular scientific magazines. This was in sharp contrast to Brinton's version of anthropology, which was avidly consumed by both the general public and the scientific community. Whereas the editors of *Popular Science*

Monthly carried a one-column summary of Boas's AAAS address, they published Brinton's entire address just months before the *Plessy* decision.[20]

Boas also attempted to attack the eugenics movement, but he was summarily dismissed by the federal government and virtually ignored by the academic community. In 1907 President Theodore Roosevelt established the U.S. Immigration Commission (or, as it was known at the time, the Dillingham Commission), consisting of three senators, three House representatives, and three scientists. The commission was charged with informing the executive and legislative branches about the impact that the "new migration" would have on the United States and judging whether they should restrict it. The commission hired an array of experts who compiled a Herculean forty-one-volume report. It cost more than $1 million and took more than three years to complete.

Franz Boas was one of the scientists employed by the commission. He began his report by questioning the commission's underlying premise that there was some sort of difference between migrants who were coming to the United States and those who were already here. He stated that "This problem is an exceedingly complicated one, on account of the great differences in type of the people that have immigrated into the United States from different parts of Europe, on account of the changes of social conditions under which these people lived at home and here, and on account of the extended intermixture of descendants of various nationalities that is taking place in the United States."[21] In *Changes in Bodily Forms of Descendants of Immigrants* (1912), his contribution to the massive congressional report, he sought to prove that the so-called inferiority of Eastern European immigrants was erroneous. His report consisted of more than 500 pages of painstaking statistics, graphs, and formulas. It documented significant differences between the growth patterns of first- and second-generation children and demonstrated that the so-called inferior racial traits of Eastern Europeans were plastic and developed differently in different environments. His statistics were impressive, rigorous, and far more sophisticated than those of any other study conducted under the rubric of eugenics.

Although Boas was characteristically cautious, he stated that "we are therefore compelled to draw the conclusion that . . . the adaptability of the immigrant seems to be very much greater than we had a right to suppose before our investigations were instituted."[22] He continued:

[N]ot even those characteristics of a race which have proved to be most permanent in their old home remain the same under the new surroundings;

and we are compelled to conclude that when these features of the body change, the whole bodily and mental make-up of the immigrants may change.

These results are so definite that, while heretofore we had the right to assume that human types are stable, all the evidence is now in favor of a great plasticity of human types, and permanence of types in new surroundings appears rather as the exception than as the rule.[23]

The U.S. Immigration Commission selectively abridged the forty-one volumes into two volumes and presented them to the Senate. Although they mentioned Boas's efforts, they summarily dismissed them, stating that there were no corroborative data. This dismissive posture toward Boas's obliteration of the pervasive myth surrounding head size or the cephalic index was summed up by the eminent Yale sociologist Henry Pratt Fairchild, who stated that "the results reached by Professor Boas are somewhat startling and challenge attention. It is to be hoped that they will be subjected to the most careful scrutiny by anthropologists qualified either to verify or correct them."[24]

At this point Boas was provoking debate in scientific circles but was virtually discredited by the federal government. Eventually, however, his concept of culture and his defense of racial equality would become the dominant paradigm in the social sciences, and it would also be integrated into the sophisticated discourse on the political economy of race articulated by Du Bois. While Boas's thought ultimately eclipsed nineteenth-century ideas about race in the academy, Du Bois's discourse emerged as the theoretical underpinning of the NAACP and its battles to overturn the doctrine of separate but equal. It is to Du Bois that I now turn to examine how Du Bois and Boas came to strikingly similar yet different understandings of racial categories and cultural patterns contemporaneously. I will return to Boas to show his activist role and contextualize his and his students' efforts to fight racial inequality.

Du Bois's early understanding of the color line was an important precursor for the paradigmatic shift in the social sciences that is rightly credited to Boas. Boas simply had more power than Du Bois in the academy to redirect scientific approaches to race. Boas was White, was viewed as an "objective" scientist, and held sway over scientific societies, editorial boards, and a prestigious department.

As St. Clair Drake explained, Du Bois's approach contributed to a special genre of intellectual activity called racial vindication. This genre originated in the eighteenth century but eventually became a scientific assault against racial oppression. The vindicationist approach to science sought to disprove slander, answer pejorative allegations, and criticize so-called scientific generalizations about Africans and people of African descent.[25]

Du Bois's Early Understanding of Race and Culture

William Edward Burghardt Du Bois was born in Great Barrington, a small, affluent town in western Massachusetts (Figure 9). He graduated from high school in 1885 and won a scholarship to attend Fisk University in Nashville, Tennessee. At Fisk, in the Jim Crow South, he experienced a sharp contrast to his upbringing in Massachusetts. But Nashville and Great Barrington had one feature in common—racial prejudice. The contrasts and consistencies of racism that he observed as a young man became a backdrop for his sagacious comprehension of the race problem in the United States and later the world. It was at Fisk University that he resolved to fight the "color line" in a forthright but peaceful manner. In 1888 he completed his undergraduate work at Fisk and embarked on work toward a second bachelor's degree, matriculating as a junior at Harvard College. He continued graduate studies at Harvard, pursuing history and philosophy. He was interested in sociology, but, at that time, Harvard did not recognize the field.

Sociology developed into a professional academic field concurrently with anthropology, and it too gleaned many ideas from Social Darwinism. Du Bois recognized that the scope of the emerging field was congruent with his vision but that the methods and theory were not. He made a decision not to pursue sociology in the same vein as Herbert Spencer, William Graham Sumner, or Lester Ward; instead, he "came to the study of sociology, by way of philosophy and history rather than by physics and biology."[26] Du Bois received his doctorate from Harvard University and was influenced in important ways by Harvard's philosophical pragmatists, William James, Josiah Royce, and George Santayana.[27]

Du Bois's contribution to the philosophical foundation of American pragmatism has recently been established,[28] but his contribution to the concept of culture has not been addressed. He made a distinction between the cultural aspects of race and the social relations of race. These ideas were informed by his training within the German philosophical rubric *Geisteswissenschaften,* which roughly translates as the humanities and explored aspects of culture.

Figure 9. W. E. B. Du Bois, 1904. (Courtesy of the Library of Congress)

Before he completed his award-winning dissertation, "The Suppression of the African Slave Trade in the United States" (1896), Du Bois attended the Friedrich-Wilhelm III Universität in Berlin. He enrolled in October 1892 with assistance provided by the Slater Fund. In Germany he had the opportunity to garner an academic approach to society and culture that emphasized a methodology relying on inductive reasoning and the empirical gathering of historical and descriptive data. This methodology was used in conjunction with a rigorous curriculum of political economy. Du Bois stated:

I was admitted my first semester to two seminars under Schmoller and Wagner, both of them at the time distinguished men in their line; . . . I sat under the voice of the fire-eating Pan-German, von Treitschke; I heard Sering and Weber; . . . Under these teachers and in this social setting, I began to see the race problem in America, the problem of the peoples of Africa and Asia, and the political development of Europe as one. I began to unite my economics and politics.[29]

This approach was drastically different from the Spencerian approach to understanding society that was being touted at Harvard University by Shaler, Putnam, and others during the same period.[30] In *Dusk of Dawn: An Essay toward an Autobiography of a Race Concept* (1943), Du Bois explained this difference:

At Harvard . . . I began to face scientific race dogma: first of all evolution and the "Survival of the Fittest." It was continually stressed in the community and classes that there was a vast difference in the development of the whites and the "lower" races; that this could be seen in the physical development of the Negro. . . . [S]tress was quietly transferred to brain weight and brain capacity, and at last to the "cephalic index." . . . [I]n Germany, the emphasis again was altered, and race became a matter of culture and cultural history.[31]

During the 1890s and the first decade of the twentieth century Du Bois, like Boas, forcefully argued that racial categories were divorced from cultural patterns by suggesting that one should analyze historically specific cultures, as opposed to hierarchical levels of culture. The two scholars emphasized different issues, but both engendered strikingly similar lines of thought even before they began to collaborate.

Du Bois's Early Attack

Du Bois committed his life to developing a theory of society interactively with and through social and political practice in order to achieve enlightenment *and* emancipation.[32] Because of the interactive nature of Du Bois's social theory, he never made a distinction between theory and practice. His theory emanated from his political activism, and his political activism emanated from his theory.[33] The world into which Du Bois was born was changing as fast as his attempts to change it. His political and theoretical strategies and orientations changed as the world changed. He explained that he lived during, and subsequently chronicled, "changes of cosmic significance." "From 1868 to 1940 . . . incidentally the years of my own life but more especially years of cosmic significance, when one remembers that they rush from the American Civil War to the reign of the second Roosevelt; from Victoria to the Sixth George; from the Franco-Prussian to the two World Wars. They contain . . . the turmoils of Asia in China, India and Japan, and the world-wide domination of white Europe."[34] Although his theory was responsive, many of his biographers have been critical because they viewed him as eclectic and contradictory or incomprehensible and inconsistent, portraying him lurching between the antithetical and contradictory goals of black nationalism and racial integration.[35] Du Bois was, however, developing ideas to combat racial inequality when America was lurching between contradictions and global changes.

Du Bois's notion of the color line was one consistent tenet in his work. Race, he declared, was a political and social relationship, an integral part of capitalism, and the ultimate paradox of democracy.[36] He remarked that "to be a poor man is hard, but to be a poor race in a land of dollars is the very bottom of hardships."[37] The color line, according to Du Bois, prevented Negroes from gaining any political, economic, or social equality. As a form of institutionalized alienation, the color line ultimately denied the "cultural and spiritual desire to be one's self without interference from others; to enjoy that anarchy of the spirit which is inevitably the goal of all consciousness."[38]

Early in his career Du Bois sought to explain the color line as it related to the daily life of Negroes, arguing that racial inequality in the United States was the direct result of the heritage of slavery—not biology. And he viewed slavery as one component in the global imperialism undertaken by the "lighter races." Racial inequality, he argued, was born from the imposition of the color line, and that imposition created the relationship between "darker to the lighter races of men," "the burden he bore upon his back, that dead-weight of social degradation partially masked behind a half-named Negro problem."[39] Du Bois explored "the experience of being a problem" in its geopolitical and economic contexts, as opposed to the capacity of humans to surmount them.[40] He usually referred only to "the concept of race" and did not define race in biological terms. He was not even satisfied with describing race as a concept, suggesting "perhaps it is wrong to speak of it [race] at all as a concept rather than as a group of contradictory forces, facts and tendencies."[41]

In 1897 Du Bois groped for the right language to express ideas about racial equality and the unique cultural contributions of different races. This was evident in "The Conservation of Races," a paper presented at the first meeting of the Negro Academy. During this address Du Bois explained that "when we thus come to inquire into the essential difference of races we find it hard to come at once to any definite conclusions."[42] His main argument was that "so far as purely physical characteristics are concerned, the differences between men do not explain all the differences of their history."[43] He used examples of the subtle variations in color, ranging from the marblelike color of the Scandinavian to the rich dark brown of the Zulu, from the creamy Slav to the yellow Chinese. He dismissed color, cranial measurements, body shape, and language as criteria for demarcating racial categories. His evidence was gleaned from the fact that the racial criteria employed to categorize the races were inconsistent and appear in various combinations and different magnitudes within each race. He argued that science has not succeeded in clearing up the "relative authority of these various and contradictory criteria."[44] Concluding the first part of this address, he denied that any specific criteria existed to define races but contended:

yet there are differences—subtle, delicate and elusive, though they may be—which have silently but definitely separated men into groups. While these subtle forces have generally followed the natal cleavage of common blood, descent and physical peculiarities, they have at other times swept across and ignored these. At all times, however they have divided human beings into races, which while they perhaps transcended scientific definition, nevertheless, are clearly defined to the eye of the Historian and Sociologist.[45]

After effacing the scientific and biological categories of race, Du Bois attempted to discern "What is the real distinction between these nations?"[46] The answer he provided for this mounting question was a precursor to the later articulation of the culture concept. He explained that the cohesiveness which races (or nations) shared was rooted in more than physical characteristics: "The deeper differences are spiritual, psychical, differences—undoubtedly based on the physical, but infinitely transcending them. The forces that bind together the Teuton nations are, then, first, their race identity and common blood; secondly, and more important, a common history, common laws and religion, similar habits of thought and a conscious string together for certain ideals of life."[47]

As early as 1897 Du Bois provided an important first step for disassociating race from language and culture when he suggested that race was not a biological category and was not necessarily associated with different nations or the genius of a people (what later would be explained as ethnic groups or culture areas). His writings anticipated ideas of cultural relativism and the critique of ideas of racial inferiority that emerged from anthropologists at Columbia University during the 1920s. In certain respects, Du Bois presaged the "emergence of a scientific 'paradigm' for the study of mankind. The idea of culture, radically transformed in meaning [and stripped from ideas of evolution that linked patterned behavior to 'race traits'], is the central element of this paradigm, and indeed much of the social science of the twentieth century may be seen as a working out in detail of the implications of the culture idea."[48]

Du Bois also anticipated and was a pioneer of urban ethnography when he undertook research for *The Philadelphia Negro* in 1896. This study was sponsored by the University of Pennsylvania and underwritten by the City of Philadelphia. He developed a holistic ethnography based on fifteen months of intensive participant observation. He "sought to ascertain something of the geographical distribution of this race, their occupations and daily life, their homes, their organizations, and, above all, their relation to their million white fellow-citizens."[49] His ultimate goal at this juncture was to combat the notions of racial inferiority because "the world was thinking wrong about race, because it did not know. The ultimate evil was stupidity. The cure for it was knowledge based on scientific investigation."[50]

Du Bois explored the history of the Negro people in Philadelphia and their condition as individuals and organized social groups, as well as their physical and social environment.[51] He gathered data from thousands of informants in a wide range of class positions and occupations, including members of the police force and social organizations, bankers, cobblers, prostitutes, and parishioners. He painstakingly wove the ethnographic data into a comprehensive historical and demographic survey.

According to Du Bois, Philadelphia was the worst governed of the ill-governed northern cities. White residents in Philadelphia blamed the mismanagement of the city on the "the corrupt, semi-criminal vote of the Negro Seventh Ward."[52] To prove these allegations the city commissioned a study, backed by a prestigious university, in an effort to study their Negro problem. What city officials received did not quite match their expectations. They received a 400-page monograph which utilized innovative sociological and anthropological methods to demonstrate that poverty, segregation, and lack of health care, not racial inferiority, disposition toward criminal activity, and bad morals were the root causes of Negro degradation. The study was summarily shelved, and the University of Pennsylvania did not grant Du Bois an academic appointment. He had hoped that the study would steer public policy and secure him a position at the university.[53]

Du Bois's ethnography blazed a trail for such theoretical problems as differences in enculturation and socialization experienced by longtime urban residents and newly arriving southern migrants. Additionally, he was the first sociologist to document and analyze the changing forms of cultural adaptation, the impact on urban social relations by rural forms of social organization, and the perils and benefits of cultural identity.[54] Faye V. Harrison and Irene Diggs have both pointed out that the method and theoretical point of view which Du Bois articulated for this study helped to lay foundations for research that changed the discourse on race and culture in the social sciences in the United States. Harrison, extending the intellectual history of Diggs, has suggested that findings in *The Philadelphia Negro* predate similar findings in both *The Mind of Primitive Man* (1911), by Franz Boas, and *The Polish Peasant in Europe and America* (1918), by William I. Thomas and Florian Znaniecki. Moreover, W. Lloyd Warner's school of community studies at Harvard and Chicago (which resulted in *Black Metropolis: A Study of Negro Life in a Northern City,* by St. Clair Drake and Horace R. Cayton [1945], and Allison Davis's *Deep South* [1941], a social anthropological study of caste and class, as well as Warner's influential *Yankee City Series* [1941–1959]) shared comparable methods and theoretical perspectives with *The Philadelphia Negro.* The argument posed by Diggs and Harrison has important ramifications. They establish Du Bois as a progenitor of the important shift in the social sciences, from ideas of society born of Social Darwinism and premised on racial inferiority, to ideas of society born of notions of cultural diversity premised on racial equality. What is at stake is who ultimately gets "credit" for the profound shift in the social sciences.[55] Although Du Bois's work in *The Philadelphia Negro* and his Atlanta University studies were innovative, they did not have the same direct influence, credibility, and prestige as did studies by White scholars who explored social relations in urban arenas.

In 1897 Du Bois was appointed professor of history and economics at Atlanta University. He wanted to change the inherent racism in the social sciences and then to let sociological knowledge "trickle down" to erode the ignorance of people who harbored racist attitudes. To do so, he developed a systematic hundred-year program of studies of Negro life. As Du Bois stated, he wanted to "study the facts, any and all facts, concerning the American Negro and his plight, and by measurement and comparison and research, work up to any valid generalization I could. I entered this primarily with the utilitarian object of reform and uplift; but nevertheless, I wanted to do the work with scientific accuracy."[56]

The Atlanta studies covered a broad spectrum of issues, ranging from the physique and health of African Americans to patterns and strategies of economic cooperation. Each year Du Bois organized a conference to present the results of that year's investigation into a specific topic. He outlined ten topics of inquiry and envisioned revisiting each topic every decade for ten decades. The result would be a massive longitudinal study of Negro life and culture.

Many White scholars at the time could not accept that Negroes could pursue "rational" research because they considered them too "emotional." Others, however, took them seriously and applauded the much-needed data. The noted author and reformer George Washington Cable praised the conferences when they were launched: "It seems to me, from the highest, broadest, most patriotic and cosmopolitan point of view, to be one of the best enterprises that could be undertaken at this time."[57] The economic historian Frank Taussig said that no better work was being done anywhere in the United States.[58] W. Montague Cobb, a physical anthropologist and anatomist at Howard University, stated that the sixth study, in 1906, on Negro health was the "first significant scientific approach to the health problems and biological study of the Negro." Cobb was clear that "neither the Negro medical profession nor the Negro educational world was ready for it. Its potential usefulness was not realized by Negroes. [And] Whites were hostile to such a study." Although this study was Du Bois's only excursion into the health field,

Cobb quipped that it "was an extraordinary forward pass heaved the length of the field, but there were no receivers."[59]

Cobb's reflection on the 1906 study was emblematic of the gravity and originality of this ground-breaking research and its marginal impact at the time. However, the studies undertaken at Atlanta University were compiled into a series of monographs that became the corpus of research from which the interdisciplinary standard of African American studies was advanced.

The first two studies were conducted and subsequently presented in conferences before Du Bois became the official director of the annual conferences. The first, "Morality among Negroes in Cities," was conducted in 1896. The second, "Physical Condition of Negroes in Cities," was conducted and presented in 1897. When Du Bois officially became the director of the conferences he tightened up the series and developed the long-range intensive program. He also began to publish the proceedings of the annual conferences in a series, *The Atlanta University Publications,* which consisted of eighteen monographs with five bibliographies.[60] Du Bois began to edit the monographs with the third study, "Some Efforts of American Negroes for Their Own Social Betterment" (1898). The fourth study, "The Negro in Business" (1899), called for the establishment of a Negro business organization. Incidentally, Booker T. Washington established the Negro Businessmen's League the following year. The fifth, sixth, and seventh studies were entitled "The College-Bred Negro" (1900), "The Negro Common School" (1901), and "The Negro Artisan," respectively. The eighth study, "The Negro Church" (1903), was one of the first attempts to advance the sociological significance of the Black church, by documenting the history and diversity of several prominent Black denominations. The ninth study, "Some Notes on Negro Crime, Particularly in Georgia" (1904), linked crime to poverty, a double standard of justice in the courts, and discriminatory laws. The study found that African Americans, and African American women in particular, had no legal defense against violence perpetrated by White men. The study also highlighted the exploitation born of the convict-lease system and southern prison labor. The tenth and eleventh studies were "A Select Bibliography of the Negro American" (1905) and "The Health and Physique of the Negro American" (1906). Franz Boas participated in this study and contributed to the proceedings. The twelfth, thirteenth, and fourteenth studies were the last edited solely by Du Bois: "Economic Co-Operation among Negro Americans" (1907), "The Negro American Family" (1908), and "Efforts for Social Betterment among Negro Americans" (1910).[61]

In 1910 Du Bois left Atlanta to become an officer of the NAACP and the editor of its official organ, the *Crisis*. The hundred-year study did not materialize, and by 1905 Du Bois began to look for other ways to fight racial inequality. He began to see that correcting people's ignorance via the social sciences did not "trickle down" and correct the social evils of institutionalized racism, racists attitudes, and the pogrom attacks on entire communities. Furthermore, the Atlanta studies were woefully underfunded. Philanthropic agents did not see a need for the research, and Booker T. Washington blocked support for the project.[62] The studies continued anyway and received a paltry annual allocation from the university of $500.

During his years in Atlanta Du Bois took charge of the annual sociological conferences, edited the annual volumes for the studies, chaired the program in sociology, and instructed an upper-division year-long course. He began to grow impatient with the slow program of Negro progress led by Booker T. Washington and with the ineffectiveness of, and lack of support for, his Atlanta studies. The problems facing African Americans remained unchanged. African Americans lacked civil rights and economic opportunity and were still largely segregated by law and practice. Even worse, pogrom attacks and lynchings continued unchecked.

In an effort to combat racial inequality through political action, Du Bois organized a Negro rights group, the Niagara Movement, in 1905. Twenty-nine members of Du Bois's so-called talented-tenth of the Negro population attended the initial conclave. The press called them "the radicals." More African American leaders were expected but, according to rumors, declined the invitation at the last minute, after being pressured by friends of Booker T. Washington.[63] The Niagara Movement was much more demanding than Washington's Tuskegee Machine. It insisted that the government meet several demands: free speech, equal employment, union opportunities, federal aid for education, an end to sharecropping, and no more federal subsidies for the Tuskegee Machine's press.[64]

Du Bois's move from the academy enabled him to focus on political activism and agitation. The move was also facilitated by an increasing rift with Washington. Du Bois was not opposed to industrial education and generally agreed with Washington in terms of economic uplift, self-help, and self-determination. However, he disagreed with Washington about how to obtain equality. Du Bois held the position that social equality and economic opportunity could be obtained only through gaining political rights.

The rift, drawn in terms of region and social status, separated the South from the North, a vocationally trained working class from the normal-school- and college-educated talented-tenth. The rift was thrown into vivid relief in 1903 with the publication of Du Bois's widely acclaimed *The Souls of Black Folk,* a collection of essays previously published in the *Atlantic Monthly* and other fifteen-cent monthlies. The book contained some of the finest prose of the day, and in it Du Bois was openly critical of Washington's agenda. Du Bois exposed differences between the young intellectuals who organized the Niagara Movement and the established leadership and summarized his criticism in a chapter entitled "Of Mr. Booker T. Washington." He curtly penned:

Mr. Washington thus faces the triple paradox of his career:

1. He is striving nobly to make Negro artisans, businessmen and property owners; but it is utterly impossible . . .
2. He insists on thrift and self-respect, but at the same time counsels a silent submission to civic inferiority . . .
3. He advocates common-school and industrial training, and depreciates institutions of higher learning.[65]

The "old-school" leadership of Washington and the Tuskegee Machine was delivered a fatal blow in 1909, when Mary White Ovington, a White social worker, issued a call to form the National Negro Committee. She wanted to merge the weak Niagara Movement with a group of White reformers.

This organization, which soon became the NAACP, first met in New York City on May 31, 1909.[66] The widely publicized meeting was viewed as a protest movement. Members of the university community, including William James, Du Bois's former professor at Harvard, thought that race prejudice might increase as a result of the publicity the committee would receive. Furthermore, powerful White friends of Washington, such as Andrew Carnegie, shunned the conclave. The meeting attempted to forge a new model for the advancement of colored people. Washington's model ignored the future role of urban African Americans and was blind to the growing horror of racial violence.[67] For these reasons, the organization convened without him.

Although the *Crisis* was the official organ of the NAACP, Du Bois exercised editorial independence. It was essentially his publication, and he made it one of the most effective tools for education, vindication, and liberation. Each issue critiqued and chronicled, provided leadership and propaganda, agitated and organized, all the while tackling the myriad issues that African Americans had to negotiate during the 1910s.[68]

Between 1896 and 1910 Du Bois made profound contributions. He laid the foundation of a new discourse on race within the social sciences, undertook an important research program at Atlanta University, published numerous articles in widely circulated periodicals, helped to establish the NAACP, and began his work as editor of the *Crisis*.

Franz Boas, in an attempt to establish a new discourse on race within anthropology, intersected each of these endeavors undertaken by Du Bois. Boas took part in the Atlanta studies, attempted to popularize his notion of race in widely circulated periodicals, spoke at the first meeting of the NAACP, and contributed to the *Crisis*.[69]

Some of their parallel experiences may illuminate the reasons why both Boas and Du Bois developed lines of thought that were inimical to the consensus about racial inferiority held by people in the mass media, the academy, southern state legislatures, and each branch of the federal government. To begin with, Boas was trained in the same German traditions that influenced Du Bois. Boas shared with Du Bois the methodological orientation that emphasized inductive reasoning and the empirical gathering of descriptive and historical data. Boas also shared with Du Bois firsthand experience with persecution and discrimination.[70] The precise experiences that influenced these two scholars to engender similar approaches may never, however, be known.

There were, of course, differences between their strategies, philosophies, and subject positions. Boas viewed racial categories in terms of biological differences. Though deeply committed to ideals of the equipotentiality of the race, he was also committed to the science that seemed to prove Blacks to be inferior to Whites. He tried to explain the differences in terms of plasticity and frequency, but his early critiques were conducted on terms laid down by Social Darwinists in previous years. As Vernon J. Williams, Jr. suggests, Boas was a "prisoner of his times."[71] Young Du Bois was imprisoned too. According to David Levering Lewis, Du Bois was imprisoned by both his own color complex, in which "mulattoes" were superior to "full-blooded" Negroes, and his adopted Victorian elitism. Although Du Bois did not view racial differences in strictly biological terms, he stood arrogantly and willfully apart from the Negro masses, who were, he envisioned, his destiny to uplift.[72] I do not dispute the claims of Williams and Lewis, but I do see both Du Bois and Boas during the first decade of the twentieth century working hard to subvert the racial discourse as reformers, not as revolutionaries. Although Boas may have been imprisoned by his empiricism, that was not what hindered his efforts to fight for racial equality.

Franz Boas in the Struggle for Racial Equality

Boas's reputation began to grow in the late 1890s, and he became viewed by African American leaders as an ally in the struggle for racial equality because of his antiracist research and theories.[73] Boas was also eager to build alliances and strengthen his ties with civil rights leaders. He appears to have been initially unaware of the various strategies used by African American leaders to alleviate racial inequality, for he attempted to build alliances with both Washington and Du Bois. Ultimately, however, he allied himself with Du Bois and became associated with the radical integrationist arm of the movement. The relationship Boas formed with Du Bois and the NAACP alienated him from the accommodationist wing of the movement led by Washington and financed by Andrew Carnegie. It, in effect, cut off Boas from possible funding from Carnegie.

While Du Bois and his associates began to gain prominence, the vast majority of African Americans continued to claim Washington as their leader. Few Whites ventured into matters of race relations without his counsel.[74] Franz Boas was no exception. In 1904 Boas wrote to Washington concerning the admission of an African American student into the graduate anthropology program at Columbia University:

Dear Sir,

> A young gentleman, Mr. J. E. Aggrey, of Livingston College, Salisbury, N.C., desires to study anthropology at Columbia University. He is a full-blood negro. . . . I very much hesitate to advise the young man to take up this work, because I fear that it would be very difficult after he has completed his studies to find a place. On the other hand, it might perhaps be possible for him to study for two or three years and take his degree of master of arts, and then to obtain a position in one of the schools for his people.[75]

Boas must not have been fully aware of Washington's strategy, which emphasized vocational training and devalued university education. If Boas had been, he would have been able to predict Washington's response:

> Judging by what you state in your letter and knowing what I do, I cannot rid myself of the feeling that the course which he [Aggrey] is planning to take, will be of little value to him.

> At the present time I know of so many cases where young colored men and women would have done well had they thoroughly prepared themselves for teachers, some kind of work in the industries, or in the applied sciences, but instead, they have made the mistake of taking a course that had no practical bearing on the needs of the race; the result being they ended up as hotel-waiters or Pullman car porters.[76]

Boas was characteristically shrewd in his professional relationships; however, this rather naive understanding of the political terrain within African American leadership proved detrimental. At least one of Boas's projects was not funded by Carnegie due to his involvement with Du Bois at Atlanta University.

Du Bois's initial contact with Boas was a letter written on October 11, 1905. In it he explained the hundred-year study and asked Boas to participate in the eleventh conference, which was on the Negro physique.[77] Boas accepted the invitation and also delivered the 1906 commencement address for Atlanta University. In the speech he empowered African Americans by saying that their ancestors contributed greatly to the civilization of the human race. He explained that "while much of the history of early invention is shrouded in darkness, it seems likely that at a time when the European was still satisfied with rude stone tools, the African had invented or adopted the art of smelting iron."[78] Boas also used other examples: the military organization of the Zulu, the advanced economic and judicial system of the Negro Kingdoms of the Sudan, and the innovative bronze casting of Benin. He further appealed: "If, therefore, it is claimed that your race is doomed to economic inferiority, you may confidently look to the home of your ancestors and say that you have set out to recover for the colored people the strength that was their own before they set foot on the shores of this continent."[79]

St. Clair Drake has suggested that the Atlanta University address clearly placed Boas and early anthropology at Columbia right in the middle of the "vindication struggle."[80] It also placed Boas squarely within the integrationist, radical, and anti-Washington wing of the struggle for racial equality. And it had a tremendous impact on Du Bois. In *Black Folk Then and Now* (1939) he reflected on what a profound contribution Boas made to his own view of the African world.

Franz Boas came to Atlanta University where I was teaching History in 1906 and said to the graduating class: You need not be ashamed of your African past; and then he recounted the history of black kingdoms south of the Sahara for a thousand years. I was too astonished to speak. All of this I had never heard and I came then and afterwards to realize how the silence and neglect of science can let truth utterly disappear or even be unconsciously distorted.[81]

It is difficult to know for certain whether Boas understood the complexities of the political debates among African American leaders or whether he even knew about Washington's contempt for both Du Bois and Atlanta University. On the other hand, the contempt Washington held for Du Bois was well known in the Black community. It was made quite clear in public arenas. For example, Washington indicted Du Bois in an open letter to the president of Atlanta University, after *Souls* was published. This 1903 letter was published in one of the most popular African American newspapers, the *Colored American*.

If Atlanta University intends to stand for Dr. Du Bois' outgivings, if it means to seek to destroy Tuskegee Institute, so that its own work can have success, it is engaged in poor business to start with; . . . Tuskegee will go on. It will succeed . . . not withstanding the petty annoyances of Du Bois and his ilk. . . . Let him [the university president] prove himself by curbing the outgivings and ill-advised criticism of the learned Doctor who is now in his employ.[82]

In November 1906 Boas exposed his lack of understanding regarding the different agendas set forth by the African American leadership. He wrote a letter to Washington requesting his support for the creation of an African and African American museum, and he enclosed his Atlanta University commencement address to prove to Washington that he was sincere about the Negro:

I am endeavoring to organize certain scientific work on the Negro race which I believe will be of great practical value in modifying the views of our people in regard to the Negro problem. I am particularly anxious to bring home to the American people the fact that the African race in its own continent has achieved advancements which have been of importance in the development of civilization of the human race. You may have seen some of my references to this matter, but I enclose an address that I gave in Atlanta last spring, which will suggest some of the matters that I have in mind.[83]

Clearly, the copy of his commencement address was not warmly received by Washington. Chances are that Boas was seeking Washington's support so that Carnegie would fund his project. Two weeks later he solicited financial support for the museum directly from the financier:

All that we can say at the present time is that it seems unfair to judge the Negro by what he has come to be in America, and that the evidence of cultural achievement of the Negro in Africa suggests that his inventiveness, power of political organization, and steadiness of purpose, equal or even excel those of other races of similar stages of culture. . . . It seems plausible that the whole attitude of our people in regard to the Negro might be materially modified if we had a better knowledge of what the Negro has really done and accomplished in his own native country. . . . The endless repetition of remarks on the inferiority of the Negro physique, of the early arrest of development of Negro children, of the tendency in the mulatto to inherit all the bad traits of both parental races, seems almost ineradicable, and in the present state of our knowledge can just as little be repudiated as supported by definite evidence. . . . There seems to be another reason which would make it highly desirable to disseminate knowledge of the achievements of African culture, particularly among the Negroes, in vast portions of our country there is a strong feeling of despondency among the best classes of the Negro, due to the economic, mental, and moral inferiority of the race in America, and the knowledge of the strength of their parental race in their native surroundings must have a wholesome and highly stimulating effect. I have noticed these effects myself in addressing audiences of Southern Negroes, to whom the facts were a complete revelation.[84]

Carnegie did not support the project.

Boas wanted to help advance African American equality. Yet his impact as an activist was limited to influencing a small number of anthropologists at Columbia University and to lending his name to a few radical intellectuals. He did not successfully negotiate the political dynamics produced by the African American leadership. His impact was also limited within the sciences and among the educated public because of the virulent racism that permeated U.S. social relations.

Even though Boas may not have realized the depth or significance of the strategic differences and polarization of African American intellectuals, he continued to struggle for racial equality. He attempted to popularize his views in magazines, in spite of the fact that writers sympathetic to Social Darwinists dominated that medium. For instance, in September 1906, the influential *Century Magazine* published an article by Robert Bean entitled "The Negro Brain." Bean wrote, "The Caucasian and the negro are fundamentally opposite extremes in evolution. Having demonstrated that the negro and the Caucasian are widely different in characteristics, due to a deficiency of gray matter and connecting fibers in the negro brain . . . we are forced to conclude that is is [*sic*] useless to try to elevate the negro by education or otherwise except in the direction of his natural endowments."[85] In response to this article

Boas wrote to the owner, editor, and publisher of this magazine, Richard Watson Gilder, explaining that such an article would "give strong support to those who deny the negro equal rights; and from this point of view . . . the paper is not just to the cause of the negro."[86] Boas's letter to Gilder did nothing to curb the racism perpetuated by Gilder's magazine. A month later, in the October issue, Gilder published another article by Robert Bean which espoused the same propaganda as "science."[87]

A year later Boas wrote to Gilder again and proposed submitting a nonscientific essay on African culture, accompanied by various pictures of native industries.[88] The article was rejected but in 1909 appeared as "Industries of African Negroes" in the *Southern Workman,* published by Hampton Institute.[89] This article had nineteen images, ranging from "Pottery made by the Bali tribe" to "Congo throwing knives." Between them were statements like the following: "A broader treatment of the question will require a consideration of the achievements of the Negro under other conditions, and particularly of the culture that he has developed in his own natural surroundings. The conditions for gaining a clear insight into this question are particularly unfavorable in North America, where loss of continuity of development and an inferior social position have made a deep impress on the race that will be slow to disappear."[90]

Boas was unable to publish this article in a magazine that promoted racism. Undaunted by the setback, he made several other attempts to popularize his views. In 1907 he published an article entitled, "The Anthropological Position of the Negro" in *Van Norden's Magazine*.[91] Its impact was diminished because it was published in the same issue as "The Race Question," written by South Carolina Senator Benjamin Tillman, who sought support for repealing the Fifteenth Amendment. Boas again attempted to popularize his position by editing an encyclopedia of the Negro, but the project was aborted.

Substantial resistance to Boas's proposals to further the cause of the Negro came from influential capitalists, such as Carnegie and Gilder—men who, through vast financial resources, controlled the media and forcefully articulated notions of racial inferiority. Boas's efforts to educate White Americans failed, but as early as 1906 his efforts did contribute to the nascent fields of African and African American Studies. He subsequently developed both a personal and a professional relationship with Carter G. Woodson, founder of the Association for the Study of Negro Life and History. Boas was a member of its Executive Council and sat on the Editorial Board of its organ, the *Journal of Negro Life and History*.[92]

The discourse on race that Boas established resonated with the vision of the political activists fighting for racial equality, and he was invited to the first conclave of the NAACP. The meeting began with a symposium that attempted to finally answer the basic question of whether or not Negroes were equal to other peoples, so Boas and Burt G. Wilder, a zoologist at Cornell University, delivered the opening address.[93] Boas also spoke the following year at the organization's annual meeting. His second address, "The Real Race Problem," was subsequently published in the *Crisis*. The subtitles in the article show how Boas had espoused racial equality since 1906: "The Negro Not Inferior," "The Handicap of Slavery," "[African] Trade Well Organized," and so forth.[94]

Boas continued to support the NAACP and its leaders. In 1911 he wrote the foreword for Mary White Ovington's book, *Half a Man: The Status of the Negro in New York*, a sociohistorical study of Negro labor relations in New York City.[95] For the next fifty years the NAACP led the fight for racial equality and integration. Boas continued to be involved with and published on issues surrounding African Americans, and he developed a lifelong friendship with Du Bois.

Boas forms a tenuous but critical link between two nascent groups who would help to change the structure and meaning of race. The first group consisted of anthropologists trained at Columbia University, who orchestrated a paradigmatic shift in the scientific discourse on race by advancing the notion of cultural relativity and refuting ideas regarding racial inferiority. The second group Boas influenced comprised the intellectuals of the NAACP, who orchestrated a juridical shift in the legal codification of racial inferiority by tenaciously fighting racial segregation in the courts.

Tightly Knit Discourse on Race

Between the world wars three distinct but closely aligned methodological approaches to anthropology were used to explore the African American experience. The first was folklore. The anthropologists who delved into African American folklore took seriously the diffusion, contribution, and cultural continuity of African cultures in the Americas. The second approach took the nexus of race and class as its central charge. These anthropologists investigated the environmental and social conditions of segregated communities and documented the cultural, social, and psychological toll of racism. This approach converged with sociology and social psychology and was active in the caste-versus-class debates. Finally, physical or biological anthropology followed and emerged as an important field for the scientific assertion of racial equality. Each of these methodological approaches was affected in important ways by African American anthropologists.

The earliest African American scholars to study anthropology were vindicationists first and anthropologists second. Invariably, they employed a multidisciplinary approach to the study of race and culture and were primarily interested in integrating scholarship with political activism and/or artistic expression. What united these scholars was a penchant for the vindication of diasporic Africans in the academic literature and a propensity to "set the record straight."

These vindicationists gravitated toward the scholars in the Department of Anthropology at Columbia University and helped to accelerate the paradigmatic shift in the understanding of race and culture. This occurred during the tumultuous social transformations in the United States between World War I and World War II, which began to slowly erode the construct of race that had solidified in the 1890s. Change was on the horizon, and once again anthropology played an integral role — this time, on both sides of the color line.

CHAPTER 6

The New Negro and
Cultural Politics of Race

The anthropological discourse on race between the world wars was not touted at world's fairs or in other vehicles of popular culture; nor was it congruent with wider currents of public discourse.[1] Yet anthropology played important roles in the process of racial formation on both sides of the color line. Holding onto its prestige as the "science" of race and culture, anthropology began to effectively counter dominant ideas about race articulated by people in the media, southern state legislatures, and all branches of the federal government. During the 1920s and 1930s artists and intellectuals of the New Negro Movement used anthropology to help form a new identity and validate African American culture. During the 1930s and 1940s, activists, educators, and lawyers appropriated the anthropology of race as scientific proof of racial equality in order to facilitate their attempts to desegregate the very institutions that fastidiously demarcated the color line.

Cultivating the New Negro

In 1927 Arthur Huff Fauset, a Philadelphia anthropologist and educator, explained that "the New Negro has been in America for a long time. Only, everyone was so used to seeing Negroes that practically no one discovered that differences were taking place under our very eyes." He recalled that it was not until Alain Locke "packed the evidence of these differences into one single volume, calling it 'The New Negro,' that people fully realized what had been taking place."[2]

Alain Locke's 1925 book was a snapshot of the intellectuals and artists who emerged during this period of rapid change. Although African American communities had existed in northern cities for centuries, the influx of massive numbers of southern immigrants who were willing to sell their labor for next to nothing transformed the United States. What has been referred to as the Great Migration consisted of 6 million African Americans moving from a rural sharecropping system in the agrarian South to become an urbanized proletariat in the industrial North. This was roughly half of the African American population at the time and one of the largest internal migrations ever.[3] No longer were there small enclaves of African Americans in northern cities and masses of exploited and disfranchised workers on the delta of the Mississippi, in the cotton fields of the Black Belt, or in the cypress swamps in Florida. New York, Philadelphia, Chicago, Boston, St. Louis, Washington, and Newark witnessed their African American populations explode after World War I. During World War II the migration intensified, and the Black population in the cities of Portland, Seattle, Oakland, and Los Angeles also increased rapidly. Racial tensions pervaded the everyday lives of residents in virtually every city and suburb; the large numbers of migrants transformed local and state politics, popular culture, residence patterns, labor markets—indeed, the very idea of what it meant to be an American.

African Americans began to forcefully contest how race was constructed and to assert their economic, political, and cultural power. Marcus Garvey and the United Negro Improvement Association (UNIA), A. Philip Randolph and the Brotherhood of Sleeping Car Porters, W. E. B. Du Bois and the NAACP, and Mary Church Terrell and the National Association of Colored Women, as well as a host of churches and a myriad other social, fraternal, and economic organizations, began to assert their collective power. Newspapers such as the Harlem *Crusader* depicted this movement by headlining "The Old Negro Goes," exclaiming, "His abject crawling and pleading have availed the Cause nothing." The Kansas City *Call* captured the movement by proclaiming "The NEW NEGRO, unlike the old time Negro 'does not fear the face of day.' "[4] With new jobs, access to high-quality education, and the development of new and varied forms of organizations, African Americans combined the strategies outlined by both Washington and Du Bois but were not limited to them. Self-determination and determined desegregation, organization and political participation, artistic and industrial production all emerged as ways of resisting the system of repression routinized by lynchings, sharecropping, and Jim Crow. But new forms of despair and oppression were found in the cities. Crime, overcrowding, disease, labor disputes, and citywide pogroms tempered the enthusiasm of the so-called New Negro.

These dramatic transformations in race and class relations created a milieu from which African American intellectuals and artists developed the New Negro Movement. Certain events quickened the pursuit of racial equality, while other events curtailed that challenge. Important events were occurring all over the world. To provide the needed context, I will provide only a cursory outline of this rich history.

The candidates for the presidential elections of 1912 offered African Americans little in substance and less in hope. African Americans generally did not trust the Republican incumbent, William Howard Taft. In addition, they were leery of Theodore Roosevelt and his newly formed Progressive Republican Party, especially in the wake of Roosevelt's blatant disregard for Blacks in 1906, when he dismissed without honor and without a proper trial a whole Negro battalion stationed at Fort Brown for allegedly shooting up the town of Brownsville, Texas. This issue notwithstanding, the NAACP drafted a plank for the platform of Roosevelt's "Bull Moose" Party. The NAACP plank asserted "that distinctions of race or class in political life have no place in democracy,"[5] denounced segregation, and demanded complete enfranchisement. Roosevelt, however, complied with the wishes of his southern supporters and rejected the plank. He even revoked seats won by African American delegates to the "Bull Moose" convention. This left Woodrow Wilson, a Democrat, and Eugene V. Debs, a Socialist. A. Philip Randolph, a labor organizer and the editor of the *Messenger*, supported Debs. Du Bois, however, believed that he "could not let Negroes throw away votes" and subsequently threw his support behind Wilson.[6] Editorials in the *Messenger* began to paint Du Bois as an opportunist.[7] The NAACP and other Black organizations gave Wilson the nod, though each organization recognized the gravity of the situation. If Wilson were elected, "the Presidency, the Senate, the House of Representatives and, practically, the Supreme court . . . [would be in] the hands of the party which a half century ago fought desperately to keep black men as real estate in the eyes of the law."[8]

Although Wilson made some overtures to "absolute fair dealing" and "justice done to the colored people," Black voters did not fully embrace the Democratic Party. In a sense they voted for Wilson by default; the field simply lacked any viable candidate. However, the African American support of Wilson, and by default the Democratic Party, is a watershed in the history of electoral politics in the United States. It signaled the imminent shift of African American support from the Republican Party to the Democratic Party.[9]

Many African Americans found Wilson's rhetoric of a new freedom encouraging and were optimistic when Wilson won the election. The *Crisis* echoed this optimism in an open letter to Wilson on inauguration day. "It was a step toward political independence," stated Du Bois, "and it was helping to put into power a man who has to-day the power to become the greatest benefactor of his country since Abraham Lincoln."[10]

This optimism quickly waned. The Congress that convened with the Wilson administration introduced more Jim Crow legislation than had any other. At least twenty bills proposed laws to racially segregate public transportation in the District of Columbia, as well as rest rooms in federal office buildings. Other bills attempted to exclude the immigration of people of African descent; still others proposed the exclusion of African Americans from officer commissions in the military. Although most of this legislation died on the floor, Wilson viewed it as a clear mandate. Less than six months after coming to office he issued an executive order that segregated the bathrooms and cafeterias of federal agencies in the District. Simultaneously, he implemented a plan to systematically phase out African Americans from most federal and civil positions.[11] The NAACP Board of Directors issued a stern reproach and drew a subtle parallel between repression in the United States and repression in Europe which had led to the outbreak of war. This statement was distributed to the Associated Press on August 14, 1914. It stated, in part:

Never before has the Federal Government discriminated against its civilian employees on the ground of color. Every such act heretofore has been that of an individual State. . . . And wherever there are men who rob the Negroes of their votes, who exploit and degrade and insult and lynch those whom they call their inferiors, there [will be] this mistaken action of the Federal Government [which] will be cited as the warrant for new racial outrages that cry out to high Heaven for redress. . . . Who can deny that every act of discrimination the world over breeds fresh injustice?[12]

In 1915 most Americans were closely watching German submarines in the Atlantic, but African Americans were closely watching a retooled,

Figure 10. The entertainment value of burning flesh. (Courtesy of the Library of Congress)

officially incorporated, and efficiently organized Ku Klux Klan (KKK) that was spreading throughout the nation. The ideological edict of the new KKK was decidedly broadened: in addition to Negroes, it now sought to persecute Jews, southern European immigrants, and Catholics. Even labor organizers and political radicals felt the wrath of the unscrupulous KKK.[13] It fueled a new surge of lynchings that reached almost a hundred that year. Tacked onto the number of African American lynchings were the murders of more than twenty-five European immigrants killed in a similar fashion.[14] Lynching via the public hanging or live burning emerged as a type of American pastime (Figure 10). In 1916, for example, there was the horrible public burning of Jesse Washington in Waco, Texas, before a mob of thousands of men, women, and children:

While a fire was being prepared of boxes, the naked boy was stabbed and the chain put over the tree. He tried to get away, but could not. He reached up to grab the chain and they cut off his fingers. The big man struck the boy on the back of the neck with a knife just as they were pulling him up on the tree. Mr.—thought that was practically the death blow. He was lowered into the fire several times by means of the chain around his neck.[15]

The birth of the revamped KKK was concurrent with the release of the first full-length feature film, *The Birth of a Nation,* produced by D. W. Griffith and based on Thomas Dixon's virulently racist book *The Clansman* (1905). The film followed the book and captured its leitmotiv. It heralded the triumphs of the KKK, which supposedly saved the South after the Civil War. Griffith's original title for the film mirrored that of the book, but he changed it to "match the picture's greatness."

Two overarching themes ran through the film: the first suggested that the KKK had been responsible for quelling the unrest in the South after the Civil War; the second suggested that African Americans had been the cause of all the problems in the United States. The film was effectively framed by the subtitle that introduced the prologue: "The bringing of the Africans to America planted the first seeds of disunion." This film emphasized repeatedly that the African presence in the United States served as the only barrier to a unified country. Du Bois observed that it "fed to the young of the nation and to the unthinking masses as well as to the world a story which twisted the emancipation and enfranchisement of the slave in great effort toward universal democracy, into an orgy of theft and degradation and wide rape of white women."[16]

Griffith's use of history paralleled Brinton's, McGee's, and Shaler's use of ethnology. The ethnologists reproduced popular images by cloaking the representation of Negro inferiority with the authority of scientific anthropology. Griffith reproduced the images by veiling the representation of Negro inferiority in the authority of documented history. In fact, he offered to contribute $10,000 to charity if the NAACP could "find a single incident in the play that was not historic."[17]

At key junctures in the plot, Griffith stopped the moving picture and inserted still photography underscored by subtitles from Woodrow Wilson's book *A History of the American People* (1902). These stills accompanied texts and were called "historic facsimiles." Ostensibly the film was authentic because it was framed by quotations from the historic record. By quoting the current president of the United States, Griffith invariably buttressed the authenticity and lent credibility to his story. Not only was Wilson president, he had academic credentials as a noted historian and as the former president of Princeton University.

Griffith's feature film functioned in the same way as Nathaniel Shaler's articles in fifteen-cent monthlies had some twenty years earlier. Both cast enduring racial stereotypes under the guise of an academic discourse within a popular medium. Griffith merely recycled the profitable images found in the Darktown comics, minstrel shows, popular fiction, advertising, cartoons, and the like. Compared with Shaler's texts, Griffith's moving picture had a far more pervasive impact on how Americans visualized ideas about racial inferiority. Griffith portrayed African American men as innately brutal, eternally sadistic, excessively drunken, lawless, and riotous—and perpetually lusting after White women. African American women, on the other hand, were depicted either as oversexed mulattoes or as bossy, overprotective, and asexual mammies. Mythical Negroes—mostly played by White actors in blackface—were shown arrogantly abusing Whites in their attempt to take over the government of the Old South. Following scenes depicting the Negro's total inability to hold power, the film vividly exploited and solidified into so-called historic fact the alleged justification for lynching Black men: the degenerate Black brute always lusts shamelessly after and rapes White women. The pure white flower of southern womanhood, then, must be defended by the chivalrous and noble Knights of the Ku Klux Klan.

Members of the press and of Congress, as well as Woodrow Wilson himself, heralded the didactic value of the film. They also attested to its veracity. Columnist Dorothy Dix called the movie "history vitalized" and urged people to "go see it . . . for it will make better Americans of you." Booth Tarkington, a notable novelist, Claude Kitchin, a congressional representative from North Carolina, and other literary and political figures all allowed themselves to be quoted in advertisements proclaiming the educational value of the film.[18] One prominent preacher from the North publicly stated that "a boy can learn more true history and get more of the atmosphere of the period by sitting three hours before the film which Mr. Griffith has produced with such artistic skill than by weeks and months of study in the classroom."[19] After viewing it at the White House, Woodrow Wilson even chimed in and stated, "It's like writing history with lighting and my only regret is that it is all so terribly true."[20]

During the first decade and a half of the twentieth century, movie houses normally held a film for only a few days. Griffith's work shattered this standard. It ran for ten months in New York City and twenty-two weeks in Los Angeles. It enjoyed similar engagements in other markets. Contemporary estimates of the numbers of people who saw it during the first year alone range upward from 5 million.[21] The feature-film industry was launched with *The Birth of a Nation* and therefore born by profiting from odious images of Black people; furthermore, it fell right in line with the other vehicles of popular culture that produced images of African Americans which ultimately reinforced Jim Crow. Feature

films were more powerful, more ubiquitous, and, in effect, more vera-
cious than other media, however. Griffith seared images of degraded
Negroes into the minds of millions. A whole new generation of con-
sumers of American mass media was fed the same old stereotypes to
shape images of African Americans. Although the NAACP led boycotts
and tried to educate the public about the film's misrepresentation, there
was a powerful synergistic relationship between its overwhelming popularity and the ideology that held firm to the belief in Negro inferiority.[22]

The NAACP became the organization that Black people looked to
for leadership and direction in the struggle for civil rights. With the
death of Booker T. Washington in 1915 the Tuskegee Machine waned.
The NAACP waxed, especially in the leadership it began to shoulder in
state and federal courts. It won its first cases before the U.S. Supreme
Court between 1915 and 1917. The first case in which it participated was
Guinn v. United States,[23] in which the Court found the "grandfather
clause" in Maryland and Oklahoma statutes unconstitutional under the
Fourteenth and Fifteenth amendments. The NAACP was party to the
case only as amicus curiae (friend of the court), but the powerful brief
submitted by Moorfield Storey, the past president of the American Bar
Association, an eminent Massachusetts jurist, and then-president of the
NAACP, proved critical to the Court's decision.[24] In 1917 Storey won
Buchanan v. Warley.[25] This case struck down a law passed by the Louisville, Kentucky, City Council that imposed residential racial segregation as part of a "de-uglification" project. It was an important case because similar statutes were springing up all over the country, especially
in the wake of the rapid increase in African American migrants to the
North and West. The Court found that the Louisville statute was in
violation of the 1870 Civil Rights Act, which clearly stated that "all citizens of the United States shall have the same right in every state and
territory as is enjoyed by white citizens thereof to inherit, purchase,
lease, sell, hold and convey real and personal property." These cases were
important beginnings, but the precedents they set were quickly eroded
or circumvented.[26]

In six years the NAACP developed from a small organization of radical agitators on the periphery to a national organization of staid lobbyists, lawyers, and organizers who moved quickly to the center. The
organization was well established, well respected, and well organized,
and it began to adopt a centrist position in order to better serve its
broadening base of constituents. Thousands of people, Black and White,
were incorporating local chapters across the nation. Charged with the

mandate to advance colored people, the leadership of the organization became entwined in the complex web of racialized politics in the United States.[27]

When the United States joined the Allies in World War I, the NAACP was forced to come out in support of U.S. involvement. The NAACP was then forced to negotiate a contradictory position: although it could support the government's entry into the war to lead the people in the Western world to social justice, self-determination, and democracy, it could not support the federal government's consistent abrogation of democratic ideals on the home front. The federal government was party to oppressing Blacks with Jim Crow laws and disfranchisement while virtually condoning mob violence. Joel Spingarn, chair of the NAACP board, believed that the war effort would provide an opportunity for African Americans at home and abroad. He was a strong advocate of American intervention. This position, however, translated into the NAACP's begging the War Department to let Negroes die for the country—a country which offered African Americans little protection under the law. The NAACP was successful in pressuring the War Department into establishing a special, segregated officer-training camp and making Negro regiments combatant, as opposed to only service, personnel.

Du Bois was critical of the war effort and was, initially, a dissident on the NAACP board, which overwhelmingly supported U.S. involvement. Exercising the editorial freedom he had over the *Crisis,* he castigated the war effort when members of 24th Colored Infantry were summarily sentenced after being provoked and, arguably, defending themselves in a race riot in Houston, Texas. The War Department and the Committee on Public Information subsequently organized a mandatory meeting for all the editors of the Black press. The committee wanted to ensure a united front. It received only perfunctory compliance, but A. Philip Randolph and Chandler Owen kept true to the leftist tradition of the *Messenger.*

Ostensibly protected by the First Amendment, they wrote that a war between capitalists, exploiters, and colonizers was not a war for the colored citizens of the United States. Predictably, both were indicted and found guilty of seditious activity. They lost their second-class mailing privileges and received sentences that included incarceration.[28] When allegations surfaced that members of the NAACP were participating in seditious activities, agents from the War Department investigated its New York offices. In a curt retort to one of the agent's queries, Du Bois leaned back in his chair and responded smugly: "We are seeking to have the Constitution of the United States thoroughly and completely enforced."[29]

Du Bois eventually came out in support of the war after being pressured by the leadership of the organization. His support, however, could be seen as a concession to President Wilson, who broke his long silence on lynching and also began to commission Negro officers on a regular basis. Du Bois wrote a famous editorial, "Close Ranks," for the July 1918 issue of the *Crisis*. The piece was written in the midst of reports that kept coming over the wires extolling the gallantry of African American troops and the patriotic fervor that was roaring through the country. Du Bois wrote: "That which the German power represents today spells death to the aspirations of Negroes and all darker races for equality, freedom and democracy. Let us not hesitate. Let us, while this war lasts, forget our special grievances and close our ranks shoulder to shoulder with our own white fellow citizens and the allied nations that are fighting for democracy."[30] What is political pragmatism for one is opportunism for another. Du Bois was quickly criticized for his position, and parallels were drawn by more radical writers between his position and the conciliatory positions of Booker T. Washington.[31]

The Black troops in the European theater were not concerned about the position of the NAACP regarding American intervention. They were more concerned with proving to the rest of the world that they could fight as well as or better than their White counterparts. African Americans served gallantly and courageously in combat and in service during the war. The 371st and 372d Infantry Regiments were welcomed and integrated into the French forces. Winning medals for distinguished service from the French as well as the American governments was commonplace for African American soldiers. Black soldiers were also awarded newfound freedom in Paris and other European cities.

Negro troops did not only win medals and appreciation. African Americans lost their lives in numbers disproportionate to those for White Americans. In addition, they endured humiliation on a daily basis and often worked and fought in the most squalid and dangerous situations. Black troops were also subjected to some of Germany's most intense propaganda schemes. For example, on September 12, 1918, the 92d Division was engaged in a campaign against the German forces. The German forces tried to persuade the Negro troops to desert their lines, lay down their weapons, and come to Germany, where they would be treated like "gentlemen." The lines were littered with circulars that stated, in part:

What is Democracy? Personal freedom, all citizens enjoying the same rights socially and before the law. Do you enjoy the same rights as the white people do in America, the land of Freedom and Democracy, or are you rather not treated over there as second-class citizens? Can you go into a restaurant where white people dine? Can you get a seat in the theater where white people sit? . . . Is lynching and the most horrible crimes connected therewith a lawful proceeding in a democratic country?[32]

None of the soldiers deserted. African Americans were also the subject of American propaganda directed at both French civilians and military personnel. For example, *Secret Information concerning Black Troops* was one of the many documents circulated widely in France. This document only reiterated the terse warning White American soldiers gave French civilians regarding their Black counterparts. It stated that the Negro troops must be segregated, lest the Negro assault and rape White women. Evidently, French soldiers, civilians, and officers ignored all of the reports, for they continued to welcome African Americans in their homes and establishments.[33]

One of the major stateside events during the war years was the great exodus of Black people from the South to the North. Although the Great Migration had begun several years earlier, hundreds of thousands of migrants were still flooding into the cities along the northeastern seaboard and up the Mississippi River to fill the industrial jobs created by the war. Most African Americans supported the war wholeheartedly. They bought war bonds and went to work in the war industries with a heightened pitch of patriotism. During the preceding years European immigration had been substantially curbed. This left a void in the labor market in the northern industrial cities. African American men and women enthusiastically filled the wage-labor shortage created by the war. Injustice in the southern courts, continued lynchings and pogroms, boll weevils that destroyed the cotton market, entrenched Jim Crow segregation, poor schools, disfranchisement, and the lose-lose cycle of tenant farming were all important reasons influencing African Americans to move North to "the Promised Land." These factors, as well as empty promises of wealth, prosperity, and security, were emphasized by agents of northern industrialists who were sent to the South to recruit workers by the thousands to fill the void left by the lack of immigrant labor.[34]

The pogroms continued. In 1917 more than 3,000 families in Tennessee responded to a newspaper advertisement to witness the public burning of a live Negro. Many children witnessed the event and were taught the entertainment value of pouring ten gallons of gasoline over an innocent man and then igniting it, while screams of helplessness and the smell of burning flesh filled the air. That same year East St. Louis exploded in race hatred. White workers in a plant that held government contracts protested the company's hiring of nonunion migrants. Notwithstanding the fact that the union did not accept Black members, their fellow laborers retaliated against the entire Black community of East St. Louis with mass destruction. One hundred and twenty-five African Americans were killed, and hundreds of others were maimed. Their homes were looted, then leveled. African Americans were shot, clubbed, stabbed, and hanged. A two-year-old child was shot and left for dead in a burning doorway.

In July 1917 the NAACP organized a march down New York's Fifth Avenue—a "Silent Protest" against the violence in East St. Louis and elsewhere. Some 15,000 Negroes marched silently to the cadence of somber drums, holding hands and placards that posed such haunting questions as "Mother, do lynchers go to heaven?" or "Mr. President, why not make America safe for democracy?"[35]

After the armistice the troops were welcomed home with pomp and circumstance. On February 17, 1919, New York's 15th Infantry Regiment, attached to the 369th and the first Negro regiment in the French army, returned home with medals of valor, distinction, and hard-won honor. The troops marched proudly up the avenues of Manhattan fully adorned in their finest regalia—the same avenues through which the NAACP had marched a year and a half earlier. Though diametrically opposed in tenor, the marchers offered an identical message: there was a *New Negro* who, collectively, was asserting and demanding social, political, and racial equality.

The New Negro: Changing Urban Space into Their Place

Congregated in densely populated urban spaces, African Americans were engaged in complex processes that sought to define their place in America's cultural landscape. In New York City they sought to create Black Manhattan, Harlem, Negro Metropolis, or simply Nigger Heaven.[36] Implicitly and explicitly, the New Negroes were engaged in constructing an empowered racial identity or a "race consciousness" and in shoring up their cultural moorings by looking to Africa to establish their cultural "heritage." Although it was happening in virtually every urban center, the residents of uptown Manhattan took the lead in raising race consciousness and validating their heritage for the rest of the country.

After World War I and the so-called Red Summer of 1919, when twenty-six race riots erupted, the African American voice took on a decidedly militant tone. Instead of knowing their place, uplifting the race, or fighting from being kept down, African Americans organized proactive institutions with increased vigor. The older and more established organizations began to reap benefits from years of agitation. The National Association for Colored Women, the NAACP, the National Urban League, the UNIA, and the Brotherhood of Sleeping Car Porters all became important associations that sought to effect change and affect lives. In concert, these organizations helped to redefine the role African Americans would play in the U.S. political landscape for the balance of the century. Although some of the African American organizations were antithetical to each other, many effectively built alliances or negotiated divisions of labor. The organizations garnered national and international support and began to transcend racial issues. Many of them built coalitions with White organizations around such key issues as women's suffrage, equal rights for women, poverty, and labor.

While the militant voice of the New Negro was heard in politics, it became deafening in the arts. The explosion of new and experimental forms of artistic expression by African Americans between the world wars redefined American art, particularly in the areas of prose, poetry, music, drama, and painting. American literature and poetry were transformed by writers like Claude McKay, Nella Larsen, Jessie Fauset, Anne Spencer, Arna Bontemps, Angelina Grimké, Langston Hughes, James Weldon Johnson, Jean Toomer, and Countee Cullen, to name only a few. There were also playwrights, actors, sculptors, and painters. Jazz came of age during this era, and Duke Ellington, Fats Waller, Count Basie, Bessie Smith, Jelly Roll Morton, and numerous others helped to redefine American music. Nonfiction was also an important genre that emerged alongside the arts. Magazines like the *Crisis, Messenger,* and *Opportunity* (the organ for the National Urban League) provided an important vehicle for both Black and White social scientists to read and write about critical issues regarding African American life and culture. In most cases African American social scientists were motivated by activism and the need to develop strategies to solve social problems.

In addition, they followed their artistic counterparts and ignored discipline-specific boundaries by blurring the lines that delineated them. In this respect the scholars who emerged during the New Negro Movement foreshadowed multidisciplinary approaches to research.

Although each engaged in research across discipline boundaries, Rayford Logan, Carter G. Woodson, and Arthur A. Schomburg were established historians, and Ralph Bunche was a trained political scientist. Ira De A. Reid, E. Franklin Frazier, Charles Johnson, Kelly Miller, and George Edmond Haynes were sociologists, while Zora Neale Hurston, Arthur H. Fauset, Irene Diggs, and Katherine Dunham were trained in cultural anthropology and folklore. Abram L. Harris, Allison Davis, and St. Clair Drake carefully pursued economics and social anthropology.

Without a doubt, the African American political, scientific, philosophical, and aesthetic movement of the interwar years changed the fabric of American culture. For the first time there was a concerted effort to challenge the derisive and stereotypical images of African Americans produced by blackface minstrelsy, magazine publishers, and racist science. Henry L. Gates, Jr. has pointed out that "to call the Harlem Renaissance a 'New Negro' movement is to describe exactly what its visual and verbal artists sought to create: a largely unregistered, unimagined image of the Noble Negro that would destroy forever the confusing, limited range of black stereotypes that every artist had to confront."[37]

The New Negro Movement was, at times, conscripted and audaciously promoted by the very intellectuals who saw themselves emerging from it. These intellectuals (far from elite, but not working in factories or keeping someone's house) were attempting to make a racial identity out of an American racial order that still shut them out. This construction was undertaken largely in cultural terms and largely for sociopolitical reasons. However, attempts to raise race consciousness led to a paradox that traumatized Du Bois and perplexed many others. What many African Americans (save for the followers of the UNIA) were struggling for was integration, equality, and, above all, to be Americans. However, in order to reach this end, the NAACP and other organizations had to mobilize people and foster a sense of us-versus-them. So, on the one hand, they espoused the rhetoric that race does not matter; but on the other hand, to reach the goal of integration, they had to promote the significance of race.[38]

To reconcile this paradox and anchor their mobilization efforts, many

Black intellectuals looked to African American culture. In effect, they strove to transform a racial identity into an ethnic identity. However, there were various tensions between the artists, shapers of public opinion, and organizers. A. Phillip Randolph, W. A. Domingo, and other labor leaders focused on quelling the exploitation of the working class across racial lines, Du Bois and the NAACP focused on ensuring full civil and political rights, and Marcus Garvey focused on securing Africa for the Africans. And, as Henry Lewis Gates, Jr. notes, the literary artists actually "transformed the militancy associated with the trope [of a New Negro] and translated this into an apolitical movement of the arts."[39] Although Gates looks to writers like the novelist Jessie Fauset to help explain how certain writers diluted Black vernacular oral traditions by "imitating those they least resembled," other writers like her sibling Arthur embellished African American culture by promoting and accentuating its African origins. Producing studies on Negro folklore emerged as an effective way to advance this particular agenda. Far from imitating Whites, Zora Neale Hurston did not even bother to collect folklore from African Americans when she deemed its origins inappropriate. From the field, she reported to Franz Boas: "I thought you might be interested in the Bahamas. The Negroes there are more African, [they] actually know the tribes from which their ancestors came. . . . Now in the stories, I have omitted all Pat and Mike [Irish] stories. It is obvious that these are not negroid, but very casual borrowings. The same goes for the Jewish and Italian stories."[40]

Collecting folklore did not necessarily reconcile but perhaps magnified the paradox of whether race mattered. Nathan Huggins, writing in the early 1970s, suggested that this paradox "crippled the art" of the movement because it led to "a provincialism which forever limits [the] possibility of achieving good art; but without it the perplexities of identity are exacerbated by confusion of a legitimate heritage."[41] Although he unabashedly stated that "good art" transcends universal themes, he argued that the Harlem Renaissance failed because integral aspects of Negro identity formation was contingent on White patrons who desired a new type of minstrel show which depicted Negro culture as exotic and primitive.[42] And although Harold Cruse indicted the New Negro Movement for "evading the issue of nationalism and its economic imperatives for the Negro community," Houston Baker identified the tricksterlike agency of the movement's promoters who "thought of black expressive culture as a reservoir from which a quintessentially Afro-American spirit flowed."[43] It is obviously difficult to generalize about the New Negro

Movement, because it was as multifarious as its many histories. One of the histories that has not been explored is the relationship between members of the American Folk-Lore Society (AFLS) and the promoters of the New Negro Movement, who together advanced an important cultural project during the interwar years.

CHAPTER 7

Looking behind the Veil
with the Spy Glass
of Anthropology

The Negro is sort of a seventh son, born with a veil, and gifted with
second-sight in this American world, — a world which yields him no
true self-consciousness, but only lets him see himself through the
revelation of the other world.

W. E. B. Du Bois, 1903

The rise and fall of Negro folklore within anthropology,
and the relationship between the JAFL and writers of the Harlem Renaissance, is a story seldom told in the annals of the history of anthropology.[1] African American scholars were attracted to anthropology during the Harlem Renaissance because they saw the discipline as a way of
documenting and celebrating their African heritage. Nathan Huggins
has explained that

the popularity of folk materials among the promoters of the New Negro
marks a significant step in the Negro intellectual's gaining self-consciousness
and self-confidence. Remarkably, this Afro-American concern with the preservation of folk materials was paralleled by a similar white effort which
began to discover value in mountain and rural folk-idiom. The American's
willingness, white and black, to parade before the world his peasant origins
was tantamount to stating his own sophistication and urbanity. One seems
to have come of age when one can discuss with detachment and pride one's
true origins.[2]

During the 1920s anthropology was used for the first time as a tool by
Black people in an effort to shape an ethnic identity, carve out a heritage,

and fight for racial equality. As part of this processes Arthur A. Schomburg, Alain Locke, Arthur H. Fauset, Zora Neale Hurston, Carter G. Woodson, and others turned to and contributed to the JAFL.

The anthropological analysis of folklore provided evidence for their claim that the rich and complex traditions and music of African Americans was the United States' most distinctive cultural gift to the rest of the world.[3] Although "country niggahs" were repudiated by both Whites and seemingly uppity Blacks, many scholars realized that it was the rural folk who were unconsciously pouring out the raw material that fueled American music and literature.[4] This understanding, in one form or another, motivated scholars to produce studies of Negro folklore. As Arthur H. Fauset penned for *The New Negro*:

There is strong need of a scientific collecting of Negro folk lore before the original sources of this material altogether lapse. Sentimental admiration and amateurish praise can never adequately preserve or interpret the precious material. It is precious in two respects—not only for its intrinsic, but for its comparative value. . . . American folk-lorists are now recognizing this, and systematic scientific investigation has begun under the influence and auspices of the Society for American Folk Lore [*sic*] and such competent ethnologists as Franz Boas, Elsie Clews Parsons, and others.[5]

There was an auspicious convergence between Black writers who wanted to promote the New Negro by collecting Negro folklore and White editors of the JAFL who wanted to promote Negro folklore by publishing issues dedicated entirely to it. To these ends, the editors of the JAFL gravitated toward the promoters of the New Negro, and the promoters gravitated toward the editors. The outcome of this timely courtship was fourteen issues, between 1917 and 1937, of the JAFL dedicated entirely to Negro folklore. Affectionately known as the "Negro Numbers," these volumes, as well as a number of books and monographs—written by both Black and White anthropologists—provided scientific evidence to validate African American cultural specificity. The editors of, and contributors to, the JAFL fashioned Negro folklore into an important thrust within the anthropological discourse on race and culture. However, African American scholars who forayed into the anthropological field of folklore immediately met with marginalization. They were limited in their access to funds and to publishers. Because of these and other factors, the study of African American folklore within anthropology did not sustain itself. After the early 1940s Negro folklore did not have much of an impact on the anthropological discourse of race and culture. Nevertheless, it had a lasting impact outside the academy because it helped to empower African Americans during the New Negro Movement and beyond.

It should not be surprising that Franz Boas played an important role in orchestrating the alliance between African American intellectuals during the New Negro Movement and folklorists in anthropology. Boas did not study folklore because it held intrinsic interest for him per se; he viewed it as an important part of "mass culture" and a manifestation of "popular life."[6]

Boas used folklore as a window to view both cultural differences and similarities, help establish local history, and develop arguments about cultural diffusion, assimilation, and adaptive change.[7] He gave considerable attention to the "local coloring" of widespread folk-tale themes that, he argued, "can be understood only in relation to the whole culture."[8] He employed this argument to reinforce his claim that each tribe had a unique cultural expression. In "Mythology and Folk-Tales of the North American Indians," for example, Boas explained that "a perusal of the available collections makes it quite clear that in this sense the expression of the cultural life of the people contained in their tales gives to them a marked individuality, no matter what the incidents constituting the tales may be."[9] Boas collected and studied folklore, in short, to help validate some of his basic tenets, including ideas that culture was a means of adapting to the environment, that customs and traits were diffused across space and time, and that cultural elements must be seen as an integrated whole.

In 1888 Boas, with a group of colleagues, founded the AFLS. He held sway over the society and its journal for the balance of his life. He was president of the organization in 1900, 1932, and 1934. In addition, he was involved in the editorial leadership and adjudication of the journal for forty-four consecutive years. First he served as an associate editor and then, between 1908 and 1923, as editor. After fifteen years at the helm he resigned from that post, only to serve again as an associate editor until 1942. Unlike the *American Anthropologist*, everyone who assumed a leadership position on the editorial board of the JAFL was either Boas's former student or a close colleague — and all adhered to his directives.[10] Reflective of Du Bois's editorial control and heavy-handed leadership at the *Crisis*, Boas used the JAFL as a vehicle for his own musings and as an organ to publish his students' work.

Negro Folklore under Newell's Editorship of the JAFL — 1888–1900

From the inception of the AFLS, African American folklore was supposed to be an integral part of both the society and its journal. The original structure of the AFLS included a department of Negro folklore, and the original editorial policy dictated that one-fourth of the space in the journal be dedicated to it. Both Boas and William Wells Newell, another founding member, were responsible for the importance afforded African American folklore by the organization.

Newell was a member of the progressive Boston elite and shared Boas's views on race and culture. Newell was the first editor of the journal and served from 1888 to 1900, but he quickly found it difficult to fulfill the organization's clearly defined mandate to collect Negro folklore. The difficulty arose because most of the contributors to the journal were culled from the members, most of whom resided in the North. Newell's editorship predated the Great Migration, so the "best" folklore remained in the South. Given these constraints, Newell did surprisingly well in adhering to the editorial policy. He was responsible for publishing more than forty articles and four memoirs that covered folklore or folk traditions from Africa, the Caribbean, and the South. The quality of the material was uneven, and the Negro folklore from the South was particularly poor.

During Newell's tenure the organization was financed by the dues of just over one hundred members, and the AFLS could not afford to send members to the South to collect material. Boas and Newell pushed to have more chapters in the South, but this only resulted in collections with explicitly racist overtones. Boas was infuriated by southern collectors' lack of professionalism and the racial epithets that punctuated most submissions.

Both Newell and Boas stuck by their editorial mandate and were committed to collecting Negro folklore, but they were running out of options. In 1894 they turned to the students and faculty of Hampton University for collecting folklore to publish.[11] Alice M. Bacon, a faculty member, organized the multiracial Hampton Folklore Society. With the help of Boas and Newell, a department of folklore and ethnology for Hampton's journal, the *Southern Workman,* was established. Boas, Newell, and Bacon also leveraged a formal affiliation between the Hampton

Folklore Society and the AFLS. By 1894 African Americans were publishing their collections in the JAFL.[12]

The JAFL Sidelines Negro Folklore—1900–1919

In 1900 Alexander F. Chamberlain became the editor of the journal. He did not have the same enthusiasm for Black folklore as Newell did. In addition, Boas began to insist that only professionals undertake anthropological investigations. Boas's insistence on professionalism curtailed African American contributions to the JAFL because there were so few professional Black anthropologists.[13] Boas also began to sideline his interest in African American folklore because of competing interests. His initial commitment to African American empowerment vis-à-vis studying Negro folklore and the great kingdoms of Africa was eclipsed by his commitment to advance his students and develop other projects. One such project was the International School of American Archeology and Ethnology in Mexico, which he tried to establish prior to World War I.[14]

In 1908, when Boas assumed the editorship, he did not canvass African American universities looking for collectors. Nor did he try to revive the relationship with the Hampton Folklore Society. Although the amount of Negro folklore increased slightly under Boas, he admitted that he only gave it "slight attention."[15] He essentially transformed the JAFL into an outlet for his students' dissertations, abrogating his own policy to publish Black folklore. During the first decade of the twentieth century the final requirement for the doctorate at Columbia University included publishing the dissertation. Boas was overseeing many advanced degrees and simply used the JAFL to publish them.[16] He actually proposed changing its name to the *American Journal of Folklore,* which would justify a broader purview. Boas failed to convince the board to change the name, but he did change the scope: the board passed a revision to the policy that favored "longer and weightier" articles, which, in effect, rationalized the publication of dissertations.[17]

Boas's neglect of African American folklore changed after World War I. In a strange twist of events, the editors of the JAFL once again began to publish Negro folklore—but this time with submissions by the first generation of African American anthropologists trained, in part, by Boas.

The Censure of Franz Boas—1919

By the time the United States entered World War I the Boasian discourse on race all but eclipsed discussions in cultural anthropology stemming from the Harvard and Washington axes. The ascension of the Boasian discourse was wedded to the veritable hostile takeover of the American Anthropological Association (AAA) by Boas and his students. By 1905 the anthropologists who were aligned with Boas constituted two-thirds of the AAA Executive Board. Boas did not orchestrate these maneuvers single-handedly. Although the coalition that Boas organized held the balance of power within the AAA, it was loosely knit and fragile. Boas depended on support from current and former students and was indebted to the loyal support of Robert Lowie and Alfred Kroeber, two of his most powerful former students.[18] Kroeber emerged as a key consensus builder and quelled the grumbling that was heard from Washington and Cambridge—but not for long.

One locus of tension was the Department of Anthropology at Harvard University, which focused on Central American archeology. By 1910 its members were conducting massive research projects excavating the Mayan ruins. The so-called Maya group wanted more control and input in the direction of the AAA. A. M. Tozzer from Harvard, Kroeber from University of California, Berkeley, and Boas worked out an amicable relationship, but Harvard anthropologists seized the opportunity to censure Boas. Kroeber also negotiated with the less numerous, but more vocal, government-agency anthropologists from Washington. The so-called Washington group exercised control over the *American Anthropologist* and remained influential within the organizational leadership until late in the decade. The Washington group believed that its power and influence had been usurped by the Columbia group.

Animosity toward Boas was also mounting outside the formal organizational structure of the AAA. In 1916 the NRC was established as part of a national war-readiness program, and it organized the Committee on Anthropology to help fulfill its mission. Boas was an adamant pacifist and an outspoken critic of the war. He was a German Jew and obdurate in his stance against eugenics, which the NRC seemed to take as its research program of choice. Scholars like Charles B. Davenport,

Madison Grant, and Aleš Hrdlička were all influential in organizing the NRC's Committee on Anthropology. The committee was actually organized to oppose the Columbia group. George Stocking noted that the NRC explicitly tried to undermine the Columbia anthropologists' antiracist program during the most pervasive nativism in the history of the United States.[19] The strategy included having biologists, eugenicists, and other so-called hard scientists challenge the authority of cultural anthropology as a science.

During late 1918 and early 1919 the scientific reaction against cultural anthropology was a matter of some concern to Boas's group. The main organizational locus of the reaction was the Galton Society of New York, which was organized by Charles Davenport and Madison Grant in March 1918. The society was dedicated to the study of "racial anthropology," and its membership was confined to "native" Americans who were anthropologically, socially, and politically "sound."[20] Boas would have failed on every criterion, given his counterhegemonic pursuits and ethnic background. Members of the Galton Society, Harvard University, and government agencies all had vested interests in realigning the discipline in a way congruent with growing nativism, racism, and patriotism prior to and following the war.

Boas became a maverick. He denounced the war repeatedly by writing editorials and newspaper articles outlining his position that the war was undeniably one of imperialism.[21] His righteousness fueled the mounting tensions that finally exploded at the 1919 AAA meetings in Cambridge, Massachusetts.

On December 20, 1919, the *Nation* published "Scientists as Spies," a letter written by Boas to the editor. The letter called Woodrow Wilson a hypocrite, said that democracy in the United States was a fiction, and alleged that several scientists had abrogated their calling by working as spies during the war. Boas held little back:

To the Editor of *The Nation*,

> Sir: In his war address to Congress, President Wilson dwelt at great length on the theory that only autocracies maintain spies, that these are not needed in democracies. At the time that the President made this statement, the government of the United States had in its employ spies of unknown number. I am not concerned here with the familiar discrepancies between the President's words and the actual facts, although we may perhaps have to accept his statement as meaning correctly that we live under an autocracy, that our democracy is a fiction. The point against which I wish to enter a vigorous protest is that a number of men who follow science as

their profession, men whom I refuse to designate any longer as scientists, have prostituted science by using it as a cover for their activities as spies.

A soldier whose business is murder as a fine art . . . accept[s] the code of morality to which modern society still conforms. Not so the scientist. The very essence of his life is the service of truth. . . . By accident, incontrovertible proof has come to my hands that at least four men who carry on anthropology work, while employed as government agents, introduced themselves to foreign governments as representatives of scientific researches. . . . Such action has raised a new barrier against the development of international friendly cooperation.[22]

This letter ignited a furor and gave factions brooding over Boas's radical positions and institutional power the excuse to level him. Just days after the *Nation* published his letter, the AAA convened and issued a public censure of Boas. The punitive censure was leveled at the behest of the Anthropological Association of Washington but ratified, in part, by the large number of Harvard-affiliated members attending that meeting. It was used as a device to usurp his power and publicly attack his anti-American and antiscientific (read: antiracist) research strategies.[23]

The Need for Black Graduate Students — 1920–1923

According to William Willis, "In view of these developments [surrounding the censure], Boas decided that the study of black folklore was needed more than ever."[24] Willis did not explicitly outline the causal relationship between Boas's censure and the increase of Negro folklore published by the JAFL (which he controlled throughout the AAA fracas). For one reason or another, Boas began to make a concerted effort to develop a new program in African American folklore within the AFLS and train Black graduate students immediately after his censure.

Why Boas felt compelled to make this effort is not entirely clear. There were a number of auspicious factors that, perhaps, obliged him to do so. Most notable were Elsie Clews Parsons's enthusiasm for Negro folklore, the rise of African American interest in folklore, and his need to collect physical data on Black people.

The new program of Negro folklore was spearheaded and financed by Elsie Clews Parsons. Independently wealthy, Parsons came to anthropology with a doctorate in sociology, but she committed substantial financial resources to the advancement of anthropology and Negro folklore. She was fascinated by Negro folklore and conducted her own fieldwork in the United States as well as the Caribbean.[25] In addition, she shared many of Boas's views regarding race, politics, and anthropology. The ingredients for a perfect relationship with Boas were unmistakable. She had money and loyalty, and she held Boas in high esteem. The relationship flourished: she financed fieldwork for several of Boas's students and paid for their publications. She also paid for Boas's personal secretary. In return, Boas respected her scholarship, assured her election as an associate editor of the JAFL, and made her an honorary member of the Department of Anthropology at Columbia University.[26] Together they revived the use of Black collectors and began to train professional anthropologists.

These efforts were quickened by factors outside their sphere of influence. First and foremost was the Great Migration. As a result of the migration, racial tensions in urban arenas heightened and then exploded with the Red Summer of 1919, which fueled efforts to better understand all aspects of the so-called Negro problem. The Harmon Foundation, the Social Science Research Council, the Rosenwald Fund, and the Association for the Study of Negro Life and History all increased funding for Negro research. Another result was the fact that a researcher could collect a wide range of African American folktales within walking distance of Columbia University. Within the cultural mosaic of Harlem was a veritable panoply of tales from the Caribbean, the South, and Africa. The Great Migration also cultivated the New Negro intellectuals, some of whom were interested in African American folklore and cultural history. Boas began to see the value of Black professionals and believed that African American researchers were "able to penetrate through that affected demeanor by which the Negro excludes the White observer" from "participating in his true inner life."[27] In addition to Parsons's funding of folklore projects, these dynamics lead to the timely courtship between the editors of the JAFL and the nonfiction writers of the New Negro Movement immediately after Boas's 1919 censure by the AAA.

However, Boas's push to recruit African American anthropologists was not driven solely by his desire to train folklorists. Boas needed someone on the "inside" to facilitate gathering physical data on Black people. He remained interested in physical anthropology and wanted his students to amass measurements of the Negro body in order to defend the claims regarding phenotypic plasticity that he put forth in *Changes in Bodily Form of Descendants of Immigrants* (1912). Boas was instrumental in securing a fellowship from the NRC for Melville Herskovits along these very lines.[28] He also believed that "excellent results might be obtained" if he recruited "a graduate Negro student who wishes to work into anthropological and psychological research" to work with "Mr. Herskovits in such a way that he [the graduate student] would become an independent investigator."[29]

Boas Solicits Support from Carter G. Woodson

During the early 1920s Boas wanted Black students to fulfill his research agenda for folklore and physical anthropology. He turned to his colleague Carter G. Woodson, a leading scholar in African American Studies, for access to and funding for Black scholars interested in pursuing anthropology. Boas and Woodson worked together to recruit and fund Black students. They organized a national contest for the most outstanding study of folklore to recruit African Americans to Columbia. The award for the contest was $200, and advertisements were dispatched to all of the leading Negro newspapers. Circulars were also given to 60 Black organizations, and it was publicized at 225 secondary schools and colleges.[30] To fund African American students at Columbia, they established a fellowship in the Department of Anthropology under the auspices of the Association for the Study of Negro Life and History (ASNLH), which Woodson directed.

Boas quickly found that the standard of excellence he set for his students paled in comparison to the standard of excellence Carter G. Woodson set for his. For example, Boas urged Woodson to fund Abram L. Harris, who wanted to pursue anthropology in concert with his interests in economics and history. Boas became interested in funding Harris in 1923. At that time, Harris was a twenty-four-year-old college graduate who spoke fluent German, was active in the Communist Party, and had a particular bent for Marxist theory.[31] Boas liked Harris, but Woodson did not. Boas wrote: "So far I have seen only one man who seems promising, Mr. Abraham [*sic*] L. Harris, who will write to you and submit his testimonials. I doubt whether he is just the ideal man for the position, but he makes a good impression, and I should be willing to risk it. I am going to make some further inquires, and unless I find a better candidate within a few days I shall recommend that you appoint Mr. Harris [to the fellowship]."[32] Woodson replied, "I know him personally. I am sorry to say that he does not make a favorable impression upon me."[33] Woodson simply demanded a record of stellar scholarship from African Americans graduate students funded by the ASNLH.[34] This posed a stumbling block for Boas: he bemoaned the fact that Woodson always felt that the students he or Parsons suggested "did not appear to be qualified."[35]

Boas mentioned to Woodson that he was going to make other inquiries regarding an assistant for Herskovits. The same day that Boas wrote to Woodson regarding Harris, he queried his longtime friend W. E. B. Du Bois. In a letter sent to the "Editorial Rooms of *The Crisis*," Boas briefed Du Bois about Herskovits's project and his need for an assistant, and he explained that "the only promising applicant whom I have seen so far is Mr. Abraham [*sic*] L. Harris. Do you happen to know him? If you know of any other young Negro who might be a promising candidate for this position, I wish you would be good enough to send him to me."[36] Du Bois quickly wrote back and stated that he only vaguely knew of Abram L. Harris and suggested contacting Arthur H. Fauset, who was pursuing his master's degree in anthropology at the University of Pennsylvania.[37]

Arthur H. Fauset (1899–1983)

The first Black anthropologist to use the JAFL to validate Black culture was Arthur H. Fauset. He took advantage of not only the JAFL but also Parsons's interest in African American folklore. Parsons underwrote Fauset's fieldwork in the South, the Caribbean, and Nova Scotia. She also underwrote the bulk of his publications and was responsible for publishing his master's thesis at the University of Pennsylvania as the twenty-fourth memoir of the JAFL.[38]

Fauset was born in Flemington, New Jersey, in 1899. He was educated in the public schools of Philadelphia and attended both Central High School and the Philadelphia School of Pedagogy. He began teaching in the Philadelphia public schools at the age of nineteen and continued to teach as he pursued his academic career at the University of

Pennsylvania, from which he received a bachelor's degree in 1921, a master's degree in 1924, and a doctoral degree in 1942.[39]

He was the youngest of the nine children who made up a large household of extended family members. One of his most notable siblings was Jessie R. Fauset, his older half-sister, who was an important novelist during the Harlem Renaissance and served as the literary editor of the *Crisis*.[40] His father was an outspoken minister for the relatively conservative African Methodist Episcopal Church. The Reverend Huff Fauset did not let the church stop him from engaging in larger political struggles or preaching political rhetoric from the pulpit. As a result, church officials curtailed his aspirations to positions of leadership within the larger church organization. All of the children in the Fauset family were raised in an atmosphere that cultivated knowledge, fostered excellence, and nourished self-worth. Reflecting on growing up in Philadelphia, Arthur Fauset explained that the "family was poor, one might say, dreadfully poor," but many considered them middle class because they "read newspapers and books, discussed politics and religion." They also "fought against the binding racial biases that made life in the City of Brotherly Love often a burden. It is in these respects that the family was middle class: working, aspiring, discussing, getting their children educated to the extent that biases would permit."[41]

Fauset emerged as one of the leading Black folklorists in the early 1920s, although he was only tangentially associated with Boas. He made a substantial contribution to the awareness of African American folklore in the New Negro Movement and to the new program of Negro folklore in the AFLS.[42] He intersected with the JAFL via Parsons and Frank Speck. The latter, a linguist and folklorist of Native American groups, served as Fauset's advisor in the Department of Anthropology at the University of Pennsylvania.[43]

Although his contributions to the study of folklore did not impart many theoretical innovations, like many of Boas's early students, he was charged only with reporting the facts. The bulk of his work included collections of tales, songs, conundrums, and jokes. It rarely included commentary. Both Willis and Drake have indicted Boas and Parsons for using Black collectors as mere technicians.[44] Ostensibly, Fauset was one of them. Another view suggests that Fauset let people speak for themselves. He dutifully recorded where the tale was told and where the teller of the tale was born, grew up, and resided. In short, he contextualized Black people's voices and then just let the voices tell the story. He did not give Negro folklore an anthropological spin. Alain Locke, Arthur

Schomburg, and other New Negroes were attracted to the actual folklore in the JAFL, not the heavy-handed theory that often littered the
pages. Fauset was exceedingly critical of the amateur and commercial
folklorist who "assumes to interpret Negro character instead of simply
telling his stories."[45] He thus acted as an archivist who deposited the
collections of Negro folklore in the JAFL to be used by the New Negro
promoters and future generations.

Fauset did employ a subtle theoretical framework in his first book,
Folklore from Nova Scotia (1931) and his contribution to Alain Locke's
The New Negro entitled "American Negro Folk Literature" (1968
[1925]).[46] In the latter he railed against Joel Chandler Harris, who collected and published Uncle Remus stories as a commercial venture. He
criticized Harris for using his own imagination and writing the tales
with "no thought of the ethnological bearing." Fauset declared that Harris's stories had "too much the flavor of the popular trend of contemporary writing of the Thomas Nelson Page portrait of the Negro. . . .
[I]t cannot be denied that such portraits as they [T. Nelson Page and
J. C. Chandler] gave were highly romanticized, presenting an interpretation of the Negro seen neither objectively nor realistically."[47]

In *Folklore from Nova Scotia* (1931) Fauset clearly articulated the theories that shaped his work. Central to his theoretical understanding of
folklore was the diffusion model, which influenced his decision to study
folklore in Nova Scotia. He even stated that it "may seem strange" to
collect Negro folklore in Canada, because the "native Nova Scotia Negro
knows little or nothing about the original folk-tales which are common
property among Negroes of the south. . . . Animal stories, so prevalent
in the lore of Africa, are almost entirely lacking among these people."[48]

Although the diffusion model was central, it was not the key theoretical element. Fauset expressed that he was documenting the diversity
of the African American experience and debunking stereotypes. He
framed his collection of Nova Scotia folklore by noting that Negro migrations had created cultural diversity within African American communities throughout the Americas. Stereotypes of Negroes, therefore,
simply did not hold up to scientific scrutiny because there were so many
African American cultures. This point was seemingly important to his
research because he highlighted it in the second paragraph of his book.
He stated that Negroes from Nova Scotia often told perfect strangers
that they " 'would go down to the States, but it is too hot down there,' —
thus giving the lie to the proverbial fondness of the Negro for warm
climes."[49] Fauset also mentioned that his informants were aware of the

perpetuation of stereotypes, and he "seemed to detect a disdainful attitude toward telling tales which put them [the informants] in the role of
minstrels."[50]

The major problem Fauset explored was neither diffusion nor African
retentions but hybridity and diversity in the African diaspora. He noted
that traditional Uncle Remus and "B're Rabbit" stories were remem-
bered only by the older members of the communities but stated that it
was like "extracting the proverbial hen's teeth to obtain anything resem-
bling a [Negro] tale."[51] Fauset recalled one of these attempts at collecting: "Old Ned Brown almost literally sweat drops of blood as he la-
bored, partly to recall the tale, and partly to deliver himself of the thing
which he recalled."[52] On the other hand, he recounted, Negroes would
tell their own variations of Irish, French, or English folktales. This hybridity or "medley," as he called it, was his basic framework for the
monograph:

Scarcely any of these stories and riddles had anything distinctive from the
general folklore of the province, and since they were obtained in part from
white as well as from colored people, I will treat the material from that
general aspect for the most part. I would say that the folklore of the province
is a medley of tales and folk notions representing cultures from all parts of
the western world, a natural situation in a maritime locality.[53]

Fauset's medley model fits within the Boasian approach because his
model advanced the idea that African American culture changed as its
context changed—all was not lost, nor was it lost for good. He stated
that "It would not be impossible, however, for the Nancy stories or
Uncle Remus tales to become the property of these Negroes once more
due to the comparatively large number of migrants from the West Indies
who have invaded the province."[54] Fauset recognized that African Americans in Nova Scotia did not simply assimilate the dominant culture and
argued that they emerged as part of the regional culture and contributed
substantially to it.

Although Fauset put forward an important thesis, he virtually ignored the class dimensions associated with "the kind of story you naturally expect" of the Negro.[55] He highlighted the fact that most of the
collecting he did occurred in biracial communities, but he did not explain the relationship between the demographic composition of the
communities he studied and the virtual lack of Negro stories. Furthermore, he glossed over the strategies employed by rural Blacks to resist
imparting their tales to a city Negro from the United States. He did,
however, hint at these strategies. For example, he noted that "where the

Negroes live for all the world like plantation folk, in their rickety cabins (not log cabins), off to themselves, with religious customs and even habits of living distinctly their own, I could not find persons who knew the animal stories. These folk were difficult to approach, and very reticent to impart information . . . while one or two thought that they knew what I meant but refused to tell what they pretended was in their heads."[56] Fauset went as far as to say that "the folklore collector must remember that his business goes on like that of the insurance agent. It is almost always, 'Call around tomorrow!' But if one calls a sufficient number of times, one is frequently rewarded for being persistent."[57]

Fauset was an important link between anthropology and the New Negro Movement. He was also an important folklore collector for the AFLS, the catalyst that allowed the society to fulfill its new mandate— to train and publish African American folklorists.[58]

Elsie Clews Parsons's Recruitment Efforts

Arthur Fauset was only one of many who contributed to the JAFL's Negro Numbers. Elsie Clews Parsons (1875–1941) solicited and received submissions by many African Americans, and she received much of the material from the ranks of Black professionals. A. E. Perkins, for example, wrote several articles for the JAFL. A school principal in New Orleans, Perkins had earned a doctorate. He collected folklore from his students and sent the collections to Parsons, who subsequently published them in the Negro Numbers.[59]

Parsons looked in earnest for Negro folklore. She was determined to locate Negro collectors and even designed a lecture on the value of Negro folklore to deliver at social organizations in Harlem. She made her pitch to organizations that served Caribbean immigrants; ostensibly, members of these organizations could collect the seemingly best folklore. Evidently, she did not make her pitch to the Harlem intelligentsia who, according to Huggins, were willing to "parade before the world" their "peasant origins." She tried to obtain folklorists among the recent immigrants from the Caribbean who, in many respects, were trying to shed their cultural baggage and embrace so-called mainstream American traditions. One successful recruit, from these otherwise fruitless ventures into the burgeoning Caribbean community, was John H. Johnson of Antigua.[60]

Parsons did not have much success recruiting working-class folklorists outside the circle of New Negro promoters. She did, however, succeed in recruiting students and faculty from agricultural schools in the South, primarily because of her collaboration with George Foster Peabody. Peabody was a powerful advocate for her in the southern schools, many of which he had graciously endowed.[61] Parsons traveled to various agricultural and normal schools in the South and found a number of educators who were willing to collect folklore from their students. The fruits of these endeavors resulted in the bulk of the texts in the Negro Numbers.[62]

When Alain Locke brought together the so-called New Negroes to write contributions for his book, he turned to Arthur H. Fauset and Arthur Schomburg to cover African and Negro folklore as it related to the New Negro. Both authors used the articles and submissions in the JAFL extensively to support their arguments about the retention of African cultural patterns by New World Negroes. Caddie S. Isham, Portia Smiley, Susan D. Spinney, Sadie E. Stewart, Clemmie S. Terrell, and Monroe N. Work were African American contributors to the JAFL who were cited in Locke's comprehensive bibliography in *The New Negro*. In addition to African American folklorists, Fauset cited seven articles by Parsons and sundry other citations by collectors associated with the AFLS in his essay on "American Negro Folk Literature."

Locke's comprehensive bibliography was a treasure trove of the New Negro Movement, and it contained more than fifty references to the JAFL. One can begin to see how the Boas-influenced program of Negro folklore implemented by the AFLS was appropriated by the promoters of the New Negro Movement to fashion their identity in terms of African cultural continuities. Perhaps the most notable promoter of the New Negro Movement to use folklore for this end was Zora Neale Hurston, who loomed large in both Harlem literary circles and Parsons's program of Negro folklore in the AFLS.[63]

Zora Neale Hurston (1891–1961)

Zora Neale Hurston was born in Eatonville, Florida, in 1891 (Figure 11).[64] Eatonville was a small African American township that celebrated the fact it was one of the first Black communities to charter and incorporate its own city. Hurston grew up listening to her father preach in the Macedonia Baptist Church, and she also grew up

Figure 11. Zora Neale Hurston, ca. 1935. (Courtesy of the Library of Congress)

listening to men swapping stories, gossiping, or, as she put it, "telling lies" in front of Joe Clarke's store.

Hurston was nine when her mother died. She later left home to be a maid in a traveling Gilbert and Sullivan show and finished high school in Baltimore. She stayed in Baltimore and began college at Morgan State

University, but she later transferred to Howard University, where she was encouraged by the faculty to pursue creative writing. She then moved to New York and finished her undergraduate studies at Barnard College, where she became interested in anthropology and folklore. Gladys Reichard introduced her to both anthropology and Franz Boas. She began to view anthropology as an effective tool for the exploration of African American culture as she developed an affectionate relationship with Boas. She penned:

In a way it would not be a new experience for me. When I pitched head-foremost into the world I landed in the crib of negroism. From the earliest rocking of my cradle, I had known about the capers Bre Rabbit is apt to cut and what the Squinch Owl says from the house top. But it was fitting me like a tight chemise. I couldn't see it for wearing it. It was only when I was off in college, away from my native surroundings, that I could see myself like somebody else and stand off and look at my garment. Then I had to have the spy-glass of Anthropology to look through at that.[65]

By the late 1920s Hurston became an important promoter of the New Negro Movement, while pursuing folklore and the rest of her Barnard curriculum. Her successes were due to the way in which she embraced the incongruities that made her enigmatic yet effective. These incongruities were based not on her being a woman in a sexist society or being a Black in a racist society but her being articulate, creative, and smart, yet dark, big, and "country" in the "color-struck" Harlem society. These same qualities gave her an entrée to patrons who supported New Negro artists.

Mrs. Rufus Osgood Mason underwrote much of Hurston's field-work. She thought of Hurston as "an unspoiled child of nature" who could bring to her the primitive and honest stories of the Negro. Hurston was not a jazz player, cabaret dancer, pimp, prostitute, or bootleg-ger; but, for all intents and purposes, she satisfied her patron the same way other Harlemites satisfied their patrons at places like the Cotton Club. Hurston gave her patron what she wanted: a slice of the exotic and erotic, honest and natural, world of the Negro.[66]

Nathan Huggins perhaps best captures the role Harlem played in satisfying Whites' deep desires fashioned out of popular renditions of Jung and Freud:

Men who sensed that they were slaves to moral codes, that they were cramped, and confined by guilt-producing norms which threatened to make them emotional cripples, found Harlem a tonic and a release. Harlem Negroes' lives appeared immediate and honest. Every thing they did—their music, their art, their dance—uncoiled deep inner tensions. Harlem seemed a cultural enclave that had magically survived the psychic fetters of Puritanism. How convenient! It was merely a taxi trip to the exotic for most white New Yorkers. In cabarets decorated with tropical and jungle motifs . . . they heard Jazz, that almost forbidden music. . . . Coffee, chocolate, and caramel-brown girls whose lithe long legs kicked high, bodies and hips rolling and tossing with insinuations; feline black men—dandies—whose intuitive grace, teased and flirted at the very edge of chaos, yet never lost aplomb. Into its vortex white ladies and gentlemen were pulled, to dance the jungle dance.[67]

This same vortex engulfed the patrons of Negro artists and compelled them to support the cultural production (or reproduction, in Hurston's case) of Negroes who were still further from civilization and closer to savagery than were their downtown counterparts.

During the late 1920s and early 1930s Hurston executed a precarious balancing act—between her fiction and scholarship, her cosmopolitan élan and southern disposition—to negotiate the complex terrain that Harlem created. She had to simultaneously exploit yet obey the needs and expectations of a variety of patrons, members of literary circles, African American critics, and academic advisors that included Franz Boas, Carter G. Woodson, Gladys Reichard, Ruth Benedict, and Melville Herskovits.

While performing this balancing act Hurston emerged as the leading Negro folklorist in the nation,[68] even though her first attempt at collecting folklore ended in failure. She then embraced the mantra of the Columbia anthropologists: the researcher must immerse him- or herself in a particular culture and understand that each particular culture was a complex integrated whole and equally sophisticated relative to the particular environment and historical experience.

She dropped her "Barnardese" and undertook ethnological fieldwork in New Orleans, Florida, Haiti, and Jamaica, becoming an active participant in each community. In a ritual in New Orleans, for example, she lay nude for sixty-nine hours while she was put through a complicated ritual that included drinking wine mixed with the blood of all present and being accepted by the spirit. When she went to the field she carried her personal effects in her suitcase and packed a pearl-handled pistol in her purse. She searched for folklore in places into which few scholars would venture. One time she was made to steal a black cat with her hands and then kill it by tossing it into a boiling cauldron. After the cat's flesh dropped away from its bones, Hurston was instructed to pass the bones through her mouth until one tasted bitter, then carry it forever.[69]

Hurston advanced the vindicationist concern for debunking stereotypes and fallacies while promoting African American culture by using Boasian ideas of culture. For her, vindication meant dismissing notions that African American culture in the South was backward and inferior. She asserted that the experiences of rural southern Negroes were rich, important, and a vital link between African American culture in Harlem and traditional West African cultures. She advanced Herskovits's concern for documenting the retention of African cultural patterns, as well as Margaret Mead's and Ruth Benedict's concern for documenting the nexus between culture and personality. Much of Hurston's work in Jamaica attempted to explore the relationship between the Jamaican national culture and the Jamaican personality. Despite these contributions to specific anthropological frameworks, she remained largely marginalized in the field of anthropology.

Her most influential nonfiction book, *Mules and Men,* was a study of Negro folklore in rural Florida. In it she shattered preconceived notions about lazy and ignorant rural Negroes by forcefully arguing that African American folklore was both complex and expressive and that folklore was an effective adaptive strategy with origins in Africa. She explained that

they [folktales] are the complex cultural communications permitted an oppressed people, their school lessons, their heroic biographies, their psychic savings banks, their children's legacies. Black folktales illustrate how an entire people adapted and survived in the new world experience, how they transformed what they found into a distinctive way of life; they describe the human behavior the group approves, indicate when the behavior is appropriate, and suggest strategies necessary for the preservation of the group in a hostile environment.[70]

The book consisted of an arduous recording of linguistic usage, a careful documentation of the social world of rural Florida, and the prose of an experienced novelist.

Another important aspect of Hurston's work was documenting African religious practices in the Americas. For example, she wrote about Haitian Voodun as a complex African belief system that integrated the Haitian worldview. She attempted to exonerate the religion from the sensational and lurid association held by the general public. She also assumed the role of a salvage ethnographer and gave voice to people whose culture was rapidly changing in the wake of twentieth-century progress.

She won critical acclaim for her fiction, but her nonfiction was not afforded attention in either academic or public forums. In his review of *Tell My Horse* (1938), her ethnography of Haiti and Jamaica, for the *Saturday Review of Literature,* Harold Courlander remarked that the book was "a curious mixture of remembrance, travelogue, sensationalism and anthropology. The remembrances are vivid, the travelogue tedious, the sensationalism reminiscent of Seabrook and the anthropology a mélange of misinterpretation and exceedingly good folklore."[71]

There were other dimensions to her work. Like her contemporaries Ruth Benedict and Margaret Mead, she focused on women and their role in cultural production. She also boldly presaged the postmodern critique and embraced the fact that writing ethnography presupposed contributions from one's own creative processes. Blurring the lines between ethnography and fiction was her signature. The following excerpts of her work are emblematic of her concern for women and her creative writing approach to ethnography:

But now Miss America, World's Champion woman, you take your promenading self down into the cobalt blue waters of the Caribbean and see what happens. You meet a lot of darkish men who make vociferous love to you, but otherwise pay you no mind. If you try to talk sense, they look at you right pitifully as if to say, "What a pity! That mouth that was made to supply some man (and why not me) with kisses, is spoiling itself asking stupidities about banana production and wages!" It is not surprising they try to put you in your place, no. They consider that you never had any.[72]

Women get no bonus just for being female down there. She can do the same labors as a man or a mule and nobody thinks anything about it. In Jamaica it is a common sight to see skinny-looking but muscular black women sitting on top of a pile of rocks with a hammer making little ones out of big ones. They look so wretched with their bare black feet all gnarled and distorted from walking barefooted over rocks. The nails on their big toes thickened like a hoof from a lifetime of knocking against stones. All covered over with the gray dust of the road, those feet look almost saurian and repellent. Of course their clothing is meager, cheap and ugly. But they sit by the roadside on their enormous pile of rocks and crackdown all day long.[73]

In 1961 Zora N. Hurston died in poverty. During the past decade, however, literary critics have championed her and her work.[74]

The Decline of Negro
Folklore in Anthropology

Elsie Clews Parsons, Franz Boas, Frank Speck, and Carter G. Woodson provided the financial and structural foundation for an important program in Negro folklore, but it flourished for only a short time. It actually contributed more to the promoters of the New Negro than to anthropological theories of race and culture. Many of the reasons for the failure of the program were circumstantial. Boas had neither the ability nor the inclination to consistently secure funds for his Black students. Moreover, he had assumed commitments and responsibilities that did not allow him to focus on or support Negro folklore projects. The AFLS project could not survive without Boas's continuous support.

Other reasons for the failure were not circumstantial, however. William Willis, Jr. highlighted the more substantive reasons for Boas's intermittent support, arguing that Boas viewed African American folklore strictly in terms of survivals from Africa and not integral to the southern Negro experience. The study of African American culture by way of folklore required symbolic interpretations and a consideration of the social environment. Boas was thwarted by his literalism. "For instance he saw animals as animals and not as persons in animal fables. . . . Boas strongly resisted symbolic interpretations. . . . Boas's distrust of folklore severely restricted his insights into the black experience in slavery and under Jim Crow."[75] Boas also failed to follow his own views that folklore must be viewed in relation to the environment. He did not view the hostile social climate of the South (and the North) endured by Negroes in the same terms as the rainy climate of the Pacific Northwest endured by Kwakiutl or the arid climate of the Southwest endured by Great Basin Shoshone — part of the environment to which cultural strategies helped people to adapt. There is a final note that perhaps led to Boas's patchy enthusiasm for Negro folklore. He may have sensed how the JAFL was becoming party to the promoters of the New Negro and their attempts to promote "race consciousness." Boas was "absolutely opposed to all kinds of attempts to foster racial solidarity."[76] He made little distinction between nationalism in Europe and "racial solidarity" among African Americans in the United States. He viewed both as roadblocks to a fully integrated society.

The Negro folklore promoted by the AFLS has been virtually erased by historians of anthropology and locked out of the anthropological canon. There were a number of other scholars who used African American folklore as a vehicle for vindication but were not associated with the JAFL. Two notable examples were Katherine Dunham and Irene Diggs.

Early African American Folklorists outside the JAFL

Katherine Dunham (1910–) used anthropology and folklore for social activism and psychosocial empowerment. She pursued anthropology, folklore, dance, and theater at the University of Chicago in the early 1930s. She studied African cultural continuities in dance traditions in the Americas, using anthropological methods and theory introduced by Robert Redfield. She also collaborated with Melville Herskovits when he was at Northwestern University. Her first fieldwork was conducted in the Caribbean, where she studied and compared the dance forms of Haiti, Jamaica, Martinique, and Trinidad. Although she studied throughout the Antilles, the bulk of her fieldwork was in Haiti.[77] She had decided to continue her studies at Chicago in anthropology after she wrote up her fieldwork. Redfield encouraged her, however, to pursue her medium of choice—dance. Although she pursued dance over anthropology, she incorporated anthropology into her scholarship and activism.[78]

The results of Dunham's research have been published in Spanish, French, and English. Although she was influenced by Herskovits, she explained and analyzed dance from a functional approach. She did not approach functionalism the way A. R. Radcliffe-Brown did; rather, she focused on the psychological functions of dance. She later successfully applied her research methods to disillusioned youth in East St. Louis, teaching them discipline as well as personal competency through dance. She developed a dance company in 1939, and in 1943 she founded a school of arts and a research institute for dance in New York City. The school of arts housed a department of cultural studies and an institute for Caribbean research, and her dance company received critical acclaim. Her activism took many forms: in addition to building institutions, she frequently worked with the NAACP and the Urban League in an effort to integrate audiences in theaters.[79]

Irene Diggs (1906–1998) began her graduate study of anthropology and sociology at Atlanta University the same year that Du Bois left the NAACP and returned to Atlanta. In 1934 she enrolled in Du Bois's seminar "Karl Marx and the Negro Problem," and the following spring she became his research assistant.[80] As such she became instrumental in Du Bois's historiography. She worked on *Black Reconstruction in America* (1935), *Black Folk Then and Now* (1939), and *Dusk of Dawn: An Essay toward an Autobiography of a Race Concept* (1940). She and Du Bois also cofounded the journal *Phylon: A Review of Race and Culture*.[81]

In the early 1940s Diggs began her anthropological career in Cuba, where she received her doctorate. She studied under Fernando Ortiz and was able to travel throughout the island analyzing and investigating the West African cultural impact on Cuban society. By collecting folklore, recording music, photographing festivals, and participating in rituals and dances, she documented how transgenerational cultural patterns affected societies. She also demonstrated how the identity of twentieth-century Afro-Cubans incorporated visible elements of Yorban Dahomeyan traditions.[82]

Diggs's work was firmly located within the tradition of Black vindicationist scholarship, and "she extended or applied Du Bois's analytical concerns and methodological orientation to the study of Latin America."[83] She relied on ethnography coupled with historiography and social history to develop a comparative analysis of race, class, and culture in African societies in the Americas.

Fauset, Hurston, Dunham, and Diggs all conducted ethnographic work throughout the Americas. The continuity of African culture in the Americas, a multidisciplinary approach, and the effort to validate African culture as rich, complex, and expressive made these individuals pioneers in anthropology and members of a long tradition of vindicationist scholar-activists who painstakingly eroded notions that African American culture was inferior, backward, or degenerate.

The Larger Impact of the New Negro Movement

Franz Boas and his students at Columbia University (on West 119th Street and Amsterdam Avenue, just up the steps of Morningside Park from Harlem) were reshaping the anthropological discourse on race literally in the middle of the Harlem Renaissance. The discourse that eclipsed anthropological ideas of racial inferiority emerged in the very space in which African Americans challenged the meaning of a racial category that imposed inequality while demonstrating that their culture was rich, complex, and far from degenerate.

Boas and several of his students at Columbia University joined activists in an effort to liberate African Americans from the grip of claims of inferiority and to establish a more rigorous academic discourse to explain race and culture. The change in the social sciences followed, and at times led, slow changes and arduous political and social struggles that would eventually topple *Plessy* in 1954 and usher in the surge of protests for civil rights during the 1960s. The social and political processes that fostered changes in the construction of race during the Great Migration and the Harlem Renaissance gave rise to changes in an American anthropology that began to espouse racial equality.

CHAPTER 8

Unraveling the
Boasian Discourse

Anthropology and Racial Politics of Culture

During the decades that enveloped the Great Depression and the New Deal, the NAACP could not rely on Democrats in Congress or the White House to pass Civil Rights legislation. Franklin D. Roosevelt could not support bills empowering African Americans; if he had, southern Democrats would make sure that his New Deal legislation did not become law. The judicial branch was the only recourse, so the NAACP turned to Charles Hamilton Houston, dean of the Howard University Law School, to pull together an elite corps of legal scholars, strategists, and litigators to fight school segregation in the federal judiciary. The NAACP led a dogged campaign to change the Supreme Court justices' interpretation of the Constitution.

The senior members of the legal staff of the NAACP were professors at the Howard School of Law and had been trained in sociological jurisprudence by Roscoe Pound and Felix Frankfurter at Harvard. In other words, they were trained in the value of using social science as a complement to precedent and logic to make their case. The NAACP developed a strategy that used current sociological and anthropological research as evidence to prove that African Americans were not given "equal protection" under the law. The LDEF employed the most authoritative science available: it presented Gunnar Myrdal's *An American Dilemma* as "Exhibit A."[1] The role anthropology played in directly changing the legal significance of racial categories, therefore, corresponds to Myrdal's use of it in 1938, when he began to compile his Herculean 1,300-page study. The work emerged as the dominant discourse on Negro and White race relations. This emergence, as well as the reasons for the NAACP's use of it, are buried in the twists and turns of the politics surrounding the New Deal, World War II, and the rise of Howard University as the center for the study of race relations.

From Hoover to the TVA—"Lily White"

In 1920 Warren G. Harding, the little-known Republican senator from Ohio, was elected president. The members of Harding's cabinet were scandalous: they lined their pockets with government contracts, accepted bribes, and refused to prosecute organized criminals who violated the prohibition of alcohol. In 1923 Harding died, and Calvin Coolidge, the vice president, presided over the executive branch for the balance of the term. In 1924 Coolidge won the presidency in his own right, because the Democratic Party was not united. It was split over whether to include an anti-Klan plank in its platform and who to nominate for president. The fissure emerged between the political machines in northern cities and the Klan defenders in southern districts. Southern Democrats held sway over considerable electoral votes in their respective states, which allowed them to reject, by one vote, the anti-Klan plank. The party also deadlocked on its nominee. On the 103rd ballot the two factions finally compromised on John W. Davis, thus ending the longest standoff in the history of national party conventions.

Coolidge did not run for a second term in 1928, which left his efficient and highly respected secretary of commerce, Herbert Hoover, as the logical nominee for the Republican Party. The political machines succeeded in nominating Alfred C. Smith from New York during the Democratic convention, but Smith lost to Hoover in a landslide. Smith failed because he was Catholic, he favored repeal of the Eighteenth (Prohibition) Amendment, he was connected to Tammany Hall (New York City's political machine), and he was a friend of the Negro and the worker.

Virtually every Black newspaper and most Black organizations endorsed Alfred C. Smith. African Americans again turned away from the "Party of Lincoln," hoping not to repeat the Wilson debacle. With the help of the Black vote, Smith carried the twelve largest U.S. cities. While African Americans cultivated an alliance with White northern Democrats, northern Republicans cultivated one with White southern

Democrats. This meant that northern Republicans had to abandon southern Black Republican officials and party members. The leadership of the Republican Party executed this shift to what Du Bois called "lily-white-ism" with aplomb.[2] In 1928 southern Whites betrayed their loyalty to the Democratic Party. They abandoned the party in droves and overwhelmingly supported Herbert Hoover. The Republican Party spoils for courting White southern Democrats included carrying Florida, Kentucky, North Carolina, Tennessee, Texas, Virginia, and West Virginia. The Republicans delivered the half-century- "solid South" from the grips of the Democratic Party.

African Americans did not, however, totally abandon the Republican Party, especially in local and congressional races. In 1928 African Americans widely supported Smith, to no avail; yet residents of the south side of Chicago sent their Republican alderman, Oscar DePriest, to the U.S. Congress. DePriest was the first African American legislator from the North. He thus represented not only his district but also the New Negro, serving as a beacon of hope and a symbol of pride.[3]

Hoover and his secretary of the treasury, Andrew Mellon, won instant acclaim from business interests. Hoover increased tariffs and reduced corporate and individual taxes. He also steered legislation through Congress that extended credit to farmers who had been hit hard by falling agricultural prices. During the 1920s the economy grew, and most Americans experienced a rapid rise in their standard of living. Relying often on credit, Americans consumed goods and invested in securities at unprecedented levels, but this pattern of conspicuous consumption and unchecked economic growth was short-lived. Agricultural profits soon lagged far behind industrial profits, and wages did not keep up with inflation. The manufacturing and industrial sectors began to produce more goods than Americans could buy, even on credit. In addition, overseas markets were quickly diminished by the high tariffs imposed by the United States. In October 1929 the stock market crashed, and the ensuing mayhem throughout the financial world ushered in a decade-long depression.[4]

In 1932 the nation was in the grip of the Great Depression. The Democratic presidential nominee, Franklin D. Roosevelt, won an impressive victory by espousing a new deal for the forgotten man. Relief, recovery, and reform were catchwords that framed Roosevelt's attempts to manage the economy in such a way that Americans could spend their way back to prosperity. The Democrats held a majority in both the House and the Senate; plus, with a clear public mandate, they passed many recovery and reform acts in Congress. To provide relief for unemployment, Congress implemented the Civilian Conservation Corps and the Civil Works Administration. To assist in the recovery of businesses and agriculture, Congress enacted the National Industrial Recovery Act, the Public Works Administration, the Agricultural Adjustment Act, and the Federal Housing Administration. To guide reform of unfair business practices and to ensure consumer protection, Congress implemented policies to reform banking procedures, price gouging, and racketeering. Most of the first programs were directed at industry, businesses, and merchants. Only after winning overwhelming public support for the New Deal did Roosevelt create agencies and policies that became effective in helping African Americans and organized labor recover from despair. These included the Works Progress Administration, the National Youth Administration, the National Labor Relations Act, and the Fair Labor Standards Act.

Franklin and Eleanor Roosevelt facilitated some political agency for African Americans by appointing many Black people to high-level positions in the administrative bodies of the New Deal. It was Harold L. Ickes, Roosevelt's secretary of the interior and the former president of the Chicago branch of the NAACP, however, who did the most to integrate the New Deal. Many African American political appointees or "advisors" were used merely as salespeople for the New Deal.[5]

Roosevelt's administration immediately embarked on the Tennessee Valley Authority (TVA), one of the largest regional programs of the New Deal era. The TVA planned to harness the power of the Tennessee River to generate inexpensive hydroelectric power, which would jumpstart the economy and make the entire region prosperous. On May 18, 1933, Congress enacted legislation creating the project. By generating cheap electricity, the planners outlined, large-scale industry would expand along the transmission lines that would in turn increase small businesses, employment, and the purchasing power of the residents in the Tennessee River Basin. TVA administrators attempted to hire African Americans in proportion to their population, but they were kept from participating in the many remedial programs implemented by the authority. For example, they were denied access to the model dairies, tree nurseries, and produce farms, as well as the model woodworking, automotive, and electrical shops. Another model program was the planned community erected at Norris, Tennessee. No expense was spared to make it represent an ideal American community.[6] In an article entitled "TVA: Lily-White Reconstruction" (1934), Charles H. Houston and

John P. Davis reported in the *Crisis* that "The authorities told us bluntly no Negroes would be permitted to occupy houses in Norris, 'Because Negroes do not fit into the program.' Thus their position is that Negroes do not belong in the 'ideal American community' built and maintained by public funds."[7] Houston and Davis concluded "that the only function that the Negro has in the T.V.A., the only recognition which the T.V.A. gives him, is as a labor commodity. And even this function is subject to certain exceptions."[8] Even though the New Deal offered recovery and relief for some unemployed workers, it was not such a great deal for Black people.

Walter White was appointed executive director of the NAACP in 1931. He immediately committed much of the organization's time and resources to pressure, agitate, organize, and lobby Congress for the Costigan-Wagner Anti-Lynching Bill. White outlined the devastating impact that lynching had on all Americans and the urgent need for federal antilynching legislation in his 1929 book *Rope and Faggot: A Biography of Judge Lynch*.[9] His book drew on ethnographic methods, statistics, psychology, and history to level a terse indictment at the continued use of lynch law. It covered an array of topics, including "the mind of the lyncher," "sex and lynching," "the economic foundations of lynch-law," "science, nordicism, and lynching," and "the price of lynching."

The NAACP aroused overwhelming public support for this legislation, and in 1934 it was finally able to spring the perennially locked bill from the Senate Judiciary Committee—but the ensuing filibusters prevented a vote. In 1935 White was again able to have the bill considered on the Senate floor, but southern senators "with cynical skill" allowed it to flounder in the quagmire of rules, procedures, and debates.[10] While the bill was on the floor, White called Eleanor Roosevelt and pleaded with her to set up a meeting between him and her husband: the bill would die without the president's public support. Mrs. Roosevelt set up the meeting. Although the president favored the bill, he could not publicly endorse it. Roosevelt explained his position to White:

"I did not choose the tools with which I must work," he told me [White]. "Had I been permitted to choose them I would have selected quite different ones. But I've got to get legislation passed by the Congress to save America. The Southerners by reason of the seniority rule in Congress are chairmen or occupy strategic places on most of the Senate and House committees. If I come out for the anti-lynching bill now, they will block every bill I ask Congress to pass to keep America from collapsing. I just can't take the risk."[11]

The New Deal seemed more and more like a raw deal for African Americans. If African Americans could not even secure an antilynching bill, which had overwhelming national support, how could African American interest groups petition Congress to pass civil rights legislation? The executive and legislative branches blocked the NAACP's efforts. The NAACP devised a strategy based on the 1923 *Margold Report* to slowly equalize segregated public education in state and federal circuit court systems.[12] If a case was appealed to the Supreme Court, however, the 1935 Hughes Court would probably have reversed any favorable decision. The judicial branch was also blocked.

A Switch in Time Saves More Than Nine

The New Deal was literally gutted by the Supreme Court. Led by newly appointed Chief Justice Charles Evans Hughes, the Court continued its century-and-a-half-long allegiance to protect property rights by welding capitalist interests to the Constitution. Hughes had sat on the Court as an associate justice from 1910 to 1916, but he resigned to run for president. In 1930 President Hoover appointed him chief justice to replace William Howard Taft. Hughes pursued a more conservative approach than he had the first time. Just weeks after he was confirmed, Hoover needed to replace Associate Justice Edward T. Sanford. He nominated Judge John J. Parker of the U.S. Court of Appeals, Fourth Circuit. Parker's confirmation was blocked by the NAACP and the American Federation of Labor.

The NAACP knew that every appointment to the Supreme Court was critical. Parker was from North Carolina and was the overseer of the South's Fourth Circuit. NAACP leaders believed that he would affirm the state court's decisions to continue Jim Crow. White, who led the fight against confirmation, discovered evidence that Parker had advocated poll taxes, literacy tests, and the grandfather clause during his 1920 bid for governor of North Carolina. White obtained a decade-old article from the *Greensboro Daily News;* dated April 19, 1920, it reported Parker's statement that "The participation of the Negro in politics is a source of evil and danger to both races and is not desired by the wise men in either race or by the Republican Party of North Carolina."

The NAACP quickly mobilized. The organization sent telegrams to all of its branches, wrote editorials, distributed press releases, spoke at rallies, and presented copies of the article to every senator and to the president. In addition, the NAACP was successful in convincing other organizations to join the effort to derail the confirmation.[13] The American Federation of Labor also weighed in to oppose Parker's confirmation because he had affirmed an opinion to uphold Yellow Dog contracts (stating that employment would terminate upon union affiliation) when the United Mine Workers appealed an injunction to revoke them.

The campaign was successful, and Parker was denied confirmation by a two-vote margin.[14] Hoover moved quickly to appoint Owen J. Roberts, who was swiftly confirmed. Roberts gravitated toward the conservative bloc that opposed any and all efforts to federally regulate business. James C. McReynolds, Willis Van Devanter, George Sutherland, and Pierce Butler constituted this bloc and were referred to as the four horsemen. To replace Oliver Wendell Holmes in 1932, Hoover appointed Benjamin N. Cardozo, who sided with the more liberal dissenters. This only left Cardozo, Harlan Fiske Stone, and Louis D. Brandeis to defend Roosevelt's New Deal.[15]

So, thanks in part to the NAACP, Roosevelt inherited the Hughes Court, which razed the hastily written New Deal legislation. Beginning with the 1933 October term and continuing through 1936, the Supreme Court held twelve of the New Deal acts unconstitutional. Two of the acts—the National Industrial Recovery Act and the Agricultural Adjustment Act—were pillars of the New Deal.

The National Industrial Recovery Act of June 1933 established the National Recovery Administration (NRA). This legislation allowed merchants and manufacturers in specified industries to write their own codes for fair business practices. In return, the agency would impose minimum wages, maximum working hours, and collective bargaining. Businesses enthusiastically advertised their compliance with the NRA Blue Eagle, which patriotically declared "We Do Our Part." However, the infamous "Sick Chicken Case," *Schechter Poultry Corp. v. United States,* put an end to federal regulation of trade practices. Chief Justice Hughes delivered the unanimous decision, stating emphatically that "Extraordinary conditions do not create or enlarge constitutional power. . . . Congress cannot delegate legislative power to the President to exercise an unfettered discretion to make whatever laws he thinks may be needed or advisable for the rehabilitation of expansion of trade or industry."[16] In *United States v. Butler* the Court struck down another pillar of the New Deal, the Agricultural Adjustment Act, which provided incentives for farmers to reduce production, thus decreasing surplus and raising the price of their goods.

In February 1937, President Roosevelt responded to these Court decisions by proposing legislation, dubbed the "Court-Packing Plan," to add up to six justices to the Supreme Court and thereby change its makeup. In an opinion read on March 29, 1937—just weeks after Roosevelt announced his plan—Roberts unexpectedly joined the less conservative side of the Court to uphold a Washington State minimum wage law.[17] After this conversion, the Court upheld every New Deal law that came before it. Bernard Schwartz has asserted that this constituted a "veritable revolution in the jurisprudence of the Supreme Court."[18] Melvin I. Urofsky has also noted that this judicial turnaround, in the midst of the Court-Packing Plan, served as a marker to delineate a shift in the Court's agenda. For 150 years the bulk of the Court's cases had concerned economic matters, and it generally favored property rights over public welfare. With the transformation of the Court, economic matters played an increasingly smaller and less important role on the agenda. The Court began to resonate with a more libertarian tenor and changed course to explore how far the Constitution would protect individual rights and liberties.[19]

The accounts explaining why the Court switched so suddenly vary, but the poignant pun that whirled through Washington that spring simply concluded that "a switch in time saves nine."[20] In the following months Roosevelt solidified his Court by appointing two more associate justices, thus hobbling the "horsemen." In August 1937 Hugo Black replaced Van Devanter, and in January 1938 Stanley Reed replaced Sutherland. Although the rapid reconstitution of the Court concerned the NAACP, it was encouraged by the gestures to secure individual rights and uphold federal regulation. Would a Roosevelt Court favor the Negro? Roosevelt had proved that he could not. What strategy would the NAACP employ now, with a less conservative Supreme Court? And who would take the leadership of the NAACP National Legal Committee from the aged Moorefield Storey?

Charles Hamilton Houston, dean of the Howard School of Law, emerged as the leader in the first round of the desegregation battles and was soon followed by his student, Thurgood Marshall. The specific strategy was slow to develop, but to win, they decided to look to the social scientists at Howard University to provide evidence that segregation was deleterious to African Americans. They packed their briefs with anthropological, sociological, and psychological data and research to demonstrate that separate could never be equal and that segregation violated both the due-process clause of the Fifth Amendment and the equal-protection clause of the Fourteenth Amendment.[21]

Rethinking Race and Culture:
The Rise of the Howard Circle

During the 1920s literary and art circles transformed American prose and art in Harlem; during the 1930s a circle of scholars transformed the study of American race relations. The hub of this activity was Howard University. Although the nucleus was the faculty at Howard, the circle extended to an array of scholars who published in Howard's *Journal of Negro Education* and participated in many university-sponsored conferences.[22]

The movement to reshape the study of race relations can be linked to Mordecai Johnson, who, in 1926, became the first African American president of Howard University. Johnson inherited a jumble of old buildings, a secondary school, a collection of undergraduate departments, and a handful of graduate and professional schools. In addition to raising faculty salaries and academic standards, toughening admission requirements, and insisting on full accreditation, he hired an impressive group of young professors in law, physical science, medicine, education, social science, and the humanities. These scholars worked closely together to redefine the study of race relations in the United States.[23] As a consequence, Howard emerged as an important center for the study of the Negro during the New Deal era.

The core of Howard's faculty in arts and sciences included E. Franklin Frazier in sociology, Abram L. Harris in economics, Rayford Logan in history, Alain Locke in philosophy, Ralph Bunche in political science, and Charles Thompson in the School of Education. This core also included Charles Hamilton Houston and William Hastie in the School of Law and Charles Drew and W. Montague Cobb in the College of Medicine.[24] In 1925 Melville Herskovits, one of Boas's most celebrated students, was an instructor at Howard; however, he became marginalized by the Howard circle because of his emphasis on African cultural continuities in the Americas.[25] Howard's faculty advanced a multidisciplinary approach to race relations that demonstrated how economic and environmental processes prevented most Negroes from fully assimilating a "legitimate culture." The Howard circle developed ideas about culture that differed markedly from those held by folklorists, anthropologists, and certain members of the New Negro Movement.

Boas, his students, and his close associates developed a tightly knit discourse that aligned theories of racial equality with notions of a historically specific cultural relativity.[26] African American intellectuals, such as Arthur H. Fauset, Zora Neale Hurston, Arthur Schomburg, Carter G. Woodson, and W. E. B. Du Bois, accepted and built on Boas's work to explain the so-called culture of the Negro. Others scholars, such as E. Franklin Frazier, Charles Johnson, Ralph Bunche, and Guy B. Johnson, all members of the Howard circle, accepted the Boasian notion of racial equality but discarded the emphasis on cultural history. This group embraced the sociological view of Negro culture that Robert Park advanced at the University of Chicago.

Robert Park maintained "that the Negro, when he landed in the United States, left behind him almost everything but his dark complexion and his tropical temperament. It is very difficult to find in the South today anything that can be traced directly back to Africa."[27] Boas, on the other hand, viewed African American culture in terms of that "peculiar amalgamation of African and European tradition which is so important for understanding historically the character of American Negro life, with its strong African background in the West Indies, the importance of which diminishes with increasing distance from the south."[28] For analytical purposes, I suggest that the scholars aligned with Park's views were maintaining a cultural legitimacy thesis and that those aligned with Boas's views were maintaining a cultural specificity thesis. This analytical framework will enable me to illustrate how these two lines of thought converged and diverged, and why attorneys for the LDEF used the Boasian discourse on racial equality and the Park discourse on Negro culture to bolster their desegregation cases.

Proponents of the Boas-influenced cultural specificity argument stressed the idea that unique historical and cultural continuities shaped African American culture. These members of the New Negro Movement were groping for a symbolic anchor other than race to ground an identity. They found it, in part, in Africa.[29] They attempted to forge an ethnic identity centered on the construction of a cultural homeland. They produced studies of folklore, cultural history, and art history in an effort to reclaim, authenticate, and validate the past as well as the present. Schomburg captured the crux of this line of thought: "The Negro has been a man without a history because he has been considered a man without a worthy culture. But a new notion of cultural attainment and potentialities of the African stocks has recently come about, partly through the corrective influence of the more scientific study of African institutions and early cultural history."[30]

In a variety of ways the idea of African culture in America provided an important symbol that tied the indigenous West African to the plantation slave to the sharecropping tenant to the urbane and cosmopolitan "New Negro." In 1925 Alain Locke articulated this line of thought from a somewhat different angle: "But even with the rude transplanting of slavery, that uprooted the technical elements of his former culture, the American Negro brought over an emotional inheritance [and] a deep-seated aesthetic endowment. And with a versatility of a very high order, this offshoot of the African spirit blended itself in with entirely different culture elements and blossomed in strange new forms."[31]

Proponents of the Park-influenced cultural legitimacy approach maintained that Negro culture had progressed far enough, especially among assimilated middle-class Negroes, to take its place among the higher civilizations of "mankind." However, proponents of this approach were forced to explain what happened to Negroes who never attained the cosmopolitan ways of the New Negro. These scholars, most of whom were sociologists, assumed that a large percentage of African Americans deviated from American cultural and behavioral standards. Such deviations, the sociologists explained, were inevitable responses to deleterious environmental conditions, racial discrimination, and the heritage of slavery.[32] Perhaps the most notable proponent of this approach was the esteemed sociologist E. Franklin Frazier, who earned his doctorate at the University of Chicago. Advancing ideas similar to Park's, Frazier explained the "simple Negro folk culture" as an "incomplete assimilation of western culture by the Negro masses." Frazier argued that "generally when two different cultures come into contact each modifies the other. But in the case of the Negro in America it meant the total destruction of the African social heritage. Therefore in the case of the family group the Negro has not introduced new patterns of behavior, but has failed to conform to patterns about him. The degree of conformity is determined by educational and economic factors as well as by social isolation."[33] Several Black sociologists even suggested that African Americans left their culture behind in the South and adopted an entirely new one in the North. Charles Johnson concluded that "A new type of Negro is evolving—a city Negro. . . . In ten years, Negroes have been actually transplanted from one culture to another."[34]

African American sociologists cited statistics that compared African Americans with a White American standard. Deviations from "the norm" included the high incidence of female-headed households, divorces, and fictive kin relations. These were correlated with high incidences of poverty, crime, delinquency, and disease. Together they became indices for deviant or pathological culture and behavior. These supposed deviations or pathologies were purportedly caused by turbulent and radical changes in the Negroes' social structure, beginning with the break from Africa, then enslavement, then plantation tenancy, then urban life in the northern and southern cities. These rapid changes, coupled with virulent racism, inhibited the development of normative patterns that would allow Negroes to assimilate Western culture.[35]

Although many scholars challenged discipline-specific boundaries, supporters of cultural specificity arguments were generally aligned with cultural anthropology—specifically the Columbia school. These arguments were primarily articulated in New York City during the New Negro Movement of the 1920s. Supporters of cultural legitimacy arguments were closely aligned with sociology—specifically the Chicago school. These arguments eventually eclipsed those from New York and were articulated from Howard University during the Great Depression. There were influential scholars, however, who contradicted this pattern, especially St. Clair Drake, coauthor of *Black Metropolis: A Study of Negro Life in a Northern City* (1945), who combined sociological and anthropological methods and theory.

An integral component of the Howard circle's approach was Park's assimilation model outlining four phases of social evolution: competition, conflict, accommodation, and assimilation. Park's 1930s version of evolution saturated the Howard circle and affirmed its obstinate position on assimilation. The model also underpinned *An American Dilemma* and the legal arguments later used for *Brown*.[36]

The Howard social scientists found the cultural specificity thesis incompatible with assimilation because it implied that the cultural patterns of African Americans were long-standing, slow to change, and ostensibly irreversible. In a speech to the Harlem Council of Social Agencies, Frazier publicly chided Herskovits, asserting that "if whites came to believe that the Negro's social behavior was rooted in African culture, they would lose whatever sense of guilt they had for keeping the Negro down. Negro crime, for example, could be explained away as an 'Africanism' rather than as due to inadequate police and court protection."[37] E. Franklin Frazier, the most influential and prolific of the Howard scholars, continued to argue that Negroes could and should assimilate "Western culture." Gunnar Myrdal employed these same ideas in *An American Dilemma*.

Myrdal Employs Howard's Ideas and Talents

Although the Supreme Court did not officially document the sources of social science that influenced *Plessy*, it specifically cited *An American Dilemma* in *Brown*.[38] Some scholars have suggested that Chief Justice Earl Warren's reference to Myrdal's work was effectively a reference to Boas's legacy in the social sciences.[39] My argument in this section directly challenges one of Dinesh D'Souza's major theses in *The End of Racism: Principles for a Multiracial Society* (1995) that "the logic of cultural relativism leads directly to proportional representation, which is the underpinning of American civil rights law."[40] He argues that this "direct" link was made by "Thurgood Marshall [who] spearheaded a direct attack on segregation, and chose to premise it on the findings of Boasian relativism."[41]

I want to demonstrate that when Earl Warren cited *An American Dilemma* he accepted the argument presented by the LDEF and that the LDEF, for its argument, used the Howard circle's approach that adopted Boas's notion of race and jettisoned his concept of culture. In its place, the NAACP used a concept of culture associated with Robert Park but developed by scholars at Howard University during the 1930s. It was Myrdal who first validated this approach a decade before *Brown*. Following the Howard circle, Myrdal used Boas's and Herskovits's evidence that there was no basis for claims of racial inferiority and their analysis that the environment caused any racial differences, but Myrdal virtually ignored the associated line of thought that cultures were historically specific and relative to one another.[42]

Myrdal's watershed study was the culmination of a massive research study of U.S. race relations sponsored by the Carnegie Corporation.[43] As director of the project Myrdal hired researchers to write book-length memoranda or reports on an array of topics, which he then synthesized for the final product. He hired Frazier and Bunche to submit reports, and together they shaped the tenor of the study. Bunche was hired as a permanent staff member for the project and was Myrdal's closest American advisor. Frazier was also an important advisor to Myrdal and was responsible for giving the manuscript of *An American Dilemma* final approval.[44]

Myrdal employed Frazier's basic arguments that all Negroes could obtain a culture as "legitimate" as that of Whites, but he articulated the notion that "the simple folk culture of the Negro" was pathological with more force than Frazier did. In this important passage Myrdal vividly painted African American culture as pathological and demonstrated his logical disdain for Boasian notions of cultural relativity:

In practically all its divergences, American Negro culture is not something independent of general American culture. It is a distorted development, or a pathological condition, of the general American Culture. The instability of the Negro family, the inadequacy of educational facilities for Negroes, the emotionalism in the Negro church, the insufficiency and unwholesomeness of Negro recreational activity, the plethora of Negro sociable organizations, the narrowness of interests of the average Negro, the provincialism of his political speculation, the high Negro crime rate, the cultivation of the arts to the neglect of other fields, superstition, personality difficulties, and other characteristic traits are mainly forms of social pathology which for the most part, are created by the caste pressure.

This can be said positively: *we assume that it is to the advantage of American Negroes as individuals and as a group to become assimilated into American culture, to acquire the traits held in esteem by the dominant white Americans. . . .*[45]

So, what *was* the specific role anthropology played in *An American Dilemma* and subsequently the *Brown* decision? Boasian anthropology established the only common denominator in studies of African American race, culture, and society during the 1920s and 1930s. It was the anchor for the consensus that there was no proof of any hereditary difference in intelligence or temperament and that historical and environmental factors—cultural factors—caused the differences between racial groups.[46] Myrdal generally followed the members of the Howard circle, who took the tightly knit Boasian discourse and separated theories of racial equality from notions of a historically specific cultural relativity. They appropriated Boas's assumption that there was no proof of racial inferiority but discarded the rest. Therefore, although all of the studies shared Boas's theory of racial equality, his idea of culture was just one of many. Various research groups with distinct methodologies explored African American culture and social structure. Most social scientists viewed African cultures in the Americas as a variant of some sort of "national" culture; some argued that blacks, especially in the rural South, had a distinct folk culture with African influences. As I have already mentioned, there was the Chicago school of sociology and its more radical variant, the Howard circle. There was also Donald Young's comparative analysis of minority groups, Howard Odum's southern sociology, John Dollard's "caste and class" approach, W. E. B. Du Bois's interdisciplinary studies of Black society and culture, Carter G. Woodson's Negro history movement, and Charles S. Johnson's more liberal variant of Chicago sociology. Finally, there was Otto Klineberg's social-cultural psychology approach to studying racial differences and Hortense Powdermaker's functional-structural studies of southern culture.[47]

Although Myrdal incorporated the discussions of class and caste articulated by Allison Davis and John Dollard, he dropped the Boasian notion of culture altogether; he did not and could not agree with Herskovits. In addition to Herskovits and Boas, Myrdal rejected the perspective of Du Bois and Woodson.[48] He nevertheless praised Herskovits's work on Negro anthropometry,[49] explaining that "it is the merit of Professor Melville J. Herskovits that he has finally approached this problem [of racial character] directly."[50] Myrdal needed to establish a premise that Negroes were not mentally or physically inferior to Whites. As evidence he provided Herskovits's anthropometric studies, Montagu's studies of characteristics of the Negro population, Klineberg's work on IQ scores, and Cobb's applied anthropology. All of these scientists were closely associated with Boas.[51]

Howard Law: Making Sociological Jurisprudence Work

Mordecai Johnson oversaw the hiring of professors in education and the social sciences that forever changed the study of Black people. He was also responsible for hiring the professors of law who would use this new research to forever change civil rights law. In 1929 Johnson received a clear mandate from Louis Brandeis to revamp Howard's law school. The Supreme Court Justice explained, "I can tell most of the time when I'm reading a brief by a Negro attorney." He persuaded the new president "to get yourself a real faculty out there or you're always going to have a fifth-rate law school. And it's got to be full-time and a day school."[52] To execute this mandate Johnson appointed Charles Hamilton Houston as dean.

Charles Houston (1895–1950) was nineteen when he graduated Phi Beta Kappa from Amherst College. In 1917 he entered the officer training camp that the NAACP had worked so vigorously to establish at Fort Des Moines. He went on to serve as an officer in World War I, and when he returned he enrolled at Harvard Law School, where he served on the *Harvard Law Review*.

Houston enjoyed working with Felix Frankfurter, the most liberal and the only Jewish member of the law school faculty. Frankfurter was a Washington insider, a founder of the American Civil Liberties Union, on the legal advisory committee of the NAACP, and a fierce defender of labor. Frankfurter, in turn, enjoyed working with Houston and encouraged him to pursue graduate study under his tutelage. Houston agreed and earned a doctorate in juridical law from Harvard. Frankfurter then recommended Houston for the Sheldon Traveling Fellowship. Houston won the fellowship and used it to attend the Universidad de Madrid, where he earned a doctorate in civil law.[53]

Houston arrived at Harvard Law School when Frankfurter and his colleague Roscoe Pound were extolling the virtues of sociological jurisprudence.[54] Pound outlined "The Scope and Purpose of Sociological Jurisprudence" in a series of articles for the *Harvard Law Review*.[55] In the series, he railed against "Mechanical Jurisprudence" that produced laws from logical deductions based on axiomatic premises, and he argued that the law was not an autonomous collection of self-contained and self-referential rules and insisted that judges be sensitive to the social purposes of the law. He urged judges and lawyers to cease being legal monks and look to economics, sociology, and philosophy for guidance. Above all, Pound called for " 'team-work' between jurisprudence and the other social sciences."[56] Pound lionized Frankfurter's mentor, Louis Brandeis, and considered the Brandeis brief to be the best method by which to employ sociological jurisprudence.

Laura Kalman suggested that the sociological jurisprudence taught at Harvard was ineffective because the law school itself was in a state of cultural lag. She has explained that proponents of sociological jurisprudence were ineffective because the social science used was twenty years old. The attorneys and scholars who used sociological jurisprudence were simply impervious to changes in social sciences that were occurring at Columbia, Chicago, Yale, and Howard.[57]

Charles Houston was trained in sociological jurisprudence at Harvard but came to Howard University when it was fast emerging as *the* institution for cutting-edge studies of race relations. The Brandeis brief and teamwork with the other social sciences were important lessons he learned from the ineffectual proponents of sociological jurisprudence. Once Houston received the appointment, he wasted no time in executing the mandate delivered by Mordecai Johnson and Louis Brandeis.

The law school earned full accreditation in a single year. Houston made two appointments that enhanced the program: William H. Hastie (also a Harvard Law School graduate) and Leon Ransom of Ohio State University. The curriculum that Houston developed included invited lectures by Clarence Darrow and other nationally recognized law professors and litigators. Houston kept close ties to Harvard, and when Roscoe Pound was in Washington he would visit the Howard School of Law to profess his views of jurisprudence.

Houston's curriculum was not limited to case studies and lectures by distinguished jurists. He also incorporated practicing attorneys' views and cases. People like James Nabrit Jr., the young civil rights attorney from Texas, were integral to the Law School and NAACP National Legal Committee.[58]

Thurgood Marshall entered Howard School of Law in 1930 and graduated first in the class of 1933. In the same year Houston started representing the NAACP as legal counsel. Walter White enlisted Houston's support after a miscalculated effort to free the Scottsboro Boys. Houston welded the law-school students, alumni, and faculty to the LDEF. Houston did not limit his efforts strictly to law. He was a social and political critic and deeply committed to African American education. In 1934 he was elected to the School Board of the District of Columbia and joined his colleagues at Howard as an ardent critic of the New Deal. He championed school desegregation and wrote prolifically in the *Journal of Negro Education* and the *Crisis*. In 1935 he was appointed chief counsel for the LDEF and won his first case before the Supreme Court.[59]

Howard University: The Keystone of Change

The people Mordecai Johnson appointed as deans were important to his efforts to reorganize the university. Houston was not the only notable dean Johnson appointed; he also named Numa P. G. Adams dean of the College of Medicine. She in turn hired R. L. McKinney, a specialist in microscopic anatomy, M. W. Young, a neuroanatomist, and the renowned medical scientist Charles Drew. Adams also provided funds for W. Montague Cobb to attend Case Western Reserve University, where he earned a doctorate in anatomy and anthropology.

W. Montague Cobb (1904–1990) initially earned a medical degree from Howard, but after he graduated, Adams underwrote additional graduate education so that he could return to teach and assemble the Laboratory of Anatomy and Physical Anthropology. Beginning in the early 1930s, he was an integral member of the intellectuals who contributed to the anthropological discourse on race and worked with the NAACP National Health Committee to shape national health-care policy. His interest in anthropology was grounded in anatomy and medicine before a separate bioanthropological field had even matured. The American Association of Physical Anthropologists was founded in November 1929 by efforts spearheaded by Aleš Hrdlička, and that same year Cobb entered Case Western Reserve to study anatomy and physical anthropology under T. Wingate Todd. As physical anthropology became a full-fledged discipline, Cobb was thrown into the middle of debates on race within the profession. He immediately took the offensive. In 1939 he published "The Negro as a Biological Element of the American Population" in the *Journal of Negro Education*. He presented evidence to contradict physical anthropologists' assertions regarding African American infertility and contended that the intellectual achievements of African Americans were quite extraordinary in light of their social and economic barriers. Cobb was part of the generation that linked the founding figures of American physical anthropology to all succeeding generations.[60] He did not claim any intellectual roots from Boas; however, he and Boas arrived independently at many of the same conclusions. They both emphasized the value of human diversity, equality, flexibility, and creativity. Furthermore, they both deplored ideas of racial determinism.

Cobb was perhaps the first physical anthropologist to conduct an applied demography study without a commitment to eugenics. In study after study and paper after paper he exposed and documented the physical toll that racism inflicted on African Americans and the high cost the nation paid for it. His research determined that ending Jim Crow hospitals and implementing health-care reform would remedy many of the nation's public health problems. Effective public health policies, Cobb demonstrated, were ultimately linked to eradicating the embedded segregation and institutionalized racism in professional schools and health-care facilities.[61] Michael Blakey and Leslie Rankin-Hill explained that Cobb's approach to health-care policy and his 1,100 publications constituted an unparalleled program of applied physical anthropology.[62] Cobb led the NAACP National Health Committee efforts on Capital Hill to bring about health-care reform and greater access to medical facilities and public health information, and he confronted the access to health-care information in the public sphere by writing prolifically in magazines such as the *Negro Digest, Journal of Negro Education,* the *Crisis,* and *Ebony.*[63]

According to Cobb, it was clear that the social processes which make racial categories have physical and biomedical implications. To confront these issues he had the NAACP National Health Committee employ the same strategy that the LDEF was developing. Following in the LDEF's footsteps, the National Health Committee marshaled the prevailing scientific and social scientific evidence to prove that segregated hospitals and restricted access to health care must be eradicated. The National Health Committee took a legislative approach, however.

Cobb was the architect of the annual Imhotep National Conferences on Hospital Integration, which he began in 1957. The conferences were jointly sponsored by the NAACP and the National Medical Association, and they attracted many of the top biomedical scientists, anthropologists, sociologists, public health officials, and legislators. President Lyndon B. Johnson even attended. The group convened for seven years until its goal, passage of the Civil Rights Act of 1964, was met. Cobb prophetically outlined a plan for national health insurance and assisted in drafting the 1965 Medicare Bill.[64]

The activist scholars who came to Howard during the 1930s changed the discourse on Negro race and culture. In the most general sense the Howard circle's view of culture was shaped by a belief that the assimilation of "mainstream" culture facilitated the struggle for racial equality. Yet whatever political factors shaped the way they conceptualized the culture concept, nothing in anthropology paralleled the sagacious critique of the political economy of race they leveled in the 1930s. Although they generally disparaged Black cultural patterns, together they developed important approaches to understanding society, political economy, and endemic power inequalities. Typifying these efforts, Ralph Bunche insightfully penned:

Through the use of the ballot and the courts strenuous efforts are put forth to gain social justice for the group [African Americans]. Extreme faith is placed in the ability of these instruments of democratic government to free the minority from social proscription and civic inequality. The inherent fallacy of this belief rests in the failure to appreciate the fact that these instruments of the state are merely the reflections of the political and economic ideology of the dominant groups, that the political arm of the state cannot be divorced from its prevailing economic structure, whose servant it must inevitably be.[65]

I do not wish to give the impression that the scholars associated with the Howard circle were monolithic thinkers. There was a tremendous diversity of thought. Often they did not even agree on what strategy to employ in their effort to secure racial equality. For example, Bunche and Harris were critical of the NAACP's efforts to fight desegregation in the courts. They wanted the NAACP to commit its resources to forging an alliance with trade and industrial unions and the White working class. Even though they were not united in their ideas, they were resolute in their commitment to have the ideals of freedom, equality, and participatory democracy finally realized. Whether in medicine, education, or law, these scholars integrated and used each other's work to effect change and affect lives.

Howard University was a keystone for change. The multidisciplinary approach to race relations challenged, documented, and defined the very structural, institutional, and political aspects of racism prohibiting African Americans from participating in everything considered American in the United States. The subsequent appropriation of that discourse in *An American Dilemma* changed how the federal and state governments structured and imposed a racial category on African Americans.

Whereas the NAACP strategy of fighting public school segregation in the courts was conceived during the 1930s, the more sweeping decisions regarding segregation were handed down by the Supreme Court after World War II and during the cold war. The Court began to dismantle the legal fabric of state-sponsored racism only after segregation posed glaring contradictions between the ideals of democracy and the United States' triumph over the state-sponsored racism of Nazi Germany and mounting cold war tensions.

CHAPTER 9

Anthropology and the
Fourteenth Amendment

I think Plessy v. Ferguson *was right and should be re-affirmed.*[1]
William H. Rehnquist, 1952

The initial strategy that the NAACP National Legal Committee pursued to challenge racial segregation was to equalize separate facilities created for African Americans. By 1935 Charles Hamilton Houston was spending most of his time with the NAACP and developing its plans to equalize public schools. He outlined, in the *Crisis,* specific objectives for the organization's new agenda in "Educational Inequalities Must Go":

At the present time the N.A.A.C.P. educational program has six specific objectives for its immediate efforts:

a. equality of school terms;
b. equality of pay for Negro teachers having the same qualifications and doing the same work as white teachers;
c. equality of transportation for Negro school children at public expense;
d. equality of buildings and equipment;
e. equality of *per capita* expenditure for education of Negroes;
f. equality in graduate and professional training.[2]

This was an important declaration for the NAACP. Houston was outlining a plan to commit the organization's resources to equalizing educational opportunity, which meant abandoning Walter White's futile attempts to pass the antilynching bill. The article was published just after White's bill was jettisoned from the Senate floor. Houston announced that the organization was "to use every legitimate means at its disposal to accomplish actual equality of educational opportunity." Houston elegantly justified the renewed campaign:

This campaign for equality of educational opportunity is indissolubly linked with all the other major activities of the association. It ties in with the antilynching fight because there is no use educating boys and girls if their function in life is to be the playthings of murderous mobs. It connects up with the association's new economic program because Negro boys and girls must be provided with work opportunities commensurate with their education when they leave school. One of the greatest tragedies of the depression has been the humiliation and suffering which public authorities have inflicted upon trained Negroes, denying them employment at their trades on public works and forcing them to accept menial low-pay jobs as an alternative to starvation. Civil rights, including the right of suffrage, free speech, jury service, and equal facilities of transportation, are directly involved.[3]

While equalizing teachers' salaries and busing schedules remained critical to its program, the LDEF began to focus on high-profile cases equalizing graduate and professional schools. Houston was reluctant to confront the Hughes Court (which had invalidated Roosevelt's New Deal legislation) with a professional-school case because it probably would not reverse on appeal. Pursuing the equalization of Black professional schools, nevertheless, was an effective strategy, for three reasons. First, southern state governments did not even put up a facade with regard to the equality of "separate-but-equal" professional schools. Second, real compliance with the separate-but-equal doctrine would create enormous expenditures from each state's Depression-ravaged budgets. The third reason was cultural: Houston and his colleagues were exploiting the peculiar southern belief that desegregation at the collegiate level seemed less pernicious than desegregation at the primary-school level. Thurgood Marshall (Figure 12) noted the irony: "Those racial supremacy boys somehow think that little kids of six or seven are going to get funny ideas about sex and marriage just from going to school together, but for some equally funny reason youngsters in law school aren't supposed to feel that way. We didn't get it but we decided that if that was what the South believed, then the best thing for the moment was to go along."[4]

Figure 12. Thurgood Marshall, ca 1938. (Courtesy of the Library of Congress)

First Fruits

Thurgood Marshall presented a solid test case for equalizing professional schools to Houston in 1935. Marshall had just completed law school at Howard University and set up a practice in his hometown, Baltimore.

This case concerned Donald Murray, a graduate of Amherst College, who had applied, in 1934, to the law school at the University of Maryland, Baltimore. The university denied him admittance because of its policy not to admit Negroes. Donald Murray first sought counsel from the local branches of Alpha Phi Alpha Fraternity and the NAACP, which were engaged jointly in a program to desegregate the University of Maryland. Marshall was a member of both organizations, so naturally they turned to him for assistance, and he enlisted the support of his mentor, Charles Houston. Several attorneys were vying to litigate *Murray v. Maryland,* but a reluctant Houston took it on.

Houston put on witness after witness and argued a brilliant case that Maryland did not provide a separate law school for African Americans so they had to admit Murray. On cross-examination, Houston riddled the testimony of the university's witnesses. He decisively reasoned that scholarships given to Negro students by the state to attend schools outside Maryland could not be construed as equal, because the University of Maryland was the only public school in which the state's unique form of Common Law was taught. The municipal court found for Murray, and he was admitted to the law school. The state court of appeals upheld the decision.[5]

After Roosevelt's 1937 threat to add more justices to the Court, Houston pondered whether the Supreme Court would reverse lower court decisions imposing segregation as zealously as it had upheld New Deal legislation. He found, in 1938, that the Court would at least question the separate-but-equal formula.

Right after *Murray* the local branch of the NAACP in St. Louis worked up a case for Lloyd Lionel Gaines, who was denied admission into the University of Missouri Law School. The case was identical to the Murray case, except that the state insisted it was going to erect a separate-but-equal law school at Lincoln University. The state of Missouri already offered excellent resources, curricula, and professors for Negroes at Lincoln. Substantively, the education at Lincoln was equal to that at the University of Missouri, and the state insisted that it would build an equally impressive law school. The U.S. Circuit Court of Appeals upheld the denial of admission, and the separate-but-equal doctrine continued to be violated.

Houston petitioned the Supreme Court to grant a writ of mandamus to force the registrar, an officer of the state, to comply with the equal-protection clause. Chief Justice Hughes granted not the writ of mandamus but a writ of certiorari, the most common way cases are heard before the Court.[6] The case was presented as *Missouri ex rel. Gaines v.*

Canada. The Court agreed with the NAACP, and Hughes wrote: "The fact remains that instruction in law for negroes is not now afforded by the State, either at Lincoln University or elsewhere within the State, and that the State excludes negroes from the advantages of the law school it has established at the University of Missouri."[7]

Cardozo had died before this decision was handed down. To replace him, in 1939, President Roosevelt appointed Felix Frankfurter, Houston's mentor and a member of the NAACP National Legal Committee. Roosevelt's appointments to the Court proved important for the NAACP's efforts to desegregate public school districts. By 1954, when the Court decided *Brown,* five of the nine justices were still Roosevelt appointees: Hugo L. Black (1937), Stanley F. Reed (1938), Felix Frankfurter (1939), William O. Douglass (1939), and Robert H. Jackson (1941).

What Will Berlin Think?

The outbreak of war in Europe spurred the United States to prepare for war. Immediately, racial discrimination took on a global perspective. When Adolf Hitler snubbed Jesse Owens at the 1936 Olympic Games, African Americans spoke out against fascism. In 1940 Congress passed the Selective Service Act, and defense policies were becoming even more exclusionist, which motivated A. Philip Randolph and Walter White to submit a seven-point program to President Roosevelt outlining the acceptable treatment of African Americans in the defense industries and the armed services.

Thousands of jobs were created when Congress appropriated $1.8 billion to prepare the armed services for war, but African Americans were kept out of the hiring frenzy because defense contractors tenaciously held onto rigid Jim Crow policies. Randolph organized a march on Washington to demand equitable hiring by defense contractors: 100,000 African Americans were to unite on the Mall on July 1, 1941.[8] Roosevelt frantically scheduled meetings with Randolph and other African American leaders and pleaded with them to call off the march. Randolph held fast and explained that he was going ahead. Washington was abuzz with the question, "What Will Berlin Think?" Randolph would call off the march only if the President issued an executive order "with teeth in it." On June 25, 1941, just days before the march, Roosevelt issued Executive Order 8802, which stated that "there shall be no discrimination in the employment of workers in the defense industries or Government because of race, creed, color, or national origin." It also established the Fair Employment Practices Committee to investigate violations of the order.[9] The protest was averted.

The international dimensions of Randolph's protest were significant. Seven years earlier, Roosevelt had refused to support the antilynching bill, fearing southern Democrat reprisals. Ostensibly, they would retaliate against the executive order, but Roosevelt had to weigh party politics against the contradiction between U.S. support of freedom abroad and the denial of it at home.[10]

As war raged in Europe, the United States was called on by the enemies of the Axis Powers to be the arsenal for democracy. Giving material support to nations that were being besieged by fascism while maintaining racial inequality required remarkable ideological ambidexterity. The inability of the United States to declare a resolute position with regard to democratic ideals and contrasts made between Jim Crow and Hitlerism weakened its position as defender of equality and freedom and damaged its creditability.[11] To compound these contradictions, almost one million African American men and women served courageously in all branches of the armed forces — in segregated departments.

Fueled again by the wartime economy, another massive wave of African Americans filled jobs created by the defense industry, now desegregated by Roosevelt's executive order. The northward migration was renewed, and for the first time there was a great movement from east to west. The number of Black people in the West tripled when large numbers migrated to Portland, Seattle, Oakland, and Los Angeles to work in shipyards and other industries.

Perhaps more than any other event, World War II illuminated the duplicity of state-sponsored racism. Allied rhetoric about the fight for the "four freedoms" encouraged African Americans to fight for freedom at home. The Holocaust, in which some 6 million Jews were murdered in the name of racial superiority, forced all Americans to confront White supremacy in the United States; more and more, predominately White organizations were making it clear that Jim Crow was unacceptable. African Americans quickened these trends by launching the popular Double-V campaign — victory for freedom abroad and at home.

An American Dilemma:
A Guidebook for the Negro Problem

An American Dilemma won instant and widespread acclaim when it was published in 1944. Myrdal's theme was palatable and timely. Frederick Keppel, president of the Carnegie Corporation, recognized that the timing of the watershed study was indeed fortunate. In the book's foreword Keppel wrote:

When the Trustees of the Carnegie Corporation asked for the preparation of this report in 1937, no one (except possibly Adolf Hitler) could have foreseen that it would be made public at a day when the place of the Negro in our American life would be the subject of greatly heightened interest in the United States. . . . [T]he eyes of men of all races the world over are turned upon us to see how the people of the most powerful of the United Nations are dealing *at home* with a major problem of race relations.[12]

Myrdal's popular theme quelled the angst many Americans felt when they considered the parallels of state-sponsored racism in the United States and in Nazi Germany.

Though our study includes economic, social, and political race relations, at the bottom our problem is the moral dilemma of the American—the conflict between his moral valuations on various levels of consciousness and generality. The "American Dilemma," . . . *is the ever-raging conflict between, on the one hand, the valuations preserved on the general plane which we shall call the "American Creed,"* . . . *and, on the other hand, the valuations on specific planes of individual and groups living, where personal and local interest; economic, social, and sexual jealousies* [exist].[13]

Myrdal's theme appealed to the American public because he fashioned the Negro problem into a moral dilemma for Whites and a formidable task for Blacks, to assimilate and work themselves out of poverty. But he raised the stakes: White Americans either had to embrace the American ideal of equality or be forced to confront the rising tide of Black militancy.

An American Dilemma effectively reshaped the discussion of race and culture in the United States for the next fifteen years. It became a guide for an array of social policies, a standard text in university curricula, and a dominant reference in nearly every forum on race relations.[14] National newspapers and magazines, including the *New Republic, Time, Life, Sat-*

urday Review, the *New York Times,* and the *Chicago Tribune,* endorsed Myrdal's theme by printing articles and reviews with headlines such as "Race Riots or Race Unity: Which Will It Be," "Dr. Myrdal's Treatment of the Negro Problem and Modern Democracy Is a 'Must' Book," "Democracy's Chance: The Negro Problem," and "Comprehensive Study of the Negro Problem: Scholar Predicts War Will Change Outlook of Negroes by Making Them Feel Entitled to Share in American Ideals of Equality." Although the book was not uniformly praised, the federal government began to see the geopolitical benefits of creating the appearance of better race relations. The NAACP was pleased with the book's public reception because it validated and certified the long struggle for racial equality. The legal arm of the NAACP began to see it as solid and well-respected evidence for overturning *Plessy.*

Mr. Civil Rights

In 1939 the LDEF was established as a separate tax-exempt organization to preserve the NAACP's right to lobby Congress. The LDEF was soon under the direction of Thurgood Marshall, and Howard law professors William Hastie and James Nabrit emerged as key members. As a spokesperson for the LDEF and its celebrated lawyer, Marshall soon became known as Mr. Civil Rights. He handled every kind of case all over the country. He fought for equal salaries for teachers in hostile Little Rock, he defended three Negroes charged with murder in a county besieged by the KKK in Florida, and he confronted South Carolina's consistent abrogation of court-ordered voting rights. As an "outsider" who had come to the South to skew the rigid color line, Marshall was routinely harassed by local police and constantly confronted fear for his life.

While the war curbed the campaign to equalize public education, it solidified public contempt of segregation, which in turn prompted the LDEF to pursue a more aggressive agenda. The LDEF had to make difficult decisions about where to focus its resources. Marshall weighed its priorities: "Without the ballot you've got no goddamned citizenship, no status, no power, in this country. But without the chance to get an education you have no capacity to use the ballot effectively."[15] The LDEF chose to focus its limited resources on attacking the entire separate-but-equal doctrine in a campaign to desegregate public schools, with the aid of social science.[16]

Cold-War Maneuvers

The sociological arguments the LDEF was developing became more attractive with the public's praise for *An American Dilemma* and the mounting need for better race relations in the United States as the cold war eclipsed World War II. The LDEF attorneys seized these opportunities and finally convinced the U.S. Department of Justice to support the NAACP with an amicus curiae brief detailing why the executive branch supported its case. In 1943, before *An American Dilemma* and the cold war, the Justice Department refused to support the LDEF's argument to end the Texas White primary in *Smith v. Allwright* (1944).[17] In 1948, however, U.S. Attorney General Tom Clark supported the LDEF argument to strike down the enforcement of homeowners' restrictive racial covenants with an amicus brief in *Shelley v. Kraemer* (1948). This dramatic shift of the executive branch concerning Jim Crow laws was essential to the success of the ensuing school-desegregation campaign. The government submitted amicus briefs in support of the LDEF for every desegregation case that followed *Shelley*.[18]

Harry Truman was ultimately responsible for the executive branch's new support of civil rights issues. After Roosevelt died, Truman moved quickly and decisively to establish the United Nations, broker Germany's unconditional surrender, and order atomic bombs dropped on Japan. He moved equally decisively to expel communists and to secure civil rights for African Americans. In 1947 he created the Federal Employee Loyalty Program to expel so-called communist sympathizers ("the reds and parlor pinks") from government service, terminating hundreds of federal workers and forcing several thousand to resign. He also established the President's Commission on Civil Rights, which first convened early that year. By October the commission had completed its report, *To Secure These Rights* (1947).

The report recommended that a permanent commission be established to enforce fair employment practices, that federal subsidies for Jim Crow health, education, and housing facilities be revoked, that Jim Crow cars on interstate transportation be prohibited, and that lynching be made a federal offense. Within months Truman had drafted legislation embodying these recommendations and demanded that Congress pass it. His own party refused. Southern Democrats blocked the legislation; in retaliation, Truman issued executive orders abolishing segregation in all government agencies, including the Federal Housing Authority and all branches of the Armed Services. Truman was up for election in 1948, and he campaigned on an anticommunist, pro-civil-rights platform.[19]

In 1948 the LDEF argued the class action suit *Shelley v. Kraemer* before the Supreme Court. The case addressed restrictive covenants, "private agreements to exclude persons of a designated race or color from the use or occupancy of real estate for residential purposes." The Court found that these covenants by themselves did not violate the Fourteenth Amendment but that state courts violate the equal-protection clause if they enforce them.[20] The LDEF was successful in convincing Truman's attorney general, Tom Clark, to direct his solicitor General to file a brief as amicus curiae. Clark was no radical; he was a leading advocate of the loyalty program and compiled the first "pink" list of alleged communist sympathizers. His brief underscored his paranoia about everything un-American. The Justice Department's brief concluded that overcrowded, demeaning ghettos promoted by the covenants "cannot be reconciled with the spirit of mutual tolerance and respect for the dignity and rights of the individual which give vitality to our democratic way of life."[21]

To argue *Shelley* the NAACP implemented two strategies that it continued to use effectively in the school-desegregation cases. The first was to solicit briefs of amicus curiae from prominent and powerful organizations as well as from the Justice Department. The second was to buttress its legal arguments with the prevailing social science, selective statistics, and other data in Brandeis briefs. The Court ultimately agreed with the arguments presented by the NAACP and the Justice Department.[22] Although the Court did not consider the sociological data in *Shelley,* there is no doubt that it took note of the briefs submitted by various organizations and the Justice Department.[23]

After *Shelley* the LDEF launched a direct attack on *Plessy* by arguing that segregation was per se unconstitutional. The time was right to attempt to overturn the separate-but-equal doctrine.[24] Three particular events worked in tandem to allow the LDEF to strategically use the rhetoric of assimilation expressed in *An American Dilemma* to exploit fears cultivated by the cold war to outmaneuver both the judicial and the executive branch. First, public opinion about the acceptability of Jim

Crow was changing after World War II. Second, the force-feeding of *An American Dilemma* to the American public by the press and the federal government made the Howard circle's cultural legitimacy thesis hegemonic by the early 1950s. Finally, the federal government and the press began to scorn anything considered "un-American."[25] These dynamics allowed the LDEF attorneys to take advantage of the discourse articulated by their former colleagues from Howard as well as the prevailing views of people in circles of power.

If an assimilationist approach proved effective, they would use it.[26] The LDEF made the case that segregation itself was un-American by couching its arguments for equality within a discourse that emphasized the assimilation of American culture and values. Additionally, they argued that segregation denied African Americans the opportunity to embrace true American values, which implied that African Americans were poised to embrace un-American values if they were not educated in desegregated schools. In a sense the LDEF strategy was like Brer Rabbit tricking Brer Fox by playing the fool: the LDEF employed a strategy that disparaged African American culture by evoking a distinctive tradition in African American culture—the trickster.

During the late 1940s and early 1950s, the LDEF gradually won desegregation cases that concerned public graduate and professional schools in the South. It eventually turned to public grade-school desegregation; that litigation culminated with *Brown* in 1954. Although the LDEF jettisoned the cultural specificity argument, the way the LDEF used the anthropological discourse on racial equality was critical to its protracted litigation. Members of the LDEF only selectively cited anthropological texts in their Brandeis briefs and were even more selective in their choices of which anthropologists to put on the stand as expert witnesses.

Anthropology and Professional-School Desegregation

After World War II African Americans were attending college in record numbers. Armed with the GI Bill, many veterans pursued college and advanced studies. Black universities were overcrowded and turned away thousands of qualified applicants. However, the large state universities in the South still refused to accept African American applicants. The NAACP filed three cases that were eventually argued before the Supreme Court: *Sipuel v. Oklahoma State Board of Regents*,[27] *Sweatt v. Painter*,[28] and *McLaurin v. Oklahoma State Regents for Higher Education*.[29] Although these were three separate cases, they became intertwined, and two were argued before the Supreme Court on the same day. Each case concerned the admission of exceptionally qualified African Americans to a state-supported law or graduate school in the South. *Sipuel* was the first case argued, and the Court did not write an opinion announcing its decision. It merely issued an unsigned per curiam order compelling the state of Oklahoma to provide Ada Sipuel with a legal education "in conformity with the equal protection clause of the Fourteenth Amendment and provide it as soon as it does for applicants of any other group."[30] To comply, the Oklahoma Board of Regents hired three law teachers and set up a law school in a room in the state capitol.[31] Thurgood Marshall was left with two cases to execute the plan. In the *McLaurin* case, a sixty-eight-year-old graduate student was admitted to the school but was forced to occupy special "reserved for coloreds" areas cordoned off in the library, cafeteria, and classrooms. In the *Sweatt* case the state had just allocated $3 million to create a "first-class" university for African Americans rather than admit Black students to its law school in Austin.

The LDEF strategy was honed to precision. Its attorneys solicited briefs as amici curiae, put anthropologists and law-school professors on the stand, and crafted powerful Brandeis briefs. They argued that there was no basis on which to classify the races as separate and no rationale for the segregation of people based on racial inferiority. Additionally, they argued that "intangibles" must be considered in any determination of equal facilities. Employing the same tactics as in *Shelley*, the NAACP was able to have the Justice Department submit a brief.

The LDEF also received briefs in support of its cases from the American Federation of Teachers, the American Veterans' Committee, the Congress of Industrial Organizations, the Japanese American Citizens' League, the American Civil Liberties Union, the Committee of Law Teachers against Segregation in Legal Education, and the American Jewish Congress (AJC). The brief filed by the AJC evoked the similarities between state-sponsored racism in Nazi Germany and the United States. The AJC, of which Thurgood Marshall and Charles Houston were advisory board members, filed a riveting amicus brief for *Sweatt*: "The discriminatory effect of such legally sanctioned inequality can be demonstrated by reference to recent tragic history. The Nazis understood it fully when they imposed on Jews the wearing of the Yellow Star of David. Polizeiverordnung über die Kennzeichnung der Juden vom 1.

September 1942, RGBI, I.S. 547, augeg. am 5. IX. 1941."[32] The AJC also cited *An American Dilemma* in outlining various arguments, stating with authority, "According to Myrdal. . . ."[33]

Robert Carter joined the LDEF in 1944 as a legal-research assistant. He continued to do much of the research and quickly became one of the most prominent attorneys in the organization. The brief that he and Marshall drafted for *McLaurin* was theoretically more rigorous than the one filed for *Shelley*. It was underpinned exclusively with Myrdal and his associates. The list of authorities included John Dollard, Arnold Rose, and Robert Park. Myrdal relied on each for specific aspects of his study. The citations that drew directly from the Howard circle include E. Franklin Frazier, Ralph Bunche, Charles Thompson, and Kenneth B. Clark. Thompson was dean of the Howard Graduate School, editor of the *Journal of Negro Education,* and a consultant for Myrdal's project. Kenneth Clark went to Howard University as an undergraduate in the early 1930s, at the same time Thurgood Marshall was attending its law school. Clark completed his doctorate in psychology at Columbia University and was also a member of Myrdal's research staff. Kenneth Clark and Mamie P. Clark, also a social psychologist, became integral to the later public-school desegregation cases.[34]

The kind of anthropologists Carter and Marshall chose to include in their bibliography shows that the LDEF mirrored the Howard circle's use of Boasian anthropology. The LDEF cited only anthropological publications on race which demonstrated that there was no scientific proof of hereditary differences in intelligence or temperament and concluded that environmental factors could explain the differences among racial groups.

The LDEF did not cite anthropological publications which demonstrated that cultures were historical or functional, adaptive or cognitive. The brief's bibliography included *Man's Most Dangerous Myth: The Fallacy of Race* (1942), by M. F. Ashley Montagu, a physical anthropologist, an advisee of Boas, and a contributor to Myrdal's project. The other anthropologist was Robert Redfield, a social anthropologist at the University of Chicago. Though not directly associated with the Myrdal study, Redfield was a program director at the Carnegie Institute.

The LDEF included three publications by Otto Klineberg, a social psychologist at Columbia University who had worked closely with Boas and pursued "research in the border-land field between psychology and ethnology."[35] Klineberg was yet another advisor to Myrdal and wrote a monograph for his study. Klineberg drew heavily from Boasian anthropology and investigated cultural differences in relation to differences in

IQ scores. The LDEF quoted Klineberg's *Negro Intelligence and Selective Migration* (1935), which concluded that "length of residence in a favorable environment plays an important part in the intellectual level of the Negro children."[36] The LDEF brief did not include Herskovits, Ruth Benedict, or any other cultural anthropologist.

The exclusion was a calculated decision. For example, William Maslow, director of the AJC's Commission on Law and Social Action, wrote to Marshall to inform him of Ruth Benedict's work. He also suggested "that Ruth Benedict would make a good witness" for the Texas case.[37] Marshall ignored the information, for he only wanted to use anthropologists to testify that no scientific rationale existed to classify the races and that African Americans were not inferior to White Americans. Apparently, he did not want anthropologists to expound on the virtues of African American culture. He expressed this position when he outlined the LDEF's strategy for the Herman Sweatt case. Marshall explained that he was only "contemplating putting on anthropologists to show that there is no difference between folks."[38] He selected Robert Redfield to testify in *Sweatt,* undoubtedly because of his knowledge of the law and his credentials. He had received a law degree and then a doctorate in social anthropology from the University of Chicago, where he served as dean of social sciences and chair of the Department of Anthropology.

Redfield proved to be an important and indefatigable expert witness during the five days of argument in the District Court of Travis County, Texas. His testimony also proved critical four years later, when the case reached the Supreme Court. In the original "petition and brief" filed at the Supreme Court, Redfield's testimony was the authority cited in the section on "The Unreasonableness of Compulsory Racial Segregation in Public Legal Education."[39] It was also cited in the brief filed for *McLaurin.*[40]

On the stand in Texas, Redfield presented, with force and candor, scientific studies which established that African Americans were not inferior. Thurgood Marshall told the court that Redfield's arguments that "there is no rational basis for the classification" of race lie "flat in the teeth of the 14th Amendment."[41] Marshall continued:

Q: Dr. Redfield, are there any recognizable differences between Negro and white students on the question of their intellectual capacity? . . .

A: We got something of a lesson there. We who have been working in the field in which we began with a rather general presumption among our common educators that inherent differences in intellectual ability of capacity to learn existed between negroes and whites, and [we] have slowly, but I think very convincingly, been compelled to come to the opposite conclusion, in the course of long history, special research in the field. . . . The conclusion, then, to which I come, is differences in intellectual capacity or inability to learn have not been shown to exist as between negroes and whites, and further, that the results make it very probable that if such differences are later shown to exist, they will not prove to be significant for any educational policy or practice.[42]

Redfield was a convincing scientist and did not waver on cross-examination, even when the attorney general tried to make him contradict himself:

Q: [Mr. Daniels] Yes, Sir. In other words, you will agree with the other eminent educators in your field, the fields in which you are acquainted, that it is impossible to force the abolition of segregation upon a community that has had it for a long number of years, in successfully obtaining the results that are best?

A: No, I don't agree to that.

Q: Do you think the laws should be changed tomorrow?

A: I think that segregation is a matter of legal regulation. Such a law can be changed quickly. . . . Segregation in itself is a matter of law.[43]

The attorney general tried to question Redfield's authority by quoting the *Encyclopædia Britannica,* but Redfield provided a different set of sources.

Q: Do you recognize the Encyclopedia Britannica and the articles on such subjects as an authority in the field?

A: No, I do not.

Q: You do not?

A: No, sir . . .

Q: Could you give us some of the authorities that you think we would be justified in taking as authorities on the subject you have testified to us about?

A: Franz Boes [*sic*], Ruth Benedict, Ashley Montague [*sic*], Otto Klineberg. Is that enough?[44]

Redfield's testimony and the specific research cited by the LDEF in its briefs for these cases confirm the important role that anthropology played in the juridical construction of race in the early 1950s. The Supreme Court did not completely overturn the separate-but-equal doctrine but reversed lower courts' decisions and desegregated state graduate and professional schools. The NAACP won a major victory and dealt an irreparable blow to Jim Crow.[45]

Footnote 11: A Social Science Statement

The use of anthropology and sociology in the arguments for *Brown* were essentially the same as those in the graduate- and professional-school cases: the LDEF selectively appropriated anthropology to debunk notions of racial inferiority and selectively appropriated sociology to demonstrate the values of assimilation. The LDEF also introduced social psychology to explain the psychosocial impact of segregation. When the class-action suit was being waged in the lower courts, Kenneth Clark was the chief expert witness, testifying about the studies he had conducted with Mamie Clark (Figure 13).

In a series of studies that assessed children's racial attitudes and knowledge, the Clarks presented three-to-seven-year-olds with two White dolls and two Black ones, identical in every respect save color. They then gave the children such instructions as, "Give me the doll that you like best," "Give me the doll that looks bad," and "Give me the doll that looks like you."[46] Although the studies produced mixed results, Clark focused his testimony on the results that found Black children choosing White dolls because they looked "pretty" or "nice" and not choosing Black dolls because they looked "bad" or "ugly."[47]

Robert Carter argued to the Court that the social science testimony and briefs were the "heart of our case." The heart of the case, then, was an "Appendix to Appellants' Briefs" entitled "The Effects of Segregation and the Consequences of Desegregation: A Social Science Statement." The introduction read: "The following statement was drafted and signed by some of the foremost authorities in sociology, anthropology, psychology and psychiatry who have worked in the area of American race relations. It represents a consensus of social scientists." The statement drew explicitly from Myrdal's theme and thesis, and *An American Dilemma* was the first reference cited. Although the brief dealt mostly with

Figure 13. Kenneth B. and Mamie P. Clark, ca. 1936. (Courtesy of the Library of Congress)

the psychological impact of segregation, the anthropological discourse on race was specifically employed to argue the idea of racial equality:

Behind this question is the assumption, which is examined below, that the presently segregated groups actually are inferior intellectually.

The available scientific evidence indicates that much, perhaps all, of the observable differences among various racial and national groups may be adequately explained in terms of environmental differences. It has been found, for instance, that the differences between the average intelligence test scores of Negro and white children decreases, and the overlap of the distributions increases, proportionately to the number of years that the Negro children have lived in the North. . . . It seems clear, therefore, that fears based on the assumption of innate racial differences in intelligence are not well founded.[48]

This was the Boasian discourse on race; the LDEF conclusion mirrored Boas's conclusion after studying the cephalic indexes of immigrants some forty years earlier. Boas concluded that "It appears in those cases that contain many individuals whose parents have been residents of America for a long time that the influence of American environment upon the descendants of immigrants increases with the time that the immigrants have lived in this country."[49]

Most of the justices found the social science evidence compelling.[50] The Court was, however, obliged to present a rational explanation for its judicial interpretation. Because the framers of the Fourteenth Amendment did not explicitly delineate whether the amendment was intended to abolish segregation in the public schools, the Court charged both sides with determining, historically, if the framers of the Fourteenth Amendment understood or did not understand it to abolish segregation in public schools.

The Court found that it could not rely on history to explain its judicial interpretation because history proved inconclusive. The only other rationale to use was the set of arguments evidenced by current social science. Earl Warren was able to craft a weak but unanimous decision to put an end to the disingenuous doctrine of separate but equal as it pertained to public-school education. To construe the Fourteenth Amendment, he stated that the Court "cannot turn the clock back to 1868 when the Amendment was adopted, or even to 1896 when *Plessy v. Ferguson* was written."[51] He then documented how the Supreme Court used social science as a rationale for establishing a new juridical construction of race:

To separate them from others of similar age and qualifications solely because of their race generates a feeling of inferiority as to their status in the community that may affect their hearts and minds in a way unlikely ever to be undone. . . . Whatever may have been the extent of psychological knowledge at the time of *Plessy v. Ferguson,* this finding is amply supported by modern authority.[11] Any language in *Plessy v. Ferguson* contrary to this finding is rejected. We conclude that in the field of public education the doctrine of "separate but equal" has no place. Separate educational facilities are inherently unequal.[52]

Figure 14. Celebrating after *Brown v. Board of Education*, 1954. Left to right: George Edmond Haynes, Thurgood Marshall, and James M. Nabrit Jr. (Courtesy of the Library of Congress)

In this passage Warren included "Footnote 11" to provide the authority and rationale for overturning *Plessy* (Figure 14). Cited in the footnote were, among others, Kenneth B. Clark and E. Franklin Frazier. It concluded "and see generally Myrdal, *An American Dilemma* (1944)." Although this decision was technically weak, it was a powerful symbolic victory. *Brown* did change the way the state imposed racial categories in the United States, and it was a clarion call for the Civil Rights movement. The following year, Rosa Parks refused to give up her seat on a bus in Montgomery, Alabama; and her community, led by Dr. Martin Luther King, Jr., launched the landmark bus strike.

Anthropology played a complex and crucial role in the desegregation movement. It was complex because the LDEF was forced to unravel the tightly knit Boasian discourse on race, language, and culture; what it appropriated from anthropology proved crucial to its success. Throughout the twentieth century, anthropology reigned over its scientific domain — race. In 1896, when ideas of racial inferiority and the law were wedded, the discipline of anthropology was appropriated whole-cloth to validate claims about racial inferiority. In 1954, when ideas of racial equality and the law became wedded, the discipline was selectively appropriated to validate claims about racial equality. The discourse produced by scholars in anthropology, in a very literal sense, was woven into the very fabric of U.S. society.

CHAPTER 10

The Color-Blind Bind

Government cannot make us equal; it can only recognize, respect, and protect us as equal before the law.
Associate Justice Clarence Thomas,
opinion in *Adarand Constructors v. Peña,* 1995

If one race be inferior to the other socially, the Constitution of the United States cannot put them upon the same plane.
Associate Justice Henry B. Brown,
opinion in *Plessy v. Ferguson,* 1896

What role does U.S. anthropology play in racial forma-
tion processes in the late 1990s? It is certainly not the same as it was a
hundred years ago, but some of the dynamics and relationships persist.
The intersection and convergence of racial politics and discourses produced by the media and social scientists remain integral to the processes
that form and reform racial constructs. Similarly, specific interest groups
selectively appropriate certain aspects of social science to help further
those interests. Whether it is *The Bell Curve,* informing restrictive welfare
reform, or a race-evading multiculturalism, reinforcing the Supreme
Court's interpretation of a "color-blind" Constitution, anthropology
looms.

From Radical to Reactionary:
Denying Racial Difference

Anthropologists have long been at the forefront of criticizing ideas about race, and, for successive generations, anthropologists have challenged the meaning of the actual concept of race.[1] There is a rich and important history with regard to how generations of anthropologists have moved to a "no-race" position. Although it perhaps began with Boas's earliest critiques, it took on practical political significance during World War II. During the war U.S. anthropologists played important roles in asserting notions of racial equality in the international arena. Gene Weltfish and Ruth Benedict, for example, wrote a pamphlet entitled *The Races of Mankind* (1943) to educate military personnel about the lack of racial differences. Congress, however, denounced the publication as subversive and recalled it after its initial distribution.[2] In the wake of the Jewish Holocaust, M. F. Ashley Montagu chaired the first of two committees of "Experts on Race Problems" for the United Nations Educational, Scientific, and Cultural Organization (UNESCO). The initial committee of scholars issued a *Statement by Experts on Race Problems,* published in 1951. It was a clear and striking declaration, from the foremost authorities, that there was no scientific basis for making racial distinctions. The UNESCO scientists recommended that "it would be better when speaking of human races to drop the term 'race' altogether and speak of ethnic groups."[3] In addition to Montagu, contributors to the UNESCO statement on race included the now-familiar E. Franklin Frazier, Gunnar Myrdal, and Otto Klineberg, as well as other notable scholars such as Claude Lévi-Strauss and Theodosius Dobzhansky.[4]

During the early 1960s politically engaged anthropologists began to team up with population geneticists, like Dobzhansky, to claim that "the employment of the term 'race' [is] inapplicable to most human populations as we find them today."[5] The assertion of racial equality couched in ideas of population genetics became a dominant discourse in anthropology. It is perhaps best typified by Sherwood Washburn's presidential address to the AAA on November 16, 1962. Washburn followed Montagu's position that new studies on population genetics challenged the very idea of biologically based racial distinctions. He concluded by stating: "All kinds of human performance—whether social, athletic, intellectual—are built on genetic and environmental elements. The level of the kinds of performance can be increased by improving the environmental situation so that every genetic constitution may be developed to its full capacity. Any kind of social discrimination against groups of people, whether these are races, castes, or classes, reduces the achievements of our species, of mankind."[6] Although many anthropologists were articulating a strong position with regard to racial equality, Washburn warned that some anthropologists still regarded races as biological types. He suggested that "this kind of anthropology is still alive, amazingly, and in full force in some countries; relics of it are still alive in our teaching today."[7] This was a subtle way of admonishing people like Carleton Coon, who still employed racial taxonomies positioned in something like the "Great Chain of Being."[8] As population geneticists began to question the biological basis for racial classification and cultural anthropologists began to focus on "ethnic groups," the social and historical significance of racial categories was sorely undertheorized.

This movement in anthropology away from race, even as an analytical and conceptual category, led many anthropologists to use ethnicity as the chief organizing principle for exploring human diversity.[9] The use of ethnicity as a surrogate for race tended to euphemize, blur, and even deny how racial categories emerge and persist. More important, by evading race and racism as integral aspects of the United States' experience, it allowed conservatives and well-meaning liberals to advance a romantic ideal of a color-blind society. In chapter 3 I outlined how politicians and pundits appropriated turn-of-the-century anthropology to advance claims about Negro inferiority in a way that reinforced the Jim Crow legislation and the denial of Black men's voting rights. In an interesting way, one hundred years later, an analogous dynamic of appropriation continues.

Fifteen-Cent Monthlies or $2.50 Weeklies: What Difference Does Difference Make?

The cover story of the February 13, 1995, issue of *Newsweek* was entitled "What Color Is Black? Science, Politics and Racial Identity." In a provocative set of articles, the writers and editors of *Newsweek* described race as a "notoriously slippery concept that eludes any serious attempt at definition."[10] Although the authors mentioned that *The Bell*

Curve revived an old controversy about racial inequality, they correctly concluded that "the bottom line, to most scientists working in these fields, is that race is a mere 'social construct'—a gamey mixture of prejudice, superstition and myth."[11] They identified race as a social construct, but they only detailed how biological ideas of race are not appropriate categories and did not adequately illustrate how the social category of race still dictates peoples' lives. In one article, an author suggested that racial categories will eventually not matter by explaining that "what we call people matters a lot less than how we treat them."[12] With articles that discussed the joys and tragedies of biracial families, the end of affirmative action, and a summary of scientists denouncing race as a biological category, the unmistakable editorial position was that racial categories are not particularly useful and that the United States, as a whole, should become more color blind or race neutral.

The authors of this collection of articles turned to biological anthropologists to support this editorial position. Sharon Begley, in "Three Is Not Enough: Surprising New Lessons from the Controversial Science of Race," quoted senior anthropologist C. Loring Brace, who stated that "There is no organizing principle by which you could put 5 billion people into so few categories in a way that would tell you anything important about humankind's diversity."[13] Begley also cited Alan H. Goodman, a biological anthropologist and critical race theorist. Begley first explained how "the notion of race is under withering attack for political and cultural reasons. . . . But scientists got there first. Their doubts about the conventional racial categories—black, white, Asian—have nothing to do with a sappy 'we are all the same' ideology. Just the reverse. 'Human variation is very, very real,' says Goodman. But race, as a way of organizing [what we know about that variation], is incredibly simplified and bastardized.' " *Newsweek* concluded this article by stating that race does not matter and that the best way to understand the meaning and origin of humankind's diversity is to use "a greater number of smaller groupings, like ethnicities."[14]

At one level the editors of *Newsweek* and *Discover* (which ran a similar cover story with an identical editorial position in its November 1994 issue) must be commended for tackling these issues head-on and in a particularly sophisticated manner.[15] In many respects public discourse is catching up with what anthropologists have been writing since the 1940s. *Newsweek* even credits Montagu with pioneering the concept that assuming biological differences have anything to with racial categories is, as the title of his book suggests, *Man's Most Dangerous Myth* (1942).

In other respects, however, the editors of these magazines are selectively appropriating particular aspects of the anthropological discourse on race to bolster the popular ideal of a color-blind, meritocratic society. This particular line of thought is difficult to criticize, yet it has emerged as the rationale for the conservative bloc of the Supreme Court, the so-called California Civil Rights Initiative, and the erosion of minority-majority voting districts.

Although biological categories of race do not exist, social categories persist, and it does not follow that U.S. society is color blind. Advocates for a color-blind society must somehow grapple with the racial disparities that include the fact that a Black baby in 1996 was almost three times as likely as a White baby to be born with no prenatal care and twice as likely to die before it was one year old. Or a Black college graduate was as likely, in 1996, to face unemployment as a White youth who never attended college. During 1996—on any given day—14 Black children under the age of twenty-five were killed by guns, 31 Black babies died before their first birthday, 723 were born into poverty, and virtually half of all Black children were living in poverty. As well, between 1995 and 1996, thirty-nine Black churches were torched.[16] I could, of course, trot out disparities in wages, prison sentencing, unemployment, and many other social indexes, or I could reflect upon the O. J. Simpson trial and the Million Man March to demonstrate that the United States is simply not a color-blind society.

One of the more prominent ways in which high-profile advocates of a color-blind society have been able to explain these racialized disparities in the 1990s is to revive the IQ debate. The gross disparities are putatively explained by the fact that racism has abated (as evidenced by the growing Black middle class), but the reason many individuals have not succeeded is that they have been endowed with bad genes.

Like a Bad Dream: The IQ Debate Is Back

In the early 1970s Arthur R. Jensen was labeled a racist by many members of the academic community because he argued that Black-White differences in IQ scores were caused by genetic differences between the races. Jensen explained that the allegations of racism were misguided because he was only dispassionately and empirically exploring "the scientific theory that there are genetically conditioned mental or behavioral differences between the races."[17] He resigned himself to the fact that his views simply ran counter to public opinion and the political climate of the late 1960s and early 1970s. He even evoked the relationship between *An American Dilemma* and *Brown* to explain: "the civil-rights movement that gained momentum in the 1950s 'required' liberal academic adherence to the theory that the environment was responsible for any individual or racial behavior differences, and the corollary belief in genetic equality in intelligence."[18] In 1994 the scenario was different: Jensen's advisees, Richard Herrnstein and Charles Murray, repackaged his ideas and published *The Bell Curve: Intelligence and Class Structure in American Life* (1994). Although charges of racism were leveled, Herrnstein and Murray were not marginalized the way Jensen had been in the early 1970s. Talk-show hosts and magazine editors afforded Murray (Herrnstein had died) exceptional latitude for expressing his views that racial and class inequalities could be explained by the quality and inequality of genes.

In their controversial book Herrnstein and Murray explained that a high IQ corresponds with "the commonly understood meaning of *smart*."[19] They argued that general intelligence is reflected by Spearman's g, which is defined as "a person's capacity for complex mental work" and constitutes the "broadest conception of intelligence." They suggested that g, IQ, or intelligence can be accurately measured by standard intelligence tests, that IQ is 40 to 80 percent heritable, and that results of IQ tests are relatively stable over an individual's lifetime. They reported that African Americans' IQ scores are significantly lower than White Americans' but then linked those numbers to ideas that low IQ is the cause of social problems such as poverty, crime, unemployment, illegitimacy, welfare dependency, and that high IQ is the only means to success. Alan H. Goodman devised a useful syllogism to summarize the particular logic that underscores the authors' argument:[20]

GENES MAKE BRAINS.
BRAINS MAKE THOUGHTS.
THOUGHTS MAKE BEHAVIORS.
BEHAVIOR MAKES SOCIETIES AND ECONOMIES.

Finally, Herrnstein and Murray posited, the world is rapidly dividing into a cognitive elite and a not-so-cognitive underclass. Persons of low IQ, they suggested, are outbreeding persons of high IQ, and measures, such as the denial of welfare benefits, must be taken to limit the population of people with low IQs in the United States. Their dire warnings are focused as much on class as on race, and they specifically target poor women as virtually the sole culprits for the burgeoning "underclass." For example, they cautioned that: "Three-quarters of all white illegitimate births are to women below average in IQ, and 45 percent are to women with IQs under 90. These women are poorly equipped for the labor market, often poorly equipped to be mothers, and there is no reason to think that the outcomes for their children will be any better than the outcomes have been for black children."[21] They also claimed that nothing can be done to raise IQs and that social programs such as Head Start, Affirmative Action, and AFDC (welfare) are useless.[22] Although they suggested that environmental factors may exist, they stated: "if a culture of poverty is at work, it seems to have influence primarily among women who are of low intelligence."[23] They concluded, *putting it all together, success and failure in the American economy and all that goes with it, are increasingly a matter of the genes that people inherit.*"[24]

The authors' style made the reader feel entitled to claim membership to the cognitive elite by slowly seducing him or her into their nativism, racism, sexism, and classism—cultivating an us-versus-them rhetorical stance. In dozens of places throughout the text they employed the pronoun "we" as a divisive tool. For example, they actually instructed the readers to look at themselves for an example of a person who is a member of the so-called cognitive elite. "You—meaning the self-selected person who has read this far into this book—live in a world that probably looks nothing like the figure [a bell curve that runs from Class V, 'the very dull' to Class I, 'the very bright']. In all likelihood, almost all of your friends and professional associates belong in that top Class I slice."[25]

Herrnstein and Murray were careful not to use outrageous stereotypes, although the researchers they used to support their arguments did not hesitate to do so. The authors' sweeping national policy proposals rested on bold claims fashioned from fragile arguments gleaned from marginal racial theorists and eccentric eugenicists. The authors drew many of their conclusions from racialist research conducted by William Shockley, Arthur Jensen, J. Philippe Rushton, and Robert Gordon.

Rushton is a professor of psychology in Western Ontario and author of *Race, Evolution, and Behavior: A Life History Perspective* (1995). In this book he focused on sexual characteristics, including breast, buttock and genital size, all of which, he stated, are largest in African Americans, middling in Whites, and smallest in Asians. He paid particular attention to penis size to argue that African American men evolved large penises to facilitate "indiscriminate sexuality," which, in an evolutionary scheme, apparently makes up for African Americans' lack of parental care.[26] In an interview with *Rolling Stone Magazine*, Rushton summed up his evolutionary theory: "it's a trade off: more brains or more penis. You can't have everything."[27] Herrnstein and Murray devoted two pages and eleven citations in *The Bell Curve* to defending Rushton: they argued that the Canadian researcher "has strengthened the case for consistently ordered race differences" in intelligence, sexual drive, and levels of parental affection.[28]

Herrnstein and Murray also used the contemporary work of sociologist Robert Gordon at Johns Hopkins University. They supported Gordon's conclusion that "virtually all of the difference in the prevalence of Black and White juvenile delinquents is explained by the IQ difference, independent of the effect of socioeconomic status."[29]

According to Michael Lind, a senior editor of *Harper's,* Shockley, Jensen, Rushton, and Gordon each received hundreds of thousands of dollars from the conservative Pioneer Fund, and, between 1986 and 1990, Rushton alone received $250,000 for his research. In the October 31, 1994, issue of the *New Republic,* Lind explained that the Pioneer Fund had been founded in 1937 with money from textile tycoon Wickliffe Draper, who also underwrote the translation of eugenics texts from German into English. Additionally, the Pioneer Fund provided annual grants to the Federation of American Immigration Reform.[30] In 1994 the federation waged a successful campaign to pass California's Proposition 187, denying public services to undocumented immigrants.

The initial purpose of the Pioneer Fund was to promote "race betterment" through the reproduction of descendants of "white persons who settled in the original thirteen colonies prior to the adoption of the Constitution and/or from related stocks." One of the fund's founders, Frederick H. Osborn, former president of the American Eugenics Society, described Nazi eugenic policy in 1937 as the "most important experiment which has ever been tried."[31] Hiding behind the guise of science, many of the studies the authors of the *Bell Curve* used to support their arguments were not awarded funding by an academic panel of peers.

As *The Bell Curve* hit the stores, the academic community immediately denounced it as a political tract, or what Stephen Jay Gould called a "dreary and scary drumbeat of claims associated with conservative think tanks."[32] Although it never represented the academic discourse on race, it masqueraded as the scientific discourse on race in the mass media.

In important respects, the tremendous response to the book reflected the fact that the "science" of race which influences public opinion does not come solely from the academy. Popular "science" is emerging from privately funded think tanks that are dedicated to formulating policy and shaping public opinion in order to reinforce particular agendas.

Nightline, the morning talk shows, and National Public Radio all featured Charles Murray. The nation's leading newspapers and magazines reviewed the book, and dozens of op-ed pieces and magazine articles explored the merits and mediocrities of the research. Although much of the media was critical of it, the authors' stark portrait of American class structure loomed as a consideration and was given a hearing. *Newsweek* called it "frightening stuff" and explained that it "plays to public anxieties over crime, illegitimacy, welfare dependency, and racial fiction." *Time* reported that the book was "845 pages of provocation-with-footnotes" and a work of "dubious premises and toxic solutions." Support was found along narrow partisan lines. The *National Review* called the book "magisterial" and reported that it "confirms ordinary citizens' reasonable intuition that trying to engineer racial equality in the distribution of occupations and social positions runs against not racist prejudice but nature, which shows no such egalitarian distribution of talents." *Forbes* and the *Wall Street Journal* both gave it positive marks; the Heritage Foundation policy studies, written explicitly for members of Congress, used it to justify welfare reform.[33]

The authors' arguments were not particularly novel: they simply recycled ideas Otto Klineberg had refuted in the 1930s. Nor did they have much influence on the Supreme Court or on Capitol Hill. During the fall of 1994 and the spring of 1995, *The Bell Curve* dominated the public discourse on race at the same time the major parties were defining their respective positions on affirmative action, welfare reform, and minority-majority voting districts and the Supreme Court was deciding on the constitutionality of virtually identical issues. The Court did not cite the work, and Congress did not use it on the House or Senate floor. In this respect *The Bell Curve* was not similar to *An American Dilemma.*

If I had to choose a historic analog for *The Bell Curve,* it would be the film *Birth of a Nation.* In a period of virulent racism, D. W. Griffith cast his narrative about White supremacy as an "authentic" reflection of the historic record for White Americans who were groping for answers about the current state of affairs. Both works should be viewed as pieces of American popular culture that resonate with contemporary fears about people of color.[34]

From the family-friendly Wal-Marts in the U.S. heartland to the tony bookstores in Harvard Square, the Free Press (its publisher) aggressively 'marketed this provocative book. Herrnstein and Murray pitched it not to the academic community or government officials but to the self-identified cognitive elite. The Free Press targeted a market (coveted by conservative talk-show hosts) of individuals hit hard by taxes and down-sizing and looking for easy answers to explain a complicated social land-scape. This same market defined the electorate in November 1994.

The *Bell Curve* hit the stores a month before the 1994 midterm con-gressional elections, in which Republicans won control of Congress for the first time in four decades. Successful Republican campaigns were waged under the banner of the "Contract with America," which in-cluded pithy-sounding legislation like the "Personal Responsibility Act" and the "Take Back Our Streets Act." The Republicans also gained nine-teen House seats across the eleven states of the old Confederacy plus Oklahoma and Kentucky. Of all the White men who voted, 62 percent supported Republican candidates.

The Bell Curve and its logic acted for the electorate as an added jus-tification for restrictive welfare reform. Although the Republican Party framed its reform in terms of engendering family values and lowering taxes, its welfare reform was explicitly designed to remove the subsidy and incentives for so-called illegitimacy, punishing poor women and children. This illegitimacy tactic was inspired by political strategist Charles Murray, before he wrote *The Bell Curve*.[35]

Although a sizable but largely uninformed swath of the American public used *The Bell Curve* rationale to explain racial disparities, the more powerful (in terms of policy and legislation) ideas that were used to explain racial disparities during the mid-1990s came from sociologists who advanced ideas about the declining significance of race and the increasing significance of class.[36] Again, the idea that race is somehow declining in significance bolsters or resonates with agendas that call for a "color-blind" society by eroding affirmative action, dismantling mi-nority-majority voting districts, and impeding efforts to desegregate schools. Social scientists like Faye Harrison, Manning Marable, and Howard Winant, who argue that although race is changing in signifi-cance, racism persists and that is why we need affirmative measures to ensure that opportunities continue, are simply not ceded the same au-thority. The anthropologists who are ceded some authority are the bi-ological anthropologists who argue that races do not exist. The companion thesis that racism persists is jettisoned—in a way (politically very different) similar to what the cultural anthropologists experienced in the 1940s.

As a way of concluding this book, I want to cautiously extend my argument that during periods of racial realignment in the United States particular approaches for understanding race come to the fore and shape public opinion, public policy, and laws and that these approaches tend to justify or quicken the realignment. I am especially intrigued by the way in which notions as diverse as multiculturalism, the declining significance of race, and the IQ redux can all be marshaled under the banner of moving toward a "color-blind" society that erodes the legislative gains made during the Civil Rights movement, which in turn quickens the current realignment.

Since the 1980s the United States has been going through another racial realignment in the way in which people view and experience racial categories. This period has been dominated economically by rapid deindustrialization and equally rapid growth in service, information, and technological production. It is also plagued by fears of downsizing, immigration, crime, and the "underclass."

Images and Realities: African American Race and Class Formation

In the context of a U.S. economy moving from an industrial and manufacturing base to one motored by finance, information, and service, all people of color have been engaged in various processes of class formation that have been influenced by desegregation, affirmative-action programs, and rising numbers of college graduates.[37] As the economy has become increasingly deindustrialized, cities have lost hundreds of thousands of manufacturing jobs and billions of dollars in federal funds. These trends have been augmented by a general pattern of uneven development that has systematically decimated many inner cities and led to an increase in violent crime, infant-mortality rates, high-school dropouts, and drug trafficking.[38] The combination of decomposing inner cities and the loss of high-paying union, manufacturing, and industrial jobs has driven an invisible wedge between the more mobile clerical and professional people of color and the structurally underemployed, underpaid, and unemployed in the inner cities.[39]

Within the African American community a structural rift has developed, accompanied by the construction of two competing images perpetuated primarily in the media. The first image—a positive one—has been formed primarily on prime-time television sitcoms such as *The Cosby Show* and through genuinely positive media personalities such as Oprah Winfrey or newscasters. In addition to television, a myriad of elected and appointed African American public officials are ensconced in popular culture and thus contribute to the idea that "Blacks have made it." This image is reified by an even larger number of upwardly mobile African Americans who are part of the so-called professional middle class.[40]

The second image of African Americans—a negative one—is framed by crime and ideas of the "underclass." This image is produced at movie theaters, on nightly newscasts, and by pundits and politicians who view illegitimacy and crime in terms of an individual's lack of family values.[41] This image of the underclass is almost always couched in terms of the criminal activity of people of color.[42] As a *Time Magazine* cover story put it, "The universe of the underclass is often a junk heap of rotting housing, broken furniture, crummy food, alcohol and drugs."[43] To round out this image, one merely needs to envision the Black male gang member contemplating his next carjacking on a dimly lit street corner riddled with graffiti and littered with garbage, forty-ounce beer bottles, and crack vials—and, of course, listening to rap music lyrics pounding "Fuck tha Police!"

These two opposing images—successful assimilated minority and "gangster–welfare mother"—serve to bifurcate prejudice along class lines, which allows individuals to circumvent specific allegations of individual racial discrimination.[44] This circumvention occurs because the construct of race that is signified by and for poor Blacks is often juxtaposed with the construct signified for and by the amorphous "Black middle class." If one begins to isolate racial inequalities in the criminal justice, welfare, and education systems along racial lines, one need only look to the burgeoning Black middle class to conclude that members of the so-called underclass can pull themselves up by their bootstraps.[45] Nevertheless, the appearance of more people of color in the professions and universities, coupled with growing numbers of unemployed or underemployed Whites due to the shrinking manufacturing and defense industries, creates an illusion that unqualified Blacks and Hispanics are stealing contracts, jobs, and admission spots from more qualified Whites, which of course makes the idea that the United States should move to color-blind contracts, applications, and admissions even more attractive. The complementary illusion is that marginally affluent African

Americans are comfortably middle class. Journalist Leanita McClain, however, explains that she is, like many, "uncomfortably middle class." McClain illustrates the tensions and incongruencies that abound in the lives of many middle-class Blacks: "Sometimes when I wait at the bus stop with my attaché case, I meet my aunt getting off the bus with other cleaning ladies on their way to do my neighbors' floors." She captures these tensions by lamenting her feeling that "I am a member of the black middle class who has had it with being patted on the head by white hands and slapped in the face by black hands for my success."[46]

The interracial-intraclass tensions are often compounded by Whites who impatiently point to the recent progress in racial equality, diversity of institutions, and representational curricula and equally impatient Blacks who counter by pointing to all the inequality that remains. The public tug-of-war has left many White Americans more sanguine about efforts to make the United States more inclusive and many Black Americans more skeptical about making democracy work for all Americans. Poor people and people of color, however, cannot reasonably expect a more inclusive democracy when Rush Limbaugh and his ditto-heads, Newt Gingrich and his army of Republicans, and William H. Rehnquist and his Supreme Court majority envision a better America with eroding affirmative-action programs, draconian welfare reform, punitive immigration policies, erasure of majority-minority congressional districts, and sharp reductions in financial aid and school lunches. The U.S. Congress and the U.S. Supreme Court are the two arenas in which the relationship between the discourses that support arguments for a putative color-blind society and the contemporary racial realignment have been most visible.

Color-Blind Republicans?

In 1985 Ronald Reagan reconstituted the U.S. Civil Rights Commission by appointing Clarence Pendleton Jr. as chair. Pendleton made the commission's number-one priority the investigation of "reverse discrimination." He reassured Reagan that the commission was "working on a color blind society that has opportunities for all and guarantees success for none."[47] The revamping of the Civil Rights Commission was a benchmark in the erosion of strides made by people of color during the Civil Rights movement.

Republicans during the 1980s undertook many initiatives to eliminate any consideration of race in decisions for hiring, promotion, state-college admissions, and contract procurement as an effort to make up for past inequities. One of the most successful ways they have reinforced these initiatives has been to appropriate the rhetoric of the Civil Rights movement. After all, it was the Rev. Dr. Martin Luther King, Jr. who had a dream that his children would be judged solely on the "content of their character." From Reagan's Civil Rights Commission in the 1980s to the California Civil Rights Initiative in the 1990s, neoconservatives have rearticulated the notion of racial equality by emphasizing equality of opportunity—not outcome.[48] Simultaneously, less conservative interests succeeded in promoting notions of multiculturalism and ethnic diversity, but this has conflated race with ethnicity, blurred racial disparities, and done little for poor people of color. The changing politics of race are not limited to assaults by Republicans; the Democrats have also used the palatable idea of a color-blind society to further their agenda. By itself, affirmative action is a political wedge; however, taken with the challenges of minority-majority congressional districts, it is a political double-edged sword that has eviscerated the Democratic Party along racial lines, adding another dimension to the changing politics of race. If Republicans' vociferous challenges of affirmative-action programs is put alongside their tacit consent to minority-majority voting districts, the true partisan nature of efforts to dismantle affirmative action becomes clear.

Opponents of affirmative action have illustrated its perils with regard to school admissions, contracting, and employment, but they have been conspicuously silent about the so-called perils of minority-majority congressional districts drawn after the 1990 decennial census. The explicit creation of minority-majority districts helped to nearly double the African American representation in Congress, arguably one of the nation's best affirmative-action programs. Although the Republican leadership wanted to achieve a color-blind society by dismantling affirmative-action programs, generally it did not want to dismantle the color-conscious congressional districts—Supreme Court Justice Sandra Day O'Connor declared that it "bears an uncomfortable resemblance to political apartheid."[49]

There are two reasons why Republicans did not link the debates about affirmative action and racial redistricting and did not incorporate the so-called perils of racial gerrymandering into their arguments for a color-blind society. First, the same political and legislative thicket that gave rise, in 1992, to the largest African American delegation to Congress also contributed to the rise of a Republican majority in Congress in 1994 and, specifically, to its stronghold in the South. David Lublin, a political scientist at the University of South Carolina, provides a conservative calculation that between six and nine House seats shifted from Democrat to Republican control since 1990 as a direct result of the creation of safe minority districts in the South.[50] In 1995 Georgia's racially polarized, eleven-member congressional delegation exemplified these dynamics: the eight Republicans were White, and the three Democrats were Black.

The second reason why members of the Republican Party did not address the quotas used for redistricting mirrors the reasons why they attacked so-called quotas with regard to affirmative action. The formation of minority-majority congressional districts formed a wedge issue in the Democratic Party. The Democratic Party was forced to grapple with the harsh reality that minority-majority districts in the South increased minority representation but decreased Democrats' overall representation in Congress.

In most of the redistricting cases the plaintiffs who challenged the constitutionality of minority-majority districts were activists within the Democratic Party. These plaintiffs were motivated by the fact that racial redistricting reduces the number of Democrats in their states' delegation to Washington. They successfully posed legal arguments that drawing congressional districts by "computerized hunting for concentrations of blacks" creates "bizarre and tortured" districts that violate the equal-protection clause. Like the affirmative-action debate, Blacks were pitted against Whites in an already fractured Democratic Party. On the last day of the Supreme Court's 1994–1995 term it ruled 5–4 that using race as a predominant factor for drawing congressional districts was unconstitutional.[51]

A Color-Blind Court!

The Court's most activist decisions during its 1994–1995 term concerned how the government could use racial classifications; it also struck down congressional term limits and allowed a veterans' group to deny a gay, lesbian, and bisexual group a spot in its St. Patrick's Day parade. With three disjointed opinions delivered in June 1995, the Court effectively dismantled hard-won measures of the Civil Rights movement. Affirmative action, court-ordered school desegregation, and minority-majority congressional districts were all hobbled by narrow 5–4 majorities.

The Court's conservative majority, consisting of Chief Justice William H. Rehnquist, Antonin Scalia, Clarence Thomas, and, often, Sandra Day O' Connor and Anthony Kennedy, practiced a form of judicial activism that ostensibly ensured that the Constitution remained color blind. On its face it sounded ideal; however, the effect of this bloc's interpretation of the Fourteenth Amendment proved constitutional scholar Derrick Bell's axiom that "racial patterns adapt in ways that maintain white dominance."[52]

As in 1896 and 1954, in 1995 the Supreme Court used its interpretation of the Fourteenth Amendment to change the significance of race under the U.S. Constitution. Since *Brown*, the Court had held that the federal government should play a special role in redressing past state-sponsored racism—but no longer.

The *New York Times* headlined "Farewell to the Old Order in the Court" and explained how "the birth struggle of a new era is not a pretty sight. It is messy, it is unstable, it is riveting."[53] Many newspapers and magazines noted the sweeping changes the Court made during its 1994–1995 term, specifically with regard to racial issues. The *Atlanta Constitution* headlined "Blacks fear return to 'dark days of the 19th Century' " and declared that the Court "pulled the rug out from under gains they have made from courthouse to Congress in the last 30 years."[54] The *New York Times'* depiction of a "new era" in race relations is particularly cogent because it captured how social and political transformations combined with the actions of the Court and Congress are contributing to a racial realignment.

Representative Major Owens (Democrat from New York) outlined the role of the federal legislative branch in this new era. From the well of the House he explained, "When you combine an assault on affirmative action with a Republican Contract With America, you create a kind of scorched earth approach to the reordering of our society. Government by an elite minority, for the benefit of the elite minority, becomes the driving philosophy. . . . [N]ow they want to spread, use that power to spread a racist, anti-immigrant brew throughout the minds of America, to poison the minds of the American voters."[55]

The Supreme Court's role in this new era of race relations can be viewed by its 1994–1995 term. In *Adarand Constructors v. Peña* (No. 93–1841) the Court ruled that federal affirmative-action programs, specifically a minority set-aside provision in a federal highway-contracting program, must be held to the same strict scrutiny standard as state and local programs. Writing for the Court, Sandra Day O'Connor declared that her decision to vacate the judgment of the court of appeals was "derive[d] from the basic principle that the Fifth and Fourteenth Amendments to the Constitution protect *persons*, not *groups*."[56] Citing *Korematsu*, she explained: "Any retreat from the most searching judicial inquiry can only increase the risk of another such error occurring in the future."[57] Justice Clarence Thomas wrote a concurring opinion, and he declared that "as far as the Constitution is concerned, it is irrelevant whether a government's racial classifications are drawn by those who wish to oppress a race or by those who have a sincere desire to help those thought to be disadvantaged." He concluded: "In my mind, government sponsored racial discrimination based on benign prejudice is just as noxious as discrimination inspired by malicious prejudice. In each instance, it is racial discrimination, plain and simple."[58] Justice Stevens, in his dissent, blasted the Court's majority: "There is no moral or constitutional equivalence between a policy that is designed to perpetuate a caste system and one that seeks to eradicate racial subordination. Invidious discrimination is an engine of oppression, subjugating a disfavored group to enhance or maintain the power of the majority. Remedial race-based preferences reflect the opposite impulse: a desire to foster equality in society."[59]

Although the *Adarand* decision did not eliminate all federal affirmative-action programs, it outlined that the government is not allowed to develop programs to ameliorate past discrimination. In another Court action, it allowed a circuit court decision to stand that invalidated the University of Maryland scholarship program for outstanding African American scholars.

With the same division, the Court ruled in *Missouri v. Jenkins* (No. 93–1823) that a federal district court in Missouri had improperly ordered the state to pay for a desegregation plan for Kansas City's schools. This case related directly to the social science used in *Brown*. After *Brown*, neither the state of Missouri nor the Kansas City Missouri School District (KCMSD) dismantled its Jim Crow schools. Twenty years after *Brown*, thirty-nine of KCMSD's seventy-seven schools had student bodies that were more than 90 percent Black, and a full 80 percent of Black schoolchildren in the district attended these schools. In 1984, thirty years after *Brown*, the district court found that KCMSD had failed to reform its segregated pubic schools. The district court concluded that both the state and the school district had "defaulted in their obligation to uphold the Constitution."[60] However, during the time it took to finally order desegregation, few White students were left in the inner-city district to integrate the schools. With uneven development and many middle-class Whites and Blacks moving to the suburbs, the court devised a interdistrict desegregation plan to increase the "desegregative attractiveness" of the district by reversing what the court called white flight to the suburbs. The court-ordered plan amounted to creating an entire magnet school district. The Supreme Court ruled in 1995, forty-one years after *Brown*, however, that the district court had exceeded its authority.

Although Thurgood Marshall, Robert Carter, and Kenneth Clark strategically used Gunnar Myrdal's and E. Franklin Frazier's ideas about the Negro's pathological culture during the late 1940s, Clarence Thomas exploited the problematic nature of this research to write a persuasive concurring opinion that forcefully articulated the Court's color-blind agenda. Thomas outlined how "the [lower] court has read our cases to support the theory that black students suffer an unspecified psychological harm from segregation that retards their mental and educational development. This approach not only relies upon questionable social science research rather than constitutional principle, but it also rests on an assumption of black inferiority."[61] As I noted in my introduction, by criticizing the work done by the Howard circle some sixty years earlier, Thomas advanced somewhat contradictory ideas that Black people do not need White people, quality schools, or government intervention. Thomas framed this important opinion by stating, "It never ceases to amaze me that the courts are so willing to assume that anything that is predominantly black must be inferior. . . . The mere fact that a school is black does not mean that it is the product of a constitutional violation."[62]

The district court that oversaw the desegregation order of the Kansas City schools cited *Brown* as its rationale that a racial imbalance in the school system constituted a constitutional violation that harmed African American children. Justice Thomas found this citation inimical to the principles of the Constitution and directly challenged *Brown* — what has come to be viewed as a sacred American text.[63] Thomas assumed that the district court's position "appears to rest upon the idea that any school that is black is inferior, and that blacks cannot succeed without the benefit of the company of whites." He substantiated this assumption by purporting: "The District Court's willingness to adopt such stereotypes stemmed from a misreading of our earliest school desegregation case. In *Brown v. Board of Education* the Court noted several psychological and sociological studies purporting to show that *de jure* segregation harmed black students by generating 'a feeling of inferiority' in them. Seizing upon this passage in *Brown*, . . . the District Court suggested that this inequality continues in full force even after the end of *de jure* segregation."[64]

Although Thomas was quick to point out that "under this theory, segregation injures blacks because blacks, when left on their own, cannot achieve," he failed to explain that this theoretical perspective is more than sixty years old and that there were various political reasons why the LDEF chose to employ this particular type of social science. He simply explained: "to my way of thinking, that conclusion [in *Brown*] is the result of a jurisprudence based upon a theory of black inferiority."[65] Although I discussed this in my introduction, I want to reiterate it in the conclusion. By only using the term "black," Thomas skillfully blurred the line between race and culture. He sidestepped explaining how that rationale in *Brown* was based on the ideas of racial equality and cultural pathology, and he merely collapsed the concepts of race and culture into a commonsense understanding of "black inferiority."

Finally, by disparaging half-century-old social science, Thomas essentially muzzled contemporary social theorists who attempt to contribute to the juridical discourse on race, even in the lower courts. He decreed with sweeping authority that "the lower courts should not be swayed by the easy answers of social science, nor should they accept the findings, and the assumptions, of sociology and psychology at the price of constitutional principle."[66]

The Court did not stop at affirmative action and school segregation; it ruled to invalidate congressional districts that were drawn to include a majority of racial minorities in its boundaries. In *Miller v. Johnson* (94–631) it invalidated Georgia's 11th Congressional District, which had been created to produce another majority-Black district. Using the same color-blind principle as O'Connor in *Adarand*, Justice Kennedy explained that

the Equal Protection Clause of the Fourteenth Amendment provides that no State shall deny to any person within its jurisdiction the equal protection of the laws. Its central mandate is racial neutrality in governmental decision making. Though application of this imperative raises difficult questions, the basic principle is straightforward: Racial and ethnic distinctions of any sort are inherently suspect and thus call for the most exacting judicial examination. . . . This rule obtains with equal force regardless of the race of those burdened or benefitted by a particular classification.[67]

The principle of a color-blind Constitution that the conservative bloc of the Supreme Court used to challenge district-court desegregation orders, minority-majority voting districts, and federal affirmative action indeed mirrors the editorial position of the special issues of *Time* and *Discover* I discussed previously, and it clearly refracts or resonates with other sources of news and commentary that evade racial constructs and the many forms of racism. Of course this is a difficult and contradictory position to take. One must weigh reifying vacuous categories whose logic stems from a history of dehumanization against the ability to identify racism, and weigh the sloppiness of racial categories against supporting pundits and politicians who promote a so-called color-blind society that rolls back important strides. Although disregarding race is logically accurate and theoretically sound in terms of biological categories, it is historically, socially, and politically problematic. It disregards the complex processes of racial formation and evades racism.

During the 1990s certain anthropologists began to advance critical race theories and began to address the complexity of persisting forms of racialization and racism.[68] However, these anthropologists are rarely featured in *Newsweek* or on *Nightline*. What is fascinating to me is the fact that the news media appropriate or skillfully subvert progressive biological anthropologists' arguments about the inanity of the biological concept of race to advance a vulgar, color-blind agenda. Critical cultural anthropologists are rarely called on to explain that even though a biological category of race is meaningless, the social category of race is very real, meaningful, and still dictates life chances and opportunities.[69] In many respects this is precisely how anthropologists were used in the 1950s. Biological anthropologists were used as influential spokespersons to argue that Blacks were not racially inferior to Whites, but cultural anthropologists were not used to explain how African American culture is rich, unique, and just as "legitimate" as any other culture in the United States.

This historical narrative raises more questions than it answers. What does it tell us about history, culture, and power? How does it help us answer historical and contemporary questions about law and legitimacy for a nation constructed in the image of democratic ideals but characterized by the divisive and explosive politics of race, culture, authenticity, and traditional values? Can anthropologists contribute to a meaningful progressive discourse in the United States? And why have anthropologists failed to bring the lessons learned abroad home to help expose problems in the United States?

There is one issue that this narrative clearly demonstrates: the scholarly critique of ideas of biological categories of race has not successfully curbed the political force of ideas of racial inferiority, which is evidenced by overwhelming response to *The Bell Curve*. Although fundamentally different, the anthropological discourse on race has been selectively appropriated for various political agendas that have shaped the meaning of race in the United States for the last century.

There are no easy answers. The public, academic, political, and juridical discourses on race converge and overlap, but each is created in political struggle. Such is politics. Anthropology is not exempt. Anthropologists have consistently engaged in advancing a liberating political agenda in the United States even though, as this narrative suggests, national politics often limits their impact. Anthropologists and other scholars must nonetheless continue to advance research that exposes the contradictions in U.S. society in an effort to reconcile the ideal of racial equality with the nagging, persistent, and seemingly perpetual forms of oppression.

Appendix

Time Line of Major Events

This cursory time line should help locate writings and events I discuss within a larger historical framework.

YEAR	NATIONAL EVENTS	EVENTS INFLUENCING ANTHROPOLOGY
1886	Haymarket Square Riot	D. G. Brinton appointed professor at the University of Pennsylvania
1887	Dawes Servility Act	F. W. Putnam appointed professor at Harvard University; F. Boas initiates museum debates in *Science*
1888	B. Harrison elected president	J. W. Powell elected president of the American Association for the Advancement of Science; Boas founds the American Folk-Lore Society
1889		F. Boas joins the faculty at Clark University
1890	Democrats win control of Congress; Massacre at Wounded Knee	D. G. Brinton's *Races and Peoples* and N. S. Shaler's "Science and the African Problem" published

YEAR	NATIONAL EVENTS	EVENTS INFLUENCING ANTHROPOLOGY
1892	G. Cleveland reelected president; Homestead Strike; 241 African Americans murdered by lynch mobs	F. Starr appointed assistant professor of anthropology at the University of Chicago
1893	Financial "Panic"	World's Fair, Chicago: anthropology introduced to the American public as popular culture
1894	Pullman Strike	D. G. Brinton elected president of the American Association for the Advancement of Science; F. W. Putnam appointed curator of anthropology at the American Museum of Natural History; F. Boas speaks on "Human Faculty as Determined by Race" before the American Association for the Advancement of Science and helps organize the Hampton Folklore Society
1895	B. T. Washington's "Atlanta Compromise" speech at the Cotton States and International Exposition	D. G. Brinton speaks on "The Aims of Anthropology" before the American Association for the Advancement of Science
1896	W. McKinley elected president; the Supreme Court decides *Plessy v. Ferguson*	F. L. Hoffman's *Race Traits and Tendencies of the American Negro,* F. A. Walker's "Immigration Restriction," and F. Boas's "The Limitations of the Comparative Method" published; F. Boas joins the staff of the American Museum of Natural History and becomes a lecturer at Columbia University

YEAR	NATIONAL EVENTS	EVENTS INFLUENCING ANTHROPOLOGY
1897	W. McKinley inaugurated president	F. Starr's "The Degeneracy of the American Negro" appears; W. E. B. Du Bois publishes "The Conservation of Races" and is appointed to the faculty of Atlanta University
1898	Spanish-American War; occupation of Cuba, Samoa, and the Philippines	F. W. Putnam elected president of the American Association for the Advancement of Science
1899	T. Roosevelt writes *The Rough Riders* in a serial for *Scribner's*	WJ McGee's "The Trend of Human Progress," T. Veblen's *The Theory of the Leisure Class,* and W. E. B. Du Bois's *The Philadelphia Negro* published; F. Boas becomes a professor at Columbia University
1900	The United States annexes Hawaii; I. B. Wells-Barnett's *Mob Rule in New Orleans* published	F. Boas becomes president of the American Folk-Lore Society
1901	W. McKinley assassinated; T. Roosevelt assumes the presidency; F. Norris's *The Octopus* published; T. Roosevelt dines with B. T. Washington	F. Galton delivers "The Possible Improvement of the Human Breed under the Existing Conditions of Law and Sentiment" as his Huxley Lecture to the British Anthropological Institution, which is reprinted in *Nature* and *Popular Science Monthly;* the U.S. eugenics movement initiated
1903	W. E. B. Du Bois's *The Souls of Black Folk* published	A. Hrdlička becomes assistant curator of physical anthropology at the U.S. National Museum

YEAR	NATIONAL EVENTS	EVENTS INFLUENCING ANTHROPOLOGY
1904	T. Roosevelt's first presidential campaign; riot in Statesboro, Ga.; Louisiana Purchase Exposition, St. Louis; *Lochner v. New York*	
1905	W. E. B. Du Bois organizes the Niagara Movement	Ota Benga, from Zaire, exhibited at the Bronx Zoo
1906	Riot in Brownsville, Ga.; U. Sinclair's *The Jungle* published; Meat Inspection Act; Pure Food and Drug Act	F. Boas delivers the commencement address at Atlanta University; R. B. Bean's "The Negro Brain" published
1907	F. Ziegfeld begins his annual Ziegfeld Follies	F. Boas's "The Anthropological Position of the Negro" and B. R. Tillman's "The Race Question" published
1908	*Muller v. Oregon*	F. Boas becomes editor of the *Journal of American Folk-Lore* and holds the position for the next 15 years
1909	M. W. Ovington organizes the National Association for the Advancement of Colored People	F. Boas's "Industries of African Negroes" published
1910		F. Boas's "The Real Race Problem" published; A. Hrdlička appointed curator at the U.S. National Museum
1911	M. W. Ovington's *Half a Man* appears	F. Boas's *The Mind of Primitive Man* appears
1912	T. Roosevelt organizes the Progressive ("Bull Moose") Party; W. Wilson elected president; R. Pound's "The Scope and Purpose of Sociological Jurisprudence" published	

YEAR	NATIONAL EVENTS	EVENTS INFLUENCING ANTHROPOLOGY
1914	W. Wilson segregates federal agencies; the National Association for the Advancement of Colored People responds by issuing a terse statement; World War I begins	F. Boas's "Mythology and Folk-Tales of the North American Indians" appears
1915	The Ku Klux Klan officially incorporated and reorganized; D. W. Griffith's *The Birth of a Nation* released; B. T. Washington dies	
1916	W. Wilson reelected president	Anthropology Committee organized at the National Research Council
1917	*Buchanan v. Warley;* race riot in East St. Louis; the United States enters World War I	*Journal of American Folk-Lore* issues its first "Negro Number"; the National Association for the Advancement of Colored People marches on Manhattan
1918	W. E. B. Du Bois writes "Close Ranks"; C. Davenport and M. Grant organize the Galton Society	A. Hrdlička founds the *American Journal of Physical Anthropology;* P. Popenoe and R. H. Johnson found *Applied Genetics*
1919	New York's 15th Infantry marches on Manhattan	F. Boas publishes "Scientists as Spies" and is censured by the American Anthropological Association; E. C. Parsons's "The Provenience of Certain Negro Folk-Tales" appears
1920	Nineteenth Amendment (women's suffrage) ratified; W. G. Harding becomes president; Senate rejects the Treaty of Versailles	

YEAR	NATIONAL EVENTS	EVENTS INFLUENCING ANTHROPOLOGY
1921		E. C. Parsons's "Folk Lore from Aiken, South Carolina" published; A. Hrdlička speaks on eugenics at American University
1922		A. E. Perkins's "Riddles from Negro School Children in New Orleans, La." appears
1923	W. G. Harding dies; C. Coolidge assumes the presidency	C. G. Woodson and F. Boas organize Negro folklore contest
1924	Immigration Restriction Act	
1925	A. Locke's *The New Negro* published	
1926	M. Johnson appointed president of Howard University	
1927		A. H. Fauset's "Negro Folk Tales from the South" and E. F. Frazier's "Is the Negro Family a Unique Sociological Unit?" appear
1928	Black organizations support A. Smith for president; northern Republicans woo southern White Republicans in the presidential campaign	M. Mead publishes *Coming of Age in Samoa*
1929	H. Hoover becomes president; the stock market crashes and the Great Depression ensues; W. White's *Rope and Faggot* appears; C. H. Houston appointed dean of Howard School of Law	A. Hrdlička establishes the American Association of Physical Anthropologists; W. M. Cobb enters Case Western Reserve University to study physical anthropology and anatomy

YEAR	NATIONAL EVENTS	EVENTS INFLUENCING ANTHROPOLOGY
1930	C. E. Hughes appointed Chief Justice; the National Association for the Advancement of Colored People blocks J. J. Parker's nomination to the Court	Z. N. Hurston's "Dance Songs and Tales from the Bahamas" published
1931	W. White appointed executive director of the National Association for the Advancement of Colored People	A. H. Fauset's *Folklore from Nova Scotia*, Z. N. Hurston's "Hoodoo in America," and A. R. Radcliffe-Brown's *The Social Organization of Australian Tribes* published
1932	F. D. Roosevelt elected president	
1933	Legislation passed for the Tennessee Valley Authority; the National Recovery Act established; T. Marshall graduates from Howard School of Law	
1934		C. H. Houston and J. P. Davis's "TVA: Lily-White Reconstruction" and R. Benedict's *Patterns of Culture* appear
1935	Antilynching bill fails in the Senate; Italy invades Ethiopia; Z. N. Hurston's *Mules and Men* published	C. H. Houston becomes chief counsel for the National Association for the Advancement of Colored People, and his "Educational Inequalities Must Go" appears; W. White meets with F. D. Roosevelt, who backs down from supporting the antilynching bill

YEAR	NATIONAL EVENTS	EVENTS INFLUENCING ANTHROPOLOGY
1936	A. Hitler snubs J. Owens in the Berlin Olympic Games; F. D. Roosevelt reelected; *Schechter Poultry Corp. v. United States; Murray v. Maryland; United States v. Butler*	
1937	F. D. Roosevelt's court-packing plan proposed	
1938	*Missouri ex rel. Gaines v. Canada;* G. Myrdal begins research on the Negro problem for the Carnegie Corporation	
1939	F. Frankfurter joins the Supreme Court; Germany invades Poland	The Legal Defense Fund of the National Association for the Advancement of Colored People becomes a separate, tax-exempt organization, with T. Marshall as director; W. M. Cobb's "The Negro as a Biological Element of the American Population" published
1940	Germany invades Scandinavia and France; F. D. Roosevelt reelected to a third term; E. Hemingway's *For Whom the Bell Tolls* and R. Wright's *Native Son* appear	
1941	F. D. Roosevelt issues Executive Order 8802, ending employment discrimination in the defense industry; the United States declares war on Japan	
1942	F. D. Roosevelt issues Executive Order 9066, establishing military areas for Japanese Americans	F. Boas dies

YEAR	NATIONAL EVENTS	EVENTS INFLUENCING ANTHROPOLOGY
1943	Allies invade Italy	
1944	*Smith v. Allwright*	G. Myrdal's *An American Dilemma* appears
1945	F. D. Roosevelt dies; atomic bombs dropped; Japan and Germany surrender	S. C. Drake and H. R. Cayton publish *Black Metropolis*
1946	H. S. Truman forms the President's Commission on Civil Rights	
1947	The President's Commission on Civil Rights Report, *To Secure These Rights,* issued	
1948	H. S. Truman desegregates federal agencies, including the military; *Shelley v. Kraemer*	
1949	Berlin Airlift; People's Republic of China established	
1950	J. R. McCarthy begins anti-communist crusade; *Sweatt v. Painter, McLaurin v. Oklahoma State Regents for Higher Education*	
1951		E. E. Evans-Pritchard's *Kinship and Marriage among the Nuer* published
1952	D. D. Eisenhower elected president	
1954	McCarthy hearings; *Brown v. Board of Education*	
1955	R. Parks refuses to give up her seat on a bus; M. L. King Jr. launches Montgomery Bus Strike	

Notes

Introduction

1. The Fourteenth Amendment to the Constitution of the United States was ratified in 1868. It was designed to restrain state governments from abridging the rights of former slaves after the Civil War, but it has been used to extend most of the personal liberties and rights granted in the Bill of Rights to protection against infringement by state governments. Although the amendment itself defines citizenship and restrains states from abridging the privileges or immunities of a citizen, it requires "due process of law" and "equal protection of the laws" for persons under its jurisdiction and reduces representation in Congress for states that deny voting rights. It also disqualified certain officials from the former Confederacy from certain offices and invalidated any war debts of the Confederate States. The changing significance of race in the United States seems to become incorporated into changing interpretations of this amendment. Whether the Court upholds racial segregation of public facilities in the 1890s, mandates the desegregation of public schools in the 1950s, or limits affirmative action in the 1990s, the Fourteenth Amendment is often the constitutional battleground.

2. Audrey Smedley, *Race in North America: Origin and Evolution of a Worldview* (Boulder, Colo.: Westview Press, 1993); Howard Winant, *Racial Conditions: Politics, Theory, Comparisons* (Minneapolis: University of Minnesota Press, 1994); Sandra Harding, *The "Racial" Economy of Science: Toward a Democratic Future* (Bloomington: Indiana University Press, 1993); Studs Terkel, *Race: How Blacks and Whites Think and Feel about the American Obsession* (New York: New Press, 1992); William A. Thomas, ed., *Science and Law: An Essential Alliance* (Boulder, Colo.: Westview Press, 1993); Derrick Bell, *Faces at the Bottom of the Well: The Permanence of Racism* (New York: Basic Books, 1992).

3. Winant, *Racial Conditions*, 13–21.

4. Faye V. Harrison, "The Persistent Power of 'Race' in the Cultural and Political Economy of Racism," *Annual Review of Anthropology* 24 (1995): 48.

5. Ibid.; Faye V. Harrison, ed., *Decolonizing Anthropology: Moving Further toward an Anthropology for Liberation* (Washington, D.C.: American Anthropological Association, 1991); Steven Gregory and Roger Sanjek, eds., *Race* (New Brunswick, N.J.: Rutgers University Press, 1994); Leonard Lieberman and Fatimah Linda C. Jackson, "Race and Three Models of Human Origin," *American Anthropologist* 97 (1995): 231–242.

6. Harrison, "Persistent Power of 'Race,' " 53.

7. Richard J. Herrnstein and Charles Murray, *The Bell Curve: Intelligence and Class Structure in American Life* (New York: Free Press, 1994).

8. *Missouri v. Jenkins*, Concur: 1–2.

9. Dinesh D'Souza, *The End of Racism: Principles for a Multiracial Society* (New York: Free Press, 1995).

10. Ibid., 18.

11. Ibid., 142–196.

12. Ibid., 19.

13. Ibid., 194.

Chapter 1

1. Audrey Smedley describes the term *race* as a symbol for a particular "cosmological ordering system" that developed from political, economic, and social dynamics produced by people who colonized and conquered the world in a quest for wealth and power (Smedley, *Race in North America*, 25). She makes a persuasive argument that race, as a worldview, is composed of "ideological ingredients" or constituent elements that can be isolated and analyzed socially and historically in an effort to map the shift from an ideological system of folk beliefs and prejudices to a systematic view of the world structured by laws and rationalized by science. Smedley identifies five constituent elements that, taken together, form the basis of a flexible and infinitely expandable construct of race. Her elegant summary of these elements warrants reproducing:

The first and most basic was a universal classification of human groups as exclusive and discrete biotic entities. The classifications were not based on objective variations in language or culture, but were categories that eclipsed these attributes and included superficial assessments and value judgements of phenotypic and behavioral variations. The categories were arbitrary and subjective and often concocted from the impressions, sometimes fanciful, of remote observers. A second element . . . was the imposition of an inegalitarian ethos that required the ranking of these groups vis-à-vis one another. Ranking was an intrinsic, and explicit, aspect of the classifying process, having derived from an ancient model of the Great Chain of Being (a hierarchical structure of all living things) that had been readapted to eighteenth-century realities.

A third constituent element was the belief that the outer physical characteristics of different human populations were but surface manifestations of inner realities, in other words, the cognitive linking of physical features with behavior, intellectual, temperamental, moral, and other qualities. Thus, what most scholars recognize today as cultural (learned)behavior was seen as an innate concomitant of biophysical form. A fourth element was the notion that all of these qualities were inheritable—the biophysical characteristics, the cultural or behavioral features and capabilities, and the social rank allocated to each group by the belief system itself. Finally, perhaps the most critical element of all was the belief that each exclusive group (race) so differentiated was created unique and distinct by nature or by God, so that the imputed differences, believed fixed and unalterable, could never be bridged or transcended. (Smedley, *Race in North America*, 27)

2. Ibid., 49.

3. Ibid., 60–87.

4. Ibid., 81.

5. Ibid., 96.

6. Ibid., 171; Thomas Gossett, *Race: The History of an Idea*, 4th ed. (New York: Schocken Books, 1970 [1963]); David Bakan, "The Influence of Phrenology on American Psychology," *Journal of the History of the Behavioral Sciences* 2, no. 2 (1966): 200–220; John C. Greene, *Science, Ideology, and World View* (Berkeley: University of California Press, 1981); William A. Tucker, *The Science and Politics of Racial Research* (Urbana: University of Illinois Press, 1994); J. S. Sloktin, "Racial Classifications of the Seventeenth and Eighteenth Centuries," *Transactions of the Wisconsin Academy of Sciences* 36 (1944): 459–467; Herbert Hovenkamp, "Social Science and Segregation before Brown," *Duke Law Journal* 1985: 624–672.

7. Thomas Jefferson became one of the leading intellectuals in the new republic who articulated scientific ideas of Indian and Negro inferiority. Although tentative and often contradictory, his writings were consistently evoked—well into the nineteenth century—to reinforce the idea that racial inferiority was simply natural (see Smedley, *Race in North America*, 196).

8. Ibid., 205.

9. George Stocking, *Race, Culture, and Evolution: Essays in the History of Anthropology* (New York: Free Press, 1968), 47; Charles Darwin, *On the Origin of Species by Means of Natural Selection* (New York: New York University Press, 1988 [1859]).

10. Stocking, *Race, Culture, and Evolution*, 144.

11. Smedley, *Race in North America*, 239; Josiah Nott and George R. Gliddon, *Types of Mankind* (Philadelphia: Lippincott, Grambo), 1854.

12. Derrick Bell, ed., *Civil Rights: Leading Cases* (Boston: Little, Brown, 1980), 7; Smedley, *Race in North America*, 248. Priscilla Wald makes an excellent comparison between *Scott v. Sandford* (1854) and *Cherokee Nation v. Georgia* (1831). The Court decided it had no jurisdiction to hear the 1831 case because it found that Indians were not members of an alien nation (for Article III purposes). The Court similarly decided that it had no jurisdiction to hear the 1854 case because it found that Negroes were not citizens. Wald argues that both cases "attempt to legislate the disappearances of the 'Indians' and the 'descendants of Africans,' respectively, by judging them neither citizens nor aliens and therefore not legally representable. In so doing, however, these cases call attention to the symbolic processes through which the United States constitutes subjects: how Americans are made" (Priscilla Wald, "Terms of Assimilation: Legislating Subjectivity in the Emerging Nation," in *Cultures of United States Imperialism* [Durham, N.C.: Duke University Press, 1993], 59).

13. Stephen Jay Gould, *The Mismeasure of Man* (New York: Norton, 1981), 45.

14. Smedley, *Race in North America*, 252, 28.

15. The long and intimate relationship between science and racial categories in the United States and Europe dates to the Enlightenment. Many scholars have explored various aspects of the relationship between science and racial categories, slavery, and colonialism before the twentieth century. Among them are Smedley, *Race in North America;* Bakan, "Influence of Phrenology"; Michael P. Banton, *The Idea of Race* (London: Tavistock, 1977); Philip D. Curtin, *The Image of Africa: British Ideas and Action, 1780–1850* (Madison: University of Wisconsin Press, 1964); Carl N. Degler, "Slavery and the Genesis of American Race Prejudice," *Comparative Studies in Society and History* 2, no. 1 (1960): 49–66; Barbara J. Fields, "Slavery, Race and Ideology in the United States," *New Left Review* 181 (1990): 95–128; George M. Fredrickson, *The Black Image in the White Mind* (Middletown, Conn.: Wesleyan University Press, 1971); Gossett, *Race*; Gould, *Mismeasure of Man;* Greene, *Science, Ideology, and World View;* John S. Haller, *Outcasts from Evolution: Scientific Attitudes of Racial Inferiority, 1859–1900* (Chicago: University of Illinois Press, 1971); Winthrop J. Jordan, *White over Black: American Attitudes toward the Negro, 1150–1812* (Chapel Hill: University of North Carolina Press, 1968); Joel Kovel, *White Racism, a Psychohistory* (New York: Pantheon Books, 1970); Leonard P. Liggio, "English Origins of Early American Racism," *Radical History Review* 3 (1976): 1–36; Arthur Lovejoy, *The Great Chain of Being* (Cambridge, Mass.: Harvard University Press, 1936); Dorothy Ross, *The Origins of American Social Science* (New York: Cambridge University Press, 1991); Alexander Saxton, *The Rise and Fall of the White Republic: Class Politics and Mass Culture in Nineteenth-Century America* (London: Verso, 1990); Walter Scheidt, "The Concept of Race in Anthropology and the Divisions into Human Races, from Linnaeus to Deniker," in *This Is Race,* ed. E. Count (New York: Henry Schuman, 1950), 354–391; Sloktin, "Racial Classifications"; William Ragan Stanton, *The Leopard's Spots: Scientific Attitudes toward Race in America, 1815–1859* (Chicago: University of Chicago Press, 1960); Joel Williamson, *The Crucible of Race* (New York: Oxford University Press, 1984); C. Vann Woodward, *The Strange Career of Jim Crow* (New York: Oxford University Press, 1957 [1955]).

16. Eric Foner, *Reconstruction: America's Unfinished Revolution, 1863–1877* (New York: Harper and Row, 1988), 276–283.

17. W. E. B. Du Bois, *Black Reconstruction in America* (New York: World Publishing, 1952 [1935]), 600.

18. Foner, *Reconstruction,* 278.

19. Du Bois, *Black Reconstruction in America,* 703; Jacquelyn Dowd Hall, *Revolt against Chivalry: Jessie Daniel Ames and the Women's Campaign against Lynching* (New York: Columbia University Press, 1979), 130–191; Ida B. Wells-Barnett, *Southern Horrors: Lynch Law in All Its Phases* (New York: New York Age, 1892), 7–15.

20. Richard M. Valelly, *The Puzzle of Disfranchisement: Party Struggle and African-American Suffrage in the South, 1867–1894,* Occasional Paper 93–4, Center for American Political Studies, Harvard University, 1993, 12.

21. The end of Reconstruction and the beginning of southern redemption is usually delineated by the partial withdrawal of federal troops from the South and the election of President Hayes, generally known as the Compromise of

1877. This compromise was struck between pragmatic southern Democrats and reform-minded Republicans over the contested 1876 presidential election. The bid for the presidency in 1876 included the Republican governor of Ohio, Rutherford B. Hayes, and the Democratic governor of New York, Samuel Tilden. Tilden won the popular vote and secured 185 electoral votes, one vote shy of the majority needed to win. Hayes secured 165 electoral votes. Both parties claimed the twenty electoral votes that hung in the balance. Southern Democrats relinquished the executive branch in exchange for their constituents' immediate concern: establishing home rule and extricating the troops from the South.

22. Valelly, *Puzzle of Disfranchisement,* 26.

23. See John Hope Franklin, *From Slavery to Freedom: A History of Negro Americans,* 4th ed. (New York: Knopf, 1974), 252; Richard Kluger, *Simple Justice: The History of Brown v. Board of Education* (New York: Knopf, 1976), 59.

24. Valelly, *Puzzle of Disfranchisement,* 28.

25. James R. Pole, *The Pursuit of Equality in American History,* rev. ed. (Berkeley: University of California Press, 1993), 229–253.

26. These restrictions included a poll tax, personal registration, and the Australian ballot. Prior to state election reforms a party ballot was given to voters. These ballots listed all of the party's candidates; one merely checked a "straight ticket" and deposited it in the ballot box. The Australian ballot had both parties' candidates on it and was distributed at polling booths. This disfranchised many illiterate people because the candidates' names had to be read and the votes cast in secret. One scheme made the Black vote ineffective by dividing areas of Black communities into several districts with a system of gerrymandering. Other schemes included the poll tax and changing polling places at the last minute without informing African American communities. The Democrats' election commissioners began to print difficult ballots, on which the voter had to write in the name of the office and the candidate within a two-and-one-half-minute time limit inside a voting booth. The White primary and the White Democratic convention were other devices that effectively made the Democratic Party the governing body of each southern state by 1896. Provisions were of course made to keep Whites eligible to vote because the schemes to disfranchise Blacks would have also disfranchised poor Whites. Such provisions included the good-character clause, the understanding clause, and the grandfather clause, devised in 1898, which made one eligible to vote if one's grandfather could (Franklin, *From Slavery to Freedom,* 267–272; Kluger, *Simple Justice,* 62). While the Democrats were disfranchising Blacks in the South, the Irish-controlled Democratic machine in Boston was disfranchising the Black Republican stronghold in New England by similar schemes.

27. Arnold S. Rice, John A. Krout, and C. M. Harris, *United States History to 1877,* 8th ed. (New York: Harper Perennial, 1991), 62.

28. Ironically, the attorneys for the railroad manager's association secured an injunction for the strike in the federal courts under the Sherman Antitrust Act.

29. Rayford W. Logan, *The Betrayal of the Negro* (New York: Collier Books, 1972 [1954]); Rice, Krout, and Harris, *United States History to 1877,* 83–84; Valelly, *Puzzle of Disfranchisement,* 30.

30. Logan, *Betrayal of the Negro,* 96.

31. 56th Cong., 1st sess., S2244.

32. John Higham, *Strangers in the Land: Patterns of American Nativism* (New York: Atheneum, 1970), 39; Richard Hofstadter, *Social Darwinism in American Thought* (Boston: Beacon Press, 1960 [1944]), 38; Leonard Wood, "The Existing Conditions and Needs in Cuba, by Major-General Leonard Wood, Military Governor of Santiago de Cuba," *North American Review* 168 (1899): 593–601.

33. John Daniels, *In Freedom's Birthplace: A Study of the Boston Negroes* (Boston: Houghton Mifflin, 1914), 114.

34. See Edward F. Waite, "The Negro in the Supreme Court," *Minnesota Law Review* 30 (March 1946): 220–304; *Plessy v. Ferguson*, 163 US 537 (1896); *Williams v. Mississippi*, 170 US 213 (1898); *Cumming v. Richmond County Board of Education*, 175 US 528 (1899); *Berea College v. Kentucky*, 211 US 45 (1909).

35. Theodore B. Wilson, *The Black Codes of the South* (Tuscaloosa: University of Alabama Press, 1965), 96–116; Barton J. Bernstein, "Case Law in *Plessy v. Ferguson*," *Journal of Negro History* 47 (1962): 192–198; Paul L. Rosen, *The Supreme Court and Social Science* (Urbana: University of Illinois Press, 1972), 23–45; Frank Freidel, "The Sick Chicken Case," in *Quarrels That Have Shaped the Constitution Court*, ed. John A. Garraty (New York: Harper and Row, 1964), 192. In one of these dissents, Oliver Wendell Holmes was actually forced to remind the Court that the U.S. "constitution was not intended to embody" Herbert Spencer's Social Darwinism (*Lochner v. New York*, 198 US 74).

36. Logan, *Betrayal of the Negro*, 106–107.

37. Bernstein, "Case Law in *Plessy v. Ferguson*," 198.

38. *Plessy v. Ferguson*, 163 US 544 (1896).

39. *Plessy v. Ferguson*, 163 US 540–541 (1896).

40. *Plessy v. Ferguson*, 163 US 541 (1896).

41. *Plessy v. Ferguson*, 163 US 541 (1896).

42. *Plessy v. Ferguson*, 163 US 538 (1896).

43. *Plessy v. Ferguson*, 163 US 543 (1896).

44. *Plessy v. Ferguson*, 163 US 552 (1896).

45. Antonio Gramsci, *Selections from the Prison Notebooks*, trans. and ed. Quintin Hoare and Geoffrey Nowell Smith (New York: International Publishers, 1971 [1935]), 12.

46. See John T. Morgan, "The Race Question in the United States," *Arena* 2 (1890): 385–398; William C. P. Breckinridge, "The Race Question," *Arena* 2 (1890): 39–56; Theodore Roosevelt, "Kidd's 'Social Evolution,'" *North American Review* 161 (1895): 94–109; John Sharp Williams, "The Negro and the South," *Metropolitan Magazine* 27, no. 2 (1907): 138–151; Benjamin R. Tillman, "The Race Question," *Van Norden's Magazine*, April 1907, 19–28.

Chapter 2

1. During the 1870s much of the institutional support for anthropology was provided by the Museum of Comparative Zoology at Harvard University and the USGS at the Department of the Interior.

2. Nancy Leys Stepan and Sander L. Gilman, "Appropriating the Idioms of Science: The Rejection of Scientific Racism," in *The Bounds of Race: Perspectives on Hegemony and Resistance*, ed. D. LaCapra (Ithaca, N.Y.: Cornell University Press), 77.

3. This period also witnessed the denial of women's rights, the destruction and assimilation of many Chicanos, violence against and exclusion of Chinese immigrants, and pogrom attacks on labor unions and Eastern European immigrants. Trade unions became battlegrounds between race and class because managers used various notions of racial inferiority to undermine working-class solidarity. These as well as many other examples contributed increasingly vivid contradictions between the pillars of democracy and the persistent articulation of sexism, racism, and nativism.

4. Stocking, *Race, Culture, and Evolution*, 22; John S. Flagg, "Anthropology: A University Study," *Popular Science Monthly* 51, no. 4 (1897): 510–513.

5. The relative authority that anthropology obtained by the mid-1890s can be gauged by the amount of money Congress appropriated for the BAE. For 1895 Congress approved $30,817.80 for BAE professional and support staff salaries, an amount equal to the salaries of the entire scientific staff at the USNM and three times the entire budget for the Astro-Physical Observatory. The Smithsonian Institution Board of Regents set these funding priorities. The chancellor was Chief Justice Melville Fuller, and other members of the board included Adlai E. Stevenson, vice president of the United States under Grover Cleveland, and William P. Breckinridge, an avowed Social Darwinist and congressman from Kentucky (J. B. Henderson, "Report of the Executive Committee of the Board of Regents of the Smithsonian Institution," in *Annual Report of the Board of Regents of the Smithsonian Institution, July 1895* [Washington, D.C.: Government Printing Office, 1896], xix–xl; Breckinridge, "Race Question," 45).

6. Daniel G. Brinton, "The Aims of Anthropology," *Popular Science Monthly* 48, no. 1 (1896): 68.

7. John Wesley Powell, "Relation of Primitive Peoples to Environment, Illustrated by American Examples," in *Smithsonian Institution Annual Report* [1895] (Washington, D.C.: Government Printing Office, 1896), 625, 631.

8. *Plessy v. Ferguson*, 163 US 552 (1896).

9. See Wilson, *Black Codes of the South*, 96–116; Bernstein, "Case Law in *Plessy v. Ferguson*," 198; Rosen, *Supreme Court*, 23–45; Freidel, "Sick Chicken Case," 192.

10. Hofstadter, *Social Darwinism*.

11. See Daniel G. Brinton, *Races and Peoples: Lectures on the Science of Ethnography* (New York: Hodges, 1890), 76; David Bloor, *Knowledge and Social Imagery* (Chicago: University of Chicago Press, 1991 [1976]), 70; Tucker, *Racial Research*, 26. Even before Charles Darwin introduced the theory of natural selection, scholars were incorporating ideas of social evolution into nascent fields like archeology, comparative law, and ethnology. Henry Sumner Maine, M. Boucher de Perthes, Lane Pitt-Rivers, Lewis Henry Morgan, John Lubbock, Edward B. Tylor, and Robert Dunn were among the scholars who advanced ideas of social evolution prior to the 1880s. See David N. Livingstone, *Nathaniel Southgate*

Shaler and the Culture of American Science (Tuscaloosa: University of Alabama Press, 1987), 79; John W. Burrow, *Evolution and Society: A Study in Victorian Social Theory* (London: Cambridge University Press), 1966; John W. Burrow, "Evolution and Anthropology in the 1860's: The Anthropological Society of London, 1863–1871," *Victorian Studies* 7 (1963): 137–154; Stanton, *Leopard's Spots;* Haller, *Outcasts from Evolution.* In Europe, where ideas of progress and evolution were in vogue much earlier, scientists used ideas about the hierarchy of races to validate the conquest and exploitation of people of color in Europe's colonial empire (Stanley Diamond, *In Search of the Primitive: A Critique of Civilization* [New Brunswick, N.J.: Transaction Books, 1987], 24–33).

12. What Social Darwinism actually encompasses has been debated. For example, Roger Bannister limited his scope to science and concluded that "the early Darwinians were not social Darwinists; likewise, many so-called social Darwinists (such as Spencer) were not Darwinians" (Robert C. Bannister, *Social Darwinism: Science and Myth in Anglo American Social Thought* [Philadelphia: Temple University Press, 1979], 16). I have followed Richard Hofstadter's and Stephen Gould's more general view, however (Hofstadter, *Social Darwinism;* Stephen Jay Gould, "Curveball," in *The Bell Curve Wars: Race, Intelligence, and the Future of America,* ed. Steven Fraser [New York: Basic Books, 1995], 12). I too view the variety of ideas regarding social, cultural, and racial evolution under the broad ideological rubric of Social Darwinism.

Jerry Watts proposed that "[t]he claim by Hofstadter and others that it was the prevailing public philosophy at the turn of the century may in fact be a significant overstatement" (Jerry Watts, "On Reconsidering Park, Johnson, Du Bois, Frazier and Reid: Reply to Benjamin Bowser's 'The Contribution of Blacks to Sociological Knowledge,' " *Phylon* 44, no. 4 [1983]: 273–291). However, Watts added that Spencer's "thought when simplified in America to the doctrine of 'the survival of the fittest' and used as an endorsement of the status quo must be considered merely an ideology" (p. 277). Although Watts depreciates the role of ideology in American society, he is correct that Social Darwinism was a bulwark for the status quo.

13. Tucker, *Racial Research,* 27.

14. Hofstadter, *Social Darwinism,* 45.

15. John S. Haller, "Race and the Concept of Progress in Nineteenth Century American Ethnology," *American Anthropologist* 73 (1971): 711.

16. Woodward, *Jim Crow,* 51; Haller, *Outcasts from Evolution,* 173–174; Du Bois, *Black Reconstruction in America,* 700; Charles H. Wesley, "The Concept of Negro Inferiority in American Thought," *Journal of Negro History* 25, no. 2 (1940): 541; Hofstadter, *Social Darwinism,* 172.

17. David Duncan, *The Life and Letters of Herbert Spencer* (New York: Appleton, 1908), 128.

18. Tucker, *Racial Research,* 27.

19. Herbert Spencer, *Principles of Psychology,* 3d ed. (New York: Appleton, 1880), 1: 136.

20. Ibid., 2: 535.

21. Herbert Spencer, "The Comparative Psychology of Man," *Popular Science Monthly* 8 (1896): 260.

22. Ibid.

23. Panchanan Mitra, *A History of American Anthropology* (Calcutta: University of Calcutta Press, 1933), 141.

24. Early ethnologists shared an understanding that all people shared a psychic unity or human nature. These ideas were influenced more by Adolph Bastion and Edward B. Tyler than by Spencer. See Adolf Bastian, *Der Mensch in Der Geschichte Zur Begrundung Einer Psychologischen Weltanschauung* (Leipzig: O. Wigand, 1860); Edward B. Tylor, *Primitive Culture: Researches into the Development of Mythology, Philosophy, Religion, Art, and Custom* (London: J. Murray, 1871).

25. Brinton, "Aims of Anthropology," 65.

26. Regna D. Darnell, "Daniel Garrison Brinton: An Intellectual Biography" (Ph.D. diss., University of Pennsylvania, 1967), 18.

27. Ibid., 3.

28. Albert Smyth, Memorial Address, in *Report of the Brinton Memorial Meeting,* ed. Albert Smyth (Philadelphia: American Philosophical Society, 1899), 18–19.

29. Daniel G. Brinton, *Notes on the Florida Peninsula, Its Literary History, Indian Tribes and Antiquities* (Philadelphia: Joseph Sabin, 1859), 172, 174, 197; Daniel G. Brinton, "The Mound-Builders of the Mississippi Valley," *Historical Magazine* 11 (1866): 33–37.

30. Darnell, "Daniel Garrison Brinton: An Intellectual Biography," 11.

31. Ibid., 9–21.

32. Ibid., 5.

33. Regna D. Darnell, *Readings in the History of Anthropology* (New York: Harper and Row, 1974), 5.

34. Brinton, *Races and Peoples,* 5.

35. Ibid., 47–48.

36. Ibid., 51.

37. Haller (*Outcasts from Evolution,* 153) and Stocking (*Race, Culture, and Evolution,* 254) have characterized Brinton's theoretical orientation as neo-Lamarckian in the tradition of Spencer. A good example of Brinton's neo-Lamarckian thought is demonstrated by his assertion that: "The Fuegian savage is one of the worst specimens of the genus; but put him when young in an English school, and he will grow up an intelligent member of civilized society. However low man is, he can be instructed, improved, redeemed; and it is this most cheering fact which should encourage us in incessant labour for the degraded and the despised of humanity" (Daniel Brinton, *The Basis of Social Relations* [New York: G. P. Putnam and Sons, 1901], 18).

38. Brinton, *Races and Peoples,* 192.

39. Ibid., 25.

40. Brinton, *Basis of Social Relations,* 133.

41. Karen C. Dalton, "Caricature in the Service of Racist Stereotypes: Evolution of Nineteenth-Century Caricatures of African Americans" (paper presented at the W. E. B. Du Bois Institute for Afro-American Studies Colloquia Series, Harvard University, March 31, 1993).

42. Brinton consistently conflated or collapsed the distinctions he made be-

tween specific African ethnolinguistic groups and African Americans. Although he is speaking of Africans on the African continent in this particular case, one can infer from all of the other examples in which he interchanges the "ethnic elements" of continental Africans and African Americans that he included African Americans in this stereotype. See Brinton, *Races and Peoples,* 180.

43. *Plessy v. Ferguson,* 163 US 552 (1896).

44. In *Mob Rule in New Orleans* ([New York: Arno Press, 1969 (1900)], 47) Ida B. Wells-Barnett reported these grim statistics created by lynch mobs:

1888, Negroes murdered by mobs 143
1889, Negroes murdered by mobs 127
1890, Negroes murdered by mobs 176
1891, Negroes murdered by mobs 192
1892, Negroes murdered by mobs 241
1893, Negroes murdered by mobs 200
1894, Negroes murdered by mobs 190
1895, Negroes murdered by mobs 171
1896, Negroes murdered by mobs 131

45. Wells-Barnett, *Southern Horrors,* 9–54.

46. See Gossett, *Race,* 270; James R. McGovern, *Anatomy of a Lynching: The Killing of Claude Neal* (Baton Rouge: Louisiana State University Press, 1982), 2.

47. Brinton, *Races and Peoples,* 287.

48. Haller, "Race and the Concept of Progress," 721; Daniel G. Brinton, "The Nation as an Element in Anthropology: From Proceedings of the International Congress of Anthropology at Chicago, 1893," in *Smithsonian Institution Annual Report* (Washington, D.C.: Government Printing Office, 1894), 589–600; Brinton, *Basis of Social Relations,* 153–157.

49. Harding, *"Racial" Economy of Science,* 12. Hall, in *Revolt against Chivalry,* explained that many White women resisted this ideology of White womanhood and documented how members of the Association of Southern Women for the Prevention of Lynching attacked the apologetics of lynching by disassociating the image of the vulnerable southern lady and the mob violence. She also explained how members of the association attacked the paternalism of chivalry. The claim that lynching was necessary as a protection of White women, they argued, masked the racism out of which mob violence really sprang. The presumptive tie between lynching and rape cast White women in the position of sexual objects—ever threatened by black lust, ever in need of rescue by their White protectors (p. 194).

50. Brinton, "Aims of Anthropology," 69; Haller, "Race and the Concept of Progress," 722.

51. Darnell, "Daniel Garrison Brinton: An Intellectual Biography," 50. The Anthropological Society of Washington had several women in its membership. For example, in 1894 the membership roster included Miss Alice C. Fletcher, Miss Katherine Foote, Dr. Anita Newcombe McGee, Miss Sarah A. Scull, and Mrs. Matilda Coxe Stevenson. See Marcus Baker, comp. *Directory of Scientific Societies of Washington: Comprising the Anthropological, Biological, Chemical, En-*

tomological, Geological, National Geographic, and Philosophical Societies (Washington, D.C.: Joint Commission, 1894).

52. Livingstone, *Shaler*, 35–39; Curtis M. Hinsley, *Savages and Scientists: The Smithsonian Institution and the Development of American Anthropology, 1846–1910* (Washington, D.C.: Smithsonian Institution Press, 1981), 139, 147–157. Powell was the founder and first president of the Cosmos Club in 1878. It was then and still remains one of Washington's most elite men's clubs (Wilcomb E. Washburn, *The Cosmos Club of Washington: A Centennial History, 1878–1978* [Washington, D.C.: Cosmos Club, 1978], 18–21). This locates Powell right at the center of the Washington's power elite, where he could cut deals and shore up his power base.

53. Grove Karl Gilbert, "John Wesley Powell," in *Smithsonian Institution Annual Report, 1902* (Washington, D.C.: Government Printing Office, 1903), 633.

54. Gilbert, "John Wesley Powell," 633–634; William Culp Darrah, *Powell of the Colorado* (Princeton, N.J.: Princeton University Press, 1951), 68.

55. Powell was an occasional cartographic advisor to Grant, and he parlayed his clout with the president into federal support for the expedition. In addition to the federal government, Powell lobbied the railroad companies to assist in transportation; American Express and Wells Fargo to carry specimens back to the museum; General William T. Sherman (his former commander) to provide a military escort across the Badlands; and Joseph Henry of the Smithsonian Institution to provide equipment for collecting specimens (Darrah, *Powell of the Colorado*, 81–83).

56. John Wesley Powell, *Exploration of the Colorado River of the West and Its Tributaries: Explored in 1869, 1870, 1871, and 1872* (Washington, D.C.: Government Printing Office, 1875).

57. Powell's primary concern was the policies of the Department of the Interior. Deploring the way in which the agency parceled out all the land west of the Mississippi River in equal allotments, without regard to its geological and ecological disposition, he argued that the West was not a monolithic, endless tract of land waiting for homesteaders, developers, railroads, and mines. He pointed out that the land was extremely diverse and that much of it could not support agriculture because of variations in precipitation and fertility.

58. On the House floor, the bill was debated along regional, not party, lines. Part of the bill was passed, and Powell was successful in consolidating the various surveying agencies under the Department of the Interior. However, he met resistance to the bill by Congress and by the various organizations that were to be centralized. For example, the consolidation was challenged by George M. Wheeler, Ferdinand Hayden, the War Department, and the Public Land Office. Powell literally orchestrated a hostile takeover of the various surveys with the aid of the National Academy of Sciences and sympathetic congressional members. The bill that Congress passed consolidated King's Geological Survey of the Fortieth Parallel, Hayden's Geological Survey of the Territories, Powell's own United States Geological and Geographical Survey of the Rocky Mountain Range, and Wheeler's Geological Surveys West of the One Hundredth Meridian (see Livingstone, *Shaler*, 35).

59. HR. 6140; 45th Cong., 3d sess., H2361.

60. Powell began his argument for the federal agency devoted to American ethnology by outlining the scientific value of studying disappearing societies: "The field of research is speedily narrowing because of the rapid change in the Indian population now in progress . . . and in a very few years it will be impossible to study our North American Indians in their primitive conditions except from recorded history. For this reason ethnologic studies in America should be pushed with utmost vigor" (John Wesley Powell, *Report on the Methods of Surveying the Public Domain* [Washington, D.C.: Government Printing Office, 1878], 15). He went on to explain the cogent reasons by touting the practical purposes of ethnology: "[T]he rapid spread of civilization since 1849 had placed the white man and the Indian in direct conflict throughout the whole area, and the 'Indian Problem' is thus thrust upon us and it *must* be solved, wisely or unwisely. Many of the difficulties are inherent and cannot be avoided, but an equal number are unnecessary and are caused by the lack of our knowledge relating to the Indians themselves" (p. 15).

61. Ibid.

62. John Wesley Powell, "From Barbarism to Civilization," *American Anthropologist* 1 (1888): 109.

63. Regna D. Darnell, *Daniel Garrison Brinton: The "Fearless Critic" of Philadelphia* (Philadelphia: Department of Anthropology, University of Pennsylvania, 1988), 43–50.

64. Daniel G. Brinton, *The American Race: A Linguistic Classification and Ethnographic Description of the Native Tribes of North and South America* (New York: Hodges, 1891), vi.

65. See John Wesley Powell, "Esthetology, or the Science of Activities Designed to Give Pleasure," *American Anthropologist* 1 (1899): 1–40; John Wesley Powell, "Sociology, or the Science of Institutions," *American Anthropologist* 1 (1899): 475–509, 695–745; John Wesley Powell, "Technology, or the Science of Industries," *American Anthropologist* 1 (1899): 319–349.

66. Powell, "Sociology."

67. Ibid., 695.

68. Darrah, *Powell of the Colorado*, 262–267; Stocking, *Race, Culture, and Evolution*, 116; Carl Resek, *Lewis Henry Morgan: American Scholar* (Chicago: University of Chicago Press, 1960), 150.

69. Lewis Henry Morgan, *Ancient Society, or Researches in the Lines of Human Progress from Savagery through Barbarism to Civilization* (New York: Henry Holt, 1877), 37.

70. Resek, *Lewis Henry Morgan*, 134.

71. Ibid., 79–81.

72. Morgan to Seward, February 2, 1850, William Henry Seward Papers, Rush Rhees Library, University of Rochester, Rochester, New York. In 1849 Seward was elected as a member of the Whig Party to serve in the U.S. Senate. During the turbulent 1850s he increasingly resisted the Whig attempt to compromise on the slavery issue, and when the party collapsed (1854–1855), Seward joined the newly organized Republican Party and made a firm stand against expansion of slavery into the territories.

73. Friedrich Engels, *Origin of the Family, Private Property and the State, in*

the Light of the Researches of Lewis H. Morgan (New York: International Publishers, 1972 [1884]). Haller ("Race and the Concept of Progress," 712) has summarized their position: "John Wesley Powell and Lewis Henry Morgan, although they spoke optimistically of progress for all peoples, actually limited the full meaning of the term to only those peoples whose race history clearly evidenced a progression out of savagery and barbarism and into civilization. The American Indian, who had not yet developed an agricultural society, contained no 'progressive spirit' from which 'there was no hope of elevation.' "

74. Resek, *Lewis Henry Morgan*, 50.

75. Livingstone, *Shaler*, 6; Haller, *Outcasts from Evolution*, 152.

76. On March 8, 1884, Powell wrote to Shaler and asked him to direct the surveying of New England for the USGS. Shaler accepted the invitation and later became director of the Atlantic Coast Division of the USGS (Papers of Nathan Southgate Shaler [1872–1914], Harvard University Archives, HUG: 1784, Cambridge, Mass.).

77. John Wesley Powell, *On the Organization of Scientific Work of the General Government: Extracts from the Testimony Taken by the Joint Commission of the Senate and House of Representatives*. Washington, D.C.: Government Printing Office, 1885.

78. Livingstone, *Shaler*, 39.

79. Alexander Agassiz, the son of Louis Agassiz, detested Powell's practical approach to science. He also supported the opposition in the congressional investigation. The contention between Powell and Alexander Agassiz was perhaps deeper than a philosophical disagreement. Agassiz's considerable fortune was tied to copper mining, and the federal land reform, which Powell advocated, would have jeopardized his wealth (John Murray, "Alexander Agassiz: His Life and Scientific Work," *Bulletin of the Museum of Comparative Zoology* 54, no. 3 [1911]: 140–141).

80. Livingstone, *Shaler*, 40; Nathaniel Southgate Shaler, "Aspects of the Earth," *Nation* 1282 (1890): 79.

81. Livingstone, *Shaler*, 40.

82. Nathaniel Southgate Shaler, "Science and the African Problem," *Atlantic Monthly* 66 (1890): 40.

83. Ibid., 37.

84. Dalton, "Caricature."

85. Shaler, "Science and the African Problem," 42.

86. Ibid., 43.

87. Lee D. Baker, "Savage Inequality: Anthropology in the Erosion of the Fifteenth Amendment," *Transforming Anthropology* 5, no. 1 (1994): 29–30.

88. Nathaniel Southgate Shaler, "The Negro Problem," *Atlantic Monthly* 54 (1884): 697.

89. Ibid., 703.

90. Haller, *Outcasts from Evolution*, 168; Shaler, "Negro Problem"; Shaler, "Science and the African Problem"; Nathaniel Southgate Shaler, "The Nature of the Negro," *Arena* 2 (1890): 660–673; Nathaniel Southgate Shaler, "Our Negro Types," *Current Literature* 29 (1900): 44–45; Nathaniel Southgate Shaler, "The Future of the Negro in the Southern States," *Popular Science Monthly* 57

(1900): 147–156; Nathaniel Southgate Shaler, "The Negro since the Civil War," *Popular Science Monthly* 57 (1900): 29–39; Nathaniel Southgate Shaler, "The Transplantation of a Race," *Popular Science Monthly* 56 (1900): 513–524.

91. Haller, *Outcasts from Evolution*, 173; Daniels, *In Freedom's Birthplace*, 114.

92. Darrah, *Powell of the Colorado*, 297.

93. A. M. Tozzer, *Frederic Ward Putnam, 1839–1915*, National Academy of Sciences Biographical Memoirs, 16 (Washington, D.C.: National Academy of Sciences, 1935), 129.

94. Ibid., 133.

95. R. B. Dixon, "Frederic W. Putnam 1839–1915," *Harvard Graduate's Magazine* 24 (1915): 305.

96. E. S. Morse, "Frederic W. Putnam, 1839–1915: An Appreciation," *Essex Institute Historical Collections* 52 (1916): 194.

97. Tozzer, *Frederic Ward Putnam*, 131. See also Franz Boas, *Anthropological Essays Presented to Frederic Ward Putnam in Honor of His Seventieth Birthday, April 16, 1909* (New York: G. E. Strechert, 1909).

98. Morse, "Frederic W. Putnam," 193.

99. Although the Harvard Corporation made the appointment in 1885, it was not confirmed by the Board of Overseers until 1887. Technically, Putnam was the second professor of an anthropological field in the United States because he followed Brinton, who had become professor of American archeology and linguistics at the University of Pennsylvania in 1886. See Tozzer, *Frederic Ward Putnam*, 128.

100. Ralph Dexter, "Putnam's Problems Popularizing Anthropology," *American Scientist* 54 (1966): 316.

101. Tozzer, *Frederic Ward Putnam*, 132.

102. Harlan Ingersoll Smith, "Man and His Works," *American Antiquarian* 15 (1893): 117

103. Alfred Kroeber, "Frederic Ward Putnam," *American Anthropologist* 17 (1915): 716.

104. Tozzer, *Frederic Ward Putnam*, 132.

105. Charles Peabody, "Frederic W. Putnam," *Journal of American Folk-Lore* 28 (1915): 304.

106. Franz Boas, "Frederic Ward Putnam," *Science* 42 (1915): 330.

Chapter 3

1. See W. E. B. Du Bois, "Dusk of Dawn: An Essay toward an Autobiography of a Race Concept," in *Du Bois Writings,* ed. Nathan Huggins (New York: Literary Classics of the United States, 1986 [1940]), 593–793; Winant, *Racial Conditions;* Cornel West, *Race Matters* (Boston: Beacon Press, 1993); Hazel V. Carby, "The Multicultural Wars," *Radical History Review* 54 (1992): 12.

2. Robert W. Rydell, *All the World's a Fair: Visions of Empire at American International Expositions* (Chicago: University of Chicago Press, 1984), 3.

3. Elliott M. Rudwick and August Meier, "Black Man in the 'White City': Negroes and the Columbian Exposition, 1893," *Phylon* 26, no. 4 (1965): 354;

Sidney M. Willhelm, "Black-White Equality," *Journal of Black Studies* 12, no. 2 (1981): 157.

4. Rydell, *All the World's a Fair,* 67.

5. William H. Dall, "The Columbian Exposition—IX: Anthropology," *Nation* 57, no. 1474 (1893): 226.

6. Ibid.

7. Otis T. Mason, "Summary of Progress in Anthropology," in *Annual Report of the Smithsonian Institution for the Year Ending July 1893* (Washington, D.C.: Government Printing Office, 1893), 606. Denton J. Snider, a contemporary literary critic, suggested that the Midway consisted of a "sliding scale of humanity." Nearest to the White City were the Teutonic and Celtic races, as represented by two German and two Irish villages. The center of the Midway contained the Muhammadan world, West Asia, and East Asia. Then, "we descend to the savage races, the African of Dahomey and the North American Indian" (Rydell, *All the World's a Fair,* 65).

8. Julian Hawthorne, "Foreign Folk at the Fair," *Cosmopolitan* 15 (1893): 568–570.

9. Ibid., 572.

10. John C. Eastman, "Village Life at the World's Fair," *Chautauquan* 17 (1893): 603.

11. Ibid., 604.

12. Edward B. McDowell, "The World's Fair Cosmopolis," *Frank Leslie's Popular Monthly* 36 (1893): 415.

13. Cesare Lombroso, "Why Homicide Has Increased in the United States," *North American Review* 165 (1897): 647–648. For an excellent discussion of Lombroso, see Gould, *Mismeasure of Man,* 113–146.

14. Starr viewed the ethnological exhibits as a great "object lesson" in anthropology (Frederick Starr, "Anthropology at the World's Fair," *Popular Science Monthly* 43, no. 5 [1893]: 621). Linking crime and morality to a naturalized inferiority of African Americans was also being put forth by sociologists. See Monroe N. Work, "Crime among the Negroes of Chicago," *American Journal of Sociology* 6 (1900): 204–223.

15. Frederick Starr, "The Degeneracy of the American Negro," 22 (1897): 17.

16. Ibid., 18.

17. Dexter, "Putnam's Problems," 323; Tozzer, *Frederic Ward Putnam,* 132.

18. Rydell, *All the World's a Fair,* 5. The idea that the representation of people of color in a primitive state would make American progress more persuasive was even articulated to children. For example, George Dorsey, in the *Youth's Companion,* explained that "This illustration of primitive life will make more apparent the material progress made in America during the past four hundred years." See George A. Dorsey, "Man and His Works," *Youth's Companion,* World's Fair no. (1893): 27.

19. Dall, "Columbian Exposition," 226.

20. Dexter, "Putnam's Problems," 327.

21. Rudwick and Meier, "Black Man in the 'White City,'" 354.

22. Ibid., 356.

23. Ibid., 359.

24. Ibid., 361.

25. August Meier, "Negro Class Structure and Ideology in the Age of Booker T. Washington," *Phylon* 23 (1962): 266.

26. August Meier and Elliott Rudwick, *Black Protest Thought in the Twentieth Century* (New York: Bobbs-Merrill, 1971), 3; Kluger, *Simple Justice*, 71.

27. Rydell, *All the World's a Fair*, 72–76; Kluger, *Simple Justice*, 69.

28. Booker T. Washington, *Up from Slavery* (New York: Doubleday, 1902 [1901]), 220.

29. Ibid.

30. Ibid., 220–221.

31. Ibid., 222.

32. Rydell, *All the World's a Fair*, 72–76; W. E. B. Du Bois, "The Souls of Black Folk," in *Du Bois Writings,* ed. Nathan Huggins (New York: Literary Classics of the United States, 1986 [1903]), 393; David J. Calista, "Booker T. Washington: Another Look," *Journal of Negro History* 49 (1964): 255.

33. Booker T. Washington, "Education Will Solve the Race Problem, A Reply," *North American Review* 171 (1900): 222. Washington's seemingly compromised agenda should be qualified. Given that African Americans were being brutally repressed in the South, Washington's agenda became an effective way to ensure that African Americans could eat, work, and obtain an education. It stressed independence and autonomy. In many respects, one can view the agenda as a strategy for resisting the overwhelming consolidation of power by Democrat interests in the South during the second Cleveland administration. Booker T. Washington placed more emphasis on access to jobs and a livelihood than on access to voting and White-only bathrooms. On the other hand, he dominated the Negro agenda and crushed any voice of protest against his strategy of accommodation. Although many writers have criticized Washington's strategy for accommodating White supremacy, there is, perhaps, another characterization. One could argue that during the processes of southern redemption the most innocuous African American strategy became validated, championed, coopted, or otherwise appropriated. See Meier and Rudwick, *Black Protest Thought,* 3; Manning Marable, *W. E. B. Du Bois, Black Radical Democrat* (Boston: Twayne, 1986), 40; Nathan Irvin Huggins, *Harlem Renaissance* (New York: Oxford University Press, 1971), 50; Ross, *Origins of American Social Science*, 360; Paul Rich, "'The Baptism of a New Era': The 1911 Universal Races Congress and the Liberal Ideology of Race," *Ethnic and Racial Studies* 7, no. 4 (1984): 539; Du Bois, "Souls of Black Folk," 393; Daniel S. Green and Edwin D. Driver, *W. E. B. Du Bois on Sociology and the Black Community* (Chicago: University of Chicago Press, 1978), 18.

Logan (*Betrayal of the Negro*) alludes to this argument. He suggests that President Harrison's appeal for Negro suffrage and education was an attempt to alleviate "the prejudices and paralysis of slavery [that] continue to hang upon the skirts of progress" (p. 63). Employing this type of rhetorical strategy, Harrison argued that concessions should be given to Negroes. If they were not given, Harrison feared, Negroes would fall prey to the Farmers Alliance or the Socialists. Logan argues that Harrison's views were precursors of the overwhelming acceptance of Washington.

34. Emmett J. Scott, "The Louisiana Purchase Exposition," *Voice of the Negro* 1, no. 8 (1904): 310.

35. Ibid., 311. Scott actually advised African Americans who wanted to visit the fair to "carry [their] knapsack and canteen" because they might not be able to purchase food.

36. W. S. Scarborough, "The Negro and the Louisiana Purchase Exposition," *Voice of the Negro* 1, no. 8 (1904): 314.

37. Ibid., 314.

38. Rydell, *All the World's a Fair*, 155–160.

39. Hinsley, *Savages and Scientists*, 236.

40. *American Anthropologist*, n.s., 1 (1899): 400.

41. WJ McGee, "The Trend of Human Progress," *American Anthropologist* 1 (1899): 415.

42. Ibid., 424.

43. Ibid., 419.

44. Ibid., 408.

45. Ibid., 412.

46. Ibid., 410.

47. Ibid.

48. Ibid., 411.

49. Ibid., 446.

50. Ibid.

51. Ibid.

52. Phillips Verner Bradford and Harvey Blume, *Ota Benga: The Pygmy in the Zoo* (New York: St. Martin's Press, 1992), 114.

53. Rydell, *All the World's a Fair*, 166.

54. Richard Handler, "Boasian Anthropology and the Critique of Culture," *American Quarterly* 42, no. 2 (1990): 252.

55. Flagg, "Anthropology," 512.

56. For example, see Daniel G. Brinton, "Professor Blumentritt's Studies of the Philippines," *American Anthropologist* 1 (1899): 122–125; Ferdinand Blumentritt, "The Race Question in the Philippine Islands," *Popular Science Monthly* 54, no. 4 (1899): 472–479.

57. G. G. Vest, "Objections to Annexing the Philippines," *North American Review* 168 (1899): 112.

58. See James E. Kerr, *The Insular Cases: The Role of the Judiciary in American Expansionism* (Port Washington, N.Y.: Kennikat Press, 1982).

59. Rydell, *All the World's a Fair*, 172.

60. Ibid., 175–176.

61. J. B. Steere, "The Civilized Indian of the Philippines," *Scientific American* 79, no. 12 (1898): 184–185.

62. Lee D. Baker, "Ota Benga, Story of a Tragic Travesty," *Teaching Anthropology Newsletter* 22–23 (1993): 5.

63. Bradford and Blume, *Ota Benga*, 155–188.

64. Frank Luther Mott, *A History of American Magazines, 1885–1905* (Cambridge, Mass.: Harvard University Press, 1957), 2.

65. Ibid.

66. Logan, *Betrayal of the Negro,* 243–244.

67. Gary Gumpert and Robert Cathcart, *Inter/Media: Interpersonal Communications in a Media World* (New York: Oxford University Press, 1982), 351.

68. Logan, *Betrayal of the Negro,* 265.

69. Morgan, "Race Question," 397. Morgan served as a U.S. senator for thirty-one years as a staunch segregationist and an advocate for states' rights. A longtime member of the Senate Foreign Relations Committee, he shaped many of the policies for the Pacific and the Caribbean and aggressively pursued a scheme to colonize the Philippine Islands with African Americans (Joseph O. Baylen and John Hammond Moore, "Senator John Tyler Morgan and Negro Colonization in the Philippines, 1901 to 1902," *Phylon* 29 [1968]: 66).

70. Morgan, "Race Question," 390.

71. Ibid., 387–389.

72. Williams, "Negro and the South," 138, 148.

73. Ibid., 146.

74. Tillman, "Race Question," 28.

75. Ibid.

76. Ibid.

77. Ibid.

78. Marion L. Dawson, "The South and the Negro," *North American Review* 172 (1901): 279–284.

79. Breckinridge, "Race Question," 45.

80. Ibid.

81. Ibid.

82. For example, see Booker T. Washington, "The Awakening of the Negro," *Atlantic Monthly* 77 (1896): 322–328; Booker T. Washington, "Signs of Progress among the Negroes," *Century Magazine* 59 (1899): 472–478; Booker T. Washington, "The Race Problem in the United States," *Popular Science Monthly* 55, no. 3 (1899): 317–325; Washington, "Education," 221–232; Booker T. Washington, "Heroes in Black Skins," *Century Magazine* 66 (1903): 724–729; "Wise Leader," *Century Magazine* 66 (1903): 796–797.

83. Between the end of the Civil War and the beginning of World War I, several large educational foundations were established in order to advance education for African Americans in the South. They included the Peabody Education Fund, the John F. Slater Fund, the General Education Board, the Anna T. Jeanes Fund, the Julius Rosenwald Fund, and the Phelps-Stokes Fund. George F. Peabody, who had endowed the Peabody Museums at Harvard, Yale, and Salem, established an education fund in 1867 "for the promotion and encouragement of intellectual, moral, or industrial education among the young people of the more destitute portions of the Southern and Southwestern States." In two separate grants Peabody gave almost $2.5 million to the fund. Franklin, *From Slavery to Freedom,* 278.

84. Albion W. Smith, "Civil History of the Confederate States, by J. L. M. Curry, LL.D.," *American Journal of Sociology* 7 (1901): 847.

85. Harvey Wish, "Negro Education and the Progressive Movement," *Journal of Negro History* 49 (1964): 185.

86. Jabez L. M. Curry, "The Negro Question," *Popular Science Monthly* 55, no. 1 (1899): 178.

87. Ibid., 179.

88. The Dawes Severalty Act, passed by the U.S. Congress in 1887, stipulated that Native Americans give up their tribal lands in return for individual land grants. It was sponsored by Senator Henry L. Dawes and was intended to advance the "progress" of Native Americans toward civilization by forcing them into a homesteading way of life. The main effect of the law was the opening up of the Indian Territory—Oklahoma, Nebraska, Kansas, and the Dakotas—to White settlers.

89. Henry L. Dawes, "Have We Failed the Indians?" *Atlantic Monthly* 84 (1989): 281.

90. Roosevelt, "Kidd's 'Social Evolution,' " 95.

91. Ibid., 109.

92. For examples, see Edward W. Blyden, "The African Problem," *North American Review* 161 (1895): 327–339; Hilton Scribner, "Brain Development as Related to Evolution," *Popular Science Monthly* 46, no. 4 (1895): 525–538; Anna Tolman Smith, "A Study in Race Psychology," *Popular Science Monthly* 50, no. 3 (1897): 354–360; E. P. Evans, "The Ethics of Tribal Society," *Popular Science Monthly* 44, no. 3 (1894): 289–307; E. P. Evans, "Semon's Scientific Researches in Australia," *Popular Science Monthly* 52, no. 1 (1897): 17–37; Charles Morris, "War as a Factor in Civilization," *Popular Science Monthly* 47, no. 6 (1895): 823–834; Lewis R. Harley, "Race Mixture and National Character," *Popular Science Monthly* 47, no. 1 (1895): 86–92; Alfred H. Stone, "The Mulatto Factor in the Race Problem," *Atlantic Monthly* 91 (1903): 658–662; James Weir Jr., "The Pygmy in the United States," *Popular Science Monthly* 49, no. 1 (1896): 47–56; Robert B. Bean, "The Negro Brain," *Century Magazine* 72 (1906): 778–784; Robert B. Bean, "The Training of the Negro," *Century Magazine* 72 (1906): 947–953; Gustave Michaud, "The Brain of the Nation," *Century Magazine* 49 (1904): 40–46; Cesare Lombroso, "The Savage Origin of Tattooing," *Popular Science Monthly* 58, no. 6 (1896): 793–803; Lombroso, "Homicide," 641–648.

93. Hoffman employed George M. Gould's *Anthropological Statistics* as evidence of Negro inferiority. The lines between what was anthropological Social Darwinism and what was not were blurred. There was a great deal of cross-fertilization of ideas and data between the budding disciplines.

94. Frederick L. Hoffman, *Race Traits and Tendencies of the American Negro* (Publications of the American Economic Association, 11 [1–3]; New York: Macmillan, 1896), 312.

95. W. E. B. Du Bois, "Race Traits of the American Negro, by Frederick L. Hoffman," *Annals of the American Academy of Political Science* 9 (1897): 133; B. S. Coler, "Reform of Public Charity," *Popular Science Monthly* 55 (1899): 750–755; Hoffman, *Race Traits*, 312.

96. For example, see Oswald G. Villard, "The Negro in the Regular Army," *Atlantic Monthly* 91 (1903): 721–728; W. S. Scarborough, "The Race Problem," *Arena* 2 (1890): 560–567; W. E. B. Du Bois, "The Southerner's Problem," *Dial* 38 (1905): 315–318; Franz Boas, "The Anthropological Position of the Negro," *Van Norden's Magazine*, April 1907, 42–47.

Chapter 4

1. Franklin, *From Slavery to Freedom,* 323.
2. That same year in Brownsville, Texas, the mayor and other White citizens made allegations that Negro troops stationed at nearby Fort Brown killed a man and wounded another. President Theodore Roosevelt dismissed without honor and without a proper investigation an entire battalion of Negro troops.
3. Franklin, *From Slavery to Freedom,* 324.
4. Elting E. Morison, ed., *The Letters of Theodore Roosevelt* (8 vols.; Cambridge, Mass.: Harvard University Press, 1951), 3: 149.
5. Ibid., 2: 1169.
6. Roosevelt needed Washington's influence in the South to combat Mark Hanna's influence vis-à-vis McKinley's appointments, and Washington needed Roosevelt to embellish his Tuskegee Machine and bolster the Negro Business League.
7. Elliott M. Rudwick, *W. E. B. Du Bois: Voice of the Black Protest Movement* (Chicago: University of Illinois Press, 1982), 87.
8. William L. Ziglar, "Negro Opinion of Theodore Roosevelt" (Ph.D. diss., University of Maine, Orono), 47.
9. Ibid., 141–142.
10. Morison, *Letters of Theodore Roosevelt,* 3: 190. Albion W. Tourgée was a famous radical Reconstruction lawyer who crusaded for Negro suffrage and desegregation. He wrote two influential books that marshaled support for African American rights in 1879. The first, *The Invisible Empire,* detailed Ku Klux Klan activity prior to the Civil War; the second, *A Fool's Errand,* was an autobiographical account of his experiences during Reconstruction in North Carolina. Tourgée was also the attorney for Aldolph Plessy in *Plessy v. Ferguson.* See Monte M. Olenick, "Albion W. Tourgée: Radical Republican Spokesman of the Civil War Crusade," *Phylon* 22 (1962): 332–345.
11. Theodore Roosevelt, "The Rough Riders and Men of Action," in *The Works of Theodore Roosevelt,* ed. Hermann Hagedorn, national ed. (New York: C. Scribner's Sons, 1926), 11: 276; Emmett J. Scott and Lyman Beecher Stowe, *Booker T. Washington, Builder of a Civilization* (New York: Doubleday, Page, 1916), ix–xiv.
12. Kwame Anthony Kwame, *In My Father's House: Africa in the Philosophy of Culture* (New York: Oxford University Press, 1992), 13.
13. Thomas G. Dyer, *Theodore Roosevelt and the Idea of Race* (Baton Rouge: Louisiana State University Press, 1980), 6. After completing his studies at Harvard University, Roosevelt came under the influence of John W. Burgess, of the Columbia University Law School, who thought that only a few races were fit to rule.
14. Ibid., 7.
15. For an excellent discussion of Roosevelt's serial in *Scribner's,* see Amy Kaplan, "Black and Blue on San Juan Hill," in *Cultures of United States Imperialism,* ed. Amy Kaplan and Donald E. Pease (Durham, N.C.: Duke University Press, 1993), 219–236.

16. Roosevelt, "Rough Riders," 93.

17. Morison, *Letters of Theodore Roosevelt*, 2: 1305.

18. Theodore Roosevelt, *Address of President Roosevelt at the Lincoln Dinner of the Republican Club of the City of New York,* February 13, 1905 (Washington, D.C.: Government Printing Office, 1905), 27–28.

19. Dyer, *Theodore Roosevelt*, 21.

20. Stocking, *Race, Culture, and Evolution*, 238–268. Roosevelt developed a sophisticated understanding of the comparative method used by Powell, McGee, and Mason. In *Through the Brazilian Wilderness and Papers on Natural History* (1914), he adroitly applied the comparative method for sweeping characterizations in his romantic travelogue.

At the Juruena [in central Brazil] we met a party of Nhambiquaras, very friendly and sociable. . . .

Nowhere in Africa did we come across wilder or more absolutely primitive savages, although these Indians were pleasanter and better featured than any of the African tribes at the same stage of culture . . . from the savage standpoint; there was no male brutality like that which forms such a revolting feature in the life of the Australian black fellows and, although to a somewhat less degree, in the life of so many negro and Indian tribes.

(Theodore Roosevelt, "Through the Brazilian Wilderness and Papers on Natural History," in *The Works of Theodore Roosevelt*, ed. Hermann Hagedorn, national ed. [New York: C. Scribner's Sons, 1926 (1914)], 5: 178).

21. Morison, *Letters of Theodore Roosevelt*, 2: 102–103.

22. Ibid., 3: 191.

23. Pole, *Pursuit of Equality*, 280.

24. Thomas Dyer (*Theodore Roosevelt*, 21–44) demonstrated that Roosevelt's ideas regarding race cannot be divorced from the pervasive Social Darwinian milieu at the turn of the century. As well, many scholars have suggested that ideas about Social Darwinism served as a theoretical underpinning for these policies. See David Burton, "Theodore Roosevelt's Social Darwinism and Views on Imperialism," *Journal of the History of Ideas* 49 (1965): 103–118; Hofstadter, *Social Darwinism*, 180; Ziglar, "Negro Opinion of Theodore Roosevelt," 60. At the end of his tenure, he became obsessed with changing what he called "race suicide," which was prompted by the decreasing birthrate of White Americans.

Teasing out specific theoretical particularities between the neo-Lamarckians, Spencerians, and Darwinists is not essential in identifying Roosevelt's adherence to Social Darwinian themes. Carl N. Degler (*In Search of Human Nature: The Decline and Revival of Darwinism in American Social Thought* [New York: Oxford University Press, 1991], 3–55) has detailed all of the variations of this evolutionary thought.

25. Meier, "Negro Class Structure and Ideology," 266; Stepan and Gilman, "Idioms of Science," 74–76.

26. Higham, *Strangers in the Land*, 21.

27. Ibid., 22.

28. Ibid., 33.

29. Thomas C. Patterson and Frank Spencer, "Racial Hierarchies and Buffer Races," *Transforming Anthropology* 5 (1994): 20–27. Something of a precursor of

this trend occurred in the early nineteenth century, when racial categories were socially constructed for Irish immigrants (Higham, *Strangers in the Land,* 4–7).

30. Michael Omi and Howard Winant, *Racial Formation in the United States* (New York: Routledge, 1986), 65.

31. Francis A. Walker, "Immigration Restriction," *Atlantic Monthly* 77 (1896): 823.

32. Ibid., 823. Francis A. Walker (1840–1897) followed in his father's footsteps and became a prominent political economist. Like his peer and colleague John Wesley Powell, Walker advanced quickly as a government scientist, becoming superintendent of the Census Bureau in 1870. In 1872 he was appointed professor of political economy and history at Yale's Sheffield Scientific School. While he continued to be involved in government affairs, he lectured part-time at Johns Hopkins University. In 1881 he left Yale University to assume the presidency of the Massachusetts Institute of Technology. Walker was struck by the 1890 census figures. He saw a "monstrous" rise in the immigration of strange peoples, coupled with a drop in the birthrate of U.S.-born, which compelled him to launch a public campaign to urge the government to restrict immigration (Ross, *Origins of American Social Science,* 55, 62, 78, 147; Patterson and Spencer, "Racial Hierarchies," 22).

33. Walker, "Immigration Restriction," 829, 828.

34. "The Presidency and Mr. Olney," *Atlantic Monthly* 77 (1896): 676.

35. Higham, *Strangers in the Land,* 62–74.

36. Pole, *Pursuit of Equality,* 284.

37. Garland E. Allen, "Eugenics and American Social History," *Genome* 31 (1989): 885–887.

38. Ibid., 888.

39. Sir Francis Galton, *Hereditary Genius: An Inquiry into Its Laws and Consequences* (London: Macmillan, 1925 [1869]), xxvii.

40. Sir Francis Galton, "The Possible Improvement of the Human Breed under the Existing Conditions of Law and Sentiment," *Popular Science Monthly* 60 (1902): 219.

41. Ibid., 218–233; Sir Francis Galton, "The Possible Improvement of the Human Breed under the Existing Conditions of Law and Sentiment," *Nature* 64 (1901): 659–665.

42. Galton, "Possible Improvement," *Popular Science Monthly,* 229.

43. Ibid., 228.

44. Ibid.

45. Ibid., 233.

46. Tucker, *Racial Research,* 52; S. Dale McLemore, *Racial and Ethnic Relations in America* (Needham Heights, Mass.: Simon and Schuster, 1991), 89.

47. Tucker, *Racial Research,* 52.

48. Ibid., 550.

49. Garland E. Allen, "The Misuse of Biological Hierarchies: The American Eugenics Movement, 1900–1940," *History and Philosophy of the Life Sciences* 5 (1983): 107.

50. Ibid., 114.

51. Ibid., 179.

52. William B. Provine, "Geneticists and Race," *American Zoology* 26 (1986): 867.

53. Paul Popenoe and Roswell Hill Johnson, *Applied Genetics* (New York: Macmillan, 1918), 292. The reason the authors gave to condemn miscegenation was similar to ideas that Lewis Henry Morgan had proposed forty-one years earlier, in *Ancient Society* (1877): "A race of nothing but mediocrities will stand still, or very nearly so; but a race of mediocrities with a good supply of men of exceptional ability and energy at the top, will make progress in discovery, invention, and organization, which is generally recognized as progressive evolution" (Popenoe and Johnson, *Applied Genetics*, 293).

54. Theodore Roosevelt, "Campaigns and Controversies," in *The Works of Theodore Roosevelt*, ed. Hermann Hagedorn, national ed. (New York: C. Scribner's Sons, 1926), 14: 167–178; Dyer, *Theodore Roosevelt*, 143–167.

55. Roosevelt to Davenport, January 3, 1913, Theodore Roosevelt Papers, Series 1, Reel 355, Manuscript Division, Library of Congress, Washington, D.C.

56. Michael L. Blakey, "Skull Doctors: Intrinsic Social and Political Bias in the History of American Physical Anthropology," *Critique of Anthropology* 7, no. 2 (1987): 12.

57. M. F. Ashley Montagu, "Aleš Hrdlička, 1869–1943," *American Anthropologist* 46 (1944): 117.

58. Blakey, "Skull Doctors," 12.

59. Aleš Hrdlička, "Lecture 27, Delivered at the American University, May 27, 1921," National Anthropological Archives, National Museum of Natural History, Washington, D.C., 16. Hrdlička also detailed this relationship in his "Physical Anthropology: Its Scope and Aims; Its History and Present Status in America," *American Journal of Physical Anthropology* 1 (1918): 21.

60. Alexander, "Prophet of American Racism," 73–90.

61. "No State shall make or enforce any law which shall abridge the privileges or immunities of citizens of the United States; nor shall any State deprive any person of life, liberty, or property, without due process of law; nor deny to any person within its jurisdiction the equal protection of the laws."

62. Examples of decisions that reflected these precepts included the dissents in the *Slaughter House Cases* (1873), which initiated the doctrine of substantive due process. *Chicago, Milwaukee & St. Paul Railway Co. v. Minnesota* (1890), *Allgeyer v. Louisiana* (1897), *Lochner v. New York* (1905), and *Adkins v. Children's Hospital* (1923) employed a doctrine derived from substantive due process known as the liberty of contract. The Court found these state laws that regulated wages and labor conditions inimical to the Constitution because they denied individuals the liberty of entering into a contract. Somehow, the Court did not find state laws denying "colored" individuals the liberty of entering into a hotel, school, or train unconstitutional, as in *Plessy v. Ferguson* (1896). Laissez-faire constitutionalism also supported federalism. In *Pollock v. Farmers' Loan & Trust Co.* (1895) the Court limited federal taxing power striking down an income tax. It also curbed federal regulatory power. The Court would not even allow federal child-labor laws, as in *Hammer v. Dagenhart* (1918) and *Bailey v. Drexel Furniture Co.* (1922). Additionally, the Court showed unconcealed hostility to labor, as in *Loewe v. Lawlor* (1908), *Adair v. United States* (1908), and *In re Debs* (1895).

In *The Chief Justiceship of Melville W. Fuller, 1888–1910* ([Columbia: University of South Carolina Press, 1995], 57–82), James W. Ely Jr. makes a compelling argument that Social Darwinism was not "written into the Constitution" during this period. However, he views Social Darwinism as only scientific theory and suggests that it was Hobbes more than Spencer who was used as the social theorist who guided the Court's jurisprudence. The point here is that Hobbes and Spencer used similar themes about the "natural" order of society. These common themes were among the constituent elements of the racial worldview that Audrey Smedley describes in *Race in North America*. Perhaps Spencer was not written into the Constitution, but the Court's interpretation of the Fourteenth Amendment reflected a racial worldview of which ideas of evolutionism formed important constituent elements, in turn structuring racial inequality and reinforcing the worldview.

63. Herbert Hovenkamp, "The Political Economy of Substantive Due Process," *Stanford Law Review* 40 (1988): 379. Substantive due processes was used in such cases as *Allgeyer v. Louisiana* (1897), where the Court overturned a Louisiana law requiring all corporations doing business with Louisiana residents to pay fees to the state. It was also used in *Lochner v. New York* (1905), where the Court found a maximum-hours statute unconstitutional. In *Adair v. United States* (1908) the Court used it to invalidate the Erdman Act of 1898, protecting union members who worked in interstate transportation from signing "yellow-dog" contracts or being blacklisted for union activities. This provided the precedent for striking down state laws protecting union employees, as in *Coppage v. Kansas* (1915). This doctrine of substantive due process, or "liberty of contract," was employed by the U.S. Supreme Court (and other courts) between 1885 and 1937, when the Court began to support New Deal regulatory reform.

Although the Court did not consistently find state regulations unconstitutional, there was a pattern. For example, the Court upheld state laws that regulated land reform and zoning laws as well as maximum working hours for women. During the progressive movement the Court generally struck down state regulations that favored working men, particularly legislation supporting union activities. Land-reform and zoning laws created disputes between merchants and manufactures, not management and labor.

64. Paul Kens, "Lochner v. New York," in *The Oxford Companion to the Supreme Court of the United States,* ed. Kermit T. Hall (New York: Oxford University Press, 1992), 509.

65. *Lochner v. New York*, 198 US 52–53 (1905).

66. *Lochner v. New York*, 198 US 57 (1905).

67. *Lochner v. New York*, 198 US 61 (1905).

68. *Lochner v. New York*, 198 US 75 (1905). Originally published in 1850, Spencer's "Social Statistics" was abridged, revised, and bound with another essay, "Man versus the State," in 1892. Together, these essays were routinely reissued (in 1892, 1893, 1896, 1897, and 1904). In "Social Statistics" Spencer attacked reform and regulatory legislation by strengthening arguments for laissez-faire with biological imperatives, discarding utilitarian ethics. He framed an ethical standard based on natural rights, in which every man has the right to do as he wishes as long as he does not abrogate the rights of other individuals. Ultimately,

the responsibility of the state is to ensure that these natural or common-law rights are not abridged.

69. Laura Kalman, "From Realism to Pluralism: Theory and Education at Yale Law School, 1927–1960" (Ph.D. diss., Yale University, 1982), 11.

70. *Muller v. Oregon*, 208 US 421 (1908). Brewer insisted that this judgment did not overturn *Lochner*. The Court in *Adkins v. Children's Hospital* (1923) did find it unconstitutional to have a law mandating a minimum wage specifically for women. However, this decision came after the Nineteenth Amendment was ratified and women were given the right to vote. Although many women viewed this as a loss for women's rights, the more radical women in the National Women's Party filed an amicus brief in favor of striking the law down. The party insisted that in the wake of the Nineteenth Amendment, women should be viewed as equal to men. See Karen O'Connor, *Women's Organizations' Use of the Courts* (Lexington, Mass.: Lexington Books, 1980).

71. Sheldon M. Novick, "Oliver Wendell Holmes," in *The Oxford Companion to the Supreme Court of the United States,* ed. Kermit T. Hall (New York: Oxford University Press, 1992), 407.

72. *Buck v. Bell,* 274 US 207 (1927).

73. Fred D. Ragan, "Buck v. Bell," in *The Oxford Companion to the Supreme Court of the United States,* ed. Kermit T. Hall (New York: Oxford University Press, 1992), 98.

74. *Buck v. Bell,* 274 US 206, 207 (1927).

75. *Buck v. Bell,* 274 US 207 (1927).

Chapter 5

1. John Dewey, *Psychology,* 3d rev. ed. (New York: Harper and Brothers, 1896); John Dewey, *The School and Society,* rev. ed. (Chicago: University of Chicago Press, 1915); John Dewey, *How We Think* (Boston: D. C. Heath, 1910); John Dewey, *Democracy and Education: An Introduction to the Philosophy of Education* (New York: Macmillan, 1916).

2. See John R. Commons and John B. Andrews, *Principles of Labor Legislation,* prepared in cooperation with the American Bureau of Industrial Research, 2d ed. (New York: Harper and Brothers, 1916).

3. Marshall Hyatt, "Franz Boas and the Struggle for Black Equality: The Dynamics of Ethnicity," *Perspectives in American History,* n.s., 2 (1985): 270; Stocking, *Race, Culture, and Evolution,* 150; Vernon J. Williams Jr., *Rethinking Race: Franz Boas and His Contemporaries* (Lexington: University Press of Kentucky, 1996), 9.

4. His 1881 dissertation was titled "Beiträge zur Erkentniss der Farbe des Wassers" (Contribution to the Understanding of the Color of Water). See also Stocking, *Race, Culture, and Evolution,* 143; Hyatt, "Franz Boas and the Struggle for Black Equality," 273.

5. Melville Jean Herskovits, *Franz Boas: The Science of Man in the Making* (New York: Scribner and Sons, 1953), 1.

6. Douglas Cole, " 'The Value of a Person Lies in his Herzensbildung': Franz

Boas' Baffin Island Letter Diary, 1883–1884," in *Observers Observed: Essays on Ethnographic Fieldwork*, ed. George W. Stocking Jr. (Madison: University of Wisconsin Press,), 37.

7. Williams, *Rethinking Race*, 8.

8. Herskovits, *Franz Boas*, 15–180.

9. Ibid., 18.

10. Franz Boas, "Museums of Ethnology and Their Classification," *Science* 9, no. 229 (1887): 614.

11. Ibid., 587–589; Franz Boas, "The Occurrence of Similar Inventions in Areas Widely Apart," *Science* 9, no. 229 (1887): 485–486.

12. Boas, "Museums of Ethnology," 589.

13. Ibid.

14. Franz Boas, "Human Faculty as Determined by Race," *Proceedings of the American Association for the Advancement of Science* 43 (1895): 326.

15. Ibid., 317.

16. Ibid., 307.

17. Ibid., 308.

18. Franz Boas, "The Limitations of the Comparative Method of Anthropology," in *Race, Language, and Culture* (New York: Macmillan, 1940 [1896]), 276.

19. Ibid., 276.

20. "Are Civilized Races Superior?" *Popular Science Monthly* 46, no. 4 (1895): 568; Brinton, "Aims of Anthropology."

21. Franz Boas, *Changes in Bodily Forms of Descendants of Immigrants* (New York: Columbia University Press, 1912), 1.

22. Ibid., 2.

23. Ibid., 5.

24. Henry Pratt Fairchild, *Immigration: A World Movement and Its Social Significance* (New York: Macmillan, 1913), 407.

25. St. Clair Drake, "Anthropology and the Black Experience," *Black Scholar* 11, no. 7 (1980): 10.

26. W. E. B. Du Bois, *The Autobiography of W. E. B. Du Bois: A Soliloquy on Viewing My Life from the Last Decade of Its First Century* (New York: International Publishers, 1968), 149.

27. Du Bois, "Dusk of Dawn," 581.

28. Cornel West, *The American Evasion of Philosophy: A Genealogy of Pragmatism* (Madison: University of Wisconsin Press, 1989), 139; Nancy Ladd Muller, "Du Boisian Pragmatism and 'The Problem of the Twentieth Century,' " *Critique of Anthropology* 12, no. 3 (1992): 319–338.

29. Du Bois, "Dusk of Dawn," 588.

30. Watts, "On Reconsidering Park," 279.

31. Du Bois, "Dusk of Dawn," 625–626.

32. Thomas C. Holt, "The Political Uses of Alienation: W. E. B. Du Bois on Politics, Race, and Culture, 1903–1940," *American Quarterly* 42 (1990): 302.

33. Anthony Monteiro, "Harvesting the Literary Legacy of W. E. B. Du Bois," *Political Affairs*, June 1990, 22.

34. Du Bois, "Dusk of Dawn," 555.

35. Holt, "Political Uses of Alienation," 305.

36. Du Bois, "Souls of Black Folk," 372.

37. Ibid., 368.

38. Du Bois, "Dusk of Dawn," 652.

39. Du Bois, "Souls of Black Folk," 368.

40. Cornel West (*American Evasion of Philosophy*, 148) has suggested that this theoretical contribution to American pragmatism allowed Du Bois to go beyond Ralph Waldo Emerson, John Dewey, C. Wright Mills, and William James in scope and depth. According to West, Du Bois developed a vision that privileged the creative powers of the subaltern, and the fragile structures of democracy throughout the world depend on how these powers were exercised.

41. Du Bois, "Dusk of Dawn," 651.

42. W. E. B. Du Bois, "The Conservation of Races," in *W. E. B. Du Bois: Writings,* ed. Nathan Huggins (New York: Library of America, 1986 [1897]), 815.

43. Ibid., 816.

44. Ibid.

45. Ibid., 816–817.

46. Ibid., 818.

47. Ibid.

48. Stocking, *Race, Culture, and Evolution,* 232.

49. W. E. B. Du Bois, *The Philadelphia Negro: A Social Study* (New York: Schocken Books, 1967 [1899]), 1.

50. Du Bois, "Dusk of Dawn," 596.

51. Du Bois, *Philadelphia Negro,* 8.

52. Ibid., 194.

53. Ibid., 199.

54. Faye V. Harrison, "The Du Boisian Legacy in Anthropology," *Critique of Anthropology* 12, no. 3 (1992): 243; Council Taylor, "Clues for the Future: Black Urban Anthropology Reconsidered," in *Clues for the Future: Black Urban Anthropology Reconsidered,* ed. P. Orleans and W. R. Ellis (Beverly Hills, Calif.: Sage Publications, 1971), 610; Faye V. Harrison and Donald Nonini, "Introduction to W. E. B. Du Bois and Anthropology," *Critique of Anthropology* 12, no. 3 (1992): 234.

55. See Diggs, cited in Harrison, "Du Boisian Legacy," 242. Some scholars have even suggested that Boas's influential chapter on "The Race Problem in Modern Society," in *The Mind of Primitive Man* (New York: Macmillan, 1911), was informed by the work of Du Bois in *The Philadelphia Negro* and the Atlanta Studies: see E. Digby Baltzell, "Introduction," in *The Philadelphia Negro,* by W. E. B. Du Bois (New York: Schocken Books, 1967), xxvi; Monteiro, "Du Bois," 22. Michel-Rolph Trouillot (*Silencing the Past: Power and the Production of History* [Boston: Beacon Press, 1995]) provides some needed insight into why Harrison's argument is embraced by many anthropologists of color but viewed as untenable by others.

56. Du Bois, "Dusk of Dawn," 591.

57. Quoted in William L. Katz, *The Atlanta University Publications* (New York: Arno Press, 1968), 50.

58. Cited in ibid., ix.

59. Quoted in ibid., vi.

60. Ibid., iv.

61. Ibid., iv–vii.

62. Elliott M. Rudwick, *W. E. B. Du Bois: A Study in Minority Group Leadership* (Philadelphia: University of Pennsylvania Press, 1960), 132.

63. Rudwick, *Du Bois: Voice of the Black Protest Movement,* 94.

64. Ibid., 96.

65. Du Bois, "Souls of Black Folk," 399.

66. Rudwick, *Du Bois: Voice of the Black Protest Movement,* 120.

67. Huggins, *Harlem Renaissance,* 22.

68. Green and Driver, *W. E. B. Du Bois,* 20.

69. See Baker, "Franz Boas," 205–215.

70. Marshall Hyatt (*Franz Boas, Social Activist: The Dynamics of Ethnicity,* Contributions to the Study of Anthropology No. 6 [Westport, Conn.: Greenwood Press, 1990], 156) has suggested that "Although his liberalism and commitment to professional science can never be overlooked in assessing his intellectual contributions and social activism, it was his own experience with anti-Semitism that usually pushed him to act. This factor led him to attack evolutionary theory, to challenge the structure of white, Anglo-Saxon Protestant science, and to defend American minority and immigrant groups." I am not totally convinced by Hyatt's argument. Boas may have been motivated by anti-Semitism, but he was a scientist first and foremost. He also worked closely with African Americans and was incensed by repression of any ilk. Du Bois, on the other hand, was driven to science because he thought that it was the best way to combat racism. He eventually moved away from science and began to call himself "a master of propaganda."

71. Williams, *Rethinking Race,* 4.

72. Davis Levering Lewis, *WEB DuBois—Biography of a Race, 1868–1919* (New York: H. Holt, 1993), 149.

73. Franz Boas and Clark Wissler, "The Statistics of Growth," in *The Report of the US Commissioner of Education for 1904* (Washington, D.C.: Government Printing Office, 1905), 25–132; Boas, "Human Faculty"; Boas, "Anthropological Position of the Negro"; Franz Boas, "Industries of African Negroes," *Southern Workman* 38 (1909): 217–229.

74. Franklin, *From Slavery to Freedom,* 290.

75. Boas to Washington, November 30, 1904, American Philosophical Society, Philadelphia, Pennsylvania (hereafter cited as APS).

76. Washington to Boas, December 9, 1904, APS.

77. Du Bois to Boas, October 11, 1905, APS.

78. Franz Boas, "Commencement Address for Atlanta University," in *A Franz Boas Reader,* ed. G. Stocking (Chicago: University of Chicago Press, 1974 [1906]), 311.

79. Ibid., 313.

80. Drake, "Anthropology and the Black Experience," 9.

81. W. E. B. Du Bois, *Black Folk Then and Now* (New York: Henry Holt, 1939), vii.

82. Rudwick, *Du Bois: Voice of the Black Protest Movement,* 332.

83. Boas to Washington, November 8, 1906, APS.

84. Boas to Carnegie, November 30, 1906, APS.

85. Bean, "Negro Brain," 784.

86. Boas to Gilder, September 18, 1906, APS. Bean often camouflaged ethnic stereotypes with science. For example, he published an inflammatory article entitled "On the Nose of the Jew and the *Quadratus Libii Superioris* Muscle" (*American Anthropologist* 15 [1913]: 106–108).

87. Bean, "Training of the Negro," 947–953.

88. Hyatt, "Franz Boas and the Struggle for Black Equality," 287.

89. Boas, "Industries of African Negroes."

90. Ibid., 219.

91. Boas, "Anthropological Position of the Negro."

92. Boas should be seen as both a contributor and a pirating interlocutor in the early tradition of African American Studies (Harrison and Nonini, "Introduction to W. E. B. Du Bois," 234).

93. Rudwick, *Du Bois: Voice of the Black Protest Movement*, 122; Edward H. Beardsley, "The American Scientist as Social Activist: Franz Boas, Burt G. Wilder, and the Cause of Racial Justice, 1900–1915," *Isis* 64, no. 1 (1973): 62.

94. Franz Boas, "The Real Race Problem," *Crisis* 1, no. 5 (1910): 22.

95. Mary White Ovington, *Half a Man: The Status of the Negro in New York* (New York: Schocken Books, 1911).

Chapter 6

1. Pole, *Pursuit of Equality*, 299. For example, we have seen that Boas's attempts to popularize the "new" anthropology were thwarted.

2. Arthur Huff Fauset, *For Freedom: A Biographical Sketch of the American Negro* (Philadelphia: Franklin Publishing and Supply, 1927), 79.

3. Nicholas Lemann, *The Promised Land* (New York: Knopf, 1991), 6; Franklin, *From Slavery to Freedom*, 291, 294.

4. David Levering Lewis, *When Harlem Was in Vogue* (New York: Knopf, 1981), 24.

5. Du Bois, "Dusk of Dawn," 725.

6. Du Bois was forced to resign from New York Local No. 1 of the Socialist Party because he did not publicly support the Debs ticket (ibid., 726).

7. Huggins, *Harlem Renaissance*, 34.

8. W. E. B. Du Bois, "An Open Letter to Woodrow Wilson," *Crisis* 5 (1913): 236.

9. Franklin, *From Slavery to Freedom*, 334; Du Bois, "Open Letter to Woodrow Wilson," 236; Du Bois, "Dusk of Dawn," 726; Huggins, *Harlem Renaissance*, 31.

10. Du Bois, "Open Letter to Woodrow Wilson," 236.

11. Herbert Aptheker, ed., *A Documentary History of the Negro People in the United States: From the N.A.A.C.P. to the New Deal* (New York: Citadel Press, 1990 [1973]), 65; Franklin, *From Slavery to Freedom*, 334.

12. Aptheker, *Documentary History*, 65.

13. See Arnold S. Rice and John A. Krout, *United States History from 1865* (New York: HarperCollins, 1991), 209; John B. Kirby, *Black Americans in the Roosevelt Era: Liberalism and Race* (Knoxville: University of Tennessee Press, 1980), 4.

14. Du Bois, "Dusk of Dawn," 730.

15. Ibid., 731.

16. Ibid., 729.

17. Daniel J. Leab, *From Sambo to Superspade* (Boston: Houghton Mifflin, 1976), 23–27.

18. Ibid., 36.

19. Ibid.

20. Aptheker, *Documentary History,* 87; Lewis Jacobs, *The Rise of American Film* (New York: Harcourt Brace, 1939), 175; Donald Bogle, *Toms, Coons, Mulattoes, Mammies & Bucks* (New York: Bantam Books, 1974), 11.

21. Leab, *From Sambo to Superspade,* 34.

22. There were wide dimensions to this film. White women were depicted as helpless, irrational, and hopeless; African American women were depicted in a different but similarly sexist way. Women's suffrage was being debated at this juncture in American history, and these portrayals of women on both sides of the color line effectively framed the notion that women were not competent to vote. The NAACP vigorously fought, protested, and launched a boycott of the movie. However, they were caught in the sticky dilemma between racist representation and censorship.

23. 238 US 347 (1915).

24. Kluger, *Simple Justice,* 104.

25. 245 US 60 (1917).

26. Kluger, *Simple Justice,* 109.

27. Toni Morrison, ed., *Race-ing Justice, En-gendering Power: Essays on Anita Hill, Clarence Thomas, and the Construction of Social Reality* (New York: Pantheon Books, 1992), ix.

28. Huggins, *Harlem Renaissance,* 38.

29. Du Bois, "Dusk of Dawn," 734.

30. W. E. B. Du Bois, "Close Ranks," in *W. E. B. Du Bois: A Reader,* edited by David Levering Lewis (New York: Henry Holt, 1995 [1918]), 697.

31. Huggins, *Harlem Renaissance,* 34. In 1944 Du Bois reflected on this admittedly "crazy" position in "My Evolving Program for Negro Freedom," first published in Rayford Logan's *What the Negro Wants* (Chapel Hill: University of North Carolina Press, 1944):

The struggle was bitter: I was fighting to let the Negroes fight; I, who for a generation had been a professional pacifist; I was fighting for a separate training camp for Negro officers; I, who was devoting a career to opposing race segregation; I was seeing the Germany which taught me the human brotherhood of white and black, pitted against America which was for me the essence of Jim Crow; and yet I was "rooting" for America; and I had to, even before my own conscience, so utterly crazy had the whole world become and I with it.

(W. E. B. Du Bois, "My Evolving Program for Negro Freedom," in *Writings by W. E. B. Du Bois in Non-Periodical Literature Edited by Others,* ed. Herbert Aptheker [Millwood, N.Y.: Kraus-Thomson Organization, 1982 (1944)], 234).

NOTES TO CHAPTER 7

32. Franklin, *From Slavery to Freedom*, 344.

33. Ibid., 346; Huggins, *Harlem Renaissance*, 54.

34. Sadie Tanner Mossell, "The Standard of Living among One Hundred Negro Migrant Families in Philadelphia," *Annals of the American Academy of Political and Social Science* 98 (1921): 173.

35. Du Bois, "Dusk of Dawn," 738; Franklin, *From Slavery to Freedom*, 352; James Weldon Johnson, *Black Manhattan* (New York: Knopf, 1930), 237; Roscoe E. Lewis, "The Role of Pressure Groups in Maintaining Morale among Negroes," *Journal of Negro Education* 12 (1943): 464.

36. Numerous authors attempted to document this process of carving out a "New Negro" from the urban landscape: Alain Locke, ed., *The New Negro* (New York: Atheneum, 1968 [1925]); Claude McKay, *Harlem: Negro Metropolis* (New York: Harcourt Brace Jovanovich, 1968 [1940]); Johnson, *Black Manhattan;* Carl Van Vechten, *Nigger Heaven* (New York: Knopf, 1926). This idea is gleaned from Benedict Anderson, *Imagined Communities: Reflections on the Origins and Spread of Nationalism* (New York: Verso, 1991) and Akhil Gupta and James Ferguson, "Beyond 'Culture': Space, Identity, and the Politics of Difference," *Cultural Anthropology* 7 (1992): 6–23. I think Anderson's notion of how groups invent imagined communities to foster a sense of nationhood was what "the promoters" or Black intellectuals were doing in Harlem during the 1920s, when they were trying to foster "race consciousness" for political purposes.

37. Henry Lewis Gates Jr., "New Negroes, Migration, and Cultural Exchange," in *Jacob Lawrence: The Migration Series,* ed. Elizabeth H. Turner (Washington, D.C.: Rappahannock Press, 1993), 20.

38. Appiah, *In My Father's House*, 30.

39. Henry Lewis Gates Jr., "The Trope of a New Negro and the Reconstruction of the Image of the Black," *Representations* 24 (1988): 147.

40. Hurston to Boas, October 20, 1929, APS.

41. Huggins, *Harlem Renaissance*, 308.

42. Ibid., 124–133.

43. Harold Cruse, *The Crisis of the Negro Intellectual: A Historical Analysis of the Failure of Black Leadership* (New York: Quill, 1967 [1984]), 25; Houston A. Baker Jr., *Afro-American Poetics: Revisions of Harlem and the Black Aesthetic* (Madison: University of Wisconsin Press, 1988), 5.

Chapter 7

1. William Willis, Jr. ("Franz Boas and the Study of Black Folklore," in *The New Ethnicity: Perspectives from Ethnology,* ed. John W. Bennett [St. Paul, Minn.: West Publishing, 1975], 307–334) is one of the few scholars to have published on this topic. He carefully analyzed Boas's role in publishing the "Negro Numbers" of the *Journal of American Folk-Lore.* I have drawn heavily from Willis's argument and findings in an attempt to develop and advance his contribution.

2. Huggins, *Harlem Renaissance*, 75.

3. Of course, this argument created a paradox. On one hand, African American intellectuals were arguing that "Negro culture" was unique because of its

cultural continuity with Africa. On the other hand, they were arguing that the rise of Negro culture in the New World was what was unique and what made it the only true American culture.

4. Huggins, *Harlem Renaissance*, 73.

5. Arthur Huff Fauset, "American Negro Folk Literature," in *The New Negro*, ed. Alain Locke (New York: Atheneum, 1968 [1925]), 241.

6. See Gladys A. Reichard, "Franz Boas and Folklore," in *Franz Boas, 1858–1942*, American Anthropological Association Memoir Series, 61 (Menasha, Wis.: American Anthropological Association, 1943), 52; Willis, "Franz Boas," 310.

7. Franz Boas, "Mythology and Folk-Tales of the North American Indians," in *Race, Language, and Culture* (New York: Macmillan, 1940 [1914]), 453; Franz Boas, "The Mind of Primitive Man," *Journal of American Folk-Lore* 14 (1901): 11.

8. Franz Boas, "Stylistic Aspects of Primitive Literature," in *Race, Language, and Culture* (New York: Macmillan, 1940 [1925]), 498.

9. Boas, "Mythology and Folk-Tales," 476.

10. Willis, "Franz Boas," 52; Reichard, "Franz Boas," 52.

11. Willis, "Franz Boas," 313–314.

12. Ronald Lamarr Sharps, "Happy Days and Sorrow Songs: Interpretations of Negro Folklore by Black Intellectuals, 1893–1928" (Ph.D. diss., George Washington University, 1991); Willis, "Franz Boas," 315.

13. Stocking, *Race, Culture, and Evolution*, 284.

14. Ricardo Godoy, "Franz Boas and His Plans for an International School of American Archeology and Ethnology in Mexico," *Journal of the History of the Behavioral Sciences* 13 (1977): 228–242.

15. The slight increase in the number of pages of African American folklore published in the journal was due largely to lengthy contributions by Howard W. and Anna K. Odum. These two social scientists were working at the University of North Carolina, Chapel Hill, and were largely independent of Boas's orbit of professional influence.

16. Stocking, *Race, Culture, and Evolution*, 285.

17. Willis, "Franz Boas," 317.

18. Stocking, *Race, Culture, and Evolution*, 285.

19. Ibid., 289.

20. Ibid.

21. Alexander Lesser, "Franz Boas," in *Totems and Teachers: Perspectives on the History of Anthropology*, ed. Sydel Silverman (New York: Columbia University Press, 1981), 13.

22. Franz Boas, "Scientists as Spies," *Nation* 109, no. 2842 (1919): 79.

23. Lesser, "Franz Boas," 18; Stocking, *Race, Culture, and Evolution*, 274.

24. Willis, "Franz Boas," 319.

25. Among Elsie Clews Parsons's publications are: "Notes on Folk Lore of Guilford County, North Carolina," *Journal of American Folk-Lore* 30 (1917): 201–208; "Folk Tales Collected at Miami, Florida," *Journal of American Folk-Lore* 30 (1917): 222–227; "The Provenience of Certain Negro Folk-Tales," *Journal of American Folk-Lore* 30 (1919): 227–234; "Folk Lore from the Cape Verde Islands," *Journal of American Folk-Lore* 34 (1921): 89–109; "Folk Lore from Aiken, South Carolina," *Journal of American Folk-Lore* 34 (1921): 1–39; *Folk-lore of the*

Sea Islands, South Carolina, American Folk-Lore Society Memoir No. 16 (Cambridge, Mass.: American Folk-Lore Society, 1923).

26. Willis, "Franz Boas," 319.

27. Franz Boas, "Introduction," in *Mules and Men,* by Zora Neale Hurston (Bloomington: University of Indiana Press, 1978 [1935]), x.

28. Melville Jean Herskovits, *The Anthropometry of the American Negro,* Columbia University Contributions to Anthropology, 11 (New York: Columbia University Press, 1930).

29. Boas to Woodson, April 30, 1923, APS.

30. Woodson to Boas, February 15, 1923, APS.

31. William Darity Jr. and Julian Ellison, "Abram Harris, Jr.: The Economics of Race and Social Reform," *History of Political Economy* 22, no. 4 (1990): 614–619.

32. Boas to Woodson, May 14, 1923, APS.

33. Woodson to Boas, May 15, 1923, APS.

34. Harris's activity as a communist may be the reason why Woodson would have favored someone else.

35. Boas to Putnam, October 8, 1923, APS.

36. Boas to Du Bois, May 14, 1923, APS.

37. Du Bois to Boas, May 21, 1923, APS.

38. Arthur Huff Fauset, *Folklore from Nova Scotia,* American Folk-Lore Society Memoir No. 25 (New York: G. E. Strechert, 1931), vi.

39. Locke, *New Negro,* 417.

40. Carolyn W. Sylvander, *Jessie Redmon Fauset, Black American Writer* (Troy, N.Y.: Whitstone Publishing, 1981).

41. Ibid., 24.

42. Among Arthur Huff Fauset's contributions are: "Folk-Lore from the Half-Breeds of Nova Scotia," *Journal of American Folk-Lore* 38 (1925): 300–315; "Negro Folk Tales from the South," *Journal of American Folk-Lore* 40 (1927): 213–303; "Tales and Riddles Collected in Philadelphia," *Journal of American Folk-Lore* 41 (1928): 529–557; *Folklore from Nova Scotia; Black Gods of the Metropolis: Negro Religious Cults of the Urban North* (New York: Oxford University Press, 1944); "American Negro Folk Literature."

43. Fauset, *Folklore from Nova Scotia,* vi.

44. Willis, "Franz Boas," 324; Drake, "Anthropology and the Black Experience," 18.

45. Fauset, "American Negro Folk Literature," 240.

46. His work on Nova Scotia was written as his master's thesis in 1925; it was published by the AFLS in 1931.

47. Fauset, "American Negro Folk Literature," 239.

48. Fauset, *Folklore from Nova Scotia,* viii.

49. Ibid., i.

50. Ibid., ix.

51. Ibid.

52. Ibid., vii.

53. Ibid., x.

54. Ibid., ix.

55. Ibid.

56. Ibid., vii–ix.

57. Ibid., ix.

58. Fauset went on to complete his doctorate at the University of Pennsylvania. His dissertation, "A Study of Five Negro Religious Cults in the Philadelphia of Today," was first published by the Philadelphia Anthropological Society in volume 3, number 2, of the Brinton Memorial Series. In 1944 Oxford University Press published it as *Black Gods of the Metropolis*. Fauset also wrote for children: for example, *For Freedom: A Biographical Sketch of the American Negro*, was one of the early Black history books written specifically for schoolchildren.

59. A. E. Perkins, "Riddles from Negro School-Children in New Orleans, La.," *Journal of American Folk-Lore* 35 (1922): 105–115; A. E. Perkins, "Negro Spirituals from the Far South," *Journal of American Folk-Lore* 35 (1922): 223–248.

60. Willis, "Franz Boas," 323.

61. Franklin, *From Slavery to Freedom*, 278.

62. Willis, "Franz Boas," 324.

63. Among Zora Neale Hurston's writings are: "Spunk," *Opportunity* 3 (1925): 171–173; "Dance Songs and Tales from the Bahamas," *Journal of American Folk-Lore* 43 (1930): 294–312; "Hoodoo in America," *Journal of American Folk-Lore* 44 (1931): 317–417; *Dust Tracks on the Road* (Philadelphia: J. B. Lippincott, 1942); *Mules and Men* (Bloomington: University of Indiana Press, 1978 [1935]); *Tell My Horse* (Berkeley, Calif.: Turtle Island Press, 1981 [1938]); *The Sanctified Church: The Folklore Writings of Zora Neale Hurston* (Berkeley, Calif.: Turtle Island Press, 1981); *Their Eyes Were Watching God* (New York: Perennial Library, 1990 [1937]); Zora Neale Hurston and Langston Hughes, *Mule Bone: A Comedy of Negro Life* (New York: Harper Perennial, 1991 [1931]).

64. Rampersad states that Hurston was born on January 7, 1891, but she so willfully misrepresented herself that her major biographer believed that she was born in 1901 (Arnold Rampersad, "Forward," in *Mules and Men*, by Zora Neale Hurston [New York: Harper Perennial, 1990 (1935)], xix).

65. Hurston, *Mules and Men*, 3.

66. Robert E. Hemenway, *Zora Neale Hurston* (Urbana: University of Illinois Press, 1980 [1977]), 107–108; Benjamin P. Bowser, "The Contribution of Blacks to Sociological Knowledge," *Phylon* 42, no. 2 (1981): 189.

67. Huggins, *Harlem Renaissance*, 89.

68. Hemenway, *Zora Neale Hurston*, 4.

69. Hurston, *Mules and Men*, 190–236.

70. Ibid., xxii.

71. Harold Courlander, "Witchcraft in the Caribbean Islands," *Saturday Review of Literature*, October 15, 1938, 6.

72. Hurston, *Tell My Horse*, 75.

73. Ibid., 77.

74. Hemenway, *Zora Neale Hurston*, 320–348.

75. Willis, "Franz Boas," 326.

76. Boas to Andron, October 26, 1933, APS.

77. Joyce Aschenbrenner, "Katherine Dunham," in *Women Anthropologists,*

ed. Ute Gacs and Aisha Khan (Westport, Conn.: Greenwood Press, 1989), 80–87.

78. Ibid., 84.

79. Ibid.

80. A. Lynn Bolles, "Irene Diggs," in *Women Anthropologists,* ed. Ute Gacs and Aisha Khan (Westport, Conn.: Greenwood Press, 1989), 60.

81. Ibid., 61; Harrison, "Du Boisian Legacy," 243.

82. Bolles, "Irene Diggs," 61.

83. Harrison, "Du Boisian Legacy," 245; Irene Diggs, "The Negro in the Viceroyalty of the Rio de la Plata," *Journal of Negro History* 36 (1951): 281–301.

Chapter 8

1. Mark V. Tushnet, *The NAACP's Legal Strategy against Segregated Education, 1925–1950* (Chapel Hill: University of North Carolina Press, 1987), 19; Walter Jackson, *Gunnar Myrdal and America's Conscience* (Chapel Hill: University of North Carolina Press, 1990), 95.

2. W. E. B. Du Bois, "Herbert Hoover," *Crisis* 39 (1932): 362.

3. Walter White, *A Man Called White* (New York: Viking Press, 1969 [1948]), 99–101; Franklin, *From Slavery to Freedom,* 394–397; Rice and Krout, *United States History from 1865,* 185–189; Du Bois, "Herbert Hoover," 362–363.

4. Rice and Krout, *United States History from 1865,* 194–196.

5. Ibid., 233–238; Franklin, *From Slavery to Freedom,* 402–403.

6. Charles H. Houston and John P. Davis, "TVA: Lily-White Reconstruction," *Crisis* 41 (1934): 290–291.

7. Ibid., 291.

8. Ibid.

9. Walter White, *Rope and Faggot: A Biography of Judge Lynch* (New York: Arno Press, 1969).

10. Ibid., 168.

11. Ibid., 169–170.

12. In 1923 the NAACP received a grant of $100,000 from a liberal foundation to implement a legal campaign. The organization hired Nathan Margold to outline a strategy. His lengthy report detailed a specific course of action to eliminate segregation in the schools and residential districts.

13. White, *Man Called White,* 106.

14. Parker continued to serve on the U.S. Court of Appeals, Fourth Circuit. He evolved into a moderate on racial issues. In addition, the NAACP won major victories before Parker. For example, Parker reversed a Virginia District Court that denied equal salaries to African American teachers and affirmed a lower court's decisions that the "White-only" primary in South Carolina was unconstitutional. However, he cautiously denied the NAACP's appeal for an injunction to end segregation in the schools of Clarendon County, South Carolina, in *Briggs v. Elliott,* 103 F. Supp. 920 (1952). *Briggs* became the second of five cases that made up the class-action suit of *Brown.*

15. Kluger, *Simple Justice,* 138–145; White, *Man Called White,* 102–112; Alpheus T. Mason, *The Supreme Court from Taft to Warren* (Baton Rouge: University of Louisiana Press, 1958), 74.

16. Freidel, "Sick Chicken Case," 204.

17. *West Coast Hotel Co. v. Parrish,* 300 US 379 (1937).

18. Bernard Schwartz, *The Supreme Court: Constitutional Revolution in Retrospect* (New York: Ronald Press, 1957), 16.

19. Melvin I. Urofsky, "The Depression and the Rise of Legal Realism," in *The Oxford Companion to the Supreme Court,* ed. Kermit L. Hall (New York: Oxford University Press, 1992), 394.

20. Freidel, "Sick Chicken Case," 191–209; Mason, *Supreme Court,* 70–118; Urofsky, "Legal Realism," 398–390; Peter H. Irons, *The New Deal Lawyers* (Princeton, N.J.: Princeton University Press, 1982), 17–181; William E. Leuchtenburg, "FDR's Court-Packing Plan: A Second Life, A Second Death," *Duke Law Journal* 1985: 673–689.

21. Although the "equal-protection" clause of the Fourteenth Amendment is a more explicit safeguard, it applies only to states. The District of Columbia and Puerto Rico are not states. Therefore, the NAACP had to rely on the Fifth Amendment and forced the Court to find racial segregation unconstitutional in its interpretation of "due process," as well. In *Bolling v. Sharpe,* 347 US 497 (1954), a companion decision to *Brown,* the Court explained this distinction: "The legal problem in the District of Columbia is somewhat different. . . . But [in terms of] the concepts of equal protection and due process, both stemming from our American ideals of fairness, . . . this Court has recognized [that] discrimination may be so unjustifiable as to be violative of due process."

22. W. E. B. Du Bois, "The Position of the Negro in the American Social Order: Where Do We Go from Here?" *Journal of Negro Education* 8 (1939): 551–570.

23. Ibid.

24. Jackson, *Gunnar Myrdal,* 104–105; Kirby, *Black Americans,* 202.

25. Melville Jean Herskovits, *The Myth of the Negro Past* (Boston: Beacon Press, 1958 [1941]), 2–5; Walter Jackson, "Melville Herskovits and the Search for Afro-American Culture," in *Malinowski, Rivers, Benedict, and Others: Essays on Culture and Personality,* ed. George W. Stocking Jr., History of Anthropology, 4 (Madison: University of Wisconsin Press, 1986), 95–126.

26. Some of Boas's associates who had a large impact on the study of the Negro problem were Otto Klineberg, Melville Herskovits, Ruth Benedict, Zora Neale Hurston, Gene Weltfish, Hortense Powdermaker, Eugene L. King, and M. F. Ashley Montagu.

27. Robert Park, "The Conflict and Fusion of Cultures with Special Reference to the Negro," *Journal of Negro History* 4, no. 2 (1919): 116.

28. Boas, "Introduction," x.

29. Alain Locke, "The Legacy of the Ancestral Arts," in *The New Negro,* ed. Alain Locke (New York: Atheneum, 1968 [1925]), 262.

30. Arthur A. Schomburg, "The Negro Digs up His Past," in *The New Negro,* ed. Alain Locke (New York: Atheneum, 1968 [1925]), 237.

31. Locke, "Legacy," 254. Locke eventually shifted on this view. In 1942 he

criticized Herskovits's work on African cultural continuities within Negro culture. He stated that if White people came to believe that Negroes have a strong African heritage they would think that Negroes could not assimilate ("Who and What Is a Negro?" *Opportunity*, March 1942, 84). Interestingly, Herskovits shifted on this view too. Herskovits was one of the few White scholars who contributed an essay to Locke's *New Negro*. In it he suggested that the Black community is "essentially not different from any other American community. . . . [It is] a case of complete acculturation"(Melville Jean Herskovits, "The Negro's Americanism," in *The New Negro*, ed. Alain Locke [New York: Atheneum, 1968 (1925)], 360). He argued then that Negroes did not articulate any unique cultural patterns, but he later developed a completely different understanding about how African cultural patterns were "tenaciously" held onto by the New World Negro (see Jackson, "Melville Herskovits").

32. Vernon J. Williams Jr., *From a Caste to a Minority: Changing Attitudes of American Sociologists toward Afro-Americans, 1896–1945* (Westport, Conn.: Greenwood Press, 1989), 113–148.

33. E. Franklin Frazier, "Is the Negro Family a Unique Sociological Unit?" *Opportunity* 5 (1927): 166.

34. Charles S. Johnson, "New Frontage on American Life," in *The New Negro*, ed. Alain Locke (New York: Atheneum, 1968 [1925]), 285.

35. Charles S. Johnson, "Black Housing in Chicago," in *The Negro in Chicago: A Study of Race Relations and a Race Riot*, by the Chicago Commission on Race Relations (Chicago: University of Chicago Press, 1922), 152–186; Charles S. Johnson, "New Frontage," 278–298; E. Franklin Frazier, *The Negro Family in the United States* (Chicago: University of Chicago Press, 1939), 12–145; E. Franklin Frazier, *The Negro Family in Chicago* (Chicago: University of Chicago Press, 1939); Anthony M. Platt, *E. Franklin Frazier Reconsidered* (New Brunswick, N.J.: Rutgers University Press, 1991), 41–52; Richard Robbins, "Charles Johnson," in *Black Sociologists: Historical and Contemporary Perspectives*, ed. James E. Blackwell and Morris Janowitz (Chicago: University of Chicago Press, 1974), 56–84; G. Edward Franklin, "E. Franklin Frazier," in *Black Sociologists: Historical and Contemporary Perspectives*, ed. James E. Blackwell and Morris Janowitz (Chicago: University of Chicago Press, 1974), 85–117; Nathan Glazer, "Forward," in *The Negro Family in the United States*, by E. Franklin Frazier, rev. and abr. ed. (Chicago: University of Chicago Press, 1966), vii–xvii.

36. Ross, *Origins of American Social Science*, 348–349, 358–361; Jackson, *Gunnar Myrdal*, 95; Williams, *From a Caste to a Minority*, 113–149; Fred H. Matthews, *Quest for an American Sociology: Robert E. Park and the Chicago School* (Montreal: Magill-Queen's University Press, 1977), 39.

37. Gunnar Myrdal, *An American Dilemma* (New York: McGraw-Hill, 1962 [1944]), 2: 1242.

38. US 494–495 (1954).

39. Carleton Putnam, *Race and Reality: A Search for Solutions* (Washington, D.C.: Public Affairs Press, 1967), 70; Hyatt, *Franz Boas, Social Activist;* D'Souza, *End of Racism*, 149–196.

40. D'Souza, *End of Racism*, 19.

41. Ibid., 194.

42. Myrdal was a Swede who was known as a social engineer. In Sweden, Myrdal helped to design the social welfare state, was a professor of economics at the University of Stockholm, and served as a member of the upper house in the Swedish Parliament. He was hired by the Carnegie Corporation to conduct a comprehensive study of the Negro problem. He began the project in 1938 with an aim to help reform racial policies and practices in order to slowly alleviate the menacing Negro problem (Jackson, *Gunnar Myrdal,* xi–xxi). Myrdal commissioned a number of studies by several scholars. Each study was submitted as a book-length memorandum. Together, the memoranda formed the corpus of original research.

43. Ibid., 194; Sidney W. Mintz, "Introduction," in *The Myth of the Negro Past,* by Melville Jean Herskovits (Boston: Beacon Press, 1990 [1941]), xv.

44. Myrdal, *American Dilemma,* 1: ix; Jackson, *Gunnar Myrdal,* 123.

45. Myrdal, *American Dilemma,* 2: 928–929 (emphasis in the original).

46. Williams, *From a Caste to a Minority,* 59–80; Myrdal, *American Dilemma,* 1: 90–91, cxx–cxxii.

47. Jackson, *Gunnar Myrdal,* 95. Jackson did not mention Otto Klineberg's social-cultural psychology approach to studying racial differences (see Otto Klineberg, "The Question of Negro Intelligence," *Opportunity* 9 [1931]: 366–367; Otto Klineberg, "Cultural Differences in Intelligence Tests," *Journal of Negro Education* 3 [1934]: 478–483; Otto Klineberg, *Negro Intelligence and Selective Migration* [New York: Columbia University Press, 1935]) and Hortense Powdermaker's functional-structural study of southern culture, *After Freedom: A Cultural Study in the Deep South* (Madison: University of Wisconsin Press, 1993 [1939]).

48. This may explain why Myrdal belittled the value of Black history. Myrdal characterized Carter G. Woodson's efforts to promote Negro History Week as propaganda. In a patronizing tone, Myrdal (*American Dilemma,* 2: 752) tried to explain:

When we call the activities of the Negro History movement "propaganda," we do not mean to imply that there is any distortion in the facts presented. Excellent historical research has accompanied the efforts to publicize it. But there has been a definite distortion in the emphasis and the perspective given the facts: mediocrities have been expanded into "great men"; cultural achievements which are no better—and no worse—than any others are placed on a pinnacle; minor historical events are magnified into crisis. This seems entirely excusable. . . . As propaganda, Negro history serves . . . as a counter poison to the false and belittling treatment of the Negro in newspapers and books written by whites.

Myrdal (*American Dilemma,* 2: 753) considered the ethnological view of culture as mere grist for Negro History propagandists:

[D]uring the New Negro movement of the 1920's there developed something of an appreciation for modified African music and art. One white anthropologist, Melville J. Herskovits, has recently rendered yeoman service to the Negro History propagandists. He has not only made excellent field studies of certain African and West Indian Negro groups, but has written a general book to glorify African culture generally and show how it has survived in the American negro community.

Myrdal and Herskovits argued so intensely over these issues that Ralph Bunche jokingly remarked, "[T]hose boys just can't break down—they don't know how to relax" (Jackson, *Gunnar Myrdal,* 108). Myrdal and Herskovits respected each other as scientists, and Myrdal invited Herskovits to submit a research memorandum—which was published as *The Myth of the Negro Past* (Mintz, "Introduction," xvi). Guy B. Johnson, who helped to assemble Myrdal's team, suggested that it was much more important to make Herskovits feel like a participant "than to get what he was actually going to contribute to the study" (Jackson, *Gunnar Myrdal,* 110).

49. Myrdal, *American Dilemma,* 1: 133; 2: 753.

50. Ibid., 1: 132.

51. Ibid., 1: cii–cxxii, 150. Lesley M. Rankin-Hill and Michael L. Blakey demonstrate how W. Montague Cobb was influenced by Boas (Lesley M. Rankin-Hill and Michael L. Blakey, "W. Montague Cobb (1904–1990): Physical Anthropologist, Anatomist, and Activist," *American Anthropologist* 96 [1994]: 1–23).

52. Kluger, *Simple Justice,* 125.

53. William H. Hastie, "Charles Hamilton Houston, 1895–1950," *Journal of Negro History* 35 (1950): 355–357; Kluger, *Simple Justice,* 115.

54. Frankfurter came to Harvard in 1915 because Roscoe Pound campaigned vigorously for his appointment. The men remained close until 1927, when the fate of Nicola Sacco and Bartolomeo Vanzetti tore them asunder.

55. Roscoe Pound, "The Scope and Purpose of Sociological Jurisprudence," *Harvard Law Review* 24 (1911): 591–619; 25 (1912): 140–168, 489–514.

56. Ibid., 510.

57. Kalman, "From Realism to Pluralism," 64.

58. Kluger, *Simple Justice,* 128.

59. Ibid., 122–151; Hastie, "Charles Hamilton Houston," 355–358; Houston and Davis, "TVA"; Charles H. Houston, "Educational Inequalities Must Go," *Crisis* 41 (1935): 300–316; Charles H. Houston, "Don't Shout Too Soon," *Crisis* 43 (1936): 79–91.

60. Rankin-Hill and Blakey, "W. Montague Cobb," 1.

61. W. Montague Cobb, "Physical Anthropology and the American Negro," *American Journal of Physical Anthropology* 29 (1942): 113–222; W. Montague Cobb, "Medical Care for Minority Group," *Annals of the American Academy of Political and Social Science* 273 (1951): 169–175; W. Montague Cobb, "The National Health Program of the N.A.A.C.P.," *Journal of the National Medical Association* 45 (1953): 333–339.

62. Rankin-Hill and Blakey, "W. Montague Cobb," 14.

63. Ibid., 15.

64. Ibid.

65. Ralph J. Bunche, "A Critical Analysis of the Tactics and Progress," *Journal of Negro Education* 4, no. 3 (1935): 308.

Chapter 9

1. In 1952 William Rehnquist, the current chief justice of the Supreme Court, was a clerk for Justice Robert H. Jackson, when the Supreme Court was deciding

Brown v. Board of Education. This quotation is in Rehnquist's two-page memorandum to Jackson outlining his support of *Plessy* and separate-but-equal education.

2. Houston, "Educational Inequalities," 300.

3. Ibid.

4. Alfred H. Kelly, "The School Desegregation Case," in *Quarrels That Have Shaped the Constitution*, ed. John A. Garraty (New York: Harper and Row, 1964), 254.

5. Kluger, *Simple Justice*, 188–193; Houston, "Don't Shout," 79, 91; Charles H. Houston, "How to Fight for Better Schools," *Crisis* 43 (1936): 59.

6. Petitioning the Court for a writ of certiorari is the primary way in which cases come before the U.S. Supreme Court. The other way the Court will review a case is on appeal, but the process of appealing a Circuit Court's decision to the U.S. Supreme Court is limited to a congressional mandate for a particular category of case.

7. *Missouri ex rel. Gaines v. Canada*, 305 US 345 (1938).

8. Randolph was also the architect of the 1963 March on Washington.

9. Franklin, *From Slavery to Freedom*, 439.

10. Lewis, "Pressure Groups," 464–473.

11. Franklin, *From Slavery to Freedom*, 440.

12. Myrdal, *American Dilemma*, 1: 1.

13. Ibid., 1: lxxi (italics in the original).

14. David D. Southern, *Gunnar Myrdal and Black-White Relations: The Use and Abuse of An American Dilemma, 1944–1969* (Baton Rouge: Louisiana State University Press, 1987), 71–125. The book was not embraced uniformly around the country, and many southern politicians and their constituents disagreed with its findings. For entirely different reasons, a number of intellectuals, such as Carter G. Woodson, Melville Herskovits, and Herbert Aptheker, also denounced its findings. However, neither group had much impact on the public's reception.

David Southern explained that Myrdal's work was employed as "trickledown" social theory. As President Bill Clinton reminded us, "For twelve years of trickle-down economics, we tried to build a false prosperity on a hollow base" (William J. Clinton, *Address before a Joint Session of Congress on the State of the Union*, January 25, 1994 [*http://library.whitehouse.gov/*]). In a similar fashion, the Eastern establishment circulated a convenient discourse to create an illusion that the United States was actually coming to terms with its racial contradictions.

15. Carl T. Rowan, *Dream Makers, Dream Breakers: The World of Justice Thurgood Marshall* (Boston: Back Bay Books, 1993), 129.

16. Tushnet, *NAACP's Legal Strategy*, 82–138; Jackson, *Gunnar Myrdal*, 95.

17. The White primary elections of Texas had effectively disfranchised African Americans for nearly a hundred years: the winner of the Democratic primary was certain to win the general election. The Texas legislature continued to circumvent the Supreme Court, which invalidated its White primary with *Nixon v. Herndon*, 273 US 536 (1927), and *Nixon v. Condon*, 286 US 73 (1932). In a final attempt to get around the rebukes of the Supreme Court, Texas legislators repealed all of the statutes concerning primary elections, which made the Demo-

cratic Party a private enterprise. The Supreme Court, in *Grovey v. Townsend,* 295 US 45 (1935), finally validated the Texas White primary because discrimination in private organization was beyond the purview of the Constitution. Thurgood Marshall, however, found a hole provided by a recent decision to make his case. He argued that Congress must regulate primaries for federal elections because the party, even though private, performed a public function or state action. Marshall won the case, which curbed the wholesale disfranchisement of African Americans. After *Allwright,* disenfranchisement was limited to poll taxes, literacy tests, and other devices imposed on individuals.

18. Thomas Baker, "Smith v. Allwright," in *The Oxford Companion to the Supreme Court of the United States,* ed. Kermit T. Hall (New York: Oxford University Press, 1992), 800; Kluger, *Simple Justice,* 233–238; Mark V. Tushnet, *Making Civil Rights Law: Thurgood Marshall and the Supreme Court, 1936–1961* (New York: Oxford University Press, 1994), 99–103.

19. Rice and Krout, *United States History from 1865,* 303.

20. *Shelley v. Kraemer,* 334 US 1 (1948).

21. Kluger, *Simple Justice,* 253.

22. *Shelley v. Kraemer,* 334 US 1 (1948). The decision was 6–0. Reed, Jackson, and Rutledge recused themselves from the case, probably because they had signed restrictive covenants.

23. Francis Allen, "Shelley v. Kraemer," in *The Oxford Companion to the Supreme Court of the United States,* ed. Kermit T. Hall (New York: Oxford University Press, 1992), 781; Kluger, *Simple Justice,* 250–255; *Shelley v. Kraemer,* 334 US 1 (1948).

24. Charles Thompson, "Southern Intransigence and the Sweatt and McLaurin Decisions," *Journal of Negro Education* 19 (1950): 430.

25. Emblematic of the conflation of cold-war fears of communism and civil rights was this editorial published in the *New York Times* on January 15, 1948. It was entitled "Equal Rights in Education":

If the United States is to stand before the world as an exemplar of equality of rights, if it is to urge with integrity the acceptance by the rest of the world of the tenets and practices of a democratic society, then it would be well if we set our own record straight. It seems to us that the language of the Fourteenth Amendment must be tortured out of common meaning to make segregation practices in education anything except unconstitutional.

26. Robert Carter, "Reassessment of Brown v. Board," in *Shades of Brown,* ed. Derrick Bell (New York: Teachers College Press, 1980), 27.

27. US 631 (1948).

28. US 629 (1950).

29. US 637 (1950).

30. *Sipuel v. Oklahoma State Board of Regents,* 332 US 633 (1948).

31. Kluger, *Simple Justice,* 259.

32. William Maslow and Shad Polier, "Memorandum of American Jewish Congress, as Amicus Curiae, in Support of the Petition," *U.S. Supreme Court, October Term, 1948, Sweatt v. Painter,* 14. Here they are citing Nazi legislation, translated as "The police ordinance to mark to the Jews."

33. Ibid., 7.

34. Robert Carter, Amos T. Hall, and Thurgood Marshall, "Brief for the Appellant," *U.S. Supreme Court, October Term, 1949, McLaurin v. Oklahoma State Regents for Higher Education,* iv–vii.

35. Klineberg to Boas, February 16, 1929, APS.

36. Klineberg, *Negro Intelligence and Selective Migration,* 61. This conclusion mirrored Boas's conclusion in *Changes in Bodily Form of Descendants of Immigrants.* It was also recited almost verbatim in the brief that the NAACP LDEF filed for *Brown.*

37. Maslow to Marshall, April 28, 1947, NAACP Papers, Group II, Box 206, File "Sweatt v. Painter Legal Papers and Background," Manuscript Division, Library of Congress, Washington, D.C.

38. Marshall to Hastie, April 3, 1947, NAACP Papers, Group II, Box 205, File "Sweatt v. Painter Correspondence," Manuscript Division, Library of Congress, Washington, D.C.

39. W. J. Durham, Bill Hastie, W. R. Ming, J. Nabrit, and T. Marshall, "Petition and Brief in Support of Petition for Writ of Certiorari to the Supreme Court of the State of Texas," *U.S. Supreme Court, October Term, 1948, Sweatt v. Painter,* 9.

40. Carter, Hall, and Marshall, "Brief for the Appellant," vii.

41. Supreme Court of the United States, "Transcript of Record," *Sweatt v. Painter,* 399 US 629 (1950), 192.

42. Ibid., 193–194.

43. Ibid., 198.

44. Ibid., 204–205. After Redfield finished his testimony, the courtroom started to become crowded, so the bailiff began to racially segregate it to make room for more White people. The NAACP was already sitting on the Negro side, but when the bailiff asked Redfield to move, he refused. The refusal was grounds for contempt of court.

45. Prior to the Supreme Court decision in the university cases, the LDEF had begun its campaign in the lower courts to desegregate public-school districts. The LDEF executed with great aplomb its formula of packing briefs with social science, putting expert witnesses on the stand in the lower courts, and soliciting briefs as amici curiae from influential organizations and the U.S. government. By the end of 1952 the LDEF successfully appealed three public-school-district desegregation cases to the Supreme Court. The cases came from Kansas, South Carolina, and Virginia. In addition, the Court granted two writs of certiorari for desegregation cases in Delaware and the District of Columbia. These five cases comprised the class-action suit that the LDEF first argued before the Supreme Court on December 9, 1952; the Court wrote its final decision two years later, without any mechanism to force its compliance.

46. The complete list of questions used by the Clarks (Kenneth B. Clark and Mamie P. Clark, "Racial Identification and Preference in Negro Children," in *Readings in Social Psychology,* ed. T. M. Newcomb and E. L. Hartley [New York: Norton, 1947], 169) is as follows:

1. Give me the doll that you like to play with—(a) like best.
2. Give me the doll that is a nice doll.

3. Give me the doll that looks bad.
4. Give me the doll that is a nice color.
5. Give me the doll that looks like a white child.
6. Give me the doll that looks like a colored child.
7. Give me the doll that looks like a Negro child.
8. Give me the doll that looks like you.

Other published research along these lines includes: Kenneth B. Clark and Mamie P. Clark, "The Development of Consciousness of Self and the Emergence of Racial Identification in Negro Pre-school Children," *Journal of Social Psychology* 10 (1939): 591–599; Kenneth B. Clark and Mamie P. Clark, "Segregation as a Factor in the Racial Identification of Negro Pre-School Children: A Preliminary Report," *Journal of Experimental Education* 11 (1939): 161–163; Kenneth B. Clark and Mamie P. Clark, "Skin Color as a Factor in the Racial Identification of Negro Pre-School Children," *Journal of Social Psychology* 11 (1940): 159–169; Kenneth B. Clark and Mamie P. Clark, "Emotional Factors in Racial Identification and Preference in Negro Children," *Journal of Negro Education* 19 (1950): 341–350; Kenneth B. Clark, *The Effect of Prejudice and Discrimination on Personality Development,* The 1950 Mid-Century White House Conference on Children and Youth (Washington, D.C.: Federal Security Agency, Children's Bureau, 1950).

47. Sara Lightfoot, "Families as Educators: The Forgotten People," in *Shades of Brown: New Perspectives in School Desegregation,* ed. Derrick Bell (New York: Teachers College Press, 1980), 5; Leon Friedman, ed., *Argument: The Oral Argument before the Supreme Court in Brown v. Board of Education of Topeka, 1952–1955* (New York: Chelsea House, 1969), 13; Layli D. Phillips, "A Re-Examination of the Clark Doll Studies at the 40th Anniversary of the Brown v. Board of Education Case: Implications for a Critique of the Efficacy of a Landmark Decision" (paper presented at the annual meeting of the Association for the Study of Afro-American Life and History, Atlanta, Ga., October 12–16, 1994); Sabrina L. Thomas, "Doll Choice Studies and Black Youth Self-Concept: A Reexamination" (M.A. thesis, University of Rochester, 1989); Ellen Herman, *The Romance of American Psychology: Political Culture in the Age of Experts* (Berkeley: University of California Press, 1995), 194–198.

48. Robert Carter, Thurgood Marshall, and Spottswood Robinson III, "Appendix to Appellants' Briefs: The Effects of Segregation and the Consequences of Desegregation: A Social Science Statement," *U.S. Supreme Court, October Term, 1952, Brown v. Board of Education,* 12.

49. Boas, *Changes in Bodily Forms,* 7.

50. Associate Justice Felix Frankfurter was skeptical of the evidence. Frankfurter, an early proponent of sociological jurisprudence, an early member of the NAACP legal committee, and the mentor of Charles Houston, began to tear the heart out of its case. In the first argument of *Brown,* Frankfurter questioned, "If a man says three yards, and I have measured it, and it is three yards, there it is. . . . But if a man tells you [what is] inside of your brain and mine, and how we function, that is not a measurement, and there you are. . . . [This may bring the Court to] a domain which I do not yet regard as science in the sense of

mathematical certainty. . . . I simply know its character" (Friedman, *Argument*, 172–173). Frankfurter indeed knew its character. He knew how a totally different social science was used in a similar fashion within a totally different social and political context. In 1908 his mentor Louis Brandeis "proved" the inferiority of women by using the prevailing social science (the original Brandeis brief). He knew that times change and that a new scientific discourse could shape public policy.

51. *Brown v. Board of Education*, 347 US 492 (1954).

52. *Brown v. Board of Education*, 347 US 494–495 (1954).

Chapter 10

1. Leonard Lieberman, B. W. Stevenson, and L. T. Reynolds, "Race and Anthropology: A Core Concept without Consensus," *Anthropology and Education Quarterly* 20, no. 2 (1989): 67–73.

2. Margaret Mead, *An Anthropologist at Work: Writings of Ruth Benedict* (Boston: Houghton Mifflin, 1919), 353; Sidney W. Mintz, "Ruth Benedict," in *Totems and Teachers: Perspectives on the History of Anthropology*, ed. Sydel Silverman (New York: Columbia University Press, 1981), 151.

3. M. F. Ashley Montagu, *Statement on Race* (New York: Henry Schuman, 1951), 13.

4. Ibid., 18–19.

5. M. F. Ashley Montagu, "The Concept of Race," *American Anthropologist* 64 (1962): 919.

6. Sherwood Washburn, "The Study of Race," *American Anthropologist* 65 (1963): 530.

7. Ibid., 522.

8. Donna Haraway, *Primate Visions: Gender, Race, and Nature in the World of Modern Science* (New York: Routledge, 1989), 204.

9. Harrison, "Persistent Power of 'Race,' " 48; Lee D. Baker, "Racism in Professional Settings: Forms of Address as Clues to Power Relations," *Journal of Applied Behavioral Sciences* 31 (1995): 187; Alan H. Goodman, "The Problematics of 'Race' in Contemporary Biological Anthropology," in *Biological Anthropology: The State of the Science*, ed. N. T. Boaz and L. D. Wolfe (Bend, Oreg.: International Institute for Human Evolutionary Research, 1995), 216; Lieberman and Jackson, "Race and Three Models of Human Origin"; Smedley, *Race in North America*, 6.

10. Tom Morganthau, "What Color Is Black?" *Newsweek*, February 13, 1995, 63.

11. Ibid.

12. Ellis Cose, "One Drop of Bloody History," *Newsweek*, February 13, 1995, 70.

13. Sharon Begley, "Three Is Not Enough," *Newsweek*, February 13, 1995, 67.

14. Ibid., 69.

15. Jared Diamond, "Race without Color," *Discover*, November 1994, 83–92;

Stephen Jay Gould, "The Geometer of Race," *Discover,* November 1994, 65–69; Joan C. Gutin, "End of the Rainbow," *Discover,* November 1994, 71–75; James Shreeve, "Terms of Estrangement," *Discover,* November 1994, 57–64; Christopher Wills, "The Skin We Are In," *Discover,* November 1994, 77–81.

16. Fred Gaboury, "State of Black America: 'Bad Getting Worse,' " *People's Weekly World,* February 3, 1996 (*http://hartford-hwp.com/*); Kevin Sack, "Burning of Black Churches to Be Investigated by Congress," *New York Times,* May 21, 1996. More churches were torched as the summer of 1996 progressed.

17. Arthur R. Jensen, "The Differences Are Real," in *The Bell Curve Debate,* ed. R. Jacoby and N. Glauberman (New York: Random House, 1995 [1973]), 618.

18. Ibid., 618.

19. Herrnstein and Murray, *Bell Curve,* 21.

20. Alan H. Goodman, "The Bell Curve: Good Ol' Racism and Classism Meet Bad Science," *Current Anthropology* 37 (1996): 162.

21. Herrnstein and Murray, *Bell Curve,* 521.

22. Ibid.; Morton M. Kondracke, "Inside Story behind GOP's Turn to Right on Welfare Reform," *Role Call,* October 24, 1994, Pennsylvania Avenue section.

23. Herrnstein and Murray, *Bell Curve,* 191.

24. Ibid., 91 (emphasis in the original).

25. Ibid., 121.

26. Ibid., 643.

27. Jeffery Rosen and Charles Lane, "The Sources of the Bell Curve," in *The Bell Curve Wars: Race, Intelligence, and the Future of America,* ed. Steven Fraser (New York: Basic Books, 1995), 60.

28. Herrnstein and Murray, *Bell Curve,* 643.

29. Ibid., 338.

30. Michael Lind, "Brave New Right," *New Republic,* October 31, 1994, 24–26.

31. Ibid., 24.

32. Gould, "Curveball," 32. The *National Review* collected several essays by scholars and columnists who generally supported the findings of *The Bell Curve* in a particularly partisan fashion ("The Bell Curve: A Symposium," *National Review,* December 5, 1994, 33–61).

33. Steven Fraser, "Introduction," in *The Bell Curve Wars: Race, Intelligence, and the Future of America,* ed. Steven Fraser (New York: Basic Books, 1995), 1.

34. There is actually another historic analog that may be more appropriate. Like Sir Francis Galton's initial research on eugenics, Richard Herrnstein's work on IQ only received substantial public attention during a period of racial realignment, when it resonated with particularly salient themes. In 1973 Herrnstein had published a book similar to *The Bell Curve* entitled *I.Q. in the Meritocracy* (Boston: Little, Brown). Although it caused a stir, it did not dominate public discourse the way his 1994 *The Bell Curve* did. Both Herrnstein's and Galton's work became very popular when it began to resonate with the heightened pitch of nativism in Galton's case and racism in Herrnstein's case.

35. Lee D. Baker, "For Whom the Bell Curve Tolls: Power, Money, and Multiculturalism," *Identities* 1 (1995): 443; Newt Gingrich and Dick Armey, *Con-*

tract with America: The Bold Plan to Change the Nation (New York: Random House, 1994), 70; Robert Rector, *Combating Family Disintegration, Crime, and Dependence: Welfare Reform and Beyond,* Cultural Policy Studies Project No. 983 (Washington, D.C.: Heritage Foundation, 1994); Mickey Kaus, "The 'It-Matters-Little' Gambit," in *The Bell Curve Wars: Race, Intelligence, and the Future of America,* ed. Steven Fraser (New York: Basic Books, 1995), 130.

36. William Julius Wilson, *When Work Disappears: The World of the New Urban Poor* (New York: Knopf, 1996).

37. David Harvey, *The Condition of Postmodernity: An Enquiry into the Origins of Cultural Change* (London: Blackwell, 1989); Roy L. Brooks, *Rethinking the American Race Problem* (Berkeley: University of California Press, 1992), 34–66.

38. M. Kennedy, M. Gastón, and C. Tilly, "Roxbury: Capital Investment or Community Development?" in *Fire in the Hearth: The Radical Politics of Place in America,* ed. Mike Davis (London: Verso, 1990), 97–136.

39. Thomas Byrne Edsall and Mary D. Edsall, *Chain Reaction: The Impact of Race, Rights, and Taxes on American Politics* (New York: Norton, 1992), 27–28; William J. Wilson, *The Declining Significance of Race* (Chicago: University of Chicago Press, 1978).

40. Brooks, *American Race Problem,* 34–66.

41. Gingrich and Armey, *Contract with America,* 37–39, 70–71.

42. Brett Williams, "Babies and Banks: The Reproductive 'Underclass' and the Raced, Gendered Masking of Debt," in *Race,* ed. S. Gregory and R. Sanjek (New Brunswick, N.J.: Rutgers University Press, 1994), 348.

43. Raymond S. Franklin, *Shadows of Race and Class* (Minneapolis: University of Minnesota Press, 1991), 98.

44. Many people structure their racist attitudes and prejudice along class lines. Because they do not feel any animosity toward middle-class people of color, they consider themselves exempt from allegations of racism. This dynamic is clearly demonstrated in Terkel's *Race.* Animosity is rising, however, among the so-called middle-class White Americans who believe that their jobs are being taken away with "preference" programs and affirmative action. Yet the allegation of racism is still circumvented, because people couch animosity in terms of meritocracy. The affirmative-action debate is where these animosities are expressed. These issues were at the center of partisan debates that shaped the presidential campaigns during the 1996 elections. Speaking as a presidential candidate, Bob Dole questioned on ABC's *This Week with David Brinkley:* "Why did 62 percent of white males vote Republican in 1994? I think it's because of things like this [affirmative-action programs], where sometimes the best qualified person does not get the job because he or she may be of one color" (104th Cong., 1st sess., S2154). Robyn Wiegman offers a powerful theoretical discussion of these competing images in *American Anatomies: Theorizing Race and Gender* ([Durham, N.C.: Duke University Press, 1995], 1–17).

45. Political scientists, sociologists, and legal scholars have all demonstrated that institutional racism often persists in various workplaces, marketplaces, legislative bodies, and courtrooms, despite efforts to manage or institute ethnic diversity. See Edsall and Edsall, *Chain Reaction;* Lani Guinier, *The Tyranny of the Majority: Fundamental Fairness and Representative Democracy* (New York:

Free Press, 1994); Bernard Grofman, Lisa Handley, and Richard Niemi, *Minority Representation and the Quest for Voting Equality* (New York: Cambridge University Press, 1992); Terkel, *Race;* Winant, *Racial Conditions.* The other line of reasoning is, of course, Herrnstein and Murray's: that the few Blacks who are very bright have succeeded and will continue to succeed and that the others are simply shackled by their own cognitive inability. Both lines of thought eschew structural racism as a cause of racial inequality.

46. Leanita McClain, *A Foot in Each World: Essays and Articles* (Evanston, Ill.: Northwestern University Press, 1986), 13, 12.

47. Omi and Winant, *Racial Formation,* 1.

48. An excellent example of this dynamic is welfare reform as it has been outlined in the Personal Responsibility Act for the "Contract with America" (see Gingrich and Armey, *Contract with America;* Edsall and Edsall, *Chain Reaction*).

49. David I. Lublin, "Gerrymander for Justice? Racial Redistricting and Black and Latino Representation" (Ph.D. dissertation, Harvard University, 1994).

50. *Shaw v. Reno,* 509 US 645 (1993).

51. *Miller v. Johnson,* [US Docket] No. 94–631 (1995).

52. Bell, *Faces at the Bottom of the Well,* 12.

53. Linda Greenhouse, "Farewell to the Old Order in the Court: The Right Goes Activist and the Center Is Void," *New York Times,* July 2, 1995, E1.

54. Edsall and Edsall, *Chain Reaction;* Mike Christensen, "Blacks Fear Return to 'Dark Days of the 19th Century,' " *Atlanta Journal/Constitution,* June 30, 1995, A1.

55. 104th Cong., 1st sess., H2380.

56. *Adarand Constructors v. Peña,* [US Docket] No. 93–1841 (1995), Opinion: 25 (emphasis in the original).

57. *Adarand Constructors v. Peña,* Opinion: 35.

58. *Adarand Constructors v. Peña,* Concur: 2–3.

59. *Adarand Constructors v. Peña,* Dissent: 2.

60. *Missouri v. Jenkins,* Dissent: 3.

61. *Missouri v. Jenkins,* Concur: 2.

62. *Missouri v. Jenkins,* Concur: 1–2.

63. David J. Garrow, "On Race, Its Thomas v. an Old Ideal," *New York Times,* July 2, 1995, E1.

64. *Missouri v. Jenkins,* Concur: 6.

65. *Missouri v. Jenkins,* Concur: 10.

66. Ibid.

67. *Miller v. Johnson,* [US Docket] No. 94–631 (1995), Opinion: 1, citations omitted.

68. Harrison, "Persistent Power of 'Race' "; Gregory and Sanjek, *Race.*

69. Judith Goode, "On Sustainable Development in the Mega-City," *Current Anthropology* 37, no. 1 (1996): 131–132; Ida Susser, "Sex, Drugs and Videotape: The Prevention of AIDS in a New York City Shelter for Homeless Men," *Medical Anthropology* 14, nos. 2–4 (1992): 307–322; Steven Gregory, "Race, Rubbish, and Resistance: Empowering Difference in Community Politics," *Cultural Anthropology* 8, no. 1 (1993): 24–48; Helán Page and Thomas R. Brooke, "White

Public Space and the Construction of White Privilege in US Health Care: Fresh Concepts and a New Model of Analysis," *Medical Anthropology Quarterly* 8, no. 1 (1994): 109–116; Karen Brodkin Sacks, "Toward a Unified Theory of Class, Race and Gender," *American Ethnologist* 16, no. 3 (1989): 534–550; Brett Williams, "Poverty among African Americans in the Urban United States," *Human Organization* 51, no. 2 (1992): 164–174.

Bibliography

Primary and Secondary Sources

Alexander, Charles C. "Prophet of American Racism: Madison Grant and the Nordic Myth." *Phylon* 23, no. 1 (1962): 73–90.

Allen, Francis. "Shelley v. Kraemer." In *The Oxford Companion to the Supreme Court of the United States,* edited by Kermit T. Hall, 781–782. New York: Oxford University Press, 1992.

Allen, Garland E. "Eugenics and American Social History." *Genome* 31 (1989): 885–889.

———. "The Misuse of Biological Hierarchies: The American Eugenics Movement, 1900–1940." *History and Philosophy of the Life Sciences* 5 (1983): 105–128.

American Anthropologist, n.s., 1 (1899): 400.

Anderson, Benedict R. *Imagined Communities: Reflections on the Origins and Spread of Nationalism.* New York: Verso, 1991.

Appiah, Kwame Anthony. *In My Father's House: Africa in the Philosophy of Culture.* New York: Oxford University Press, 1992.

Aptheker, Herbert, ed. *A Documentary History of the Negro People in the United States: From the N.A.A.C.P. to the New Deal.* New York: Citadel Press, 1990 [1973].

"Are Civilized Races Superior?" *Popular Science Monthly* 46, no. 4 (1895): 568.

Aschenbrenner, Joyce. "Katherine Dunham." In *Women Anthropologists,* edited by Ute Gacs and Aisha Khan, 80–87. Westport, Conn.: Greenwood Press, 1989.

Bakan, David. "The Influence of Phrenology on American Psychology." *Journal of the History of the Behavioral Sciences* 2, no. 2 (1966): 200–220.

Baker, Houston A., Jr. *Afro-American Poetics: Revisions of Harlem and the Black Aesthetic.* Madison: University of Wisconsin Press, 1988.

Baker, Lee D. "For Whom the Bell Curve Tolls: Power, Money, and Multi-culturalism." *Identities* 1 (1995): 443–445.

———. "Franz Boas within the Struggle for Racial Equality." *Critique of Anthropology* 14, no. 2 (1994): 199–217.

———. "Ota Benga, Story of a Tragic Travesty." *Teaching Anthropology Newsletter* 5 (1993): 21–22.

———. "Racism in Professional Settings: Forms of Address as Clues to Power Relations." *Journal of Applied Behavioral Sciences* 31 (1995): 186–201.

———. "Savage Inequality: Anthropology in the Erosion of the Fifteenth Amendment." *Transforming Anthropology* 5, no. 1 (1994): 28–33.

Baker, Marcus, comp. *Directory of Scientific Societies of Washington: Comprising the Anthropological, Biological, Chemical, Entomological, Geological, National Geographic, and Philosophical Societies.* Washington, D.C.: Joint Commission, 1894.

Baker, Ray Stannard. *Following the Color Line: An Account of Negro Citizenship in the American Democracy.* New York: Doubleday, Page, 1908.

Baker, Thomas. "Smith v. Allwright." In *The Oxford Companion to the Supreme Court of the United States,* edited by Kermit T. Hall, 800–801. New York: Oxford University Press, 1992.

Baltzell, E. Digby. "Introduction." In *The Philadelphia Negro,* by W. E. B. Du Bois, ix–xliv. New York: Schocken Books, 1967.

Bannister, Robert C. *Social Darwinism: Science and Myth in Anglo American Social Thought.* Philadelphia: Temple University Press, 1979.

Banton, Michael. *The Idea of Race.* London: Tavistock, 1977.

Bastian, Adolf. *Der Mensch in Der Geschichte Zur Begrundung Einer Psychologischen Weltanschauung.* Leipzig: O. Wigand, 1860.

Baylen, Joseph O., and John Hammond Moore. "Senator John Tyler Morgan and Negro Colonization in the Philippines, 1901 to 1902." *Phylon* 29 (1968): 65–75.

Bean, Robert B. "The Negro Brain." *Century Magazine* 72 (1906): 778–784.

———. "On the Nose of the Jew and the *Quadratus Libii Superioris* Muscle." *American Anthropologist* 15 (1913): 106–108.

———. "The Training of the Negro." *Century Magazine* 73 (1906): 947–953.

Beard, Charles Austin. *An Economic Interpretation of the Constitution of the United States.* New York: Macmillan, 1913.

Beardsley, Edward H. "The American Scientist as Social Activist: Franz Boas, Burt G. Wilder, and the Cause of Racial Justice, 1900–1915." *Isis* 64, no. 1 (1973): 50–65.

Begley, Sharon. "Three Is Not Enough: Surprising New Lessons from the Controversial Science of Race." *Newsweek,* February 13, 1995, 67–69.

Bell, Derrick. *Faces at the Bottom of the Well: The Permanence of Racism.* New York: Basic Books, 1992.

———, ed. *Civil Rights: Leading Cases.* Boston: Little, Brown, 1980.

"The Bell Curve: A Symposium." *National Review,* December 5, 1994, 33–61.

Benedict, Ruth. *Patterns of Culture.* Boston: Houghton Mifflin, 1934.

Benedict, Ruth, and Gene Weltfish. *The Races of Mankind.* Public Affairs Pamphlet 85. New York: Public Affairs Committee, 1943.

Benjamin, Marcus. "Frederic Ward Putnam." *Scientific American* 79, no. 9 (1898): 131.

Bernstein, Barton J. "Case Law in *Plessy v. Ferguson*." *Journal of Negro History* 47 (1962): 192–198.

Blackwell, James E., and Morris Janowitz, eds. *Black Sociologists: Historical and Contemporary Perspectives.* Chicago: University of Chicago Press, 1974.

Blakey, Michael L. "Skull Doctors: Intrinsic Social and Political Bias in the History of American Physical Anthropology." *Critique of Anthropology* 7, no. 2 (1987): 7–35.

Bloor, David. *Knowledge and Social Imagery.* Chicago: University of Chicago Press, 1991 [1976].

Blumentritt, Ferdinand. "The Race Question in the Philippine Islands." *Popular Science Monthly* 54, no. 4 (1899): 472–479.

Blyden, Edward W. "The African Problem." *North American Review* 161 (1895): 327–339.

Boas, Franz. "The Anthropological Position of the Negro." *Van Norden's Magazine,* April 1907, 42–47.

———. *Changes in Bodily Forms of Descendants of Immigrants.* New York: Columbia University Press, 1912.

———. "Commencement Address for Atlanta University." In *A Franz Boas Reader,* 311–316. Edited by G. Stocking. Chicago: University of Chicago Press, 1974 [1906].

———. "Frederic Ward Putnam." *Science* 42 (1915): 330–332.

———. "Human Faculty as Determined by Race." *Proceedings of the American Association for the Advancement of Science* 43 (1895): 301–327.

———. "Industries of African Negroes." *Southern Workman* 38 (1909): 217–229.

———. "Introduction." In *Mules and Men,* by Zora Neale Hurston, x. Bloomington: University of Indiana Press, 1978 [1935].

———. "The Limitations of the Comparative Method." In *Race, Language, and Culture,* 270–280. New York: Macmillan, 1940 [1896].

———. "The Mind of Primitive Man." *Journal of American Folk-Lore* 14 (1901): 1–21.

———. *The Mind of Primitive Man.* New York: Macmillan, 1911.

———. "Museums of Ethnology and Their Classification." *Science* 9, no. 228 (1887): 587–589; no. 229 (1887): 612–614.

———. "Mythology and Folk-Tales of the North American Indians." In *Race, Language, and Culture,* 451–490. New York: Macmillan, 1940 [1914].

———. "The Occurrence of Similar Inventions in Areas Widely Apart." *Science* 9, no. 229 (1887): 485–486.

———. "The Real Race Problem." *Crisis* 1, no. 5 (1910): 22–25.

———. "Scientists as Spies." *Nation* 109, no. 2842 (1919): 79.

———. "Stylistic Aspects of Primitive Literature." In *Race, Language, and Culture,* 491–502. New York: Macmillan, 1940 [1925].

———, ed. *Anthropological Essays Presented to Frederic Ward Putnam in Honor of His Seventieth Birthday, April 16, 1909.* New York: G. E. Strechert, 1909.

Boas, Franz, and Clark Wissler. "The Statistics of Growth." In *The Report of the Commissioner of Education for 1904*, 25–132. Washington, D.C.: Government Printing Office, 1905.

Bogle, Donald. *Toms, Coons, Mulattoes, Mammies & Bucks*. New York: Bantam Books, 1974.

Bolles, A. Lynn. "Irene Diggs." In *Women Anthropologists*, edited by Ute Gacs and Aisha Khan, 59–63. Westport, Conn.: Greenwood Press, 1989.

Bowser, Benjamin P. "The Contribution of Blacks to Sociological Knowledge." *Phylon* 42, no. 2 (1981): 180–193.

Bradford, Phillips Verner, and Harvey Blume. *Ota Benga: The Pygmy in the Zoo*. New York: St. Martin's Press, 1992.

Breckinridge, William C. P. "The Race Question." *Arena* 2 (1890): 39–56.

Brinton, Daniel G. "The Aims of Anthropology." *Popular Science Monthly* 48, no. 1 (1896): 59–72.

———. *The American Race: A Linguistic Classification and Ethnographic Description of the Native Tribes of North and South America*. New York: Hodges, 1891.

———. *The Basis of Social Relations*. New York: G. P. Putnam and Sons, 1901.

———. "The Mound-Builders of the Mississippi Valley." *Historical Magazine* 11 (1866): 33–37.

———. "The Nation as an Element in Anthropology: From Proceedings of the International Congress of Anthropology at Chicago, 1893." In *Smithsonian Institution Annual Report*, 589–600. Washington, D.C.: Government Printing Office, 1894.

———. *Notes on the Florida Peninsula, Its Literary History, Indian Tribes and Antiquities*. Philadelphia: Joseph Sabin, 1859.

———. "Professor Blumentritt's Studies of the Philippines." *American Anthropologist* 1 (1899): 122–125.

———. *Races and Peoples: Lectures on the Science of Ethnography*. New York: Hodges, 1890.

Brooks, Roy L. *Rethinking the American Race Problem*. Berkeley: University of California Press, 1992.

Bunche, Ralph J. "A Critical Analysis of the Tactics and Progress." *Journal of Negro Education* 4, no. 3 (1935): 309–320.

Burrow, John W. "Evolution and Anthropology in the 1860's: The Anthropological Society of London, 1863–1871." *Victorian Studies* 7 (1963): 137–154.

———. *Evolution and Society: A Study in Victorian Social Theory*. London: Cambridge University Press, 1966.

Burton, David. "Theodore Roosevelt's Social Darwinism and Views on Imperialism." *Journal of the History of Ideas* 49 (1965): 103–118.

Calista, David J. "Booker T. Washington: Another Look." *Journal of Negro History* 49 (1964): 240–255.

Carby, Hazel V. "The Multicultural Wars." *Radical History Review* 54 (1992): 7–18.

Carroll, Charles W. *"The Negro a Beast"; or, "In the Image of God."* St. Louis, Mo.: American Book and Bible House, 1900.

Carter, Robert. "Reassessment of Brown v. Board." In *Shades of Brown*, edited by Derrick Bell, 20–29. New York: Teachers College Press, 1980.

Carter, Robert, Amos T. Hall, and Thurgood Marshall. "Brief for the Appellant." *U.S. Supreme Court, October Term, 1949, McLaurin v. Oklahoma State Regents for Higher Education.*

Carter, Robert, Thurgood Marshall, and Spottswood Robinson III. "Appendix to Appellants' Briefs: The Effects of Segregation and the Consequences of Desegregation: A Social Science Statement." *U.S. Supreme Court, October Term, 1952, Brown v. Board of Education.*

Christensen, Mike. "Blacks Fear Return to 'Dark Days of the 19th Century.' " *Atlanta Journal/Constitution,* June 30, 1995, A1.

Clark, Kenneth B. *The Effect of Prejudice and Discrimination on Personality Development.* The 1950 Mid-Century White House Conference on Children and Youth. Washington, D.C.: Federal Security Agency, Children's Bureau, 1950.

Clark, Kenneth B., and Mamie P. Clark. "The Development of Consciousness of Self and the Emergence of Racial Identification in Negro Pre-school Children." *Journal of Social Psychology* 10 (1939): 591–599.

———. "Emotional Factors in Racial Identification and Preference in Negro Children." *Journal of Negro Education* 19 (1950): 341–350.

———. "Racial Identification and Preference in Negro Children." In *Readings in Social Psychology,* edited by T. M. Newcomb and E. L. Hartley, 69–178. New York: Norton, 1947.

———. "Segregation as a Factor in the Racial Identification of Negro Pre-School Children: A Preliminary Report." *Journal of Experimental Education* 11 (1939): 161–163.

———. "Skin Color as a Factor in the Racial Identification of Negro Pre-School Children." *Journal of Social Psychology* 11 (1940): 159–169.

Clinton, William J. *Address before a Joint Session of Congress on the State of the Union,* January 25, 1994 (*http://library.whitehouse.gov/*).

Cobb, W. Montague. "Medical Care for Minority Group." *Annals of the American Academy of Political and Social Science* 273 (1951): 169–175.

———. "The National Health Program of the N.A.A.C.P." *Journal of the National Medical Association* 45 (1953): 333–339.

———. "The Negro as a Biological Element in the American Population." *Journal of Negro Education* 8 (1939): 336–348.

———. "Physical Anthropology and the American Negro." *American Journal of Physical Anthropology* 29 (1942): 113–222.

Cole, Douglas. " 'The Value of a Person Lies in His Herzensbildung': Franz Boas' Baffin Island Letter Diary, 1883–1884." In *Observers Observed: Essays on Ethnographic Fieldwork,* edited by George W. Stocking Jr., 13–52. Madison: University of Wisconsin Press.

Coler, B. S. "Reform of Public Charity." *Popular Science Monthly* 55 (1899): 750–755.

Commons, John R., and John B. Andrews. *Principles of Labor Legislation.* Prepared in cooperation with the American Bureau of Industrial Research. 2d ed. New York: Harper and Brothers, 1916.

Cose, Ellis. "One Drop of Bloody History." *Newsweek,* February 13, 1995, 70–72.

Courlander, Harold. "Witchcraft in the Caribbean Islands." *Saturday Review of Literature,* October 15, 1938, 6.

Cox, Oliver. *Caste, Class, & Race: A Study in Social Dynamics.* New York: Modern Reader Paperbacks, 1948.

Cruse, Harold. *The Crisis of the Negro Intellectual: A Historical Analysis of the Failure of Black Leadership.* New York: Quill, 1967 [1984].

Curry, Jabez L. M. "The Negro Question." *Popular Science Monthly* 55, no. 1 (1899): 177–185.

Curtin, Philip D. *The Image of Africa: British Ideas and Action, 1780–1850.* Madison: University of Wisconsin Press, 1964.

Dall, William H. "The Columbian Exposition—IX: Anthropology." *Nation* 57, no. 1474 (1893): 224–226.

Dalton, Karen C. "Caricature in the Service of Racist Stereotypes: Evolution of Nineteenth-Century Caricatures of African Americans." Paper presented at the W. E. B. Du Bois Institute for Afro-American Studies Colloquia Series, Harvard University, March 31, 1993.

Daniels, John. *In Freedom's Birthplace: A Study of the Boston Negroes.* Boston: Houghton Mifflin, 1914.

Darity, William, Jr., and Julian Ellison. "Abram Harris, Jr.: The Economics of Race and Social Reform." *History of Political Economy* 22, no. 4 (1990): 611–623.

Darnell, Regna D. "Daniel Garrison Brinton: An Intellectual Biography." Ph.D. diss., University of Pennsylvania, 1967

———. *Daniel Garrison Brinton: The "Fearless Critic" of Philadelphia.* Philadelphia: Department of Anthropology, University of Pennsylvania, 1988.

———. *Readings in the History of Anthropology.* New York: Harper and Row, 1974.

Darrah, William Culp. *Powell of the Colorado.* Princeton, N.J.: Princeton University Press, 1951.

Darwin, Charles. *On the Origin of Species by Means of Natural Selection.* New York: New York University Press, 1988 [1859].

Davis, Allison. *Deep South: A Social Anthropological Study of Caste and Class.* Chicago: University of Chicago Press, 1941.

Dawes, Henry L. "Have We Failed the Indians?" *Atlantic Monthly* 84 (1899): 280–285.

Dawson, Marion L. "The South and the Negro." *North American Review* 172 (1901): 279–284.

Degler, Carl N. *In Search of Human Nature: The Decline and Revival of Darwinism in American Social Thought.* New York: Oxford University Press, 1991.

———. "Slavery and the Genesis of American Race Prejudice." *Comparative Studies in Society and History* 2, no. 1 (1960): 49–66.

Dewey, John. *Democracy and Education: An Introduction to the Philosophy of Education.* New York: Macmillan, 1916.

———. *How We Think.* Boston: D. C. Heath, 1910.

———. *Psychology.* 3d rev. ed. New York: Harper and Brothers, 1896.

———. *The School and Society.* Rev. ed. Chicago: University of Chicago Press, 1915.

Dexter, Ralph. "Putnam's Problems Popularizing Anthropology." *American Scientist* 54 (1966): 315–332.

Diamond, Jared. "Race without Color." *Discover,* November 1994, 83–92.

Diamond, Stanley. *In Search of the Primitive: A Critique of Civilization.* New Brunswick, N.J.: Transaction Books, 1987.

Diggs, Irene. "The Negro in the Viceroyalty of the Rio de la Plata." *Journal of Negro History* 36 (1951): 281–301.

Dixon, R. B. "Frederic W. Putnam 1839–1915." *Harvard Graduate's Magazine* 24 (1915): 305–308.

Dixon, Thomas. *The Clansmen; an Historical Romance of the Ku Klux Klan.* New York: Doubleday, 1905.

Dorsey, George A. "Man and His Works." *Youth's Companion,* World's Fair no. (1893): 27.

Drake, St. Clair. "Anthropology and the Black Experience." *Black Scholar* 11, no. 7 (1980): 2–31.

Drake, St. Clair, and Horace R. Cayton. *Black Metropolis: A Study of Negro Life in a Northern City.* New York: Harcourt, Brace, 1945.

D'Souza, Dinesh. *The End of Racism: Principles for a Multiracial Society.* New York: Free Press, 1995.

Du Bois, W. E. B. *The Autobiography of W. E. B. Du Bois: A Soliloquy on Viewing My Life from the Last Decade of Its First Century.* New York: International Publishers, 1968.

———. *Black Folk Then and Now.* New York: Henry Holt, 1939.

———. *Black Reconstruction in America.* New York: World Publishing, 1952 [1935].

———. "Close Ranks." In *W. E. B. Du Bois: A Reader,* 697. Edited by David Levering Lewis. New York: Henry Holt, 1995 [1918].

———. "The Conservation of Races." In *W. E. B. Du Bois: Writings,* 815–826. Edited by Nathan Huggins. New York: Library of America, 1986 [1897].

———. "Dusk of Dawn: An Essay toward an Autobiography of a Race Concept." In *W. E. B. Du Bois: Writings,* 550–802. Edited by Nathan Huggins. New York: Library of America, 1986 [1940].

———. "Herbert Hoover." *Crisis* 39 (1932): 362–363.

———. "My Evolving Program for Negro Freedom." In *Writings by W. E. B. Du Bois in Non-Periodical Literature Edited by Others,* 216–241. Edited by Herbert Aptheker. Millwood, N.Y.: Kraus-Thomson Organization, 1982 [1944].

———. "An Open Letter to Woodrow Wilson." *Crisis* 5 (1913): 236–237.

———. *The Philadelphia Negro: A Social Study.* New York: Schocken Books, 1967 [1899].

———. "The Position of the Negro in the American Social Order: Where Do We Go from Here?" *Journal of Negro Education* 8 (1939): 551–570.

———. "Race Traits of the American Negro, by Frederick L. Hoffman." *Annals of the American Academy of Political Science* 9 (1897): 127–133.

———. "The Souls of Black Folk." In *W. E. B. Du Bois: Writings,* 358–547. Edited by Nathan Huggins. New York: Library of America, 1986 [1903].

———. "The Southerner's Problem." *Dial* 38 (1905): 315–318.

———. "The Suppression of the African Slave Trade in the United States." In

W. E. B. Du Bois: Writings, 3–356. Edited by Nathan Huggins. New York: Library of America, 1986 [1896].

Duncan, David. *The Life and Letters of Herbert Spencer*. New York: Appleton, 1908.

Durham, W. J., Bill Hastie, W. R. Ming, J. Nabrit, and T. Marshall. "Petition and Brief in Support of Petition for Writ of Certiorari to the Supreme Court of the State of Texas." *U.S. Supreme Court, October Term, 1948, Sweatt v. Painter.*

Dyer, Thomas G. *Theodore Roosevelt and the Idea of Race*. Baton Rouge: Louisiana State University Press, 1980.

Eastman, John C. "Village Life at the World's Fair." *Chautauquan* 17 (1893): 602–604.

Edsall, Thomas Byrne, and Mary D. Edsall. *Chain Reaction: The Impact of Race, Rights, and Taxes on American Politics*. New York: Norton, 1992.

Ely, James W. *The Chief Justiceship of Melville W. Fuller, 1888–1910*. Columbia: University of South Carolina Press, 1995.

Engels, Friedrich. *Origin of the Family, Private Property and the State, in Light of the Researches of Lewis Henry Morgan*. New York: International Publishers, 1972 [1884].

"Equal Rights in Education." *New York Times*, January 15, 1948.

Evans, E. P. "The Ethics of Tribal Society." *Popular Science Monthly* 44, no. 3 (1894): 289–307.

———. "Semon's Scientific Researches in Australia." *Popular Science Monthly* 52, no. 1 (1897): 17–37.

Evans-Pritchard, E. E. *Kinship and Marriage among the Nuer*. Oxford: Clarendon Press, 1951.

Fairchild, Henry Pratt. *Immigration: A World Movement and Its Social Significance*. New York: Macmillan, 1913.

Fauset, Arthur Huff. "American Negro Folk Literature." In *The New Negro*, edited by Alain Locke, 238–244. New York: Atheneum, 1968 [1925].

———. *Black Gods of the Metropolis: Negro Religious Cults of the Urban North*. New York: Oxford University Press, 1944.

———. "Folk-Lore from the Half-Breeds of Nova Scotia." *Journal of American Folk-Lore* 38 (1925): 300–315.

———. *Folklore from Nova Scotia*. American Folk-Lore Society Memoir No. 25. New York: G. E. Strechert, 1931.

———. *For Freedom: A Biographical Sketch of the American Negro*. Philadelphia: Franklin Publishing and Supply, 1927.

———. "Negro Folk Tales from the South." *Journal of American Folk-Lore* 40 (1927): 213–303.

———. "Tales and Riddles Collected in Philadelphia." *Journal of American Folk-Lore* 41 (1928): 529–557.

Fields, Barbara J. "Slavery, Race and Ideology in the United States." *New Left Review* 181 (1890): 95–128.

Flagg, John S. "Anthropology: A University Study." *Popular Science Monthly* 51, no. 4 (1897): 510–513.

Foner, Eric. *Reconstruction: America's Unfinished Revolution, 1863–1877*. New York: Harper and Row, 1988.

Franklin, G. Edward. "E. Franklin Frazier." In *Black Sociologists: Historical and Contemporary Perspectives,* edited by James E. Blackwell and Morris Janowitz, 85–117. Chicago: University of Chicago Press, 1974.

Franklin, John Hope. *From Slavery to Freedom: A History of Negro Americans.* 4th ed. New York: Knopf, 1974.

Franklin, Raymond S. *Shadows of Race and Class.* Minneapolis: University of Minnesota Press, 1991.

Fraser, Steven. "Introduction." In *The Bell Curve Wars: Race, Intelligence, and the Future of America,* edited by Steven Fraser, 1–10. New York: Basic Books, 1995.

Frazier, E. Franklin. "Is the Negro Family a Unique Sociological Unit?" *Opportunity* 5 (1927): 155–168.

———. *The Negro Family in Chicago.* Chicago: University of Chicago Press, 1932.

———. *The Negro Family in the United States.* Chicago: University of Chicago Press, 1939.

Fredrickson, George M. *The Black Image in the White Mind.* Middletown, Conn.: Wesleyan University Press, 1971.

Freidel, Frank. "The Sick Chicken Case." In *Quarrels That Have Shaped the Constitution,* edited by John A. Garraty, 191–209. New York: Harper and Row, 1964.

Friedman, Leon, ed. *Argument: The Oral Argument before the Supreme Court in Brown v. Board of Education of Topeka, 1952–1955.* New York: Chelsea House, 1969.

Gaboury, Fred. "State of Black America: 'Bad Getting Worse.' " *People's Weekly World,* February 3, 1996 (*http://hartford-hwp.com/*).

Galton, Sir Francis. *Hereditary Genius: An Inquiry into Its Laws and Consequences.* London: Macmillan, 1925 [1869].

———. "The Possible Improvement of the Human Breed under the Existing Conditions of Law and Sentiment." *Nature* 64 (1901): 659–665.

———. "The Possible Improvement of the Human Breed under the Existing Conditions of Law and Sentiment." *Popular Science Monthly* 60 (1902): 218–233.

Garrow, David J. "On Race, Its Thomas v. an Old Ideal." *New York Times,* July 2, 1995, E1, E5.

Gates, Henry Lewis, Jr. "New Negroes, Migration, and Cultural Exchange." In *Jacob Lawrence: The Migration Series,* edited by Elizabeth H. Turner, 17–22. Washington, D.C.: Rappahannock Press, 1993.

———. "The Trope of a New Negro and the Reconstruction of the Image of the Black." *Representations* 24 (1988): 129–155.

Gilbert, Grove Karl. "John Wesley Powell." In *Smithsonian Institution Annual Report, 1902,* 633–640. Washington, D.C.: Government Printing Office, 1903.

Gingrich, Newt, and Dick Armey. *Contract with America: The Bold Plan to Change the Nation.* New York: Random House, 1994.

Glazer, Nathan. Forward. In *The Negro Family in the United States,* by E. Franklin Frazier, rev. and abr. ed., vii–xvii. Chicago: University of Chicago Press, 1966.

Godoy, Ricardo. "Franz Boas and His Plans for an International School of American Archeology and Ethnology in Mexico." *Journal of the History of the Behavioral Sciences* 13 (1977): 228–242.

Goode, Judith. "On Sustainable Development in the Mega-City." *Current Anthropology* 37, no. 1 (1996): 131–132.

Goodman, Alan H. "The Bell Curve: Good Ol' Racism and Classism Meet Bad Science." *Current Anthropology* 37 (1996): 161–165.

———. "The Problematics of 'Race' in Contemporary Biological Anthropology." In *Biological Anthropology: The State of the Science*, edited by N. T. Boaz and L. D. Wolfe, 215–239. Bend, Oreg.: International Institute for Human Evolutionary Research, 1995.

Gossett, Thomas. *Race: The History of an Idea*. 4th ed. New York: Schocken Books, 1970 [1963].

Gould, Stephen Jay. "Curveball." In *The Bell Curve Wars: Race, Intelligence, and the Future of America*, edited by Steven Fraser, 11–22. New York: Basic Books, 1995.

———. "The Geometer of Race." *Discover*, November 1994, 65–69.

———. *The Mismeasure of Man*. New York: Norton, 1981.

Gramsci, Antonio. *Selections from the Prison Notebooks*. Translated and edited by Quintin Hoare and Geoffrey Nowell Smith. New York: International Publishers, 1971 [1935].

Green, Daniel S., and Edwin D. Driver. *W. E. B. Du Bois on Sociology and the Black Community*. Chicago: University of Chicago Press, 1978.

Greene, John C. *Science, Ideology, and World View*. Berkeley: University of California Press, 1981.

Greenhouse, Linda. "Farewell to the Old Order in the Court: The Right Goes Activist and the Center Is Void." *New York Times*, July 2, 1995, E1, E4.

Gregory, Steven. "Race, Rubbish, and Resistance: Empowering Difference in Community Politics." *Cultural Anthropology* 8, no. 1 (1993): 24–48.

Gregory, Steven, and Roger Sanjek, eds. *Race*. New Brunswick, N.J.: Rutgers University Press, 1994.

Grofman, Bernard, Lisa Handley, and Richard Niemi. *Minority Representation and the Quest for Voting Equality*. New York: Cambridge University Press, 1992.

Guinier, Lani. *The Tyranny of the Majority: Fundamental Fairness and Representative Democracy*. New York: Free Press, 1994.

Gumpert, Gary, and Robert Cathcart. *Inter/Media: Interpersonal Communications in a Media World*. New York: Oxford University Press, 1982.

Gupta, Akhil, and James Ferguson. "Beyond 'Culture': Space, Identity, and the Politics of Difference." *Cultural Anthropology* 7 (1992): 6–23.

Gutin, Joan C. "End of the Rainbow." *Discover*, November 1994, 71–75.

Hall, Jacquelyn Dowd. *Revolt against Chivalry: Jessie Daniel Ames and the Women's Campaign against Lynching*. New York: Columbia University Press, 1979.

Haller, John S. *Outcasts from Evolution: Scientific Attitudes of Racial Inferiority, 1859–1900*. Chicago: University of Illinois Press, 1971.

———. "Race and the Concept of Progress in Nineteenth Century American Ethnology." *American Anthropologist* 73 (1971): 710–722.

Handler, Richard. "Boasian Anthropology and the Critique of Culture." *American Quarterly* 42, no. 2 (1990): 252–273.

Haraway, Donna. *Primate Visions: Gender, Race, and Nature in the World of Modern Science.* New York: Routledge, 1989.

Harding, Sandra. *The "Racial" Economy of Science: Toward a Democratic Future.* Bloomington: Indiana University Press, 1993.

Harley, Lewis R. "Race Mixture and National Character." *Popular Science Monthly* 47, no. 1 (1895): 86–92.

Harrison, Faye V. "The Du Boisian Legacy in Anthropology." *Critique of Anthropology* 12, no. 3 (1992): 239–260.

———. "The Persistent Power of 'Race' in the Cultural and Political Economy of Racism." *Annual Review of Anthropology* 24 (1995): 47–74.

———, ed. *Decolonizing Anthropology: Moving Further toward an Anthropology for Liberation.* Washington, D.C.: American Anthropological Association, 1991.

Harrison, Faye V., and Donald Nonini. "Introduction to W. E. B. Du Bois and Anthropology." *Critique of Anthropology* 12, no. 3 (1992): 229–237.

Harvey, David. *The Condition of Postmodernity: An Enquiry into the Origins of Cultural Change.* London: Blackwell, 1989.

Hastie, William H. "Charles Hamilton Houston, 1895–1950." *Journal of Negro History* 35 (1950): 355–358.

Hawthorne, Julian. "Foreign Folk at the Fair." *Cosmopolitan* 15 (1893): 567–576.

Hemenway, Robert E. *Zora Neale Hurston.* Urbana: University of Illinois Press, 1980 [1977].

Hemingway, Ernest. *For Whom the Bell Tolls.* New York: Scribner's Sons, 1940.

Henderson, J. B. "Report of the Executive Committee of the Board of Regents of the Smithsonian Institution." In *Annual Report of the Board of Regents of the Smithsonian Institution, July 1895,* xix–xl. Washington, D.C.: Government Printing Office, 1896.

Herman, Ellen. *The Romance of American Psychology: Political Culture in the Age of Experts.* Berkeley: University of California Press, 1995.

Herrnstein, Richard J. *I.Q. in the Meritocracy.* Boston: Little, Brown, 1973.

Herrnstein, Richard J., and Charles Murray. *The Bell Curve: Intelligence and Class Structure in American Life.* New York: Free Press, 1994.

Herskovits, Melville Jean. *The Anthropometry of the American Negro.* Columbia University Contributions to Anthropology, 11. New York: Columbia University Press, 1930.

———. *Franz Boas: The Science of Man in the Making.* New York: Scribner and Sons, 1953.

———. *The Myth of the Negro Past.* Boston: Beacon Press.

———. "The Negro's Americanism." In *The New Negro,* edited by Alain Locke, 353–360. New York: Atheneum, 1968 [1925].

Higham, John. *Strangers in the Land: Patterns of American Nativism.* New York: Atheneum, 1970.

Hinsley, Curtis M. *Savages and Scientists: The Smithsonian Institution and the Development of American Anthropology, 1846–1910.* Washington, D.C.: Smithsonian Institution Press, 1981.

Hoffman, Frederick L. *Race Traits and Tendencies of the American Negro.* Publications of the American Economic Association, 11 (1–3). New York: Macmillan, 1896.

Hofstadter, Richard. *Social Darwinism in American Thought.* Boston: Beacon Press, 1960 [1944].

Holt, Thomas C. "The Political Uses of Alienation: W. E. B. Du Bois on Politics, Race, and Culture, 1903–1940." *American Quarterly* 42 (1990): 301–323.

Houston, Charles H. "Don't Shout Too Soon." *Crisis* 43 (1936): 79–91.

———. "Educational Inequalities Must Go." *Crisis* 41 (1935): 300–316.

———. "How to Fight for Better Schools." *Crisis* 43 (1936): 52–59.

Houston, Charles H., and John P. Davis. "TVA: Lily-White Reconstruction." *Crisis* 41 (1934): 290–291, 311.

Hovenkamp, Herbert. "The Political Economy of Substantive Due Process." *Stanford Law Review* 40 (1988): 379–448.

———. "Social Science and Segregation before Brown." *Duke Law Journal* 1985: 624–672.

Hrdlička, Aleš. "Lecture 27, Delivered at the American University, May 27, 1921." National Anthropological Archives, National Museum of Natural History, Washington, D.C.

———. "Physical Anthropology: Its Scope and Aims; Its History and Present Status in America." *American Journal of Physical Anthropology* 1 (1918): 3–23.

Huggins, Nathan Irvin. *Harlem Renaissance.* New York: Oxford University Press, 1971.

Hurston, Zora Neale. "Dance Songs and Tales from the Bahamas." *Journal of American Folk-Lore* 43 (1930): 294–312.

———. *Dust Tracks on the Road.* Philadelphia: J. B. Lippincott, 1942.

———. "Hoodoo in America." *Journal of American Folk-Lore* 44 (1931): 317–417.

———. *Mules and Men.* Bloomington: University of Indiana Press, 1978 [1935].

———. *The Sanctified Church: The Folklore Writings of Zora Neale Hurston.* Berkeley, Calif.: Turtle Island Press, 1981.

———. "Spunk." *Opportunity* 3 (1925): 171–173.

———. *Tell My Horse.* Berkeley, Calif.: Turtle Island Press, 1981 [1938].

———. *Their Eyes Were Watching God.* New York: Perennial Library, 1990 [1937].

Hurston, Zora Neale, and Langston Hughes. *Mule Bone: A Comedy of Negro Life.* New York: Harper Perennial, 1991 [1931].

Hyatt, Marshall. *Franz Boas, Social Activist: The Dynamics of Ethnicity.* Contributions to the Study of Anthropology No. 6. Westport, Conn.: Greenwood Press, 1990.

———. "Franz Boas and the Struggle for Black Equality: The Dynamics of Ethnicity." *Perspectives in American History,* n.s., 2 (1985): 269–295.

Irons, Peter H. *The New Deal Lawyers.* Princeton, N.J.: Princeton University Press, 1982.

Jackson, Walter. *Gunnar Myrdal and America's Conscience*. Chapel Hill: University of North Carolina Press, 1990.

———. "Melville Herskovits and the Search for Afro-American Culture." In *Malinowski, Rivers, Benedict, and Others: Essays on Culture and Personality,* edited by George W. Stocking Jr., 95–126. History of Anthropology, 4. Madison: University of Wisconsin Press, 1986.

Jacobs, Lewis. *The Rise of American Film*. New York: Harcourt, Brace, 1939.

Jensen, Arthur R. "The Differences Are Real." In *The Bell Curve Debate,* edited by R. Jacoby and N. Glauberman, 617–629. New York: Random House, 1995 [1973].

Johnson, Charles S. "Black Housing in Chicago." In *The Negro in Chicago: A Study of Race Relations and a Race Riot,* by the Chicago Commission on Race Relations, 152–186. Chicago: University of Chicago Press, 1922.

———. "New Frontage on American Life." In *The New Negro,* edited by Alain Locke, 278–298. New York: Atheneum, 1968 [1925].

Johnson, James Weldon. *Black Manhattan*. New York: Knopf, 1930.

Jordan, Winthrop J. *White over Black: American Attitudes toward the Negro, 1150–1812*. Chapel Hill: University of North Carolina Press, 1968.

Kalman, Laura. "From Realism to Pluralism: Theory and Education at Yale Law School, 1927–1960." Ph.D. diss., Yale University, 1982.

Kaplan, Amy. "Black and Blue on San Juan Hill." In *Cultures of United States Imperialism,* edited by Amy Kaplan and Donald E. Pease, 219–236. Durham, N.C.: Duke University Press, 1993.

Katz, William L., ed. *The Atlanta University Publications*. New York: Arno Press, 1968.

Kaus, Mickey. "The 'It-Matters-Little' Gambit." In *The Bell Curve Wars: Race, Intelligence, and the Future of America,* edited by Steven Fraser, 130–138. New York: Basic Books, 1995.

Kelly, Alfred H. "The School Desegregation Case." In *Quarrels That Have Shaped the Constitution,* edited by John A. Garraty, 243–268. New York: Harper and Row, 1964.

Kennedy, M., M. Gastón, and C. Tilly. "Roxbury: Capital Investment or Community Development?" In *Fire in the Hearth: The Radical Politics of Place in America,* edited by Mike Davis, 97–136. London: Verso, 1990.

Kens, Paul. "Lochner v. New York." In *The Oxford Companion to the Supreme Court of the United States,* edited by Kermit T. Hall, 508–511. New York: Oxford University Press, 1992.

Kerr, James E. *The Insular Cases: The Role of the Judiciary in American Expansionism*. Port Washington, N.Y.: Kennikat Press, 1982.

Kidd, Benjamin. *Social Evolution*. New York: Macmillan, 1894.

Kirby, John B. *Black Americans in the Roosevelt Era: Liberalism and Race*. Knoxville: University of Tennessee Press, 1980.

Klineberg, Otto. "Cultural Differences in Intelligence Tests." *Journal of Negro Education* 3 (1934): 478–483.

———. *Negro Intelligence and Selective Migration*. New York: Columbia University Press, 1935.

———. "The Question of Negro Intelligence." *Opportunity* 9 (1931): 366–367.

Kluger, Richard. *Simple Justice: The History of Brown v. Board of Education.* New York: Knopf, 1976.

Kondracke, Morton M. "Inside Story behind GOP's Turn to Right on Welfare Reform." *Roll Call,* October 24, 1994, Pennsylvania Avenue section.

Kovel, Joel. *White Racism, a Psychohistory.* New York: Pantheon Books, 1970.

Kroeber, Alfred. "Frederic Ward Putnam." *American Anthropologist* 17 (1915): 712–718.

Leab, Daniel J. *From Sambo to Superspade.* Boston: Houghton Mifflin, 1976.

Lemann, Nicholas. *The Promised Land.* New York: Knopf, 1991.

Lesser, Alexander. "Franz Boas." In *Totems and Teachers: Perspectives on the History of Anthropology,* edited by Sydel Silverman, 1–34. New York: Columbia University Press, 1981.

Leuchtenburg, William E. "FDR's Court-Packing Plan: A Second Life, A Second Death." *Duke Law Journal* (1985): 673–689.

Lewis, Davis Levering. *WEB DuBois—Biography of a Race, 1868–1919.* New York: H. Holt, 1993.

———. *When Harlem Was in Vogue.* New York: Knopf, 1981.

Lewis, Roscoe E. "The Role of Pressure Groups in Maintaining Morale among Negroes." *Journal of Negro Education* 12 (1943): 464–473.

Lieberman, Leonard, and Fatimah Linda C. Jackson. "Race and Three Models of Human Origin." *American Anthropologist* 97 (1995): 231–242.

Lieberman, Leonard, B. W. Stevenson, and L. T. Reynolds. "Race and Anthropology: A Core Concept without Consensus." *Anthropology and Education Quarterly* 20, no. 2 (1989): 67–73.

Liggio, Leonard P. "English Origins of Early American Racism." *Radical History Review* 3 (1976): 1–36.

Lightfoot, Sara. "Families as Educators: The Forgotten People." In *Shades of Brown: New Perspectives in School Desegregation,* edited by Derrick Bell, 2–19. New York: Teachers College Press, 1980.

Lind, Michael. "Brave New Right." *New Republic,* October 31, 1994, 24–26.

Livingstone, David N. *Nathaniel Southgate Shaler and the Culture of American Science.* Tuscaloosa: University of Alabama Press, 1987.

Locke, Alain. "The Legacy of the Ancestral Arts." In *The New Negro,* edited by Alain Locke, 254–267. New York: Atheneum, 1968 [1925].

———. "Who and What Is a Negro?" *Opportunity,* March 1942, 84.

———, ed. *The New Negro.* New York: Atheneum, 1968 [1925].

Logan, Rayford W. *The Betrayal of the Negro.* New York: Collier Books, 1972 [1954].

———. *What the Negro Wants.* Chapel Hill: University of North Carolina Press, 1944.

Lombroso, Cesare. "The Savage Origin of Tattooing." *Popular Science Monthly* 58, no. 6 (1896): 793–803.

———. "Why Homicide Has Increased in the United States." *North American Review* 165 (1897): 641–648.

Lovejoy, Arthur. *The Great Chain of Being.* Cambridge, Mass.: Harvard University Press, 1936.

Lublin, David I. "Gerrymander for Justice? Racial Redistricting and Black and Latino Representation." Ph.D. diss., Harvard University, 1994.

Marable, Manning. *W. E. B. Du Bois, Black Radical Democrat.* Boston: Twayne, 1986.

Maslow, William, and Shad Polier. "Memorandum of American Jewish Congress, as Amicus Curiae, in Support of the Petition." *U.S. Supreme Court, October Term, 1948, Sweatt v. Painter.*

Mason, Alpheus T. *The Supreme Court from Taft to Warren.* Baton Rouge: University of Louisiana Press, 1958.

Mason, Otis T. "Summary of Progress in Anthropology." In *Annual Report of the Smithsonian Institution for the Year Ending July 1893,* 601–629. Washington, D.C.: Government Printing Office, 1893.

Matthews, Fred H. *Quest for an American Sociology: Robert E. Park and the Chicago School.* Montreal: McGill-Queen's University Press, 1977.

McClain, Leanita. *A Foot in Each World: Essays and Articles.* Evanston, Ill.: Northwestern University Press, 1986.

McDowell, Edward B. "The World's Fair Cosmopolis." *Frank Leslie's Popular Monthly* 36 (1893): 407–416.

McGee, WJ. "The Trend of Human Progress." *American Anthropologist* 1 (1899): 401–447.

McGovern, James R. *Anatomy of a Lynching: The Killing of Claude Neale.* Baton Rouge: Louisiana State University Press, 1982.

McKay, Claude. *Harlem: Negro Metropolis.* New York: Harcourt Brace Jovanovich, 1968 [1940].

McLemore, S. Dale. *Racial and Ethnic Relations in America.* Needham Heights, Mass.: Simon and Schuster, 1991.

Mead, Margaret. *An Anthropologist at Work: Writings of Ruth Benedict.* Boston: Houghton Mifflin, 1959.

———. *Coming of Age in Samoa: A Psychology Study in Primitive Youth for Western Civilization.* New York: W. Morrow, 1928.

Meier, August. "Negro Class Structure and Ideology in the Age of Booker T. Washington." *Phylon* 23 (1962): 259–266.

Meier, August, Elliott Rudwick, and Francis L. Broderick, eds. *Black Protest Thought in the Twentieth Century.* New York: Bobbs-Merrill, 1971.

Michaud, Gustave. "The Brain of the Nation." *Century Magazine* 49 (1904): 40–46.

Mintz, Sidney W. "Introduction." In *The Myth of the Negro Past,* by Melville Jean Herskovits, i–xliii. Boston: Beacon Press, 1990 [1941].

———. "Ruth Benedict." In *Totems and Teachers: Perspectives on the History of Anthropology,* edited by Sydel Silverman, 141–170. New York: Columbia University Press, 1981.

Mitra, Panchanan. *A History of American Anthropology.* Calcutta: University of Calcutta Press, 1933.

Montagu, M. F. Ashley. "Aleš Hrdlička, 1869–1943." *American Anthropologist* 46 (1944): 113–117.

———. "The Concept of Race." *American Anthropologist* 64 (1962): 919–928.

———. *Man's Most Dangerous Myth: The Fallacy of Race*. New York: Columbia University Press, 1942.

———. *Statement on Race*. New York: Henry Schuman, 1951.

Monteiro, Anthony. "Harvesting the Literary Legacy of W. E. B. Du Bois." *Political Affairs*, June 1990, 22–27.

Morgan, John T. "The Race Question in the United States." *Arena* 2 (1890): 385–398.

Morgan, Lewis Henry. *Ancient Society, or Researches in the Lines of Human Progress from Savagery through Barbarism to Civilization*. New York: Henry Holt, 1877.

Morganthau, Tom. "What Color Is Black? Science, Politics and Racial Identity." *Newsweek*, February 13, 1995, 63–65.

Morison, Elting E., ed. *The Letters of Theodore Roosevelt*. 8 vols. Cambridge, Mass.: Harvard University Press, 1951.

Morris, Charles. "War as a Factor in Civilization." *Popular Science Monthly* 47, no. 6 (1895): 823–834.

Morrison, Toni, ed. *Race-ing Justice, En-gendering Power: Essays on Anita Hill, Clarence Thomas, and the Construction of Social Reality*. New York: Pantheon Books, 1992.

Morse, E. S. "Frederic W. Putnam, 1839–1915: An Appreciation." *Essex Institute Historical Collections* 52 (1916): 193–196.

Morton, Samuel. *Crania Ægyptiaca; or, Observations on Egyptian Ethnography, Derived from Anatomy, History and the Monuments*. Philadelphia: J. Penington, 1844.

———. *Crania Americana; or, a Comparative View of the Skulls of Various Aboriginal Nations of North and South America*. Philadelphia: J. Dobson, 1839.

Mossell, Sadie Tanner. "The Standard of Living among One Hundred Negro Migrant Families in Philadelphia." *Annals of the American Academy of Political and Social Science* 98 (1921): 173–222.

Mott, Frank Luther. *A History of American Magazines, 1885–1905*. Cambridge, Mass.: Harvard University Press, 1957.

Muller, Nancy Ladd. "Du Boisian Pragmatism and 'The Problem of the Twentieth Century.' " *Critique of Anthropology* 12, no. 3 (1992): 319–338.

Murdoch, John. "Eskimo Bows and Arrows." *Popular Science Monthly* 51, no. 5 (1897): 645–648.

Murray, John. "Alexander Agassiz: His Life and Scientific Work." *Bulletin of the Museum of Comparative Zoology* 54, no. 3 (1911): 139–158.

Myrdal, Gunnar. *An American Dilemma*. 2 vols. New York: McGraw-Hill, 1962 [1944].

Norris, Frank. *The Octopus: A Story of California*. Garden City, N.Y.: Doubleday, 1901.

———. *The Pit: A Story of Chicago*. New York: Doubleday, Page, 1903.

Nott, Josiah, and George R. Gliddon. *Types of Mankind*. Philadelphia: Lippincott, Grambo, 1854.

Novick, Sheldon M. "Oliver Wendell Holmes." In *The Oxford Companion to the Supreme Court of the United States,* edited by Kermit T. Hall, 405–410. New York: Oxford University Press, 1992.

O'Connor, Karen. *Women's Organizations' Use of the Courts.* Lexington, Mass.: Lexington Books, 1980.

Olenick, Monte M. "Albion W. Tourgée: Radical Republican Spokesman of the Civil War Crusade." *Phylon* 22 (1962): 332–345.

Omi, Michael, and Howard Winant. *Racial Formation in the United States.* New York: Routledge, 1986.

Ovington, Mary White. *Half a Man: The Status of the Negro in New York.* New York: Schocken Books, 1911.

Page, Helán, and Thomas R. Brooke. "White Public Space and the Construction of White Privilege in US Health Care: Fresh Concepts and a New Model of Analysis." *Medical Anthropology Quarterly* 8, no. 1 (1994): 109–116.

Park, Robert. "The Conflict and Fusion of Cultures with Special Reference to the Negro." *Journal of Negro History* 4, no. 2 (1919): 111–133.

Parsons, Elsie Clews. "Folk Lore from Aiken, South Carolina." *Journal of American Folk-Lore* 34 (1921): 1–39.

———. "Folk Lore from the Cape Verde Islands." *Journal of American Folk-Lore* 34 (1921): 89–109.

———. *Folk-lore of the Sea Islands of South Carolina.* American Folk-Lore Society Memoir No. 16. Cambridge, Mass.: American Folk-Lore Society, 1923.

———. "Folk Tales Collected at Miami, Florida." *Journal of American Folk-Lore* 30 (1917): 222–227.

———. "Notes on Folk Lore of Guilford County, North Carolina." *Journal of American Folk-Lore* 30 (1917): 201–208.

———. "The Provenience of Certain Negro Folk-Tales." *Journal of American Folk-Lore* 30 (1919): 227–234.

Patterson, Thomas C., and Frank Spencer. "Racial Hierarchies and Buffer Races." *Transforming Anthropology* 5 (1994): 20–27.

Peabody, Charles. "Frederic W. Putnam." *Journal of American Folk-Lore* 28 (1915): 302–306.

Perkins, A. E. "Negro Spirituals from the Far South." *Journal of American Folk-Lore* 35 (1922): 223–248.

———. "Riddles from Negro School-Children in New Orleans, La." *Journal of American Folk-Lore* 35 (1922): 105–115.

Phillips, Layli D. "A Re-Examination of the Clark Doll Studies at the 40th Anniversary of the Brown v. Board of Education Case: Implications for a Critique of the Efficacy of a Landmark Decision." Paper presented at the annual meeting of the Association for the Study of Afro-American Life and History, Atlanta, Ga., October 12–16, 1994.

Platt, Anthony M. *E. Franklin Frazier Reconsidered.* New Brunswick, N.J.: Rutgers University Press, 1991.

Pole, James R. *The Pursuit of Equality in American History.* Rev. ed. Berkeley: University of California Press, 1993.

Popenoe, Paul, and Roswell Hill Johnson. *Applied Genetics.* New York: Macmillan, 1918.

Pound, Roscoe. "The Scope and Purpose of Sociological Jurisprudence." *Harvard Law Review* 24 (1911): 591–619; 25 (1912): 140–168, 489–514.

Powdermaker, Hortense. *After Freedom: A Cultural Study in the Deep South.* Madison: University of Wisconsin Press, 1993 [1939].

Powell, John Wesley. "Esthetology, or the Science of Activities Designed to Give Pleasure." *American Anthropologist* 1 (1899): 1–40.

———. *Exploration of the Colorado River of the West and Its Tributaries: Explored in 1869, 1870, 1871, and 1872.* Washington, D.C.: Government Printing Office, 1875.

———. "From Barbarism to Civilization." *American Anthropologist* 1 (1888): 97–123.

———. *On the Organization of Scientific Work of the General Government: Extracts from the Testimony Taken by the Joint Commission of the Senate and House of Representatives.* Washington, D.C.: Government Printing Office, 1885.

———. "Relation of Primitive Peoples to Environment, Illustrated by American Examples." In *Smithsonian Institution Annual Report* [1895], 625–637. Washington, D.C.: Government Printing Office, 1896.

———. *Report on the Methods of Surveying the Public Domain.* Washington, D.C.: Government Printing Office, 1878.

———. "Sociology, or the Science of Institutions." *American Anthropologist* 1 (1899): 475–509, 695–745.

———. "Technology, or the Science of Industries." *American Anthropologist* 1 (1899): 319–349.

"The Presidency and Mr. Olney." *Atlantic Monthly* 77 (1896): 676–682.

President's Commission on Civil Rights. *To Secure These Rights.* Washington, D.C.: Government Printing Office, 1947.

Provine, William B. "Geneticists and Race." *American Zoology* 26 (1986): 857–887.

Putnam, Carleton. *Race and Reality: A Search for Solutions.* Washington, D.C.: Public Affairs Press, 1967.

Radcliffe-Brown, Alfred Reginald. *The Social Organization of Australian Tribes.* Melbourne: Macmillan, 1931.

Ragan, Fred D. "Buck v. Bell." In *The Oxford Companion to the Supreme Court of the United States,* edited by Kermit T. Hall, 97–98. New York: Oxford University Press, 1992.

Rampersad, Arnold. "Foreword." In *Mules and Men,* by Zora Neale Hurston, xv–xxiii. New York: Harper Perennial, 1990 [1935].

Rankin-Hill, Lesley M., and Michael L. Blakey. "W. Montague Cobb (1904–1990): Physical Anthropologist, Anatomist, and Activist." *American Anthropologist* 96 (1994): 1–23.

Rector, Robert. *Combating Family Disintegration, Crime, and Dependence: Welfare Reform and Beyond.* Cultural Policy Studies Project No. 983. Washington, D.C.: Heritage Foundation, 1994.

Reichard, Gladys A. "Franz Boas and Folklore." In *Franz Boas, 1858–1942,* 52–57. American Anthropological Association Memoir Series, 61. Menasha, Wis.: American Anthropological Association, 1943.

Resek, Carl. *Lewis Henry Morgan: American Scholar.* Chicago: University of Chicago Press, 1960.

Rice, Arnold S., and John A. Krout. *United States History from 1865.* New York: HarperCollins, 1991.

Rice, Arnold S., John A. Krout, and C. M. Harris. *United States History to 1877.* 8th ed. New York: Harper Perennial, 1991.

Rich, Paul. " 'The Baptism of a New Era': The 1911 Universal Races Congress and the Liberal Ideology of Race." *Ethnic and Racial Studies* 7, no. 4 (1984): 534–550.

Robbins, Richard. "Charles Johnson." In *Black Sociologists: Historical and Contemporary Perspectives,* edited by James E. Blackwell and Morris Janowitz, 56–84. Chicago: University of Chicago Press, 1974.

Roosevelt, Theodore. *Address of President Roosevelt at the Lincoln Dinner of the Republican Club of the City of New York.* February 13, 1905. Washington, D.C.: Government Printing Office, 1905.

———. "Campaigns and Controversies." In *The Works of Theodore Roosevelt,* edited by Hermann Hagedorn, national ed., vol. 14. New York: C. Scribner's Sons, 1926.

———. "Kidd's 'Social Evolution.' " *North American Review* 161 (1895): 94–109.

———. "The Rough Riders and Men of Action." In *The Works of Theodore Roosevelt,* edited by Hermann Hagedorn, national ed., vol. 11. New York: C. Scribner's Sons, 1926 [1899].

———. "Through the Brazilian Wilderness and Papers on Natural History." In *The Works of Theodore Roosevelt,* edited by Hermann Hagedorn, national ed., vol. 5. New York: C. Scribner's Sons, 1926 [1914].

Rosen, Jeffery, and Charles Lane. "The Sources of the Bell Curve." In *The Bell Curve Wars: Race, Intelligence, and the Future of America,* edited by Steven Fraser, 58–61. New York: Basic Books, 1995.

Rosen, Paul L. *The Supreme Court and Social Science.* Urbana: University of Illinois Press, 1972.

Ross, Dorothy. *The Origins of American Social Science.* New York: Cambridge University Press, 1991.

Rowan, Carl T. *Dream Makers, Dream Breakers: The World of Justice Thurgood Marshall.* Boston: Back Bay Books, 1993.

Rudwick, Elliott M. *W. E. B. Du Bois: A Study in Minority Group Leadership.* Philadelphia: University of Pennsylvania Press, 1960.

———. *W. E. B. Du Bois: Voice of the Black Protest Movement.* Chicago: University of Illinois Press, 1982.

Rudwick, Elliott M., and August Meier. "Black Man in the 'White City': Negroes and the Columbian Exposition, 1893." *Phylon* 26, no. 4 (1965): 354–361.

Rushton, J. Philippe. *Race, Evolution, and Behavior: A Life History Perspective.* New Brunswick, N.J.: Transaction Publishers, 1995.

Rydell, Robert W. *All the World's a Fair: Visions of Empire at American International Expositions.* Chicago: University of Chicago Press, 1984.

Sack, Kevin. "Burning of Black Churches to Be Investigated by Congress." *New York Times,* May 21, 1996.

Sacks, Karen Brodkin. "Toward a Unified Theory of Class, Race and Gender." *American Ethnologist* 16, no. 3 (1989): 534–550.

Saxton, Alexander. *The Rise and Fall of the White Republic: Class Politics and Mass Culture in Nineteenth-Century America*. London: Verso, 1990.

Scarborough, W. S. "The Negro and the Louisiana Purchase Exposition." *Voice of the Negro* 1, no. 8 (1904): 312–315.

———. "The Race Problem." *Arena* 2 (1890): 560–567.

Scheidt, Walter. "The Concept of Race in Anthropology and the Divisions into Human Races, from Linnaeus to Deniker." In *This Is Race,* edited by E. Count, 354–391. New York: Henry Schuman, 1950.

Schomburg, Arthur A. "The Negro Digs up His Past." In *The New Negro,* edited by Alain Locke, 231–237. New York: Atheneum, 1968 [1925].

Schwartz, Bernard. *The Supreme Court: Constitutional Revolution in Retrospect.* New York: Ronald Press, 1957.

Scott, Emmett J. "The Louisiana Purchase Exposition." *Voice of the Negro* 1, no. 8 (1904): 305–312.

Scott, Emmett J., and Lyman Beecher Stowe. *Booker T. Washington, Builder of a Civilization.* New York: Doubleday, Page, 1916.

Scribner, Hilton. "Brain Development as Related to Evolution." *Popular Science Monthly* 46, no. 4 (1895): 525–538.

Shaler, Nathaniel Southgate. "Aspects of the Earth." *Nation* 1282 (1890): 79.

———. "The Future of the Negro in the Southern States." *Popular Science Monthly* 57 (1900): 147–156.

———. "The Nature of the Negro." *Arena* 2 (1890): 660–673.

———. "The Negro Problem." *Atlantic Monthly* 54 (1884): 696–709.

———. "The Negro since the Civil War." *Popular Science Monthly* 57 (1900): 29–39.

———. "Our Negro Types." *Current Literature* 29 (1900): 44–45.

———. "Science and the African Problem." *Atlantic Monthly* 64 (1890): 36–45.

———. "The Transplantation of a Race." *Popular Science Monthly* 56 (1900): 513–524.

Sharps, Ronald Lamarr. "Happy Days and Sorrow Songs: Interpretations of Negro Folklore by Black Intellectuals, 1893–1928." Ph.D. diss., George Washington University, 1991.

Shine, S. Walter, and Theodore C. Sorensen. "Brief for Amicus Curiae." *U.S. Supreme Court, October Term, 1952, Bolling v. Sharpe, American Council on Human Rights, et al.*

Shreeve, James. "Terms of Estrangement." *Discover,* November 1994, 57–64.

Shufeldt, Robert Wilson. *The Negro: A Menace to American Civilization.* Boston: R. G. Badger, 1907.

Sinclair, Upton. *The Jungle.* New York: Doubleday, Page, 1906.

Sloktin, J. S. "Racial Classifications of the Seventeenth and Eighteenth Centuries." *Transactions of the Wisconsin Academy of Sciences* 36 (1944): 459–467.

Small, Albion W. "Civil History of the Confederate States, by J. L. M. Curry, LL.D." *American Journal of Sociology* 7 (1901): 847–849.

Smedley, Audrey. *Race in North America: Origin and Evolution of a Worldview.* Boulder, Colo.: Westview Press, 1993.

Smith, Anna Tolman. "A Study in Race Psychology." *Popular Science Monthly* 50, no. 3 (1897): 354–360.

Smith, Harlan Ingersoll. "Man and His Works." *American Antiquarian* 15 (1893): 115–117.

Smith, William Benjamin. *The Color Line: A Brief in Behalf of the Unborn.* New York: McClure, Phillips, 1905.

Smyth, Albert. "Memorial Address." In *Report of the Brinton Memorial Meeting,* edited by Albert Smyth, 16–29. Philadelphia: American Philosophical Society, 1899.

Southern, David D. *Gunnar Myrdal and Black-White Relations: The Use and Abuse of An American Dilemma, 1944–1969.* Baton Rouge: Louisiana State University Press, 1987.

Spencer, Herbert. "The Comparative Psychology of Man." *Popular Science Monthly* 8 (1896): 257–269.

———. *Principles of Psychology.* 2 vols. 3d ed. New York: Appleton, 1880.

———. *Social Statistics, Abridged and Revised; Together with the Man versus the State.* London: Williams and Norgate; New York: D. Appleton, 1892 [1850].

Stanton, William Ragan. *The Leopard's Spots: Scientific Attitudes toward Race in America, 1815–1859.* Chicago: University of Chicago Press, 1960.

Starr, Frederick. "Anthropology at the World's Fair." *Popular Science Monthly* 43, no. 5 (1893): 611–621.

———. "The Degeneracy of the American Negro." *Dial* 22 (1897): 17–18.

Steere, J. B. "The Civilized Indian of the Philippines." *Scientific American* 79, no. 12 (1898): 184–185.

Steffens, Lincoln. *The Shame of the Cities.* New York: P. Smith, 1948 [1904].

Stepan, Nancy Leys, and Sander L. Gilman. "Appropriating the Idioms of Science: The Rejection of Scientific Racism." In *The Bounds of Race: Perspectives on Hegemony and Resistance,* edited by D. LaCapra, 73–103. Ithaca, N.Y.: Cornell University Press, 1991.

Stocking, George W. *Race, Culture, and Evolution: Essays in the History of Anthropology.* New York: Free Press, 1968.

Stone, Alfred H. "The Mulatto Factor in the Race Problem." *Atlantic Monthly* 91 (1903): 658–662.

Supreme Court of the United States. "Transcript of Record." *October Term, 1949, Sweatt v. Painter,* 399 US 629 (1950).

Susser, Ida. "Sex, Drugs and Videotape: The Prevention of Aids in a New York City Shelter for Homeless Men." *Medical Anthropology* 14, nos. 2–4 (1992): 307–322.

Sylvander, Carolyn W. *Jessie Redmon Fauset, Black American Writer.* Troy, N.Y.: Whitstone Publishing, 1981.

Taylor, Council. "Clues for the Future: Black Urban Anthropology Reconsidered." In *Clues for the Future: Black Urban Anthropology Reconsidered,* edited by P. Orleans and W. R. Ellis, 219–227. Beverly Hills, Calif.: Sage Publications, 1971.

Terkel, Studs. *Race: How Blacks and Whites Think and Feel about the American Obsession.* New York: New Press, 1992.

Thomas, Sabrina L. "Doll Choice Studies and Black Youth Self-Concept: A Reexamination." M.A. thesis, University of Rochester, 1989.

Thomas, William A., ed. *Science and Law: An Essential Alliance.* Boulder, Colo.: Westview Press, 1993.

Thomas, William I., and Florian Znaniecki. *The Polish Peasant in Europe and America.* Chicago: University of Chicago Press, 1918.

Thompson, Charles. "Southern Intransigence and the Sweatt and McLaurin Decisions." *Journal of Negro Education* 19 (1950): 427–430.

Tillman, Benjamin R. "The Race Question." *Van Norden's Magazine,* April 1907, 19–28.

Tozzer, A. M. *Frederic Ward Putnam, 1839–1915.* National Academy of Sciences, Biographical Memoirs, 16, 1935. Washington, D.C.: National Academy of Sciences.

Trouillot, Michel-Rolph. *Silencing the Past: Power and the Production of History.* Boston: Beacon Press, 1995.

Tucker, William A. *The Science and Politics of Racial Research.* Urbana: University of Illinois Press, 1994.

Tushnet, Mark V. *Making Civil Rights Law: Thurgood Marshall and the Supreme Court, 1936–1961.* New York: Oxford University Press, 1994.

———. *The NAACP's Legal Strategy against Segregated Education, 1925–1950.* Chapel Hill: University of North Carolina Press, 1987.

Tylor, Edward B. *Primitive Culture: Researches into the Development of Mythology, Philosophy, Religion, Art, and Custom.* London: J. Murray, 1871.

Urofsky, Melvin I. "The Depression and the Rise of Legal Realism." In *The Oxford Companion to the Supreme Court,* edited by Kermit T. Hall, 390–398. New York: Oxford University Press, 1992.

Valelly, Richard M. *The Puzzle of Disfranchisement: Party Struggle and African-American Suffrage in the South, 1867–1894.* Occasional Paper 93–4. Center for American Political Studies, Harvard University, 1993.

Van Vechten, Carl. *Nigger Heaven.* New York: Knopf, 1926.

Veblen, Thorstein. *The Theory of the Leisure Class: An Economic Study of Institutions.* New York: Macmillan, 1908 [1899].

Vest, G. G. "Objections to Annexing the Philippines." *North American Review* 168 (1899): 112–120.

Villard, Oswald G. "The Negro in the Regular Army." *Atlantic Monthly* 91 (1903): 721–728.

Waite, Edward F. "The Negro in the Supreme Court." *Minnesota Law Review* 30 (March 1946): 220–304.

Wald, Priscilla. "Terms of Assimilation: Legislating Subjectivity in the Emerging Nation." In *Cultures of United States Imperialism,* edited by Amy Kaplan and Donald E. Pease, 59–84. Durham, N.C.: Duke University Press, 1993.

Walker, Francis A. "Immigration Restriction." *Atlantic Monthly* 77 (1896): 822–829.

Warner, W. Lloyd. *Yankee City Series.* 5 vols. New Haven, Conn.: Yale University Press, 1941–1959.

Washburn, Sherwood. "The Study of Race." *American Anthropologist* 65 (1963): 521–531.

Washburn, Wilcomb E. *The Cosmos Club of Washington: A Centennial History, 1878–1978*. Washington, D.C.: Cosmos Club, 1978.

Washington, Booker T. "The Awakening of the Negro." *Atlantic Monthly* 77 (1896): 322–328.

———. "Education Will Solve the Race Problem, A Reply." *North American Review* 171 (1900): 221–232.

———. "Heroes in Black Skins." *Century Magazine* 66 (1903): 724–729.

———. "The Race Problem in the United States." *Popular Science Monthly* 55, no. 3 (1899): 317–325.

———. "Signs of Progress among the Negroes." *Century Magazine* 59 (1899): 472–478.

———. *Up from Slavery*. New York: Doubleday, 1902 [1901].

Watts, Jerry. "On Reconsidering Park, Johnson, Du Bois, Frazier and Reid: Reply to Benjamin Bowser's 'The Contribution of Blacks to Sociological Knowledge.' " *Phylon* 44, no. 4 (1983): 273–291.

Weir, James, Jr. "The Pygmy in the United States." *Popular Science Monthly* 49, no. 1 (1896): 47–56.

Wells-Barnett, Ida B. *Mob Rule in New Orleans*. New York: Arno Press, 1969 [1900].

———. *A Red Record: Tabulated Statistics and Alleged Causes of Lynchings in the United States, 1892–1893–1894*. Chicago: Donohue and Henneberry, 1895.

———. *Southern Horrors: Lynch Law in All Its Phases*. New York: New York Age, 1892.

Wesley, Charles H. "The Concept of Negro Inferiority in American Thought." *Journal of Negro History* 25, no. 2 (1940): 540–560.

West, Cornel. *The American Evasion of Philosophy: A Genealogy of Pragmatism*. Madison: University of Wisconsin Press, 1989.

———. *Race Matters*. Boston: Beacon Press, 1993.

White, Walter. *A Man Called White*. New York: Viking Press, 1969 [1948].

———. *Rope and Faggot: A Biography of Judge Lynch*. New York: Arno Press, 1969 [1929].

Wiegman, Robyn. *American Anatomies: Theorizing Race and Gender*. Durham, N.C.: Duke University Press, 1995.

Willhelm, Sidney M. "Black-White Equality." *Journal of Black Studies* 12, no. 2 (1981): 142–165.

Williams, Brett. "Babies and Banks: The Reproductive 'Underclass' and the Raced, Gendered Masking of Debt." In *Race,* edited by S. Gregory and R. Sanjek, 348–365. New Brunswick, N.J.: Rutgers University Press, 1994.

———. "Poverty among African Americans in the Urban United States." *Human Organization* 51, no. 2 (1992): 164–174.

Williams, John Sharp. "The Negro and the South." *Metropolitan Magazine* 27, no. 2 (1907): 138–151.

Williams, Vernon J., Jr. *From a Caste to a Minority: Changing Attitudes of American Sociologists toward Afro-Americans, 1896–1945*. Westport, Conn.: Greenwood Press, 1989.

———. *Rethinking Race: Franz Boaz and His Contemporaries.* Lexington: University Press of Kentucky, 1996.

Williamson, Joel. *The Crucible of Race.* New York: Oxford University Press, 1984.

Willis, William, Jr. "Franz Boas and the Study of Black Folklore." In *The New Ethnicity: Perspectives from Ethnology,* edited by John W. Bennett, 307–334. St. Paul, Minn.: West Publishing, 1975.

Wills, Christopher. "The Skin We Are In." *Discover,* November 1994, 77–81.

Wilson, Theodore B. *The Black Codes of the South.* Tuscaloosa: University of Alabama Press, 1965.

Wilson, William Julius. *The Declining Significance of Race.* Chicago: University of Chicago Press, 1978.

———. *When Work Disappears: The World of the New Urban Poor.* New York: Knopf, 1996.

Wilson, Woodrow. *A History of the American People.* New York: Harper and Brothers, 1902.

Winant, Howard. *Racial Conditions: Politics, Theory, Comparisons.* Minneapolis: University of Minnesota Press, 1994.

"Wise Leader." *Century Magazine* 66 (1903): 796–797.

Wish, Harvey. "Negro Education and the Progressive Movement." *Journal of Negro History* 49 (1964): 184–200.

Wood, Leonard. "The Existing Conditions and Needs in Cuba, by Major-General Leonard Wood, Military Governor of Santiago de Cuba." *North American Review* 168 (1899): 593–601.

Woodward, C. Vann. *The Strange Career of Jim Crow.* New York: Oxford University Press, 1957 [1955].

Work, Monroe N. "Crime among the Negroes of Chicago." *American Journal of Sociology* 6 (1900): 204–223.

Wright, Richard. *Native Son.* New York: Harper and Row, 1940.

Ziglar, William L. "Negro Opinion of Theodore Roosevelt." Ph.D. diss., University of Maine, Orono, 1972.

Principal Cases Cited

Adair v. United States, 208 US 161 (1908).

Adarand Constructors v. Peña, [US Docket] No. 93–1841 (1995).

Adkins v. Children's Hospital, 261 US 491 (1923).

Allgeyer v. Louisiana, 165 US 578 (1897).

Berea College v. Kentucky, 211 US 45 (1909).

Bolling v. Sharpe, 347 US 497 (1954).

Briggs v. Elliott, 103 F. Supp. 920 (1952).

Brown v. Board of Education, 347 US 483 (1954).

Buchanan v. Warley, 245 US 60 (1917).

Buck v. Bell, 274 US 200 (1927).

Cherokee Nation v. Georgia, 30 US 1 (1831).

Coppage v. Kansas, 236 US 1 (1915).

Cumming v. Richmond County Board of Education, 175 US 528 (1899).

Grovey v. Townsend, 295 US 45 (1935).

Guinn v. United States, 238 US 347 (1915).

Hirabayashi v. United States, 320 US 81 (1943).

Korematsu v. United States, 323 US 214 (1944).

Lochner v. New York, 198 US 45 (1905).

McLaurin v. Oklahoma State Regents for Higher Education, 339 US 637 (1950).

Miller v. Johnson, [US Docket] No. 94–631 (1995).

Missouri ex rel. Gaines v. Canada, 305 US 337 (1938).

Missouri v. Jenkins, [US Docket] No. 93–1823 (1995).

Muller v. Oregon, 208 US 412 (1908).

Murray v. Maryland, 182 A590 (1936).

Nixon v. Condon, 286 US 73 (1932).

Nixon v. Herndon, 273 US 536 (1927).

Plessy v. Ferguson, 163 US 537 (1896).

Regents of the University of California v. Bakke, 438 US 265 (1978).

Schechter Poultry Corp. v. United States, 295 US 495 (1936).

Scott v. Sandford, 60 US 393 (1857).

Shaw v. Reno, 509 US 630 (1993).

Shelley v. Kraemer, 334 US 1 (1948).

Sipuel v. Oklahoma State Board of Regents, 332 US 631 (1948).

Smith v. Allwright, 321 US 649 (1944).

Sweatt v. Painter, 339 US 629 (1950).

United States v. Butler, 297 US 1 (1936).

United States v. Cruikshank, 92 US 214 (1876).

United States v. Reese, 92 US 214 (1876).

West Coast Hotel Co. v. Parrish, 300 US 379 (1937).

Williams v. Mississippi, 170 US 213 (1898).

Index

Compositor:	Binghamton Valley Composition
Type:	10/13 Galliard
Display:	Galliard
Printer and binder:	Maple-Vail Book Manufacturing Group